Why Do You Need this New Edition?

The abilities to think critically, analyze, and produce strong, effective arguments are necessary to fully engage society—from the public arena to personal relationships. We argue daily. We use arguments to persuade others to act and we are persuaded by the arguments of others. *Critical Thinking and Communication* encourages students to develop skills for constructing and refuting arguments in a variety of contexts from informal conversations to structured debates. Through exercises and examples, students learn how to create arguments, how to develop extended argument cases, and how to critically understand and interpret them.

For more than 20 years, *Critical Thinking and Communication* has helped students be effective arguers and critical recipients by relating common theoretical models to true-to-life examples from law, ethics, education, and business. It helps students conceptualize argumentation in the larger framework of verbal and written communication, from public speaking and debating to interpersonal, intercultural, and small group communication. Its examples and exercises are intended to help students master their abilities to think and act purposefully about complex issues and ideas. The Sixth Edition of *Critical Thinking and Communication*

1. Has been **extensively reorganized** and reoriented to focus on communicating and analyzing arguments from multiple perspectives. Greater attention is paid to topics such as ethics, arguer-recipient relationships, and how culture affects argument.

2. Provides **new extended case studies about contemporary issues** drawn from student arguments and classroom discussions. The topics for the case studies range from politics to economics to personal-interest issues showing students how issues that affect them can be argued in multiple spheres.

3. Develops an **updated and extended treatment of argument theory** with more exploration of traditional forms as well as contemporary, collaborative types of argument. These theories are used to analyze issues and cases drawn from wide-ranging topics that affect students.

4. Offers **more study aids for students** from updated exercises to chapter key concepts to chapter glossaries. These aids help focus reading and support better understanding of the most important concepts and theories.

5. Focuses more on **argument as communication** and examines examples and issues from both communicator and recipient points of view. In an extensively reorganized and redeveloped unit, the text provides a detailed examination of the relationship between arguer and recipient and how understanding the character of that relationship affects how arguments are produced and received.

6. Extends the discussion of **argument ethics** to help students develop their own ethical code as both an arguer and a receiver.

PEARSON

SIXTH EDITION

CRITICAL THINKING AND COMMUNICATION

The Use of Reason in Argument

EDWARD S. INCH

Pacific Lutheran University

BARBARA WARNICK

University of Pittsburgh

Allyn & Bacon

Boston   New York   San Francisco
Mexico City   Montreal   Toronto   London   Madrid   Munich   Paris
Hong Kong   Singapore   Tokyo   Cape Town   Sydney

Acquisitions Editor: *Jeanne Zalesky*
Editorial Assistant: *Megan Lentz*
Marketing Manager: *Suzan Czajkowski*
Production Assistant: *Maggie Brobeck*
Editorial Production Service: *Prepare, Inc.*
Manufacturing Buyer: *JoAnne Sweeney*
Electronic Composition: *Prepare, Inc.*
Cover Designer: *Joel Gendron*

Library of Congress Cataloging-in-Publication Data

Inch, Edward S.
  Critical thinking and communication : the use of reason in argument / Edward S. Inch, Barbara Warnick.—6 ed.
       p. cm.
  ISBN 0-205-67293-0
 1. Reasoning—Textbooks. 2. Critical thinking—Textbooks. 3. Interpersonal communication—Textbooks. I. Warnick, Barbara, 1946- II. Title.

 BC177.W35 2010
 168—dc22

                                            2008047413

10 9 8 7 6 5 4 3 2 1   HAM   13 12 11 10 09

**Allyn & Bacon
is an imprint of**

www.pearsonhighered.com

ISBN-10: 0-205-67293-0
ISBN-13: 978-0-205-67293-6

TO OUR STUDENTS

CONTENTS

PREFACE

The Sixth Edition of *Critical Thinking and Communication* reflects many current developments in the teaching and learning of argumentation. During the past five years, the field has continued to adapt to the needs and interests of an increasingly diverse society and interconnected world. Although we have continued to focus on a rhetorical perspective on argument, we do so in the context of building communities of argument and acceptance of culturally diverse practices.

We decided to write this edition to highlight the importance of culturally sensitive and co-orientational forms of argument. We think that the ways in which we have organized this text in addition to new glossary and study aids will make this a more readable and study-friendly edition. The organizational approach to the text begins with concepts, moves to analysis, then examines the role of arguer and recipient, and finally develops approaches for presenting extended argument cases. Each chapter now begins with case studies adapted from student debates and presentations focusing on topics that are current and part of ongoing classroom discussions.

The book is divided into four sections. The first section focuses on a conceptual framework for argument. Chapter 1 examines the relationship between argument and critical thought and explores how argumentation can improve the ability to examine complex issues. The chapter introduces two significant theoretical constructs that are used throughout the rest of the book: argument spheres and fields. Argument spheres are central to our understanding of how argument situations and contexts develop and can be used to adapt and analyze arguments. Argument fields provide us with a way of understanding the guiding rules and norms that can be used to shape arguments as well as criticize them. This section also introduces, in Chapter 2, a co-orientational model of argument. It is developed along with traditional arguer-based models including formal logic and the Toulmin Model.

Section I ends with a discussion of how culture and ethics shape arguments. As the world becomes more interconnected and arguments cross cultural boundaries, there is a greater need to develop cultural appreciation and sensitivity toward other approaches to argument. These are explored in Chapter 3 along with strategies for understanding and developing ethical codes for argumentation. Although we continue to use the logical perspective as both a critical approach in Chapter 8 and a constructive method in Chapter 6, the focus of this edition is on creating opportunities for arguers to develop common goals and outcomes while improving their communication skills.

Section II, The Parts of An Argument, parses the model developed in the first section to examine how claims and propositions, evidence, and reasoning work together to form argument units. Each chapter in this section considers the nature and function of each argument component, provides approaches for using these components to construct arguments, and then offers tests to ensure that each part is soundly designed. The tests for each part, especially evidence in Chapter 5 and reasoning in Chapter 6, are used later in Chapter 8 to help analyze and criticize arguments.

The focus of Section III, Presenting and Critically Evaluating Arguments, examines arguments from both the advocate's and the recipient's perspectives. In Chapter 7 we consider how arguers can design and adapt their presentations in ways that enhance credibility, develop trustworthiness, and help recipients understand and accept other points of view. Chapter 8 explores approaches for critically evaluating arguments with the goal of enhancing critical thinking and analytic skills used to comprehend arguments before believing or acting upon them.

We have provided many study tools in this book—lists of key concepts, answers to selected exercises (Appendix A), chapter summaries, chapter glossaries, and exercises that require students to apply chapter concepts. Appendix B, Intercollegiate Debate, is intended to provide resources for students who want to learn about intercollegiate debate and, perhaps, try attending a debate tournament. And, Appendix C, Research Strategies, is designed as a starting point for finding strong evidence to support arguments. Both Appendixes B and C can be accessed online at www.pearsonhighered.com. The book's study aids should enable students to review for exams, do further reading, and have handy references when reading text material. We have used a variety of examples from law, education, ethics, business, and other fields to illustrate the argument concepts introduced.

ACKNOWLEDGMENTS

We would like to conclude by thanking individuals who have helped us with the development of this textbook. We would especially like to thank Susan L. Kline of The Ohio State University and Joseph W. Wenzel of the University of Illinois, whose assistance on the First and Second Editions of the book was extensive. We would also like to acknowledge the reviewers for the Third Edition, whose comments and suggestions were excellent: Beth M. Waggenspack, Virginia Tech University; Susan L. Kline, The Ohio State University; Jim Vickrey, Troy State University; Ronald O. Wastyn, James Madison University; Dale Herbeck, Boston College; Steven Schwarze, The University of Iowa; and Mark A. Pollock, Loyola University, Chicago. We would like to acknowledge the assistance of Solveig Robinson, Pacific Lutheran University, and Amanda Feller, Pacific Lutheran University, on the Fourth Edition. We would also like to thank the reviewers of the Fourth Edition: Raymie McKerrow, University of Ohio, and Chris Miller, California State University–Sacramento. We would also like to thank the reviewers of the Fifth Edition: James David Paterson, Imperial Valley College, and Dr. Thomas Preston Jr., University of Texas–Brownville, and all those who helped so much in its development, including: Chipo Chikara, Stephanie Christopher, Nigel Barron, Minerva Rios, and Leah Sprain. We are very appreciative of the work Danielle Endres contributed to the Fifth Edition and the expertise she brought to the project. In the Sixth Edition, we want to thank Katie Picket for the work she did helping edit the text and researching some of the case studies. We would also like to acknowledge the reviewers for the Sixth Edition: Martin Mehl, California Polytechnic State University; R. Blaine Davis, California State University–Sacramento; Jason Kemnitz, South Dakota State University; Joshua Butcher, Texas A&M University; Catherine L. Langford, Texas Tech University; Mark Porrovecchio, Oregon State University.

DEVELOPING A CONCEPTUAL FRAMEWORK FOR ARGUMENT

CHAPTER ONE

ARGUMENT AND CRITICAL THOUGHT

CHAPTER OUTLINE

KEY CONCEPTS

The need for argument arises from our desire to persuade or convince others of a point of view or course of action. When we perceive that something should be done or that others fail to understand our views, we may choose to advocate for our ideas and beliefs—we make arguments to inspire change. When we advocate for change or understanding, we link together arguments to support our ideas and positions.

Often, people assume that to argue is bad—that when we have an argument with someone we are having a problem with them. This view is very limited. Argumentation and advocacy are regular features of our daily lives. We advocate about which movie to see with our friends. We argue when we negotiate over how much to pay for a car or a house. We create arguments for or against the passage of legislation or rules.

Argumentation can be used for either good or bad, depending on the choices made by the advocate. This book focuses on how to positively use the skills of argumentation to (1) help others understand differing points of view, (2) explore ideas and alternatives, and (3) convince others of a need to change or act. Consider, for instance, the exchange between students in Box 1.1. This example presents a series of arguments that illustrate how discussion and arguing can work productively in each of these three ways.

In Box 1.1, the students used arguments to help define the issues for discussion, clarify perceptions, and advocate for different points of view. Throughout the conversation, they are engaged in the two processes that will be the focus of this book: critical thinking and argumentation.

BOX 1.1
DO BEAUTY CONTESTS HARM WOMEN?

Each year, more than two billion people worldwide participate in and watch beauty contests. Although Miss America, among other pageants, has experienced declining audiences over the last thirty years, some pageants, such as Miss World, continue to attract global attention and viewers. Yet, despite their popularity, the role pageants play in our culture and questions persist about whether they harm women. The following discussion between two students addresses some of these concerns:[1]

Kaidren: Beauty contests undermine women as people. They promote an ideal of female beauty that is unrealistic, and very, very few women can achieve it. Yet, this ideal pressures all women to conform to it. This is harmful because it encourages women to diet excessively, contributes to eating disorders, and encourages risky cosmetic surgery. But the "beauty myth" is so powerful that women willingly risk their health and even their lives to achieve what these contests promote.

Ramona: Wait a minute. This argument makes it sound as though women are easily brainwashed and can't figure out fact from fiction. There is nothing wrong with watching and admiring people who are fit, well proportioned, and healthy—in fact, these kinds of messages are especially important when you consider the obesity epidemic. We should strive for fitness. Anyway, both women and men enjoy beauty pageants; more women watch them than men. Women freely choose to enter them. No one is required to participate or watch—people get to make choices. Pageants haven't been forced on anyone and they don't force anyone to make bad choices.

Kaidren: You are missing the point. Healthy lifestyles are important and we should be teaching about how to be healthy. But that is not what beauty pageants do. They single out women as different from men. Women are judged on appearance rather than any other quality. And, achieving the ideal often requires poor health habits such as extreme dieting. Judging women—not men—on their looks subjugates women because it establishes an ideal feminine form that does not include intellect or any other ability. These contests set as standard of femininity that focuses almost exclusively on outward appearance at any cost.

(continued)

BOX 1.1   CONTINUED

Ramona: What is wrong with judging people on physical appearance? We judge people on particular attributes all the time. We evaluate professors on their ability to teach, irrespective of other abilities. We judge athletes on physical abilities without any concern for their intellect or emotional balance. We judge medical doctors on their skill and not on whether they are nice people. We evaluate people all the time based on physical, mental, or emotional attributes that are appropriate for the situation. Every competition, of every kind, values certain qualities over others and that's OK. Why would we exclude giving women recognition for outward appearance any more than we would exclude awarding a prize for best tattoo or the ability to lift weights?

Consider the issues that emerged in the preceding discussion. Both Kaidren and Ramona made arguments for and against pageants. As you read through the arguments again, consider the following questions:

1. Which person did a better job: Kaidren or Ramona? Why? Is it because her arguments support a position you already agree with? Or is it because she helped you understand something new and different that convinced you?
2. If you were Kaidren, what would your next argument be if this conversation continued? How do you think Ramona would respond?
3. Do you think these are good arguments? Are any issues or ideas missing? If you had been in the conversation, what would you have added?
4. Did you find any arguments that were not very good? What made them weak? How would you have strengthened them?

CRITICAL THOUGHT

Many theorists have explored critical thinking and the role it plays in education, our understanding of the world, and our understanding of ourselves. It helps us think systematically and rigorously about issues and problems that arise. Some, for instance, have described critical thinking as the process whereby the scientific method is applied by ordinary people to the ordinary world.[2] It requires the ability to analyze and evaluate conclusions based on a complete and coherent understanding of relevant issues. Joanne Kurfiss offered a clear definition of *critical thinking* as:

> *an investigation whose purpose is to explore a situation, phenomenon, question, or problem to arrive at a hypothesis or conclusion about it that integrates all available information and that therefore can be convincingly justified.*[3]

Often, when confronted with a challenge or problem, people want to leap to a solution or find a quick resolution. Critical thinking asks us to pause. A person who has thought critically about an issue will not settle for the apparent or obvious solution but will suspend judgment while seeking out relevant arguments, facts, and reasons that promote good decision making. When we fail to pause and consider alternatives, we make mistakes. Some barriers to critical thought are described in Box 1.2.

■ ■ ■ ■ ■

BOX 1.2

FIVE BARRIERS TO EFFECTIVE CRITICAL THINKING

Thinking critically is an important skill. However, most of us have learned habits and developed thinking skills that can inhibit our ability to approach issues and problems creatively.[4] These include:

1. Finding the "Right Answer." Most issues and problems have many possible solutions. However, most of our formal education has taught us to look for the one correct answer. Focusing on finding the right answer can obscure alternatives. If we become fixated on just one answer or a single approach, we may miss opportunities. Instead, look for several "correct" approaches or answers and then evaluate which is best.

2. Using Logic and Following Rules. Logic is important and it is part of critical thinking. Chapter 2 explores some of the characteristics of logic and how it is used to make arguments. Rules allow us to live and work together and they are discussed later in this chapter when we talk about spheres and fields. However, rules and logic impose restrictions on how we think about and work toward addressing issues. They can constrain thought because they tell us what is acceptable and what is not acceptable. An alternative is to assume there are no rules and use analogies to try to see relationships and connections among things that we might not otherwise perceive. Analogies, discussed in Chapter 6, are comparisons that can be figurative or literal. Discovering alternative ways of seeing issues can help open new approaches and ideas.

3. Being Practical. Sometimes people make a decision because they believe it is practical. They might say, "We need to buy a used laptop computer because that is what we can afford." The problem with this approach is that it presumes a conclusion because of an assumed constraint without considering alternatives. While issues of practicality ultimately may prevail, try imaging approaches irrespective of practical constraints. Consider what "should" be done as opposed to the feasibility of what "could" be done.

4. Avoiding Ambiguity. Ambiguity can be frightening because it introduces uncertainty and risk about decisions. Most people prefer certainty and strive for a clear, predictable understanding of events and actions. If we don't know for sure what will happen, we may decide not to try. However, the gray areas imposed by ambiguity are where creativity and innovative thinking exist. When you find ambiguity, try imagining the many possible outcomes associated with the issues or actions that are in the gray area.

5. Being Wrong Is Bad. Much of our upbringing and education imposes an assumption that being wrong is bad. Wrong answers result in bad grades. Wrong behavior results in punishment. As a consequence, people grow to fear being wrong and work hard to avoid it even though that approach may stifle creativity and inhibit finding alternatives. The challenge about being wrong is a tendency to deny or move away from the decision. Or sometimes we simply decide to do nothing out of fear of being wrong. Instead, work to understand why a decision was wrong and what other alternatives existed that might have improved the outcome.

Model of Critical Thinking

Critical thought is a complex process and, if done well, it can help us examine intricate ideas to better understand both the issues at hand and the consequences of acting. As we will discuss in Chapter 11, the world is systemically connected, and decisions about acting in one area will often have effects on other areas. For instance, we know that exposure to ultraviolet rays can cause skin cancer. Many people, therefore, have decided to reduce their exposure to sunlight and, when in the sun, use sunscreen for protection. This action makes sense given the risks associated with UV rays. However, an important and seldom discussed side effect of this action is that many people, particularly children, do not get enough Vitamin D. Normally, sunlight causes the body to produce this vitamin, which is necessary for bone growth and strength. Without enough UV exposure, people need to take steps to ensure a sufficient intake of Vitamin D. The point here is that the world is interconnected and decisions often have consequences and implications beyond the immediate decision. A process of systematic critical thinking can help uncover connections, evaluate options, and inform action.

Although there are many ways of understanding critical thinking, it can generally be considered as a process of moving through four interrelated steps, which are illustrated in Figure 1.1.[5] The four steps are (1) assess, (2) explore, (3) evaluate, and (4) integrate. Each step involves several parts, and together they represent a process whereby quality thought and decision making can develop.

Step 1. Assess. This step involves a clear identification of a problem or issue and finds the relevant information connected with it. Specifically, it includes asking the following questions:

- What is the need? People reason and argue because a need arises. The need can be anything from "Should I do my homework or go out with my friends?" to "Should euthanasia be provided on demand?" In the case of beauty pageants, the students chose a topic for a classroom presentation: "Do beauty contests harm women?" They could have spoken on any of a number of possible topics related to pageants. They might have argued "What should be done about beauty pageants?" Or, they could have asked, "What is a good topic to get a good grade on this assignment?" The need for argument is simply the impetus for critical thought and discussion. In Chapter 2, when we discuss argument situations, we will talk about the need as the "exigence" for argument. The need helps us frame the conversation so that we know what is included and what is excluded from discussion. Why are we talking about this issue? What are we trying to figure out?

- What is the purpose? Purpose represents the goal of the discussion. It can be as simple as understanding more about beauty pageants or as complicated as statistical analyses of how pageants and the "beauty myth" affect a group's identity and feelings of adequacy. The purpose of inquiry and argument does not need to focus on a particular course of action or what decision should be reached, but it does need to identify the goal of the inquiry: What do we hope to achieve? Why are we having this conversation? In Box 1.1, the purpose of the conversation was to reach an understanding about the potential harms related to beauty contests.

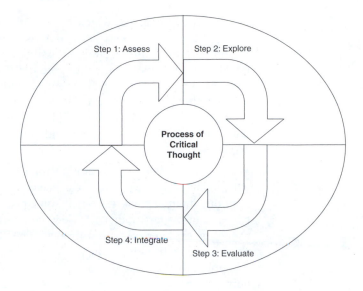

FIGURE 1.1   Critical Thought

- What information is needed? Answering questions and moving a conversation toward an outcome requires appropriate information. With beauty contests, the students needed to clearly understand what they are, how they worked, and what their effects were. They also needed to figure out if beauty contests are different from other kinds of events and contests in which people are judged for their appearance or a particular ability. Information can take many forms including statistical data, reports from eyewitnesses, individual observations, or any number of other sources of material that can help a person answer the question. Chapter 5, which focuses on evidence in argument, considers how information can be found and used. Information provides substance for thought. It is the material we draw upon to develop ideas and synthesize new thoughts.

Step 2. Explore. This step examines the interpretations and connections that occur within the issues, research, and other parts of the discussion. It includes an exploration of assumptions, biases, and the multiple points of view that affect how we understand and approach issues and ideas. Specifically, this step includes:

- *Concepts.* Concepts are the theories, definitions, rules, and laws that govern how we think and act. We know we should wear our seat belts—there are laws as well as theories of accident survival that tell us this. We know that we have a theory of fairness and equality. We have laws that protect minority rights while allowing majority rule. And we know that it is wrong to objectify or subjugate people. These concepts provide support for decisions we make about beauty contests or any other controversial subject. Concepts are constructs of the human mind.[6] They represent a framework within which we think and act. We may challenge concepts and offer replacements, but generally they inform our thinking about controversial subjects.

- *Assumptions.* Assumptions are our presuppositions and viewpoints that we take for granted. We assume, for instance, that people try to be fair. We assume that we don't want to subjugate people. And we also assume that people will watch beauty pageants, which in turn will sell products and services. This is one of the reasons contests such as Miss America and Miss World were started. It is important to understand our assumptions because they represent a "base-line," or starting point, for thought, and if they are flawed or misunderstood, the reasoning that stems from them can also be flawed. Assumptions are problematic, though, because they are part of our ways of thinking and are often unknown and unexplored by us. Therefore, revealing, testing, and challenging our assumptions help us understand our own choices and make clearer, better arguments.

- *Points of View.* People reason and think from different points of view. That is why, for instance, two people can see the same movie and have vastly different opinions about its quality. Or why some people support and others oppose beauty pageants. Our points of view come from our individual backgrounds, thoughts, experiences, and attitudes. They help us frame issues and integrate them into our thinking. The students, talking about beauty pageants, illustrate this point. Two educated people, with similar backgrounds, interpreted and understood the issues of beauty contests differently. Whenever we work with other people, we encounter different points of view. Part of critical thought involves a process of interpreting and understanding other views as well as our own.

Step 3. Evaluate. This step examines the quality of information and connections among possible solutions and considers how factors such as bias and points of view affect potential outcomes. Based on this synthesis and integration, approaches for managing issues emerge and are evaluated until a preferred approach is found. This step includes:

- *Interpretation and Inference.* When we think, we blend new information and ideas into our existing points of view, concepts, and assumptions. From this combination of questioning, examining, researching, and understanding, we reason toward a conclusion. We interpret our information and infer from it to reach our objectives. With beauty pageants, for instance, based on what the students knew, their research, and their conversations, they interpreted their data and inferred conclusions from it. The process of interpretation and inference is one of making sense of data and reasoning from it toward a goal.

- *Implications and Consequences.* Our reasoning and thinking carry with them implications and consequences. If we act on the conclusions we draw, what will happen? If we change our beliefs and attitudes, what effect will that have on future decisions we might make? Even though we often consider in-class presentations as simply another assignment, they have the potential to change classroom audiences. If the two students convince a group of students to act—or not to act—to boycott or support beauty pageants, there will be consequences. Critical thought is not a self-contained entity. It carries with it potential outcomes from the process.

Step 4. Integrate. The final step in the critical thinking process involves adopting the preferred solution, monitoring its effectiveness, and developing strategies for continued understanding and evaluation of how well the solution solves the problem and the conditions that caused it. This step, then, leads back to the first steps of monitoring, understanding, and assessing potential issues and problems.

Critical Thinking as a Skill

Critical thinking is a vital skill because it prevents people from making bad decisions and helps them solve problems. As Richard W. Paul and Gerald M. Nosich observed:

> The kind of "work" increasingly required in industry and business is "intellectual," that is, it requires workers to define goals and purposes clearly, seek out and organize relevant data, conceptualize those data, consider alternative perspectives, adjust thinking to context, question assumptions, modify thinking in light of the continual flood of new information, and reason to legitimate conclusions. Furthermore, the intellectual work required must increasingly be coordinated with, and must profit from the critique of, fellow workers.[7]

Paul and Nosich go on to comment that supervisors and employers value workers who can reason well and express themselves clearly.

Yet, as much as we claim to prize the value of critical thought and inquiry, we are generally not very good at it. Critical thinking theorists Richard Paul, Linda Elder, and Ted Bartell examined thirty-eight public universities and twenty-eight private universities to determine the level and quality of critical thinking instruction. They found that although 89 percent of teachers claimed critical thinking was a primary component of their instruction, only 19 percent could provide a clear explanation of what they taught that was critical, and only 9 percent were actually teaching critical thought.[8]

Most of us recognize the importance of critical thought. But it is not an easy skill to develop or use. It requires time and discipline. As we think, develop ideas, and argue, it is important to actively approach our questions with an intentional, critical lens. We should:

- Refine generalizations and avoid oversimplification.
- Generate and assess solutions to problems.
- Compare perspectives, interpretations, or theories.
- Read critically and seek out information that disagrees with our own perspectives.
- Listen critically, seriously considering views with which we disagree.[9]

ARGUMENTATION AND ARGUMENT

The process of argumentation engages us in a system of critical thought. *Argumentation is the process of making arguments intended to justify beliefs, attitudes, and values so as to influence others.* We see argumentation in media ads for products, campaign ads for candidates, newspaper editorials, Internet sites on public issues, business meetings where proposals are made, and in many other places. Argumentation occurs everywhere, and we deal with it as readers, listeners, writers, and speakers on a daily basis. In fact, argumentation is perhaps one of the most important skills we can develop. As participants in a world community and members of democratic communities, argument is the means by which we engage in discussion about our present and our future. Hugh Heclo, a professor of public affairs at George Mason University, took the position that American politics has been transformed in recent decades to become hypersensitive to public opinions and anxieties. Further, he noted that unprecedented access to information and the ability to disseminate opinions freely through the Internet and other media have made the individual voice and opinion more powerful than ever.[10] The importance of his observation should not be underestimated. We live in a time where the role of argument, arguers, and recipients has tremendous potential power to shape our world.

The Process of Argumentation

Argumentation is significant for the development and maintenance of a healthy society. It can occur only when people are interested in hearing or reading what others have to say and in seriously considering others' proposals. When parties engage in argumentation, they agree to certain conventions and tacit principles. They agree to rules for conducting the discussion, they make contributions as required, and they seek the approval of the other parties involved.[11] If people refuse even to listen to the other party, argumentation cannot occur.

Argumentation is a process of connecting individual arguments in ways that allow us to construct cases or overall positions. For instance, lawyers connect arguments to make a case for the prosecution or defense in courts of law. Legislators use individual arguments to argue for broad-based policies or political change. Businesses use many individual arguments to advocate for their products and services in marketing and public relations campaigns. Speeches, essays, group discussions, legislation, and political campaigns are all places where argumentation can take place. Argumentation is composed of individual arguments. *An argument is a set of statements in which a claim is made, support is offered for it, and there is an attempt to influence someone in a context of disagreement.*

It is important to understand argument in this sense—a claim, plus support for it in the form of reasoning and evidence—as distinguished from interpersonal arguments or disputes.[12] In this latter sense, "argument" is a kind of (usually unpleasant) interpersonal exchange, as when we say, "John and Mary were having an argument." Sometimes described as "quarrels" or "squabbles," these kinds of arguments usually involve two or more persons engaged in extended overt disagreement with each other.

That is not the sort of argument with which this book is concerned. Arguments of the kind described here occur when we say something like, "John made an argument in support of his proposal for the new marketing plan." This view considers whether an argument is sound and effective; it emphasizes argument as a reasoning process and considers arguments as units rather than as interactive processes.

Arguments are only one kind of communication. When we greet someone ("Hello, how are you?"), issue commands ("Shut the door"), vent our emotions ("I hate it when you do that!"), make promises ("I'll return your book tomorrow"), and so forth, we do not produce arguments. To clarify the differences between arguments and other forms of communication, we will describe the important features of argument according to our definition.

Argument Characteristics

First, to be considered an argument, a statement generally should make a claim. *A claim is an expressed opinion or a conclusion that the arguer wants accepted.* In the beauty pageant discussion, some claims were:

> Beauty contests undermine women as people.
>
> There is nothing wrong with watching and admiring people who are fit, well proportioned, and healthy.
>
> Judging women on their looks subjugates them.

Claims take on different forms in various contexts; they function as claims in relation to the support offered for them. As we will show in Chapter 4, claims in a given individual argument may themselves function as forms of support for the main claim, or thesis statement, of an extended argument. Examples of main claims include in criminal law the charge brought against the defendant by the prosecution; in the legislature the abbreviated version of a proposed bill or piece of legislation; and in medicine the diagnosis and recommended treatment regimen. In argumentation and debate, these main claims are often called *propositions* or *resolutions.*

When someone makes a claim, he or she is expected to offer further support for it in the form of reasons and information. If we issue a command or make a promise, we commit ourselves by making the statement, and no further proof is necessary.[13] Likewise, pure description ("The setting sun was reflected in a rosy haze"), small talk ("Things are so-so, could be better"), and other neutral statements generally do not make claims—they do not advance statements on which there is disagreement.

Sometimes, we can decide whether a statement is a claim only by considering its context. Arguers often leave their evidence, reasoning, or claim unstated. Do the following examples contain claims?

> When guns are outlawed, only outlaws will have guns.
> Coors Light, 'cause coffee's nasty after football.
> Every time I'm nice to him, he ignores me.

If we know that the first statement is a bumper sticker displayed by an opponent of gun control, we can conclude that it is a claim. Spelled out, it would say that "making guns illegal means that only those who circumvent the law will have guns." Knowing that the second statement occurred in a Coors ad would indicate that the claim is "[Buy] Coors Light" and that the remainder is a good reason for doing so. It is ambiguous whether the third statement is a claim or not. Knowing more about the person's relationship to her friend would help us to determine whether it is a claim. Some claims can be recognized as claims only when we know about the speaker's intention, the claim's relation to the other statements made along with it, or the situational context in which a claim is made.

The second characteristic of an argument is that support is offered for the claim. Claims are supported by evidence and by the reasoning or inferences that connect the evidence to the claim. Evidence comes in many forms, but it always functions as the foundation for argument or the grounds on which argument is based. When we make an argument, we move from statements we believe our receivers will accept (evidence) to statements that are disputable (claims). *Evidence consists of facts or conditions that are objectively observable, beliefs or statements generally accepted as true by the recipients, or conclusions previously established.*

Evidence does not consist only of objectively observable facts. From a rhetorical point of view (i.e., that arguers seek acceptance for their claims from audiences), it makes sense to regard any *proposition*, or *belief accepted by everyone in the audience*, as a starting point for argument. There are many statements ("A person is innocent until proven guilty" or "One ought to keep one's promises") that are not facts but that could function as evidence in relation to a claim.

In the beauty contest discussion at the beginning of this chapter, statements viewed as evidence by the speakers and accepted by others count as evidence. Examples of such statements include:

We have an obesity epidemic.
Both women and men enjoy beauty pageants.
We evaluate teachers, athletes, and professionals on particular attributes.

To be counted as evidence, statements should be accepted and viewed as relevant and true by the parties in a dispute or audiences to whom arguments are addressed. (If a statement is accepted by only one party—the arguer—then it is a claim, not evidence.) So, for instance, when Kaidren says that "the 'beauty myth' is so powerful that women willingly risk their health and even their lives," Ramona does not accept that as true and it does not function as evidence; rather it functions as a claim. If, however, Kaidren provided credible support from research, expert sources, or other trusted references that was accepted by Ramona, then this statement could be used as evidence. In other words, if people in an argument agree to the statement, it is evidence.

The arguer who begins by establishing claims based on statements that are not accepted will not get far. For statements to function as evidence and provide reliable grounds for claims, they must be acceptable to the recipients. For instance, if Kaidren could show specific examples of how pageants have been harmful or present credible support for how they have eroded women's rights, then Ramona's statements about their positive attributes would not be able to function as evidence because they would be in dispute. The process of argumentation begins with testing assumptions about what is true for the parties involved and then building—argument by argument—until a conclusion is reached.

Claims are also supported by the link that the arguer makes between the evidence and the claim. The part of the argument containing reasoning is frequently called the *inference*. Reasoning can take various forms. Those that occur most frequently will be described in Chapter 6, and you will become experienced at identifying them. *Reasoning constructs a rational link between the evidence and the claim and authorizes the step we make when we draw a conclusion.* Reasoning answers the question "How did you get from the evidence to the claim?"[14] It consists of general principles that explain how the evidence and the claim are connected.

The study of argument is made all the more interesting because arguers often do not explicitly state their inferences. They provide evidence and make claims, but often one can only guess how the link between the two was made. For example, if we study the evidence presented by the pageant discussants along with their claims, we will find that some of their inferences, all unstated, were functioning in the argument:

Women imitate beauty behavior seen in pageants and, as a result, engage in unhealthy practices in an attempt to achieve an idealized view of beauty.
Because both women and men enjoy pageants, women choose the consequences as opposed to having someone else impose a standard for beauty on them.
Judging people based on their physical beauty is the same thing as judging athletes and doctors on their skills.

Inferences usually make explicit a link, which enables the arguer to connect evidence with claims and thus construct an argument.

The third and last characteristic of arguments is that they are attempts to influence someone in a context where people disagree with one another. The phrase "*attempts* to influence" is important because the arguer may or may not succeed. The recipient of the argument is free not to agree with the expressed opinion of the arguer. The person to whom the argument is addressed may accept the claim, reject it, or continue to express doubts about it.

To say that arguments are "attempts to *influence*" means that there must be a recipient, or "arguee," to whom the argument is addressed who is capable of responding to it. The arguee must be open-minded and able to change her beliefs or actions because of the argument. Furthermore, in choosing argument instead of command or coercion, the arguer recognizes that the process of argument is reciprocal—that initiative and control pass back and forth as the arguer states his viewpoints and is the recipient weighs his support and decides whether to accept the argument.[15] While listening to arguments, the recipient retains the option of challenging, questioning, criticizing, or countering the expressed opinions of the arguer. The influence that arguments aim to bring about assumes many forms. Arguers may want recipients to become concerned about an issue on which they are ambivalent or neutral, to shift favorable to unfavorable attitudes or vice versa, or to change behavior.

Arguments are attempts to influence *someone*. An argument may be addressed to oneself, to another person, to a small group, to an audience, or to multiple audiences. Arguments occur in writing, in conversation, in public speeches, and in all forms of communication. Argument is a complex phenomenon that occurs in numerous forms and media of communication and that is addressed to many different kinds of audiences.

Finally, to say that argument occurs only when there is disagreement or the potential for disagreement means that the topic addressed must be controversial, capable of inciting opposing opinions from the parties involved. For example, consider the following dialogue:

John: Should we go to a movie tonight?
Mary: Fine, what would you like to see?
John: How about *Testing the Limit?*
Mary: OK. Do you want to go to the 7 o'clock showing?
John: Sure.

There is no argument here because there is no opposition. If Mary had rejected the whole idea of going to the movies, or if she had proposed another film and given reasons for preferring it, argumentation would have occurred. But as long as parties to a discussion agree with the opinions expressed, they will not produce arguments.

ARGUMENT CONTEXTS

Arguments occur in response to a question or need for inquiry. They develop among arguers, recipients, and larger communities. In the Coffee Is Hot case developed in Box 1.3, Liebeck and her advocates and McDonald's and its advocates were not alone exchanging claims and evidence. Public opinion was involved. Congress became involved. Doctors and lawyers were involved. Each group that was party to the argument

■ ■ ■ ■ ■

BOX 1.3

COFFEE IS HOT

The following story has become something of an urban legend—the story of the woman who spilled hot coffee in her lap and sued McDonald's because she was burned. Her judgment was for $2.9 million dollars. Many people have heard of the case, and most think the verdict is an indication of the decline of justice in this country and how lawyers are beginning to make it impossible for a business to manufacture anything without being sued. "Of course coffee is hot. If you spill it on yourself, you will get burned," they will say. Most people, however, are not familiar with the case; a description of it follows:

February 27, 1992, was a date on which Stella Liebeck's life changed dramatically. She was an active and energetic 79-year-old woman. She had just retired from a long career as a department store cashier.

On that morning, she did not have time for breakfast at her daughter's house. Her son, Jim, was catching an early flight out of Albuquerque, New Mexico, and to get him to the airport on time, she had to leave at dawn. After dropping off Jim at the airport, Stella and her grandson, Chris Tiano, pulled into a McDonald's restaurant drive-through to buy breakfast. Stella ordered and then went into the restaurant to add some cream and sugar to her coffee. She returned to the car and attempted to get the top off her coffee. "I took the cup and tried to get the top off," she later testified. She looked for a place to put it down, but the dashboard was slanted and there was no cup-holder in her Ford Probe. She described what happened next: "Both hands were busy. I couldn't hold it so I put it between my knees and tried to get the top off that way." With a strong tug the top came off and scalding coffee poured all over her lap. She screamed and tried desperately to get the pants from her sweat suit off as the 170-degree coffee burned. By the time she and Chris reached the emergency room, Stella had suffered second and third-degree burns across her buttocks, her thighs, and her labia. All that she remembers is the pain.

Although the jury initially awarded her $2.9 million for pain, suffering, and injuries, a judge later cut the amount to $640,000. Yet her case became one of the leading cases for tort reform in Congress—an attempt to diminish runaway damage claims in lawsuits. Was her case unjust? Was her case another example of lawyers trying to get all they can out of the system? The answer may not be as easy as it at first seems.

Liebeck spent seven days in the hospital and then three more weeks recuperating at home. During that time her movement was limited and she was in constant pain from the burns. She was again hospitalized for skin grafts over the affected areas of her body and during this time, while practically immobilized, her weight dropped 20 pounds to 83 pounds while suffering the pain from the grafts.

Initially she was not interested in suing. In a letter she wrote to McDonald's, she asked that they turn down the temperature of the coffee and requested $2,000—the amount of her out-of-pocket expenses. McDonald's offered her $800. Upon further investigation, Liebeck discovered that McDonald's had been sued in the past for keeping its coffee too hot and that McDonald's had received more than 700 burn complaints over 10 years. Yet, the coffee continued to be sold at the same, burning temperature.[16]

had its own background, assumptions, and standards for evaluating the quality and validity of the arguments produced. The types of arguments created as part of the dispute were dependent on the context that created the dispute.

When most people hear of this case, they conclude that Liebeck represents another person who was able to "beat the system." Coffee is hot—that is not the fault of

McDonald's. If people are burned, that is their own fault. We live in a litigious society where examples such as this illustrate the need to change the legal system. Sherman Joyce, president of the American Tort Reform Association, argued that Liebeck's case pointed out "a lot of the problems with the system. . . . It demonstrates that the system needs reform."[17] At the same time, Robert H. Scott, the trial judge in the case, wanted to send McDonald's a stern warning. He said that it "was appropriate to punish and deter" McDonald's given its history of burns.[18] And members of Congress moved quickly to pass legislation to reduce the amount of damages a plaintiff could collect.

This case illustrates how a common set of facts—what happened to Stella Liebeck—can be examined, reviewed, and debated among different groups of people who arrive at very different conclusions. Members of the legal community thought that punitive damages would deter McDonald's from unsafe and unnecessary practices. Political lobbyists used the case to illustrate the need for reform and argued that the punitive award was an abuse. Politicians looked for ways to act on the perceived abuses and wrote legislation to minimize any future abuses.

Cases such as this are not all that uncommon. For instance, when two teenagers from the Bronx sued McDonald's for making them obese, many responded that it was preposterous to hold a fast-food chain accountable for individual choice. Critics claimed that the girls were to blame for their own ignorance and lack of willpower. And, some said, if anyone were to blame, it should be their parents for failure to exercise reasonable control as well as family genetics.[19]

Although this case was dismissed, the arguments about the unhealthy consequences of fast food began to make their way into the public sphere. Newspaper articles, books, and even an award-winning documentary film, *Super Size Me*, made the technical arguments of the court cases part of the public debate about health.

Manufacturers of fast food and snack food began to listen. Kraft Foods, producer of Oreo cookies, announced that it would reduce the size of its portions in single-serving packages. McDonald's ended the Super size meal option and reduced the size of some of its servings. Frito-Lay decided to reduce or eliminate trans fats from their foods because of possible health risks associated with them.[20]

People from different associations and groups see different things in the world around them. They talk of different subjects and have their own rules of discourse. Lawyers, for instance, have very strict rules for what can serve as evidence for an argument. In science, certain types of reasoning are considered superior. Scientists tend to look for cause and effect and tend not to reason from analogy. Arguments should be proven objectively. This section will focus on argument contexts. It will look at why members from different fields and situations interpret arguments differently and how arguers can use knowledge of occasions to better craft arguments.

Advocates do not present their arguments in a vacuum. They adapt their arguments to their own knowledge and interest in a particular topic as well as to an audience's knowledge and interest in that topic. From an arguer's assessment of the connection between an audience and a message, arguments are formed. When scientists write about their research in academic journals, they approach their audience differently than if they were discussing the same research to a national audience on a late-night television program. When arguing before their peers, physicists or astronomers tend to employ technical proofs and reasons because the audience is expert in the field. In front of public audiences of nonexperts, the same scientists tend to employ different forms of evidence and reasoning so that a general audience can understand the claims.

Arguments develop in an environment of advocacy that we refer to as argument context. *Argument contexts grow out of the confluence of arguer, question or need, and audience.* Just as the physical environment influences how plants or animals will grow, argument contexts influence how arguments are developed and communicated.

Argument contexts can be characterized as belonging to one of three types of spheres. *Argument spheres are social constructs that guide how arguments are produced and evaluated.* Spheres may be personal, technical, or public in nature. Personal sphere arguments are made and evaluated by people who are engaged in a personal relationship. Technical sphere arguments are made among people who are experts in their fields, and the arguments are evaluated by the standards created by the members of the field. *Argument fields are sociological contexts for arguments and are marked by patterns of communication that participants in argumentative dispute can recognize.*[21] Argument fields provide their members with an understanding of the rules and conventions governing the development of arguments as well as their interpretation. Fields include many different kinds of groups, from doctors to lawyers, and from educators to scientists. Public sphere arguments are arguments made to general audiences that are evaluated using standards created by the general audiences. They are intended to be understood and evaluated using the general tools and abilities of larger, public audiences.

The variables of arguer, audience, and message are influenced by the sphere in which the arguments will take place. Whereas some audiences, such as a legal judge, require precise reasoning from specific kinds of evidence, other audiences may be moved more by their passions and feelings toward issues such as gun control or abortion and may apply very different standards to judge the value of the argument. The context for the argument informs the advocate of the rules, conventions, and constraints that should govern the development of the arguments.

Liebeck's case provides some important clues as to how argument contexts function. Liebeck's case became a fence around which arguments for and against tort reform have been debated. Although tort reform had been an issue for several years, her case provided an opportunity to bring the debate into the open. Further, it showed a clash between two powerful communities of people: lawyers and politicians. Many members of the legal profession saw this as an example of how well the justice system works in America. A single, elderly woman can beat a giant corporation when the corporation does something wrong. The political community, however, saw this case as another abuse of legal power.

The following section describes how the two concepts of argument sphere and argument field work together to create the context for argument.

Argument Spheres

The concept of argument spheres provides us with a way of understanding argument occasions by considering the elements of arguer, recipient, and message. Spheres are socially created guidelines that determine how arguers construct their arguments and how recipients evaluate them. Thomas B. Farrell and G. Thomas Goodnight, in their discussion of argument spheres, suggest that three spheres—personal, technical, and

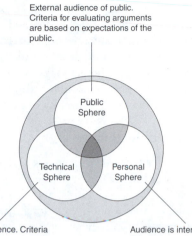

External audience of public. Criteria for evaluating arguments are based on expectations of the public.

Public Sphere

Technical Sphere

Personal Sphere

Specialized audience. Criteria for evaluating arguments are generated by member expertise (such as in law),

Audience is internal and relational. Criteria for evaluating arguments are generated by the participants.

FIGURE 1.2   The Three Argument Spheres

public—can describe argument contexts.[22] Figure 1.2 illustrates the connections among the spheres.

Personal Sphere

The personal sphere contains the relatively informal arguments among people in typically casual settings. Personal arguments are those among friends and family governed by the interpersonal rules for arguments generated in the relationship. Typically, personal arguments do not pay careful attention to evidence, reasoning, or well-framed claims. The rules and procedures for personal arguments are determined by the relationship and not by external forces.[23] For instance, when Liebeck and her daughter discussed how to arrange for in-home care while she recovered from her burns, the arguments were personal and based on a private understanding of the relationship and its needs. Personal sphere arguments are best understood by the participants because of the nature of their relationship with one another.

Technical Sphere

The technical sphere contains arguments that adhere to rules that are more formalized and rigorous and tend to be generated by particular groups of people, such as doctors or lawyers. Arguments in this sphere might include the arguments made in academic papers and essays, legal arguments, scientific arguments, and religious arguments. Arguments in this sphere are specialized and focused toward a particular audience.

Perhaps our most common exposure to technical argument is in the workplace, where people develop a language and set of rules that are unique to their own profession and interests. Professionals in any given field, from law, to medicine, to construction and manufacturing, share an understanding of what is a reasonable or unreasonable argument. Consequently, arguments that are coherent and well argued by the members of that field may be meaningless to other recipients who are not members of that field.

This is what happened in Liebeck's case. Once attorneys became involved, the arguments shifted from the personal experience of being burned and in pain to the legal implications of damage and liability. The arguments moved toward a focus on law and legal precedent, and different rules for arguing applied to the more specialized arguers and recipients. The language of the arguments changed, as did rules of evidence, reasoning, and presentation of argument. Unlike personal arguments, these arguments are evaluated by the community of people that applies the standards of the community.

Public Sphere

The public sphere contains arguments that are intended for public or general audiences. These arguments are evaluated by publicly understood and accepted standards for criticism and analysis. Public arguments include the kinds of arguments politicians might make or that a public relations officer for a corporation might present. Editorials in newspapers typically are written for the public sphere. Whereas the public sphere has relatively formalized rules for appropriateness (for example, one cannot make slanderous comments about another), the rules are understood and used by a broader public than those of the technical sphere, which focuses on a particular community of people.

The concept of the public sphere, as opposed to either the technical or personal spheres, has a dual meaning. First, the term *public* suggests that it is open and available for inspection by others. Second, public matters are those that affect a community of individuals; they are issues of common concern that are the subject of much public discourse. Politics is an example of public discourse, as is consumer product safety and foreign trade agreements.

The public sphere is also a blend of issues related to personal, technical, and public concerns. Individual values are often debated in the public arena; for example, we experience arguments over the need for gun control or the legalization of certain controlled substances. These might typically be seen as personal arguments about personal choices, yet these arguments find their way into the public arena as a means to create a social agenda and to promote certain values. Similarly, technical arguments become the substance for extended public debates. The causes of cancer or AIDS that are systematically studied and researched by scientists become the subject of public debates about policies and programs to remedy the diseases.

The public sphere provides an important venue for arguers. It offers them opportunities to extend knowledge and to focus on the plights or successes of others. People working in technical spheres may highlight issues for the public sphere by creating "events" that elevate issues to a public level. John W. Delicath and Kevin Michael Deluca offered an example of this when they wrote of the possibilities to create "image events" (staged protests designed for media dissemination) to bring environmental issues into the public sphere.[24]

This is important, because once issues reach the public sphere they can be heard by a mass audience. David Zarefsky noted that the public sphere "represents the ideal of full and equal participation and deliberation by those with interests in a decision. It shuttles between unbridled individualism and unchecked collectivism, between rampant self-interest and totalitarian rule, between freedom and social order."[25] No matter how one considers it, the public sphere is a significant domain for arguments that have the potential to affect a culture, its institutions, or its people. Zarefsky's challenge to all arguers is to find ways to enhance occasions for deliberation—to seek venues for making arguments that have the potential to transform and change culture and society by blending arguments from the personal, the technical, and the public.[26]

The Liebeck case is a good example of how public argumentation works. In the beginning, Stella Liebeck talked with her daughter and McDonald's on a personal or private level, asking that the hospital bills be covered. When she was unsuccessful, she sought the technical advice of professionals who pursued the case in the technical sphere of law. Following her award for damages, politicians created a series of public arguments to inspire tort reform and attempt to impose controls on a legal system that seemed to have gone out of control. The same event generated arguments in all three spheres and moved from the personal to the technical to the public.

The Role of Spheres in Argument

Understanding the role played by spheres is important in understanding how to produce and receive arguments. Arguments need to be adapted to the appropriate sphere for which they are intended. Arguments are shaped, understood, and judged differently depending on the sphere in which they operate. Notice, for example, how arguments changed as Liebeck's case was placed into different spheres. Initially Liebeck had no intention of suing McDonald's. She wrote them a letter asking them to reimburse her for out-of-pocket medical expenses (about $2,000) and to reduce the temperature of their coffee. This was a personal argument. It was governed by the rules created by the relationship between McDonald's and Liebeck.

McDonald's offered $800, which was not an acceptable amount. At that point, Liebeck turned to a professional who might help her persuade McDonald's to pay for her treatment. The professional was a member of the legal community who worked to focus the arguments at a technical level toward a judge and jury. The professional argued that the coffee was a defective product and that it was unsafe according to the law. The jury awarded Liebeck $2.9 million on the strength of technical arguments. The verdict and the award were based on the rules established in the legal profession. These were highly formalized rules developed and understood by a highly specialized community.

The media then carried the story to the public, which heard that a person was awarded almost $3 million for burning herself with hot coffee. The standards for judging the argument at a public level were very different, and the award was seen as unreasonable because commonly held public standards and beliefs are that coffee is hot. This is why pro–tort reform protesters later carried signs saying, "She spilled it on herself." To the public, the trial and award did not make sense.

Certain arguments have an appeal beyond the sphere in which they were produced. In such cases, arguments may be criticized and evaluated by multiple sets of standards as different communities attempt to understand and evaluate them. An interesting example of an argument that was adapted to both the technical and public spheres is the one presented in Rachel Carson's book *Silent Spring.*[27] This book was written initially for a technical audience about the dangers of a pesticide, DDT, in the environment. Carson warned that DDT was destroying the integrity of robins' eggs and posed a serious long-term threat to the ecosystem. Her argument was heard beyond the technical community to which it was addressed; the book soon found its way to bookstore shelves, and her arguments became the basis for public legislation to ban the pesticide in the United States. Similarly, technical works such as dissertations or academic papers may occasionally attract a general reader when they put forth ideas that appeal to different communities.

Arguments do not reside in a given sphere forever. For any subject of argument, the sphere can become larger or smaller as time progresses. Arguments may move from public discussion to technical to personal discussion and back again. Argument contexts change over time, depending on the audiences and the salient or important issues that affect them. Carson's book today would receive less attention than it did in 1970 because the public sphere for that argument is very small; DDT has already been banned, and the time for the argument has passed. Similarly, the arguments in the book would exist in a relatively small technical sphere because the claims in the book have already been accepted. Other arguments, however, may find that their opportunities within any given sphere are large as interest increases.

Groups of people interested in similar topics and issues may be able to identify and facilitate argument transitions among spheres. These groups, which Archon Fung of the John F. Kennedy School of Government at Harvard University referred to as "mini-publics," act as an educational forum, a participatory and advisory group, or a problem-solving entity.[28] In any case, the idea is that small groups of people can help transition ideas from technical and often hidden arenas to public spheres that attain national or global attention. Skilled arguers have this capacity.

An interesting study conducted by sociologist Gianpaolo Baiocchi examined this idea when he wrote about how small publics—groups of people with similar interests— can work together to create an impetus for change in a larger, broader public discussion. His study focused on participatory governance in Brazil, and his conclusion demonstrated an important link between the technical and public spheres. People may band together to fight poverty or injustice for their own neighborhood and community. They may also attain a sufficient critical mass to then take those issues to the larger, policy-making sphere.[29] The following section considers how the rules of specific fields shape argument spheres.

Argument Fields

The preceding discussion of argument spheres developed the idea that arguments are constrained by the norms or rules for appropriate argument as established by the sphere. In other words, arguments in the personal sphere are shaped by standards for evaluation that the participants decide to use. Technical arguments, however, are shaped and evaluated by external criteria generated by the members of the technical sphere. And public arguments are evaluated by standards appropriate for judging common arguments targeted at the general populace.

The Role of Fields in Argument

The concept of argument fields focuses on the expertise generated by experts for the purposes of analysis and understanding. Argument fields provide arguers with a context for making and interpreting argument, as well as common ground or a framework for conducting dispute. Perhaps argumentation theorist Joseph Wenzel put it best when he said to think of fields as representing "*some* sort of universe of discourse."[30] Different professions—such as law, education, medicine, or politics—have a language and set of rules for argument that govern how arguments are made and judged. These rules may be external to the arguers in the sphere, and they provide a basis by which the arguments can be developed and evaluated.

The very fact that an argument takes place in a law court, a corporate boardroom, a medical care setting, or an art class may influence the procedures that are used and the standards that are applied to make arguments and judgments about arguments. Argument fields define the rules for engagement and resolution. In other words, they determine what kind of evidence and support will be considered appropriate for a claim. Some fields are highly defined with very rigid rules, whereas other fields are loosely defined with norms for arguing.

In *The Uses of Argument* and subsequent works, philosopher Stephen Toulmin emphasized the importance of argument fields in understanding and interpreting argument.[31] The arenas in which arguments are developed influence the forms of argument, the bases on which inferences are made, and the means for deciding disputes. These fields are both social and communicative phenomena. In other words, fields for argument are made by people through interaction; they act as the source for the conventions and criteria used in conducting arguments, and they are an important feature of arguments.[32] Of the three spheres, the technical sphere is the one most rigidly defined by fields.

Field Characteristics

Argument fields include such examples as law, ethics, medicine, science, and aesthetics. Furthermore, each of these fields has subfields (e.g., tort law, family law, criminal law) that function as fields of argument. Describing what fields exist at any given moment can be difficult because we are constantly surrounded by and involved in many different fields. Nevertheless, the field in which arguments are produced affects the nature of the argument; as the field changes, so does the way the argument is constructed. Robert Rowland made the point that it "seems obvious that arguments vary by field."[33]

Although they can be complex and difficult to isolate, generally fields share five common characteristics:

- They are a human creation.[34] This means that fields develop over time through social interaction. People create them, shape them, and change them.
- They are developed by people with shared goals.[35] People sustain interaction and develop fields when they share objectives and purposes. In science, for example, the purpose is to identify the laws of nature; in ethics, the purpose is to distinguish what is good and morally right from what is not; and in medicine, the purpose is to promote health by preventing and curing illness.
- They develop specialized language and rules.[36] When people converse to achieve their objectives, there are certain rules of conduct as well as language that facilitate their objectives. We may call such specialized language *jargon*, but for the members of a field, the language carries unique meanings.

- People may belong to many fields.[37] Humans share many different objectives and adhere to many different sets of rules. There are, for instance, attorneys to abide by the rules of the legal profession who also teach and follow those rules. They may also belong to a political party and follow the ideology of the organization. Any single person may belong to and practice the standards of many different fields. We can be members of as many fields as serve our interests or objectives.
- Fields survive only as long as they serve the common purpose of their members and as long as they can adapt to changing objectives.[38] When a field no longer serves its members and cannot adapt to meet their needs, it will disappear.

Any field can be described by these five dimensions. For example, if we look at the field of law, we would say first that law is a human creation. Lawyers were not needed until human beings began developing rules and laws for governance and discovered a need to have a group of people interpret and apply the rules. Second, the legal field consists of people with shared goals. Lawyers and judges work to apply the law in civil and criminal matters to punish wrongdoers and seek justice. Third, members of the legal field develop their own specialized language to describe activities and directions in their field. They talk about writs (any legal documents used for court action), habeas corpus (a type of document used to release someone from unlawful imprisonment because of lack of due process), praecipe (writs that command a defendant to do the thing required or show just reason why he or she cannot), and estoppel (a document that prevents someone from acting in contradictory ways to the detriment of another party), among many other terms. A field develops a unique language that unites and binds its members and gives them a language within a language (in this case a legal language within English) that identifies them as members of a community or field. Fourth, members of the legal fields may also belong to many other fields. For instance, many politicians are either practicing or former attorneys and judges. Some lawyers move into education and teach at law schools. Finally, lawyers need to be able to adapt to changing conditions and times for the field to survive. As new laws are passed, members of the legal community need to remain current so that the correct rules and precedents are applied to their cases. As laws become more complex, attorneys often find themselves in very specialized areas within the field. They may, for instance, specialize in laws pertaining to intellectual property or the preservation of the environment, among many other areas. Failure to adapt to changing rules and laws can lead to individual members of the field being disbarred or to the dissolution of the field itself.

Using Fields to Evaluate Arguments

Toulmin, among others, has concluded that arguments are judged according to the standards of the field for which they are produced.[39] Different standards are applied in the field of law than in the field of politics. And standards used in either of these fields are different from those in medicine or education. For example, consider the debate that has surrounded President John F. Kennedy's assassination for decades. The FBI and prosecutor's office (legal field) in 1963 believed there was sufficient evidence to indict Lee Harvey Oswald for the murder. Witnesses saw him rush by with a panicked expression. He fit the general description of a man who left the school book depository building, and when he was arrested Oswald yelled, "Well, it is all over now," and tried to shoot one of the arresting officers.[40] The legal field has rules for evidence and is swayed particularly by physical evidence (the rifle, Oswald's finger-prints) and eyewitness testimony (what he said before the shooting, his behavior after the shooting). In the legal field, these were enough for an indictment.

Yet the scientific community did not think Oswald could have acted alone. An 8-mm home movie of the assassination recorded by Abraham Zapruder showed precisely when the shots were fired and showed which bullets hit the president. Rifle experts timed the lapse between the shots and then tested the rifle allegedly used to assassinate Kennedy. The rifle, they concluded, required a minimum of 2.3 seconds between shots to operate the bolt and re-aim. Because Oswald shot three times—and assuming the first bullet was in the chamber—the total time required by Oswald if he acted alone was a minimum of 4.5 seconds; yet Zapruder's film shows that 4.8 seconds were necessary, which made it possible but not very likely that Oswald could have re-loaded, aimed, and fired in the time allowed. Furthermore, the second bullet fired has been dubbed by conspiracy theorists as the "magic bullet." What made this bullet appear magical is that it appeared to strike Kennedy and then change direction and hit Governor John Connally. Because bullets travel in straight lines, and because few thought that one bullet could do as much damage as this one appeared to have done, the scientific community was unconvinced of the single assassin theory.[41]

In 1964, the Warren Commission (political field) was convened, and in 1978 the House Select Committee on Assassination was created. Their conclusions were that one man had the time to aim and fire and that even the "magic bullet" could have passed through both President Kennedy and Governor Connally. There was no second gunman, the two panels found, and there was no one other than Oswald who could have committed the crime.[42]

A few years ago, a British television company attempted to stage the trial of Lee Harvey Oswald, which never actually took place. The program's producers flew all the participants to London for the mock trial. Defending Oswald was Gerry Spence, who was a very successful defense attorney and known for defending high-profile clients such as Karen Silkwood and Imelda Marcos. Vincent Bugliosi, the prosecutor in the Charles Manson case, prosecuted Oswald. The jury was drawn from a pool of Dallas voters, and the judge was also drawn from Texas. The witnesses in the case were either eyewitnesses at the time, the recorded testimony of eyewitnesses, or experts who had testified in either the Warren or House Select Committee hearings. At the conclusion of the trial, the jury concluded that Oswald was the assassin and returned a unanimous verdict of "guilty."[43]

It is interesting that for several decades, more than two hundred books, a dozen documentary films, and a Hollywood feature film have been dedicated to this one event in history. Although there are many explanations for the continued interest in Kennedy's assassination, one reason is that members of different fields continue to offer conflicting opinions and support them with different forms of evidence and reasoning. In the field of medicine, pathologists have suggested that the bullet's path is inconsistent with the lone assassin theory. Yet, legal and political fields seem to have enough evidence to conclude Oswald's guilt. And members of the scientific community argue that one person did not have time to fire all of the shots. Conflicts among fields are brought about by different rules of what constitutes acceptable reasoning or evidence and can lead to confusion among different audiences.

Field Standards

Argument fields are important for arguers and critics alike because they provide us with a means of judging arguments. When we evaluate arguments to determine whether they are true or false, good or bad, valid or invalid, we apply two sets of tests: field-dependent standards and field-invariant standards.[44] *Field-dependent standards are the rules, norms, and prescriptions guiding the production of arguments in a particular field.* These are the standards that the particular field identifies as appropriate for evaluating arguments. Therefore, legal standards pertaining to hearsay evidence applied to legal arguments would constitute field-dependent standards.

Field-invariant standards apply generally, regardless of the field of argument. Although arguments in the personal sphere seldom come under rigorous scrutiny, public arguments do. For the most part, this means that when general audiences consider arguments in the public sphere, they apply certain common standards to the quality of the argument. Arguments, for instance, should not attempt to deceive recipients. Arguments should also have the required parts of an argument: claim, evidence, reasoning, and an attempt to influence.

The notion of an argument field is valuable because understanding fields helps arguers understand many of the rules and conventions for judging between competing claims in a controversy. Depending on which standards from which fields are applied to arguments, the results can be very different. This is why it is important for advocates to be aware of the fields from which they argue and to learn as much about the field for argument as the subject of argument.

SUMMARY

This book focuses on critical thinking and argumentation. Critical thinking, a vital skill in today's society, enables a person to investigate a situation, problem, question, or phenomenon to arrive at a viable hypothesis or conclusion. It includes such skills as clearly stating a question for discussion, clarifying the meaning of terms, developing and applying evaluative criteria, and evaluating the credibility of sources. Once you have gathered information on a topic and analyzed it using these processes, you must communicate your reasoning to others.

This process is called argumentation, which involves making arguments intended to justify beliefs, attitudes, and values so as to influence others. Argumentation is the second focus of this book. It involves constructing cases for or against a proposal. Argumentation occurs in law court cases, governmental legislation, marketing campaigns, and business proposals. Such extended cases are made up of individual arguments. An argument is a set of statements in which a claim is made, support is offered for it, and there is an attempt to influence someone in a context of disagreement. A person making a claim is expected to offer further support by using evidence and reasoning. Evidence consists of facts or conditions that are objectively observable, beliefs or statements generally accepted as true by the recipients, or conclusions previously established. Reasoning is frequently expressed in the form of inferences, constructs a rational link between the evidence and the claim, and authorizes the step we make when we draw a conclusion.

Arguments are produced for particular contexts, and they are generally evaluated with respect to their time and place. These contexts influence the way arguments are created, understood, and evaluated. Contexts are an important part of the argument's development because they shape the way arguers attempt to influence recipients. Generally, argument contexts are the intersection of two concepts: argument spheres and argument fields. These two concepts help us understand how to produce and evaluate arguments.

Argument spheres are the specific contexts in which people argue. Recipients understand arguments and coordinate them through their own frames of reference through the use of argument sphere. Generally, argument spheres are of three types: personal, technical, and public. When people argue in personal spheres, the arguments are relatively informal and casual. Arguments in the technical sphere are governed by rigorous and specialized rules, which serve to specify the types of acceptable evidence and reasoning. Public-sphere arguments are arguments that are produced and evaluated in a public arena. They are intended for public audiences and are criticized using public standards. Depending on the sphere the arguer operates in, arguments are adapted and criticized using the rules or conditions of the given sphere.

Argument fields help provide a context for making and interpreting arguments. Fields are specialized contexts that determine the rules for acceptable evidence, the types of issues to be considered, the rules or procedures for conducting arguments, the requirements for proving a case, and even the specialized language in which arguments are expressed. Examples of such fields are law, medicine, and science. Fields are important in judging between competing claims because they provide the basic principles in which many forms of reasoning are based. Some standards for judging arguments are field dependent and arise from the particular context in which the argument is made. Other standards are field invariant and apply to all arguments regardless of their contexts.

GLOSSARY

Argument (p. 10) is set of statements in which a claim is made, support is offered for it, and there is an attempt to influence someone in a context of disagreement.

Argument contexts (p. 16) grow out of the confluence of arguer, question or need, and audience.

Argument fields (p. 16) are sociological contexts for arguments and are marked by patterns of communication that participants in argumentative dispute can recognize.

Argument spheres (p. 16) are social constructs that guide how arguments are produced and evaluated.

Argumentation (p. 9) is the process of making arguments intended to justify beliefs, attitudes, and values so as to influence others.

Claim (p. 10) is an expressed opinion or a conclusion that the arguer wants accepted.

Critical thinking (p. 4) is an investigation whose purpose is to explore a situation, phenomenon, question, or problem to arrive at a hypothesis or conclusion about it that integrates all available information and that therefore can be convincingly justified.

Evidence (p. 11) consists of facts or conditions that are objectively observable, beliefs or statements generally accepted as true by the recipients, or conclusions previously established.

Field-dependent standards (p. 24) are the rules, norms, and prescriptions guiding the production of arguments in a particular field.

Field-invariant standards (p. 24) apply generally, regardless of the field of argument.

Personal sphere (p. 17) contains the relatively informal arguments among people in typically casual settings.

Public sphere (p. 18) contains arguments that are intended for public or general audiences.

Reasoning (p. 12) constructs a rational link between the evidence and the claim and authorizes the step we make when we draw a conclusion.

Technical sphere (p. 17) contains arguments that adhere to rules that are more formalized and rigorous and tend to be generated by particular groups of people, such as doctors or lawyers.

EXERCISES

(Please note: Throughout the book, exercise items marked with an asterisk have answers provided in Appendix A.)

Exercise 1 Can you distinguish a statement that is an argument from one that is not? Remember that an argument

  A. Puts forth a claim
  B. Offers support for it, and
  C. Makes an attempt to influence someone.

Now, consider the following statement:

  If it rains tomorrow, I'm going home.

This is not an argument because the speaker offers neither a claim nor support for it. Rather, he merely states his intention, which does not depend on the other person's acceptance. Furthermore, the speaker does not explicitly try to influence anyone else but merely states what he himself intends to do. Consider the following statements, decide whether or not they are arguments, and explain the reasons for your decision. Remember that statements of one's emotional state or pure descriptions are not generally viewed as arguments.

  ∗1. There is a plethora of credible scenarios for achieving human-level intelligence in a machine. We will be able to evolve and train a system combining massively parallel neural nets with other paradigms to understand language and model knowledge, including the ability to read and understand written documents. . . . We can then have our computers read all of the world's literature—books, magazines, scientific journals, and other available material. Ultimately, the machines will gather knowledge on their own by venturing into the physical world, drawing from the full spectrum of media and information services, and sharing knowledge with each other (which machines can do far more easily than their human creators).

  Ray Kurzweil, *The Age of Spiritual Machines: When Computers Exceed Human Intelligence* (New York: Viking, 1999), 3.

  2. Fred: Why are you leaving so early for the meeting?
      Gale: Sue asked me to pick her up on the way. Are you going to watch that movie at 8 o'clock?
      Fred: Yeah. It lasts until 10 and then I thought I'd go to bed early.
      Gale: Fine. I'll see you in the morning.

3. Today's students are no longer the people our educational system was designed to teach . . . today's students *think and process information fundamentally differently* from their predecessors. These differences go far further and deeper than most educators suspect or realize. "Different kinds of experiences lead to different brain structures," says Dr. Bruce D. Perry of Baylor College of Medicine. . . . It is very likely that *our students' brains have physically changed*—and are different from ours—as a result of how they grew up. But whether or not this is *literally* true, we can say with certainty that their *thinking patterns* have changed.

   Marc Prensky, "Digital Natives, Digital Immigrants," *On the Horizon* 9 (October 2001).

4. I try to remember when this rivalry between my daughter and me first began. I can't. It sometimes seems that we have always been this way with each other, that we have never gotten along any better or differently. I would like to make my daughter less miserable if I can, to help her be happier and much more pleased with herself, I don't know how.

   Joseph Heller, *Something Happened* (New York: Ballantine Books, 1974), 179.

✳5. As a linguist, [Mr. McWhorer, a professor of linguistics at the University of California at Berkeley and a senior fellow at the Manhattan Institute, a policy research group in New York City], he knows that grammatical rules are arbitrary and that in casual conversation people have never abided by them. Rather, he argues, the fault lies with the collapse of the distinction between the written and the oral. Where formal, well-honed English was once de rigueur in public life, he argues, it has all but disappeared, supplanted by the indifferent cadences of speech and ultimately impairing our ability to think.

   Emily Eakin, "Going at the Changes in, Ya Know, English," *New York Times* (November 15, 2003), www.nytimes.com.

6. The good news is that students care deeply about the issues of the day, and they wish that politics gave them a way to act on their concerns. Colleges could help them by offering a different kind of political education—not just an education *about* politics but an education *for* politics, for the practice of democratic citizenship. For that to happen, colleges will have to broaden their definition of politics. Citizens have a larger role to play than voting and trying to influence their officials. We have to present political life in its larger dimensions so that students can find a variety of roles to play.

   David Mathews, "Why Students Hate Politics," *Chronicle of Higher Education* (July 7, 1993): A56.

7. The immense suffering by animals in connection with the fur industry is staggering and it pains me that so many men and women seem to be so totally indifferent to this fact. Maybe someday people will wake up and remember what Jesus said about the animals. "What you do unto them, you do unto me."

   Letter to the Editor, *Seattle Times* (December 29, 1985): A19.

8. John: Should we figure the raises on a 3 percent cost of living increase plus merit?
   Judy: That will work as long as we have enough in the budget to cover it. How much is available to us?
   Dan: Well, we do have a reserve fund to cover any excesses. I think we should start out with what the staff ought to receive and concern ourselves with what's available later on.
   Judy: That sounds fine to me, as long as we have some excess.

9. At our most basic level, we humans are animals; we have animal impulses and drives. We communicate, we eat, we relieve ourselves, we tire, we sleep—and we have sex. Ultimately, what makes us human is our ability to transcend our animal composition. What makes us human is our ability to channel and curb our God-given impulses in such a way that elevates the human spirit. Sexuality is one in a series of healthy life forces.

   Michael Gotlieb, "Sex and Sin: There Is a Difference," *New York Times* (December 20, 1994): A23.

*10. Many people seeking help [from Consumer Credit Counseling Service of Southern New England] have been able to rack up $12,000 to $15,000 in credit card debts before running out of options. One reason it goes so far is there's little stigma about being in debt among young adults. Groups of twentysomethings will go out drinking and joke about the credit card payments they can't make. "We egg each other on and encourage each other, like, 'Come on, you can just make the minimum payment.'"

Margaret Webb Pressler, "Young and In Debt," www.msnbc.com (accessed December 12, 2003).

Exercise 2 Developing Critical Thinking

In this chapter, we reported that McDonald's had been subjected to several lawsuits because of asserted health consequences associated with its menu. McDonald's is not alone. Many food companies have been scrutinized as potentially damaging the health of consumers.

Recently Starbucks was compared unfavorably with McDonald's because many of its specialty coffee drinks had more fat and more calories than a Big Mac. In fact, items on the Starbucks menu have the following characteristics:

MENU ITEM (16 OZ. SIZES)	CALORIES	GRAMS OF FAT
Drip Coffee (Black)	5	0
Nonfat Latte	130	0
Vanilla Latte with Whole Milk	280	11
Chai Latte with Nonfat Milk	200	0
Mocha with Whole Milk and Whipped Cream	360	19
Strawberries & Crème Frappuccino Blended Crème with Whipped Cream	570	15
Java Chip Frappuccino	460	19
Coffee Frappuccino Blended Coffee	240	3

With diabetes reaching epidemic proportions and the United States being the most obese country in the world, if you were in charge of Starbucks, how would you respond? Or would you? Frame your answer by using critical thinking processes:

1. *Question at issue.* What is the need that has arisen?
2. *Purpose.* What is your goal with this inquiry?
3. *Information.* You have some information from the chapter, but what additional information would you need to reach a reasonable answer?
4. *Concepts.* What laws, rules, and principles guide our inquiry as we look for an answer?
5. *Assumptions.* What are our presuppositions? Do any need to be questioned?
6. *Points of view.* What perspectives come into play here? Consumers? Starbucks? Other companies?
7. *Interpretations and inference.* What conclusions can you reach given the material you have available to you? How did you arrive at them?
8. *Implications and consequences.* What would be likely to happen if Starbucks responded as you recommend?

Allison Linn, "Starbucks tries to lighten the lattes," *Tacoma News Tribune* (June 29, 2004): D3.

*Exercise 3 We have discussed the role of argument fields in

- Providing grounds for decisions
- Implying requirements for what audiences expect from argument
- Implying rules arguers will follow in conducting arguments

One example of a field in which argument occurs is medicine. Based on what you know about argument fields, how would you answer the following questions?

- What kinds of grounds do medical doctors use in their research papers, public presentations, or the diagnosis of a disease?
- What constitutes acceptable evidence for medical arguments?
- In what spheres do medical doctors operate?
- What are the audience expectations of this field?
- What are some conventions or rules followed by doctors?

Exercise 4 What argument fields are you associated with? Using the description of fields presented in the text, how would you characterize these fields?

NOTES

1. A valuable resource for reading and reviewing contemporary topics that are used in competitive academic debate can be found at Debatepedia at http://wiki.idebate.org. This conversation was adapted from Debatepedia contributors, "Are beauty contests harmful?" http://wiki.idebate.org/index.php/Debate: Beauty_Contests (accessed April 13, 2008). See also Colleen Ballerino Cohen, Richard Wilk, Beverly Stoeltje (eds.), *Beauty Queens on the Global Stage: Gender, Contests, and Power* (New York: Routledge, 1996); Sarah Banet-Weiser, *The Most Beautiful Girl in the World: Beauty Pageants and National Identity* (Berkeley and Los Angeles: University of California Press, 1999); and Naomi Wolf, *The Beauty Myth* (New York: HarperCollins, 2002).

2. Steven D. Schafersman, "An Introduction to Critical Thinking," January 1991, http://www. freeinquiry.com/critical-thinking.html (accessed on June 30, 2008).

3. Joanne Kurfiss, *Critical Thinking: Theory, Research, Practice, and Possibilities* (Washington, D.C.: Association for the Study of Higher Education, 1975), 2.

4. Adapted from Brian Clark, "Do You Recognize These 10 Mental Blocks to Creative Thinking?" http://www.copyblogger.com/mental-blocks-creative-thinking/ (accessed July 1, 2008).

5. Much has been written about critical thinking as a process for systematically evaluating issues and their interrelationships. This section and Figure 1.1 are adapted from Richard Paul and Linda Elder, *The Nature and Functions of Critical and Creative Thinking* (Dillon Beach: The Foundation for Critical Thinking, 2004); Joan Trabandt, "Critical Thinking in Online Discussions," 2002, http://www.nvcc.edu/home/jtrabandt/discussion/default .html (accessed on June 30, 2008); Peter A. Facione, "Critical Thinking: What It Is and Why It Counts," 2007 Update, http://www.insightassessment.com/ pdf_files/what&why98.pdf (accessed on July 1, 2008). There are also many resources available through Paul

and Elder at the Foundation for Critical Thinking (www.criticalthinking.org).

6. Paul and Elder, 25–26.

7. Richard W. Paul and Gerald M. Nosich, "A Model for the National Assessment of Higher Order Thinking," in A. J. A. Binker, ed., *Critical Thinking: What Every Person Needs to Survive in a Rapidly Changing World* (Santa Rosa, Calif.: Foundation for Critical Thinking, 1992), 87–88.

8. Dr. Richard Paul, Dr. Linda Elder, and Dr. Ted Bartell, "Study of 38 Public Universities and 28 Private Universities. To Determine Faculty Emphasis on Critical Thinking in Instruction," www. criticalthinking.org/schoolstudy.htm (accessed June 8, 2004).

9. Paul and Nosich, 101; see also, James H. McMillan, "Enhancing College Students' Critical Thinking: A Review of Studies," *Research in Higher Education* 26 (1987): 3–29.

10. Hugh Heclo, "Hyperdemocracy," *The Wilson Quarterly* 23 (1999): 62.

11. H. P. Grice, "Logic and Conversation," in Peter Cole and Jerry L. Morgan, eds., *Syntax and Semantics: Vol 3. Speech Acts* (New York: Academic Press, 1975), 45.

12. Daniel J. O'Keefe, "Two Concepts of Argument," *Journal of the American Forensic Association* 13 (1977): 121–128; and "The Concepts of Argument and Arguing," in J. Robert Cox and Charles Arthur Willard, eds., *Advances in Argumentation Theory and Research* (Carbondale, Ill.: Southern Illinois University Press, 1982), 3–23.

13. Frans H. van Eemeren, Rob Grootendorst, and Francisca Snoeck Henkemans, *Fundamentals of Argumentation Theory* (Mahwah, N.J.: Erlbaum, 1996), 2–4.

14. Stephen Toulmin, *The Uses of Argument* (Cambridge: Cambridge University Press, 1969), 98.

15. Douglas Ehninger, "Argument as Method: Its Nature, Its Limitations, and Its Uses," *Speech Monographs* 37 (1970): 102–103.

16. Adapted from Aric Press, Jenny Carrol, and Steven Waldman, "Are Lawyers Burning America?" *Newsweek* (March 20, 1995): 32–35.

17. Aric Press, Jenny Carroll, and Steven Waldman, "Are Lawyers Burning America?" *Newsweek* (March 20, 1995): 32–35.

18. Press et al., 35.

19. McDonald's Corp. and Kraft Foods Inc., "'Big Food' Gets the Obesity Message," *New York Times* (July 10, 2003): A.22.

20. The Wall Street Journal. "Obesity Suit Against McDonald's Is Dismissed by Federal Judge," Shirley Leung. *Wall Street Journal* (September 5, 2003): B-4.

21. A discussion of fields, definitions, and function can be found in: Robert C. Rowland, "The Influence of Purpose on Fields of Argument," *Journal of the American Forensics Association* 18 (1982): 229–245; David Zarefsky, "'Reasonableness' in Public Policy Argument: Fields as Institutions," *Dimensions of Argument: Proceedings of the Second Summer Conference on Argumentation*, George Ziegelmueller and Jack Rhodes, eds. (Annandale, Va.: SCA, 1981): 89; Thomas A. Hollihan and Kevin T. Baaske, *Arguments and Arguing: The Products and Process of Human Decision Making* (New York: St. Martin's Press, 1994): 35.

22. Thomas B. Farrell and G. Thomas Goodnight, "Accidental Rhetoric: The Root Metaphors of Three Mile Island," *Communication Monographs* 48 (1981): 271–300.

23. Very good discussions of the types of spheres and their definitions can be found in Theodore O. Prosise and Greg R. Miller, "Argument Fields as Arenas of Discursive Struggle," *Argumentation & Advocacy* 32 (Winter 1996): 111–129; and David Zarefsky, "The Decline of Public Debate," *USA Today Magazine* 126 (March 1998): 56–59.

24. John W. Delicath and Kevin Michael Deluca, "Image Events, the Public Sphere, and Argumentative Practice: The Case of Radical Environmental Groups." *Argumentation* (August 2004): 315.

25. Zarefsky, 1998, 56.

26. The loss of the public sphere and the need to reclaim public arenas for discussion were developed in D. Ambrozas, "The University as Public Sphere," *Canadian Journal of Communication* 23 (Winter 1998): 73–89; Gordon R. Mitchell, "Pedagogical Possibilities for Argumentative Agency in Academic Debate,"

Argumentation & Advocacy 35 (Fall 1998): 41–61; Carol Winkler and David M. Cheshier, "Revisioning Argumentation Education for the New Century: Millennial Challenges," *Argumentation & Advocacy* 36 (Winter 2000): 101–105.

27. Rachel Carson, *Silent Spring* (Boston: Houghton Mifflin, 1994).

28. Archon Fung, "Survey Article: Recipes for Public Spheres: Eight Institutional Design Choices and Their Consequences," *The Journal of Political Philosophy* (2003): 338.

29. Gianpaolo Baiocchi, "Emergent Public Spheres: Talking Politics in Participatory Governance," *American Sociological Review* (February 2003): 52.

30. Joseph Wenzel, "On Fields of Argument as Prepositional Systems," *Journal of the American Forensic Association* 18 (1982): 204.

31. Stephen Toulmin, *The Uses of Argument* (Cambridge: Cambridge University Press, 1958), 13–15. Further information can be found in Charles A. Willard, "Argument Fields and Theories of Logical Types," *Journal of the American Forensic Association* 17 (1981): 129–145.

32. Charles Kneupper, "Argument Fields: Some Social Constructivist Observations," in *Dimensions of Argument: Proceedings of the Second Summer Conference on Argumentation*, George Ziegelmueller and Jack Rhodes, eds. (Annandale, Va.: Speech Communication Association/American Forensic Association, 1981), 80–87.

33. Robert Rowland, "The Influence of Purpose on Fields of Argument," 228.

34. Charles A. Willard, "Argument Fields" in *Dimensions of Argument*, 21–42.

35. Willard, 41.

36. R. Rowland, "Argument Fields" in *Dimensions of Argument*, 56–79; and "The Influence of Purpose on Fields of Argument," 228–245.

37. Rowland, "Argument Fields," 64.

38. Kneupper, 82.

39. Toulmin, 33.

40. Gerald Posner, "It Was Him All Along," *Night & Day* (October 17, 1993): 8.

41. Posner, 12–13.

42. Posner, 12–13.

43. Vincent Bugliosi, *And the Sea Will Tell* (New York: Ivy, 1991), 632–634.

44. Toulmin, 33.

CHAPTER TWO

CO-ORIENTATIONAL VIEW OF ARGUMENT

As we discussed in Chapter 1, arguments occur in contexts that are defined by their fields and spheres. This chapter examines how arguments occur in the relationships among arguers and recipients. Box 2.1, "Does a College or University Have the Right or

■ ■ ■ ■ ■

BOX 2.1

DOES A COLLEGE OR UNIVERSITY HAVE THE RIGHT OR RESPONSIBILITY TO CENSOR THE ARTS?

Most countries around the world have grappled with issues related to censorship and what expression should be allowed and what expression should be banned. Sometimes, when artists push at accepted cultural norms to make political or social points clear, they are seen as crossing some threshold of appropriateness. This occurred in 2005 when the Danish newspaper *Jyllands-Posten* published editorial cartoons depicting the Islamic prophet Muhammad in a manner that linked Islam to terrorism. Demonstrations and outbreaks of violence ensued, and many college newspapers debated whether or not to reprint any of the cartoons. In most cases, however, sexual content and its appropriateness for public viewing are primary reasons for censoring art. In 2002, for instance, Attorney General John Ashcroft refused to be photographed in front of two partially nude statues in the Great Hall of the Department of Justice and spent $8,000 on blue drapes to hide them.[1]

On occasion, schools are pressured to remove an art exhibit or end a controversial performance or production. The pressure may come from the school's administration or from community members who object to the art. High schools, colleges, and universities often struggle with decisions about what artworks can be shown and what should not be open to public view. For example, in 2006, Penn State University student Josh Stulman was informed that the university had cancelled his upcoming art exhibition because it violated the university's policies related to nondiscrimination, harassment, and hate. His exhibition was based primarily on the conflict in the Palestinian territories and raised questions concerning the destruction of Jewish religious shrines, anti-Semitic propaganda, disregard for the treatment of prisoners, and the indoctrination of youth into terrorist acts.[2]

There are many examples across the world and across campuses that illustrate how groups work to balance the needs for expression with issues related to public decency and safety. Consider the following conversation between two college students, Juli and Steve, as they grapple with when and where colleges and universities have a right to censor artistic expression.[3]

Steve:	I can't believe the college is thinking about banning the *Laramie Project*.[4] We are adults and this is a college. We should be able to see and hear what we want, when we want. This play addresses important social issues that should be discussed on our campus. It should not be banned just because it makes some people in the community uncomfortable.
Juli:	Our rights to see this play or have a controversial art exhibition are not more important than someone else's rights—even when it comes to free speech. People have threatened to protest this play and our campus police are worried about violence and vandalism. We have no right to put others at risk and if a protest turns ugly, that's what could happen. If our freedoms potentially hurt others, they should be limited. Ironically, this play makes that point. We limit hate speech—we don't allow people to say what they want because it may have harmful consequences.

(continued)

BOX 2.1   CONTINUED

	Artistic work is like any other form of speech; it should have limits if it hurts others. Artistic expression should not be exempted from censorship any more than any other kind of speech.

Steve: Maybe, but people's rights should not be limited or eliminated unless there is a very, very clear and present threat to the safety of others. With art—and with this play—no one has proved a clear danger to our campus or our community. Protests don't hurt anyone—the opposite is true. Protests could highlight the dangers of homophobia and discrimination.

     And, if this play might offend someone, they don't have to see it. As long as people have a choice to see it or not, there should be no problem and no limitation on expression.

     My only point here is that all art forms—this play, music, art exhibitions—can all have significant and important messages that combat hate, stereotypes, and serve to bring us to a better understanding of one another. Before it is censored, the school, the government, or whoever has a burden to prove there would be some harm.

Juli: Fair enough. I think, though, that it is important to remember that censorship can be targeted so that some classes of people are protected—like kids. After all, movies have ratings to allow some people to see them while keeping others out. Censorship can be used to protect kids from excessive sex and violence or having to deal with issues in this play.

     The issue is that not all content is appropriate for everyone. And, in our community, maybe this play is not a wise choice. That should have been taken into consideration.

Steve: Censorship, even with age ratings or using a community standard, is a problem because it seeks to limit what people can see and think. This is bad. When we allow others to tell us what is OK to see or not, we are giving away our rights to think freely and we are allowing community sensitivity to influence our education and our thoughts. People are not forced to see this play or any other potentially offensive art. They get to choose—and they should make the choice—not the college, not the community, and not the government.

Consider the arguments that emerged in this discussion and think about the following questions:

1. If you were editing a college newspaper asked to print some potentially offensive editorial cartoons that could be considered as discriminatory or hateful, would you? What if they were a significant story such as the ones published in *Jyllands-Posten*?
2. If you were a college administrator and a major contributor to the college threatened to withdraw significant support for student scholarships unless you cancelled a controversial exhibition, would you? How would you make that decision? What would you tell the students? What would you tell the contributor?
3. What are the conditions under which you would support a ban on an art exhibition? Where is your threshold? In other words, at what point and with what evidence do you make a decision?

Responsibility to Censor the Arts?" illustrates how sometimes relationships among arguers and recipients can become complex because of multiple needs and multiple goals. The question of whether or not a school or the government has a right or responsibility to censor expression is difficult because of the varied needs of those involved. Students, for instance, may want to broaden their understanding of controversial and challenging issues through the arts, demonstrations, and discussion. Yet, others may fear the message because it challenges accepted beliefs and practice or may cause protests and violence.

The conversation developed in Box 2.1 suggests some of these issues. Steve makes the argument that the decision to ban a play or any form of speech should meet a very high threshold that demonstrates an immediate threat. For Steve, especially as a student, controversial and potentially disturbing messages are an important part of education. Juli takes a different point of view. Although she recognizes the need for controversial expression, her perspective is that it should be balanced against the interests of multiple audiences and constituents. In both cases, the advocates build their arguments on a broad base of evidence and use a variety of reasons to support their claims.

If you look at their arguments as simply a collection of parts and if you try only to identify each of the claims, reasons, and pieces of evidence that compose the total series of arguments, it would be easy to miss how the complete arguments are structured or the connections among the smaller, individual arguments. And you would miss how the argument might affect an audience. When we seek to persuade people or advocate for a position, we make use of individual arguments that, when combined, make an overall persuasive case that has an effect on the recipients.

A co-orientational approach to argument presumes that the relationship between arguer and recipient is as important as the content of the argument. Arguments may be strong and well substantiated, but if the hearer does not trust the arguer or suspects that the arguments are being used inappropriately, then even the best arguments will fail. This chapter explores traditional perspectives of argumentation, examines arguer-based approaches toward the construction of arguments, and, finally, turns to a co-orientational approach toward the design of arguments.

PERSPECTIVES ON ARGUMENTATION

Argumentation is a complex process with many dimensions, and for centuries scholars have differed on how it should be described and explained. Some hold the view that arguers have an obligation to determine the truth through the use of true premises (evidence) and sound reasoning.[5] Others argue that the "truth" frequently cannot be decisively determined and that argumentation should be studied as a means of influence in the social and political marketplace.[6] Still others, noting the tension between rational and nonrational factors of influence, have concluded that "a central focus of argumentation is on discovering and applying the general standards for determining what is true or reasonable."[7]

Joseph W. Wenzel summarized the various perspectives on argument and concluded that they could be put into three categories—*logical, dialectical,* and *rhetorical.*[8]

These are not three different kinds of arguments; they are three different ways of looking at argumentation. Each perspective emphasizes a different set of functions and features of argumentation. They might best be understood if we examine the following argument from each of the three perspectives. This argument, which appeared in the conservation column of a wilderness organization's monthly newsletter, argues that the spotted owl, an endangered species that the U.S. Forest Service is mandated to protect, is being ill-served by Forest Service policies.

> The Forest Service wants to save only 1,000 acres per breeding pair, but scientists think they require an average of over 2,000 acres. The discrepancies between USFS acreage allowances and biologists' minimum recommended acreage has meant further study and a supplemental environmental impact statement to be issued sometime this summer. . . .
>
> Spacing of spotted owl management areas is also controversial. Scientists think they should be spaced from 1–6 miles apart, and the Forest Service plans to place them at the maximum of this range—6 miles apart, which will make it difficult for young owls to disperse from their original nest sites. . . .
>
> If scientists' recommendations and Forest Service plans are so disparate, perhaps there should be a moratorium placed on all harvest of spotted owl habitat. The burden of proof that harvest can continue without endangering the survival of the species should rest on the Forest Service.[9]

The author here presents two sets of evidence—Forest Service recommendations and scientists' findings regarding the spotted owl. She then shows that the two are not in agreement—that there are discrepancies that might affect the owls' well-being and even their survival. From this she concludes that a moratorium on habitat harvesting should be declared until the discrepancies can be resolved and there is agreement about what measures are needed to ensure the owls' survival.

Logical Perspective

The logical perspective asks, "Is the argument sound?" The dialectical perspective asks, "Has the discussion been handled so as to achieve a candid and critical examination of all aspects of the issue in question?" And the rhetorical perspective asks, "Has the arguer constructed the argument so as to successfully influence a particular audience?" All three perspectives are useful and necessary, and the significance of any one perspective at any time depends on the arguer's purpose and the situation in which the argument is made.

If we are to use a *logical* approach to this example, we will view it as a set of statements made up of premises and a claim or conclusion. *The logical perspective emphasizes the accuracy of the premises and the correctness of the inferences linking premises and evidence to the claims they support.* An argument favorably evaluated from the logical perspective will be based on correct evidence and will use reasoning that is sound according to the standards of logic. Dividing the preceding argument into its parts—claim, evidence, and inference—we might ask the following:

Is the evidence correct?	■ Are scientists' recommendations accurately summarized?
	■ Do the recommendations reported cover all the studies that have been done?
Does the influence justify the move to the conclusion?	■ Will maximum placement of the management areas actually interfere with dispersal?
	■ Will placing a moratorium resolve the discrepancy between the scientists' recommendations and the Forest Service's plans?

The logical perspective views argumentation as addressed to an audience of rational individuals well informed on the topic of the dispute.[10] It removes arguments from their situational contexts and considers them primarily as statements connected by logical inferences. The inferences are identified, classified, analyzed, and critiqued by comparing their structure and adequacy with prescriptions from logical theory.

Dialectical Perspective

Viewing the example from the dialectical perspective leads us to consider this argument as one move in an ongoing process of inquiry about policies concerning the spotted owl. By refraining from deciding on a position or course of action until all aspects of the question have been thoroughly explored, a dialectical approach to argumentation searches for significant issues, identifies alternatives, generates standards or criteria for selection, and uses them to test proposals. *The dialectical perspective focuses on and enhances a candid, critical, and comprehensive examination of all positions relevant to the topic.* It makes a concerted effort to seek out all points of view. In the spotted owl controversy, the arguer articulated the environmentalist position on the issue. A dialectical perspective on the argument would seek out the viewpoints of the scientific community, the Forest Service, and the timber industry. In regard to the argument in the example, we would be led to ask such questions as:

- What is the spotted owl's present situation? Is it in immediate danger? Is the decline in old-growth forests the primary threat to the species, or are there other threats?
- What will be the impact of a harvest moratorium on the timber industry?
- Will the promised supplemental environmental impact statement provide information to resolve the disparity?
- Are there alternatives to the proposed moratorium?

Argumentation viewed from a dialectical perspective focuses primarily on the process of reaching the best conclusion. The assumption is that the best conclusion will be accepted if all points of view and issues have been carefully considered and discussed.

Rhetorical Perspective

Viewing the example from a *rhetorical* perspective means that we see it as addressed to an audience in a particular social and political context. In the *rhetorical perspective, arguments are viewed as appeals to an audience, and we must take account of the circumstances in which the argument was made and the strategies used to influence its audience.* Considering the argument this way might lead us to ask:

- Is the author aware of the interests and values of the newsletter's readers?
- What strategies does she use to structure and present the argument?
- Are there other arguments that might appeal to the readers' values and interests more successfully?
- Does the author appear knowledgeable and trustworthy? Will the readers believe her?

The rhetorical perspective on argument is important because of its emphasis on arguments as forms of communication. By taking account of the circumstances in which the argument was produced, the arguer's intent, and the beliefs and values of those to whom arguments are addressed, the rhetorical perspective enables one to interpret and evaluate the content of the arguments themselves.

HOW ARGUMENT PERSPECTIVES ARE USED

Understanding that any argument can be viewed from any of these three perspectives is important. Each of the perspectives implies a different purpose and a different emphasis. The logical perspective focuses on the structure of an argument and on its logical soundness when removed from a context. (This is the perspective of many courses in formal and informal logic.) The dialectical perspective considers especially the capacity of any given procedure for argumentation to contribute to reasoned and careful deliberation about an issue. The rhetorical perspective emphasizes the argument's effectiveness in persuading its audience. When individual arguments and argumentation are viewed from each of these three perspectives, different dimensions of the process of arguing are featured.

Understanding argument perspectives is important because at different times the use of one perspective makes more sense than use of another. For instance, in Chapters 6 and 8 when we discuss reasoning and argument analysis, we focus on the logical perspective. In Chapters 9, 10, and 11 when we discuss the construction of argumentative cases, we emphasize the dialectical perspective and its usefulness in discovering vital questions on a given topic. In Chapters 3 and 7 we are particularly concerned with the kinds of questions raised by a rhetorical perspective, which is concerned with the arguer's relationship to other parties and how arguments can be persuasive.

ARGUER-BASED ARGUMENT

Much of the study of argument has centered on the use of arguer-based models that emphasize the logical or dialectical perspectives. This approach considers how an advocate develops and produces an argument, and it focuses on finding and presenting sound evidence and strong reasoning. The assumption behind an arguer-based approach is that careful research, strong argument construction, and skillful presentation should sway an audience to accept the claims presented. This approach has its roots in the field of formal logic. During the first half of the twentieth century, most students studied logic in a philosophy course, where they concentrated on the forms and application of formal and symbolic logic.[11] Logic in these courses was considered to be a formal science, a type of theoretical study free from any immediate practical application. Such study reduced arguments to their basic elements and expressed the relationship among the parts in a standardized form for the purposes of comparison and analysis. There are times when using an arguer-based approach is appropriate. In fact, Chapter 9 is designed around how arguments are constructed and linked together. The problem with this approach, however, arises when arguers use it and ignore the relationship between arguer and recipient.

Formal Logic

Formal logic is defined by its form. And, although many ancient civilizations such as Babylon, China, and India employed elaborate systems of reasoning and logic, the most sophisticated and enduring understanding of logic is generally recognized as coming from ancient Greece and the work of theorists such as Aristotle.[12] In formal logic, arguments are reduced to their basic elements and expressed in standardized forms for purposes of building, comparing, and analyzing arguments and advocacy.[13] *Formal logic is the study of how conclusions are reached using structured statements.* The structured statements are the premises or grounds for arguments that—provided they are true and valid—lead recipients to a conclusion. Generally, when we speak of formal logic and the use of structured, formal statements, we are talking about the syllogism. Syllogisms work deductively from broadly stated premises to specific conclusions. *Deductive reasoning is the process of moving from general statements to specific conclusions.*

Over many centuries, theorists and philosophers have used and modified the theories and study of formal logic. In the seventeenth century, for instance, Sir Francis Bacon argued that the Aristotelian view of the syllogism was fallible and illogical and he offered alternatives that stressed inductive forms of reasoning.[14] *Inductive reasoning is a process of moving from particular examples, observations, or instances to general conclusions.* By the nineteenth century, logicians had begun to modify the syllogism further to include new types such as hypothetical and disjunctive forms that will be discussed shortly.

A complete discussion of the reasoning forms of formal logic would be quite lengthy and beyond the purpose or scope of this book. Extensive explanations of this topic are available in other sources for those interested in studying the applications of syllogistic reasoning in everyday argument.[15] This discussion is intended as an introduction to formal logic, which can provide a useful theoretic background to informal logic that will be developed in Chapter 6.

The Syllogism

Aristotle's model of the syllogism is the original foundational unit of logic study. He focused on deductive reasoning using a categorical form that will be discussed shortly. Generally, a *syllogism is made up of three statements, includes three terms associated in pairs with each other through the statements, and draws a conclusion from a major and minor premise.* Syllogisms can be portrayed with a simple, mathematic elegance as follows:

Major Premise:	All A are B
Minor Premise:	All C are A
Conclusion:	All C are B

In this illustration, there are three statements (major premise, minor premise, and conclusion) and three terms A, B, and C (middle term, major term, and minor term). The major term, B, is the predicate term of the conclusion. The middle term, A, occurs in both premises but not in the conclusion. The minor term, C, functions as the subject of the conclusion. Notice how each term is used exactly twice and, provided that the premises are true and valid, the conclusion is also true and valid. The following example makes this point:

Major Premise:	All mammals (A) are warm-blooded (B)
Minor Premise:	All whales (C) are mammals (A)
Conclusion:	Therefore, all whales (C) are warm-blooded (B)

Essentially, Aristotelian syllogisms work by means of classification or categorization. If the statements made in the major and minor premises are true and if the form of the syllogism is correct, the conclusion necessarily follows. The categories in this example were "mammals" and "warm-blooded." If it is true that all mammals are warm-blooded and that all whales are mammals, then it always follows that every whale is warm-blooded. One could not reach the conclusion "Therefore, all whales are fish" given the premises. By identifying the "middle term"—mammal—with the other two terms, one can reliably connect the remaining terms together in a necessary relationship.

Although this example is straightforward—all whales are warm-blooded—it depends on the certainty of the premises. If the premises were only probably true or if there is doubt whether they are always true, the conclusion, too, would be probable. Consider the following:

Major Premise:	Steven Spielberg makes great movies.
Minor Premise:	*Hook* was made by Steven Spielberg.
Conclusion:	Therefore, *Hook* is a great movie.

While the "greatness" of *Hook* may be debatable, because there are exceptions to the major premise—Steven Spielberg makes *mostly* great movies—the conclusion is also only probably true.

Because most premises have exceptions or are only probably true, the conclusions are also only probably true. Generally, there are three forms of the syllogism that are used by arguers seeking to draw probable although not necessary conclusions from premises. The three forms are categorical, disjunctive, and hypothetical.

Categorical Syllogism

The first type of syllogism providing a form of argument that can be used in practical reasoning is the categorical syllogism. *The categorical syllogism is a logical argument that draws a necessary conclusion from two premises stated as simple propositions containing categorical terms that designate classes.* The categorical syllogism works from a principle of classification, that is, by putting objects or people into groups and assigning characteristics to them, a conclusion can be drawn. Here are some examples of categorical syllogisms:

Major Premise:	All tests are biased (category = tests).
Minor Premise:	The SAT is a test (SAT = member of category).
Conclusion:	Therefore, the SAT is biased.
Major Premise:	No gravesites should be robbed (category = gravesites)
Minor Premise:	The *Titanic* is a gravesite (Titanic = member of category)
Conclusion:	Therefore, the *Titanic* should not be robbed.

For arguments of this type to be sound, two conditions must be met. First, the initial statement must be true. That is, the predicate of the statement must apply to all the persons or things named in the subject. Second, the instance named in the second or minor premise must fall within the class with which it is associated. As long as the categories are true and accurately described—that the SAT is really a test and that the *Titanic* is really a gravesite—then the conclusion is also likely to be true.

Disjunctive Syllogism

A second form of syllogism that provides a basis for argument is the disjunctive syllogism. Unlike the categorical syllogism in which we make a judgment about something based on its membership or inclusion in a class, a disjunctive syllogism uses a process of exclusion or elimination. *Disjunctive syllogisms set forth two or more alternatives in the major premise, deny all but one in the minor premise, and affirm the only remaining alternative in the conclusion.* We can state this form of reasoning symbolically as follows:

Major Premise:	Either A or B.
Minor Premise:	Not A.
Conclusion:	Therefore, B.

For example:

Major Premise:	Dr. Jones said I would receive either an "A" or a "B" for the semester depending on how well I did on the final.
Minor Premise:	I failed the final.
Conclusion:	Therefore, I will receive a "B."
Major Premise:	Next year I will study away in either China or Australia.
Minor Premise:	I don't think I should study in China because I don't speak the language.
Conclusion:	Therefore, I will study in Australia.

Disjunctive syllogisms present two or more alternatives. One by one, each alternative is eliminated until the option that remains is selected in the conclusion. For this type of argument to be sound, two conditions must be met. First, all possible alternatives must be identified. If they are not, an unnoticed alternative that is not considered may turn out to be the best. During gasoline shortages in the late 1970s, many people claimed that we must either ration gas or entirely deplete our oil reserves. As it turned out, the increased price of oil led to many energy-saving measures that made rationing unnecessary. In the first part of the twenty-first century, people were again faced with the question—drill for oil in environmentally sensitive areas or face economic collapse. But these arguments fall short because they do not consider other energy resources, conservation, or new alternatives.

Second, any proposed choices must be separate and distinct. Otherwise, they cannot be eliminated one by one. For example, suppose we assume that we could go to either the mountains or the seashore on vacation and that we made a choice based on that belief. In some areas of the country, however, mountains and seashore are within a day's drive of each other, and both can be included in a single vacation, so use of disjunctive reasoning to choose between them might lead to a poor conclusion.

Hypothetical Syllogism

A third type of syllogism is known as the hypothetical syllogism. *Hypothetical syllogisms are arguments that do not involve a direct comparison; rather they contain a conditional major premise that is either affirmed or denied in the minor premise. The conclusion is what remains.* They take this form:

Major Premise:	If A then B.
Minor Premise:	A will occur.
Conclusion:	Therefore, B will happen.

An example of a hypothetical syllogism, then, looks like this:

Major Premise:	If I oversleep, I will be late for work.
Minor Premise:	I overslept.
Conclusion:	Therefore, I will be late for work.
Major Premise:	If college tuition continues to rise, fewer students will be able to attend college.
Minor Premise:	Tuition is continuing to rise.
Conclusion:	Fewer students will be able to attend college.

We typically use this kind of argument to express causality or predict what might happen in the future. For instance:

Major Premise:	If I smoke, I will suffer negative health consequences.
Minor Premise:	I choose to smoke.
Conclusion:	Therefore, I will suffer from negative health consequences.

As with other forms of syllogisms, the hypothetical syllogism is only as strong as its premises.

Enthymeme

Argument forms in everyday discourse do not often conform to the relatively neat and rigid mathematical structure of syllogisms outlined in the previous pages—most arguers are less precise and they tend to omit a premise or even the conclusion because they assume the recipients already know it. This means that the argument form is probably not as obvious or clear as in a formal syllogism. These types of arguments are called enthymemes, and they depend on the recipients' ability to supply the missing statement. In his *Rhetoric*, Aristotle described a *rhetorical* form of the syllogism to be used in speeches and public discourse.[16] *An enthymeme is a rhetorical syllogism that calls upon the audience's existing beliefs for one or both of its premises.* Aristotle said that in most forms of public speaking, one would not want explicitly to state all of one's premises, for that would belabor the point and bore the audience. To see how an enthymeme works, consider the following example:

Mario is an Italian, so he is probably Roman Catholic.

Here the major premise, "Most Italians are Roman Catholic," is implied because the arguer believes that most recipients already know and accept this fact.

The Toulmin Model

Formal logic dominated the study of argument for centuries. It treated reasoning forms as if they had the consistency and rigor of mathematical equations, and as if the relationship between terms and premises was as simple and unequivocal as in algebra and geometry. However, it should be apparent from the preceding discussion that human beings do not argue, reason, or communicate with such precision—and even if they did, people might disagree with conclusions even if, logically, they should be accepted. Emotion, deeply held beliefs, and personal assumptions can all play significant roles in how arguments are understood and accepted.

Formal logic and the syllogism are not very adequate for studying and learning the forms of reasoning employed by people in daily arguments using imprecise language and evidence. Although formal logic can help us critically understand how a particular argument functions, it is not very useful for studying and learning the forms of practical argument.

In the 1950s and 1960s, a number of scholars in philosophy and other fields began to criticize formal logic and to propose alternatives for the study of argument. For example, Stephen Toulmin, in his book *The Uses of Argument*, criticized formal logic for several reasons.[17] He noted that everyday arguments could never be held to be as universally valid as the reasoning forms in a syllogism.

Because formal logical relations depend on the use of symbols ("A," "B," and "C"), they strip arguments of their everyday meanings, ambiguities, and equivocations. Therefore, they could mislead students by assuming that the use of terms is always clear and never varies. Toulmin also said that statements in "real" arguments have more functions than three (major premise, minor premise, conclusion), and he presented a model of argument to show some of these other functions. As Toulmin observed, substantive everyday claims are usually viewed as *probably* true rather than as *certainly* and *always* true, as implied by formal logic.

Toulmin wrote that an argument is like an organism.[18] Its individual parts each have a different function in relation to the claim. If an argument "works" (that is, is acceptable to the recipients in the audience), it is because all its parts perform their functions and work together to form an organic whole. Toulmin's model identifies the ways in which each statement in an argument bears on the claim and does justice to all the things an argument ought to do in order to be cogent. If important parts of the argument are implied or omitted, the Toulmin model directs an arguer or critic to determine what they are and to supply them.

Parts of the Model

Toulmin's model contains six parts that are defined primarily by their function in an argument. These six parts are:

1. Data. The term data is synonymous with the term *evidence* as defined in Chapter 1 as *facts or conditions that are objectively observable beliefs or premises accepted as true by the audience, or conclusions previously established.*

2. Claim. Toulmin's concept of claim is the same as defined in Chapter 1. Claims consist of the expressed opinion or conclusion that the arguer wants accepted.

3. Warrant. *The warrant expresses the reasoning used to link the data to the claim.* According to Toulmin, if the data answer the question, "What information do you have to go on to reach your conclusions?" then the warrant answers the question, "How did you get there from that data?"[19] Warrants may take the form of rules, principles, or conventions. They may also be explicit statements of reasoning such as will be discussed in Chapter 6. It is important to remember that the warrant expresses the reasoning that enables us to connect the data to the claim.

4. Backing. *The backing consists of further facts or reasoning used to support or legitimate the principle contained in the warrant.* Backing often consists of accepted principles or facts arising from the field in which the argument takes place. For example, the field of medicine universally accepts the principle that treatment regimens should be based on what has proved effective in prior clinical practice. Backing supports the warrant in very much the same way that data support the claim.

5. Qualifier. *The qualifier is a colloquial adverb or adverbial phrase that modifies the claim and indicates the rational strength the arguer attributes to it.*[20] In other words, how certain is the arguer of the claim? When arguers make claims, they attribute greater or lesser degrees of strength to them. Some warrants authorize an unequivocal acceptance of the claim, whereas others may have much weaker force. The person making the diagnosis on the head wound in the following example recommends a certain treatment "strongly." Other qualifiers frequently used to modify claims are "probably," "certainly," and "possibly." When they occur in arguments, qualifiers fulfill an important function because they indicate the degree of certainty that arguers feel regarding their claims.

6. Reservation. Sometimes there are expectations of limitations that invalidate the application of the warrant. Toulmin includes these in his model as the reservation. *The reservation states the circumstances or conditions that undermine the argument.* It is the

exception to the rule expressed in the warrant. In the example below, the arguer says that penicillin is recommended unless the patient is allergic to it. An allergic reaction, then, is a condition that would invalidate the recommendation to administer antibiotics. In the Toulmin model, the qualifier and reservation are linked because, to the extent that circumstances or conditions restricting the claim exist, the strength of the claim is limited.

Using the Model

Of these six parts, three are the most important: claim, evidence, and warrant. As with the enthymeme, an arguer may omit parts that recipients are likely to supply. However, when we diagram and analyze arguments, minimally all three of these parts must be expressed. Consider the following example:

> Twelve hours ago, the patient fell from a motorcycle and had a severe blow to the head accompanied by a deep scalp wound. He is pale, dizzy, and lethargic and has a low fever. The treatment strongly recommended includes flushing and stitching up the wound, administering antibiotics, and bed rest. Clinical experience has shown that without such treatment, infection will set in within approximately 48 hours. Penicillin is most effective unless the patient is allergic to it.

What functions as data or evidence in this argument? Clearly, the circumstances of the accident and that patient's symptoms are readily knowable or observable facts. The claim—the conclusion or end point of the argument—is the specific recommended treatment. The warrant, or reasoning connection linking the data to the claim, is a causal prediction about what will happen to the patient if measures to prevent infection are not used. This prediction is based on a background and understanding of medicine and is based on prior experience with patients in similar conditions and circumstances.

The Toulmin model is set out in a spatial pattern that is intended to show how the statements in the argument are linked to each other—what supports what and what leads to what. Generally, the first three parts are displayed as in Figure 2.1. This arrangement indicates that the data lead to the claim and that the step made from one to the other is supported by the warrant. The data, warrant, and claim of the specific argument we've been considering would therefore be diagrammed as in Figure 2.2.

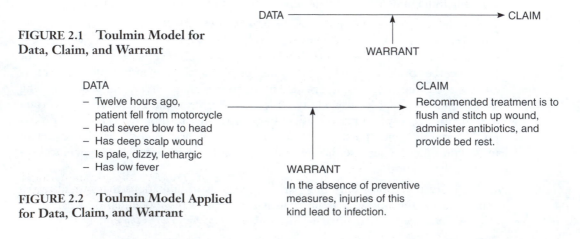

FIGURE 2.1   Toulmin Model for Data, Claim, and Warrant

FIGURE 2.2   Toulmin Model Applied for Data, Claim, and Warrant

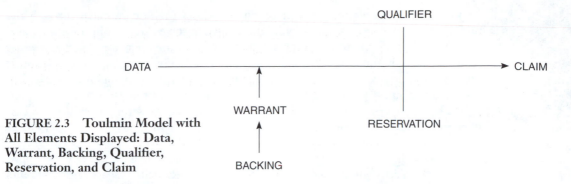

**FIGURE 2.3   Toulmin Model with
All Elements Displayed: Data,
Warrant, Backing, Qualifier,
Reservation, and Claim**

Figure 2.2 demonstrates how the Toulmin model is useful in identifying each statement's function in the argument. It indicates that the data serve as the argument's grounds
and starting point; the claim as its end point; and the warrant as its rational support.

Toulmin recommends that the six parts of the model should be set out to show
their interrelationships, as in Figure 2.3. When the additional three parts are added to
the diagram, we can see more clearly how they function in the argument. The backing
undergirds or supports the warrant. The qualifier modifies the claim by shoring the
strength the arguer attributes to it. And the qualifier is related to any reservations that
express exceptions to the claim by stating conditions that undermine the force of
the argument.

Applying the model to the example we have just discussed yields the diagram in
Figure 2.4. The elegance and usefulness of the model become clear when we see how

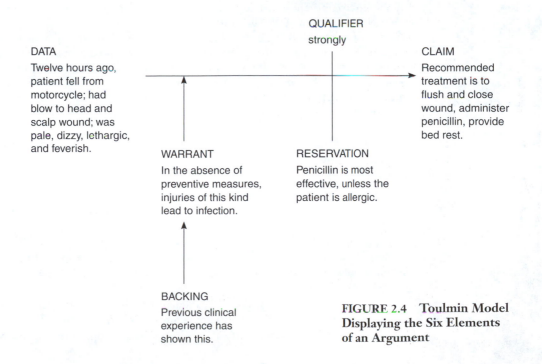

**FIGURE 2.4   Toulmin Model
Displaying the Six Elements
of an Argument**

the functions of the various statements in the arguments are revealed through the model. As we have observed, the diagram reveals that the existence of previous clinical experience backs up the prediction made in the warrant. Furthermore, we can see that penicillin is recommended "strongly" but not "absolutely." The recommendation is tempered by the reservation "unless the patient is allergic to penicillin" and is thus functionally connected to the qualifier because it limits its strength.

This argument from the field of medicine was relatively straightforward and easily comprehended. To test the capacity and usefulness of the Toulmin model, let us consider this more complex argument from the field of law:

> On the thirteenth day of August, 1880, George R. Falls made his last will and testament in which he gave small legacies to his two daughters, Mrs. Smith and Mrs. Phillips, the plaintiffs in this case, and the remainder to his grandson, John E. Falls. The testator, at the date of his will, owned a farm and considerable personal property. He was a widower and thereafter, in June 1902, he was married to Mrs. Jones. At the date of the will, and subsequently to the death of the testator, his grandson lived with him as a member of his family.
>
> At the time of his grandfather's death, John was 16 years old. John knew of the provisions made in his favor in the will. To prevent his grandfather from revoking such provisions, which his grandfather had manifested some intention to do, and to obtain speedy possession of his grandfather's property, John murdered his grandfather by poisoning him. John now claims the property, and the sole question for our determination is, can he have it?
>
> It is quite true that statutes regulating the making, proof, and effect of wills and the devolution of property, if literally construed, and if their force and effect can in no way and no circumstances be controlled or modified, give this property to the murderer. It was the intention of the lawmakers that the donees in a will should have the property given to them. But it never could have been their intention that a donee who murdered the testator to make the will operative should have any benefit under it. It is a familiar canon of construction that a thing which is within the intention of the makers of a statute is as much within the statute as if it were within the letter; and a thing which is within the letter of the statute is not within the statute unless it be within the intention of the makers.[21]

The *data* in this argument are stated by the judge before he states his decision. Briefly, they include the following: The deceased left small legacies to two daughters and the remainder of his estate to his grandson; he remarried; he was considering changing his will; he was poisoned by his grandson; the grandson now claims the estate. The *claim*, or end point, of this argument, does not seem to be explicitly stated but clearly would take the form of the judge's decision in the case. Because the entire passage justifies denial of the property to the donee, we can safely assume that the implied claim is "The donee in this case shall not have the property that has been willed to him." In the Toulmin model, if the claim is not explicitly stated, it is represented with dashed lines, as in Figure 2.5.

In seeking out the warrant linking the data and claim in this argument, we must discover the reasoning that would link the data and the claim together. In this particular argument, the warrant is explicitly stated in the judge's opinion: "It never could

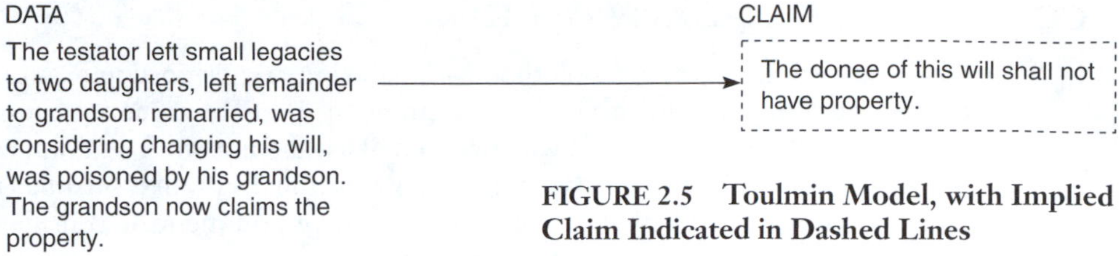

DATA

The testator left small legacies to two daughters, left remainder to grandson, remarried, was considering changing his will, was poisoned by his grandson. The grandson now claims the property.

CLAIM

The donee of this will shall not have property.

FIGURE 2.5   Toulmin Model, with Implied Claim Indicated in Dashed Lines

have been [the lawmakers'] intention that a donee who murdered a testator to make the will operative should have any benefit under it." The judge believes this to be a statement of principle inherent in the American legal tradition, and, if there is a precedent for it, he can thereby justify his decision that the property will be denied to the murderer. It is important to note that this warrant arises from the principle that legal statutes should be applied in ways congruent with the intentions of the lawmakers who proposed and approved them.

Only one remaining part of the Toulmin model is expressly stated in this argument. It is the *backing;* the principle that undergirds the warrant is expressly stated in the decision ("A thing which is within the letter of the statute is not within the statute unless it be within the intention of the makers"). The judge alludes to this as a "familiar canon of construction," which would be common knowledge among legal professionals. Because of its status as knowledge, this statement can function as support for the warrant. The finished diagram—which contains four of the Toulmin model's six parts—is shown in Figure 2.6.

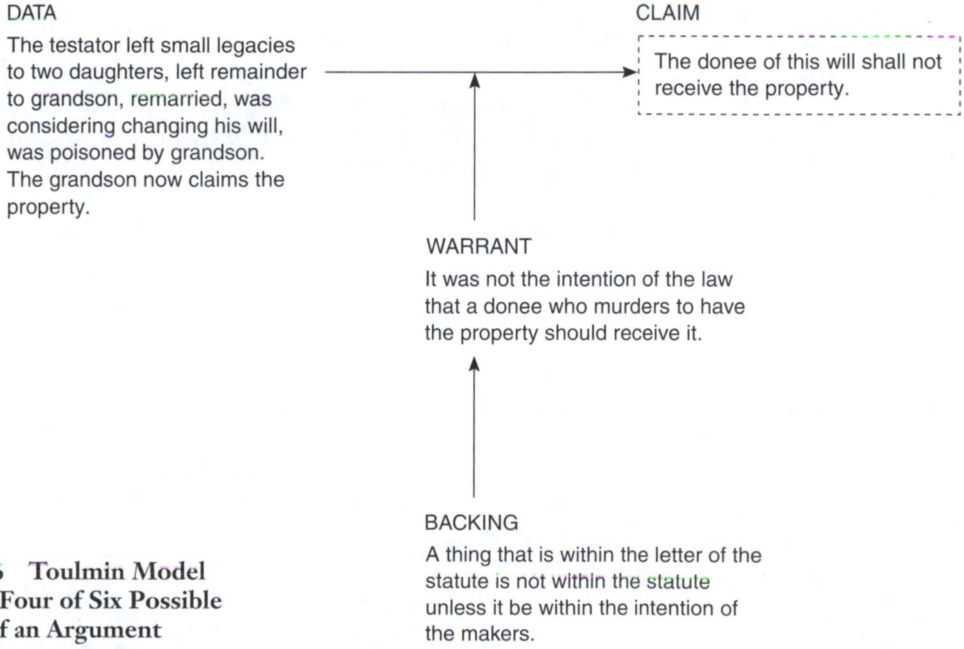

DATA

The testator left small legacies to two daughters, left remainder to grandson, remarried, was considering changing his will, was poisoned by grandson. The grandson now claims the property.

CLAIM

The donee of this will shall not receive the property.

WARRANT

It was not the intention of the law that a donee who murders to have the property should receive it.

BACKING

A thing that is within the letter of the statute is not within the statute unless it be within the intention of the makers.

FIGURE 2.6   Toulmin Model Displaying Four of Six Possible Elements of an Argument

A CO-ORIENTATIONAL APPROACH

The Toulmin model offers a method for analyzing and criticizing argument. Critics can examine passages for each of the component parts of an argument, assess their strength, and offer a critique of what worked, what did not work, and what might have been improved in any given argument. However, the Toulmin model has two important limitations. First, it focuses on a static view of argument. It considers that each part of the argument—claim, warrant, data, backing, reservation, and qualifier—can be expressed in a statement with a defined function. And, second, it focuses on the producer of the argument more than on the recipient.

A co-orientational approach to argument builds on Toulmin's model and incorporates three additional elements: process, situations, and relationship. In a co-orientational model, arguments function as rhetorical processes in which the components of an argument blend together in an attempt to influence recipients. Rather than viewing arguments as a set of separate, discrete, and definable statements, a co-orientational approach holds that the parts of an argument can be fluid and changing as the argument evolves during the interaction of arguer and recipient. For instance, argument claims may become evidence for subsequent arguments. Warrants can have both claim and evidence characteristics. Arguments also depend on their situations. Argument situations shape how arguments are understood. Time, place, and people all affect how arguments are understood and evaluated. In the 1970s, for instance, many arguments were traded back and forth among consumer advocates and automobile manufacturers about whether air bags in cars added to safety or undermined it. Some suggested that the cost of requiring air bags would destroy the auto industry. For that situation, the argument was timely and important. Today, the situation has changed and the argument would no longer be considered relevant. Finally arguments occur in relationships. Arguer and recipient interact to shape and change the direction and outcome of ideas, actions, and beliefs. Arguments, therefore, are interactive. Both arguer and recipient persuade each other as they move toward a conclusion. The quality and stability of their relationship affects what arguments are made, heard, and acted upon.

Co-Orientational Model

One defining aspect of how arguments function using a co-orientational approach is the level of agreement that separates an argument's starting point (or premise) from its claims, and whether the amount of agreement between arguer and recipient regarding the claims allows statements to be accepted without further support or evidence.

There is almost universal agreement that free speech is an important, essential element for democratic societies. Without freedom of expression, freedom of thought is compromised, and once that happens, critical thinking and decision making are significantly undermined or curtailed. Almost all recipients can readily accept this as evidence. But the question of whether a college or the government has the right or responsibility to regulate or limit any form of free speech is much more controversial—some argue that the First Amendment to the U.S. Constitution guarantees the right to

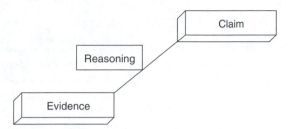

FIGURE 2.7   A Model of an Argument

say anything or behave in any way a speaker chooses. And, even those who recognize that limits must be placed on free speech are uncertain where to draw the line. Should pornography be banned? When and under what conditions? Should speakers be allowed to use "hate speech" to get their message across? If not, under what conditions should restrictions be made? Should the neo-Nazi party be allowed to parade in Jewish communities and on public streets? Should a college show a play that might prompt violent demonstrations?

These are all difficult questions, and they depend on a complex relationship among the speakers, recipients, and community standards. Many of these ideas are too controversial to be accepted as evidence and are themselves argument claims that need to be proved. The relationship between evidence and claim is represented in Figure 2.7. In this figure, evidence functions to ground the claim, and reasoning is used to connect the two parts of the argument.

The discussion in Box 2.1 provides a good illustration of how arguments work. Both Juli and Steve develop different arguments as they move through a discussion of whether or not it is appropriate to ban a play. Consider, for example, Juli's argument in which she suggested there are occasions when limiting speech or art is justified:

> Our rights to see this play or have a controversial art exhibition are not more important than someone else's rights—even when it comes to free speech. People have threatened to protest this play, and our campus police are worried about violence and vandalism. We have no right to put others at risk, and if a protest turns ugly, that's what could happen. If our freedoms potentially hurt others, they should be limited. Ironically, this play makes that point. We limit hate speech—we don't allow people to say what they want because it may have harmful consequences.
>
> Artistic work is like any other form of speech; it should have limits if it hurts others. Artistic expression should not be exempted from censorship any more than any other kind of speech.

Figure 2.8 shows how Juli moved from her evidence (facts about censorship and free speech) to her claim that there are times when censorship of artistic expression is justified. This diagram provides an easy way to see how the parts of the argument function in relation to each other within a co-orientational framework and how they work together as a whole.

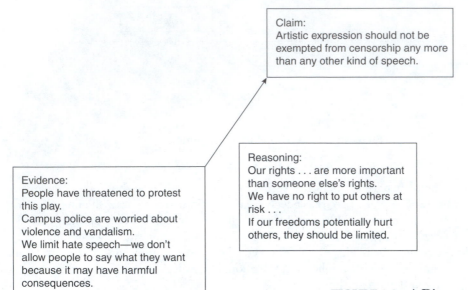

FIGURE 2.8   A Diagrammed Argument

The Level of Dispute

Arguments occur where there are disagreements about issues within a topic. If, for instance, everyone agreed that the *Laramie Project* should be banned from campus, there would be no need for Juli's arguments. Arguments occur only when people disagree with one another. This separation—what the arguer and recipient agree to and what are the points of disagreement—describes an imaginary line that separates the statements of belief and value with which recipients agree from those with which they disagree. In other words, for any issue we can think of, there is a line that separates what we are willing to accept from what we are unwilling to accept initially.

For instance, we might discuss the relative strengths of President Franklin D. Roosevelt and his four-term presidency. Even if you were a staunch political conservative and truly believed Roosevelt almost destroyed American freedoms through a strong centralized government, there is some aspect of Roosevelt's presidency you would accept. You might not agree with the arguer who says Roosevelt was the best president, but you would probably accept that he was president. You would also probably accept that he was elected to four terms and that under Roosevelt many government programs for economic reform were passed. Although you might not accept the value of such programs, you would probably agree with the facts of his administration (the WPA was established; the United States entered World War II). The point to be made here is that for any issue you can think of, there is a level of agreement about certain facts.

The level of dispute is an imaginary line that separates what is accepted by the audience from what is not accepted. Arguments that occur below the line are already accepted by the audience, and those that occur above it are not accepted. The term *line* may be a little misleading here. We are not suggesting that all issues have clearly demarcated lines that all recipients of argument acknowledge. Such a position would fail to recognize that people do not have their minds made up on all issues. Rather, we can think of

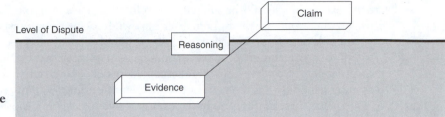

FIGURE 2.9   The Level of Dispute

this line or level of dispute as a not clearly defined area in which people neither accept nor reject arguments immediately. Therefore, the level of dispute is the lowest common level that an audience is willing to accept. The claim of an argument must always fall above the level of dispute. Otherwise, the argument is already accepted.

Figure 2.9 helps illustrate the role played by the level of dispute. Evidence in this model falls below the level of dispute because if evidence were disputed and fell above the line, then the evidence itself would need to be proved and anchored to the audience's accepted knowledge. In other words, the evidence would become the subject of an argument. The key is simply that arguments seek to move the audience from positions already accepted to new and different positions. An advocate, then, seeks to use acceptable evidence in order to reason with the audience to accept a new claim.

The level of dispute exists and is drawn in the minds and perceptions of argument recipients. An arguer's objective is to adapt the evidence, reasoning, and claims to the recipient's understanding of the subject being argued. Although this may appear to be a relatively straightforward task, it can become more complex as the number of listeners increases. Someone with a great deal of experience in one area may have a relatively high level of dispute. Someone with little knowledge of the area will have a relatively low level of dispute. When these two people are in the same audience, the arguer has the difficult task of adapting to the different levels of dispute of the different individuals. Often the result is argument directed toward the lowest common denominator that everyone in the audience can understand and agree with. Although the lowest-common-denominator approach may appeal to some, it is just as likely to bore the other recipients.

The arguer chooses and adapts the level of dispute to the audience. This is a choice unique for each situation and audience. If an arguer receives feedback indicating confusion or disagreement, he or she may decide to raise or lower the level while arguing. For a critic examining the argument, understanding the level of dispute is important because its location implies the type of recipients assumed by the arguer and offers a better understanding of the argument context.

The Role of Reasoning

Reasoning connects the evidence and the claim. It serves as a logical and persuasive bridge between the two ends of an argument. By means of the inferences made, reasoning acts to draw a strong relationship between that which is known and accepted by the recipients and that which is unknown or unaccepted by the recipients. Juli makes the argument that potentially offensive artistic expression could be equated with hate speech or other kinds of expression that can lead to violence or threaten community interests. If it causes vandalism or violence, or if it diminishes the rights of others in the community, artistic expression should be limited. Therefore, because everyone has rights and because no one group has the right to assert its own free-speech interests ahead of others', certain kinds of expression such as a controversial play could be censored.

In a co-orientational model, reasoning is important because it is a process that draws recipients from the known and accepted evidence toward the claim. As a process, reasoning plays the significant role of connecting the arguer with the recipient over a set of issues and ideas. In this case, Juli's position is one that many recipients might initially reject without much discussion or thought. Most people believe that free speech is important and banning anything—especially art—carries with it a high burden to prove it is harmful. Juli's reasoning, though, provided an approach for Steve to understand her perspective. By comparing staging the *Laramie Project* to other instances where most recipients would accept regulated speech, she offered reasoning that connected the evidence to the claim. This is not to say, however, that Juli is correct or that recipients will unquestioningly accept her argument. But it provides a good illustration of how reasoning works to link the parts of the argument together and raise the level of dispute.

Argument Chains

Once an argument is proved, what happens to the level of dispute? If Steve accepts Juli's claim, what happens next? Logically, if the claim is proved and those to whom it is addressed accept it as a valid conclusion, then the level of dispute rises such that the claim now falls below the line, as illustrated in Figure 2.10. This means that an advocate can now use a proved argument as evidence for another argument. The process of linking proven claims to unproven claims is called chaining, and it is shown in Figure 2.11. *An argument chain uses a proved argument as evidence for an unproved claim.* For example, Juli responds to Steve's comments and builds new arguments grounded in her original statements while accounting for Steve's reservations:

> Fair enough. I think, though, that it is important to remember that censorship can be targeted so that some classes of people are protected—like kids. After all, movies have ratings to allow some people to see them while keeping others out. Censorship can be used to protect kids from excessive sex and violence or having to deal with issues in this play. The issue is that not all content is appropriate for everyone. And, in our community, maybe this play is not a wise choice. That should have been taken into consideration.

In this argument, Juli links her new reasoning and claims to her original statements by adding that censorship could be adapted to particular situations and for specific audiences. That way, she suggests, community standards can be addressed as well as

**FIGURE 2.10
Level of Dispute
in a Proved
Argument**

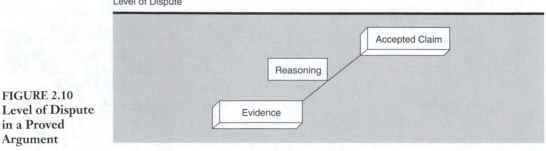

Level of Dispute

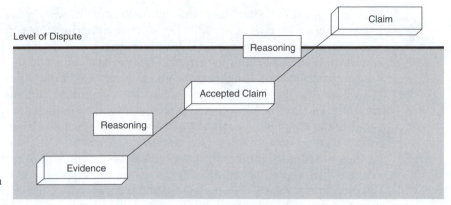

FIGURE 2.11 An Argument Chain

the interests of individual audiences such as children. She modified her argument to address issues raised by Steve and introduced evidence and reasoning to build on her original claim and reach a conclusion that the censorship could be targeted to specific types of expression.

The concept of chained arguments holds many important implications for building *macro arguments*, or extended argumentative cases, which will be developed more fully in Chapters 9, 10, and 11. In an extended case, the arguer's central thesis or claim in a macro argument may lie far above the level of dispute, and many preliminary claims may have to be established before the central claim is adequately supported. If the arguer begins with facts and premises accepted by everyone to whom the argument is addressed and builds arguments one step at a time, the level of dispute can be raised in increments until the central claim is proved.

Argument Situations

As with so many other human events, in argumentation, timing is everything. Arguments (or any form of communication) may be interpreted very differently at different times. Communication is generally bound by its particular situation. For example, the first edition of this book was published in 1989 and used many examples of arguments about the Soviet Union and the Cold War. If these same arguments were made today, they would be considered outdated and inapplicable given current events and the dissolution of the U.S.S.R. *Argument situation refers to the rhetorical situation of the argument.* Perhaps the person most noted for his development of the "rhetorical situation" is a theorist named Lloyd F. Bitzer.[22]

The rhetorical situation is a natural context of persons, events, objects, relations, and an exigence that strongly invites arguments. Therefore, every argument exists in a particular and unique situation. The situation is made up of the audience, the arguer, the experiences of the audience and arguer, and what Bitzer refers to as exigence. *Exigence* can be defined as *"an imperfection marked by urgency; it is a defect, an obstacle, something waiting to be done, a thing that is other than it should be."*[23] In other words, arguments are not developed randomly but are instead called into existence by some exigence—there is some cause or reason for us to argue. When Martin Luther King Jr. delivered his "I Have a Dream" speech, he presented it to a particular audience at a particular time.

He was responding to decades of discrimination, and he was urging action on a pending comprehensive civil rights bill. His audience comprised more than 250,000 people who had come to Washington, D.C., to protest for civil rights. It was the largest demonstration ever held in the United States to that time, and the situation required a cornerstone address. King's address met the exigence of the situation.

Not all exigencies, however, require such important arguments. Presenting an argument in class to fulfill the requirements of an assignment may address the exigence of the assignment, but it also addresses an exigence in a larger sense. *An exigence is also a contemporary problem or issue that needs to be addressed.* This is why classroom assignments address significant or important issues as opposed to trivial ones. The exigence is like a question waiting for an answer. The point is simply that particular situations call for particular arguments, and speakers who are able to identify and understand the requirements of the rhetorical situation may be able to develop arguments that fit the needs of the argument context.

Over time, argument situations change. Issues that might have been relevant and important at one time in the personal sphere may develop and move into a technical or public sphere. Some arguments drop out of all three spheres over time as arguments are accepted, rejected, or become irrelevant. Box 2.2 provides some examples of how time changes the kinds of issues that people discuss. As argument contexts change, the people involved in them change, different participants become engaged in the issues discussed. For instance, in 1981 when Bill Gates claimed, "640K ought to be enough for anybody," his audience was a relatively small group of people in a relatively technical field. As computers and discussions about them entered the public sphere, more people became involved in arguments over the technology.

Generally, argument situations have four characteristics. First, the situation invites arguments. Our arguments are in response to some problem, proposition, or other issue that is important for our recipients. Without a problem or issue that needs to be considered, there is little reason for argument. King's "I Have a Dream" speech was designed in response to a problem of racial inequality. It was adapted to a particular audience at a particular time and place. If the United States were truly integrated—if King's "dream" had already been fulfilled and equal rights were enjoyed by all—there would have been no need for the speech, and it is unlikely that King would have presented it.

Second, arguments must be fitting to the situation. Even though arguers may be able to identify a problem, not just any argument will fit. If King, for instance, had written a speech about the need for more space exploration or better pay for migrant farm workers, the speech would not have fit the situation because the audience and occasion would not have been appropriate for the subject. Similarly, if an advocate makes an argument that is not relevant to the recipients or that does not address the important issues of a dispute, then the argument does not fit.

Third, situations prescribe the criteria for a fitting response. If we agree that a response must fit the situation, the requirements for the fit should be clear: the context for the argument, the issues involved, and that the participants understand the demands of the situation. Those demands—the needs of the situation—represent criteria for evaluating how well an argument fits. This means that if King's speech fit the situation, then the criteria for judging the fit must be identifiable such that King could have understood them and adapted the speech to them. King knew that he was expected to offer a message of hope to those engaged in the struggle for civil rights,

▪ ▪ ▪ ▪ ▪

BOX 2.2
HOW SITUATIONS CHANGE WITH TIME

Timing makes a great deal of difference in when and where arguments are made. Consider the following claims:

"Computers in the future may weigh no more than 1.5 tons."—*Popular Mechanics*, 1949

"I think there is a world market for maybe five computers."—Thomas Watson, chair of IBM, 1949

"There is no reason anyone would want a computer in their home."—Ken Olson, president of Digital Equipment Corporation, 1977

"Who the hell wants to hear actors talk?"—H. M. Warner, Warner Brothers, 1927

"Stocks have reached what looks like a permanently high plateau."—Irving Fisher, Professor of Economics, Yale University, 1929

"Everything that can be invented has been invented."—Charles H. Duell, Commissioner, U.S. Office of Patents, 1899

"640K ought to be enough for anybody."—Bill Gates, 1981

acknowledge the sacrifices many had made, call for redress of discrimination against persons of color, and emphasize the importance of nonviolent protest. He did all this so admirably and his speech so fit the occasion that it has come to be regarded as one of the most masterful speeches of the twentieth century.

Fourth, argumentative situations are impermanent. This means that just as situations arise and invite argument, they also dissolve or become unimportant. Just as some questions go unanswered, so do situations. Situations, then, are temporary and, if unanswered, will dissipate and lose their significance. Had King chosen not to speak during the demonstration, his opportunity for argument would have been lost, and "I Have a Dream" might have been nothing more than a manuscript somewhere. Even if he had spoken a day later, the situation would have dissipated as the demonstration broke up and people went home.

Argument Relationships

Because arguments evolve through the interaction among arguers and recipients, the connection or relationship among the participants is important. Every message involves a content (what is being discussed) and a relationship (what is the connection among the participants).[24] Earlier we discussed the content of arguments and examined how all of the pieces are put together to move people toward a claim. This section examines the relationships among argument participants.

Argument relationships are the interdependent connections that exist between arguers and recipients. In other words, we create arguments with people who we believe can affect the outcome or change their own beliefs or behaviors—we do not tend to create arguments for people who cannot shape or enact the claims. Therefore, an attorney will make an argument to a judge because the judge has the power to make a decision. The same arguments would be irrelevant at the attorney's home because the recipients there would have no ability to act on the claim. In Box 2.1, Steve argued that the college should not be allowed to ban the production of the *Laramie Project*. Even though

Juli probably cannot change whatever decision the college makes, Steve's arguments may affect her own behavior or beliefs, which, in turn, may affect the way she talks and thinks about issues related to censorship.

Steve's argument is that controversial productions on a college campus should be allowed because of their potential positive influence on discussions and decisions at the college. He and Juli are interdependent with respect to this argument. Their developing conversation and series of arguments affect the other's point of view. If you examine the sequence of arguments, you will notice that Steve begins with a broad statement about censorship that, through his interaction with Juli, becomes more refined and focused. The arguments develop in a way that shapes and focuses the thinking of each arguer.

In any argument, the participants evaluate how to manage the content of the dispute as well as their relationships. If the relationship is very important and the content is less important, an arguer may choose to be less forceful and direct than if the content of the argument was very important. In the discussion between Juli and Steve, for instance, the content was important, but both protected the relationship. Both arguers listened to and incorporated elements of the other's ideas into their own arguments. If their focus was on content over relationship, we would probably not see as much agreement or movement toward a common understanding. Some arguments, while important, focus on enhancing the relationship. For instance, what to have for dinner or what movie to see are arguments in which the relationship is considerably more important than the particular content. Other arguments, particularly those with a fast-approaching deadline or in which the content is so important that there needs to be a decision, may undermine the relationship in favor of specific action. Arguments about safety, security, or life-and-death decisions all carry a significant weight based on their content that may override the relationship.

How arguers treat the connection of relationship and content can be referred to as a style. *An argument style is the orientation arguers choose to use to balance content and relationship needs in an argument situation.* In other words, people make a choice when they argue: Is having the claim accepted more or less important than the relationship with the recipients? Although there is almost infinite variation on this balance, argument styles can generally be classified in five types: competing, collaborating, avoiding, compromising, and accommodating.[25] These are illustrated in Figure 2.12 and are defined as follows:

> *Competing.* Arguers use this style when they are seeking to win over another person or group. A competitive approach prizes the content far more than the relationship, and it seeks to demonstrate that a particular set of arguments is superior to alternatives. This style is often seen in courts of law where one attorney seeks to win by discrediting or undermining the arguments of another attorney. Generally, a competing style views arguments as winning or losing.
>
> *Collaborating.* A collaborative style seeks to find ways in which all of the participants to an argument can succeed mutually. This style values both strong content and strong relationships. When arguers use a collaborative style, they approach an argument situation with the belief that the other parties have equally important arguments and ideas that need to be discussed and understood. People engaged in this approach see argument as an opportunity to explore

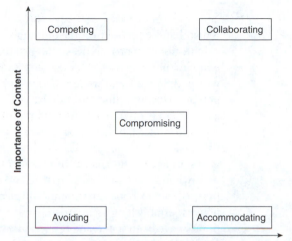

FIGURE 2.12   **Argument Styles**

ideas and develop strong relationships. This approach is used in mediation settings and in problem-solving groups. A collaborative style looks to argumentative outcomes that allow all parties to win or succeed.

Avoiding. Arguers may use this style to withdraw and escape becoming involved in an argument. This approach is used when neither the content nor the relationship is considered very important because it means that issues needing resolution are ignored or abandoned. When this style is used, arguers allow the argument situation to pass and the issues to go unaddressed.

Compromising. Arguers use this style when their content goals and relationship goals are both moderately important. When this approach is used, arguers are willing to negotiate both content and relationship such that all of the involved parties will give something up but also receive something of value. The goal is to find a middle ground among the positions advocated. Examples of this approach can be found in most negotiation settings, such as in sales or between management and unions about pay and benefits.

Accommodating. Arguers use this style when the importance of the relationship is much greater than the importance of the content. In such cases, arguers will tend to back down against other viewpoints in an effort to maintain a strong relationship. When people accommodate, they elect not to be involved in argument but rather strive for harmony in the relationship. Examples can be found in many situations, but often politicians will back down on a particular argument in favor of preserving a strong relationship for a future argument when the relationship may be needed.

Each style discussed here has advantages and disadvantages associated with it. Generally, we hope that argument allows for collaborative decision making in which multiple ideas are examined in a spirit that embraces the importance of argument as a vehicle for developing both understanding and relationship. However, different situations often call for other styles.

SUMMARY

This chapter focused on developing a co-orientational approach to argument. A co-orientational approach presumes a significant relationship between arguer and recipient. Further, the particular context and situation in which arguments occur shape the way people view and understand arguments. We began with a discussion of argument perspectives, examined arguer-based models, and concluded with the development of a co-orientational model for argument.

Argumentation can be viewed from three different but complementary perspectives, each of which emphasizes different aspects of argument. The logical perspective views an argument as a set of premises and a conclusion, and it is primarily concerned with whether the premises are true and the inference is correctly stated. The dialectical perspective describes argumentation as a process of discovering issues, generating alternatives, establishing standards for judgment, and withholding a decision until all viewpoints have been stated and tested. The rhetorical perspective emphasizes argumentation as a method of influence, and it considers whether arguers seem aware of the interests and values of the audience and state their arguments appropriately and effectively.

Arguer-based approaches focus on the production of arguments and have been linked to the study of formal logic. Syllogisms are a model of argument described by Aristotle and are probably the earliest model published. In this model, arguments are composed of three statements (major premise, minor premise, conclusion) and three terms (major term, middle term, minor term). The three terms are placed in pairs in each of the three statements such that each term is used twice. Provided that the major and minor premises are true and valid, the conclusion of a syllogism is also true and valid.

Stephen Toulmin criticized the syllogism for its formal adherence to logic as opposed to practical forms of reasoning. He argued that in conversation and informal arguments, syllogisms did not provide a useful model for how people actually argued. Toulmin's model includes three parts that are explicitly or implicitly present in every argument (data, warrant, claim) and three parts that are included in many arguments (reservation, qualifier, backing). These parts work together and describe how advocates adapt their arguments to different situations and contexts.

The chapter concluded with the development of a co-orientational approach. Using this approach, arguments are designed with an audience in mind and for a particular situation. In this model, arguments are based on statements accepted by the recipients and for which no further support is needed. Because these statements provoke no disagreement, they fall below the level of dispute. When they are successively and successfully used to support new claims, the level of dispute rises, and the formerly contested claim becomes a premise for a new argument. When a proven argument is used as evidence for an unproven claim, the result is an argument chain. The concept of a level of dispute is useful because it illustrates how the extent of the recipient's agreement with the arguer's claims may vary as the argument is being made.

Arguments are produced for particular situations and are judged by their time and place. These situations influence the way arguments are created, understood, and evaluated. Situations are an important part of an argument's development because they shape the relationship among arguers and recipients.

Argument situations change over time. Arguments that would have been appropriate for a given audience at a given time may not be appropriate years or even days later. Arguments change as people, issues, and knowledge about the world change. Argument situations refer to the rhetorical situation of the argument. Bitzer contended that a rhetorical situation arises from the context of person, events, objects, relations, and exigence, which together call for an argument to be produced. Argument situations have four characteristics. First, they ask for an argument to be offered. Just as a question invites an answer, an argument situation invites an argument. Second, the argument must be a fitting answer to the situation. The answer offered should be relevant to the question asked. Third, the standards for judging a fitting response should be embodied in the situation. The arguer should know how to adapt the arguments to the situation. And fourth, argument situations are temporary. Situations arise, they exist, and, if left unanswered, they disappear.

Finally, argument relationship describes the interdependent connection among arguers and recipients. Every argument carries both a content and a relationship component. When arguments are made, arguers choose how to balance these two variables and typically use one of five styles: collaborating, competing, accommodating, avoiding, and compromising.

GLOSSARY

Argument chain (p. 52) uses a proved argument as evidence for an unproved claim.

Argument relationships (p. 55) are the interdependent connections that exist between arguers and recipients.

Argument situation (p. 53) refers to the rhetorical situation of the argument.

Argument style (p. 56) is the orientation arguers choose to use to balance content and relationship needs in an argument situation.

Backing (p. 43) consists of further facts or reasoning used to support or legitimate the principle contained in the warrant.

Categorical syllogism (p. 39-40) is a logical argument that draws a necessary conclusion from two premises stated as simple propositions containing categorical terms that designate classes.

Co-orientational approach (p. 34) presumes that the relationship between arguer and recipient is as important as the content of the argument.

Data (p. 43) are facts or conditions that are objectively observable beliefs or premises accepted as true by the audience, or conclusions previously established.

Deductive reasoning (p. 38) is the process of moving from general statements to specific conclusions.

Dialectical perspective (p. 36) focuses on and enhances a candid, critical, and comprehensive examination of all positions relevant to the topic.

Disjunctive syllogism (p. 40) sets forth two alternatives in the major premise, denies one of them in the minor premise, and affirms the other in the conclusion.

Enthymeme (p. 42) is a rhetorical syllogism that calls upon the audience's existing beliefs for one both of its premises.

Exigence (p. 53) is an imperfection marked by urgency; it is a defect, an obstacle, something waiting to be done, a thing that is other than it should be. It is also a contemporary problem or issue that needs to be addressed.

Formal logic (p. 38) is the study of how conclusions are reached using structured statements.

Hypothetical syllogism (p. 41) is an argument that does not involve a direct comparison, rather it contains a conditional major premise that is either affirmed or denied in the minor premise.

Inductive reasoning (p. 38) is a process of moving from particular examples, observations, or instances to general conclusions.

Level of dispute (p. 50) is the level of agreement or imaginary line that separates what is accepted by the audience from what is not accepted.

Logical perspective (p. 35) emphasizes the accuracy of the premises and the correctness of the inferences linking premises and evidence to the claims they support.

Qualifier (p. 43) is a colloquial adverb or adverbial phrase that modifies the claim and indicates the rational strength the arguer attributes to it.

Reservation (p. 43) states the circumstances or conditions that undermine the argument.

Rhetorical perspective (p. 36-37) holds that arguments are viewed as appeals to an audience, and we must take account of the circumstances in which the argument was made and the strategies used to influence its audience.

Rhetorical situation (p. 53) is a natural context of persons, events, objects, relations, and an exigence that strongly invites arguments.

Syllogism (p. 38) is made up of three statements, includes three terms associated in pairs with each other throughout the statements, and draws a conclusion from a major and a minor premise.

Warrant (p. 43) expresses the reasoning used to link the data to the claim.

EXERCISES

Exercise 1 Using the arguments developed in Box 2.1, diagram any of the arguments using Toulmin's model. Include claims, data, warrant, backing, qualifiers, and reservations. Take the same argument and use the co-orientational model to diagram it. Identify the claim, evidence, reasoning, and level of dispute.

   1. What similarities and differences did you find?

   2. Which model offers you a better way to understand the argument?

   3. Use the critical thinking process discussed in Chapter 1: What issues would you expect Juli and Steve to address? Does they address them? How does this affect the quality of the arguments?

Exercise 2 Diagram each of the following arguments using both the Toulmin model and the co-orientational model of argument. Then, based on what you know, criticize each argument. What makes it strong? What makes it weak? For example:

   Capital punishment for murderers is widely supported by the general population. A Harris Poll in 1975 reported 59 percent of the public was in favor of capital punishment, and that proportion reportedly was increasing. Another poll in 1978 asked the question, "Are you in favor of the death penalty for persons convicted of murder?" The results showed 66 percent of the populace in favor of the death penalty.

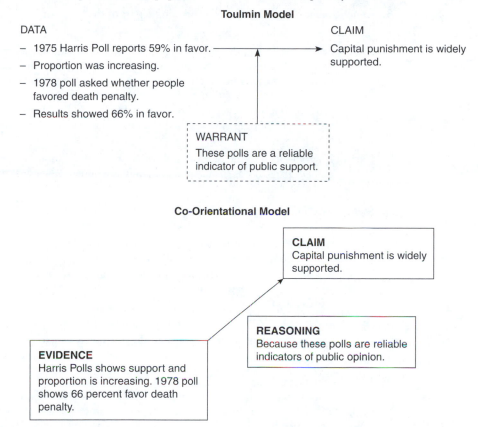

Toulmin Model

DATA

– 1975 Harris Poll reports 59% in favor.

– Proportion was increasing.

– 1978 poll asked whether people favored death penalty.

– Results showed 66% in favor.

CLAIM

Capital punishment is widely supported.

WARRANT

These polls are a reliable indicator of public support.

Co-Orientational Model

CLAIM
Capital punishment is widely supported.

REASONING
Because these polls are reliable indicators of public opinion.

EVIDENCE
Harris Polls shows support and proportion is increasing. 1978 poll shows 66 percent favor death penalty.

Criticism

These polls are very outdated. Perhaps public opinion has shifted since the 1970s. Besides, just because the public supports something does not mean that it should be favored.

Arguments for Analysis and Criticism

*1. It is the chemical firms that release the most troubling types of molecules into the environment. In Baton Rouge, according to company data, an Exxon chemical plant was leaking 560,000 pounds of benzene yearly, while just south of there, according to a survey by the Sierra Club, eighteen plants in and around St. Gabriel and Geismar dumped about 400 billion pounds of toxic chemicals into the air during the first nine months of 1986.

Michael H. Brown, "The Toxic Cloud," *Greenpeace Magazine* (October–December 1987): 17.

2. But it was when Abbado had the orchestra to himself in the Tchaikovsky *Marche Slave* that the real magic showed. This hackneyed piece was treated with respect, and Abbado built it steadily to one final climax rather than playing each eruption as a show-stopping event.

[The following two arguments are excerpted from a group discussion on the right to die. Assume that all the participants are working together to construct *one* argument and are pursuing a shared thoughtline.]

3. Anne: Technology has affected every single part of the program.

Carrie: Yes, technology is a big one.

Anne: I don't really feel that technology is just the mechanical aspect. It's chemical, biological, physical, everything. The advances in technology have gone so far that it can prolong life, yeah, but when you get in the position of an irreversibly comatose-type state, it's out of step with what man is. You know, should he be prolonged just to vegetate? Are they prolonging ill health, or are they prolonging life? Technology has reached the outer limits where it's gone beyond what man is.

Carrie: It's gone beyond the purpose for which medical technology was originally intended. Its goal was to enhance human life, whereas now it just prolongs death, dying, and pain.

4. Steve: The Hippocratic Oath, which states doctors must do everything within their power to keep the patient alive, is also a problem.

Carrie: But the idea of the Hippocratic Oath is a problem. It says, "So far as power and discernment shall be mine, I will carry out the regimen for the benefit of the sick and will keep them from harm and wrong." Now the doctors or the law, . . . someone should explain the Hippocratic Oath to everyone, what exactly those words mean.

Anne: But it's an archaic document. I mean, it talks about Greek gods. . . .

Leigh: It's so ambiguous. It doesn't have to do with today's society.

Steve: It's been outgrown by technology.

5. Is it not the great defect of our education today . . . that although we often succeed in teaching our pupils "subjects," we fail lamentably on the whole in teaching them how to think: they learn everything except the art of learning. It is as though we had taught a child mechanically and by rule of thumb to play "The Harmonious Blacksmith" upon the piano, but had never taught him the scale or how to read music; so that, having memorized "The Harmonious Blacksmith," he still had not the faintest notion how to proceed from that to tackle "The Last Rose of Summer."

Dorothy L. Sayers, "The Lost Tools of Learning," *National Review* (January 19, 1979): 91.

6. It's not too late. We can act. Today there are some 500 million women in the Third World who have told the World Fertility Survey that they want no more children. Most of them didn't want their last child, but they lacked the knowledge and the means to do something about it—whether it happens to be the three condoms for a penny that the United Nations Population Fund buys and distributes, or a cycle of oral contraceptives which the United Nations buys for 15 cents a cycle, or whether it's Norplant or vasectomy equipment.

Werner Fornos, "The Environmental Crisis: A Humanist Call for Action," *The Humanist* (November/December 1991): 31.

7. The 1991 statistics from the Carnegie Foundation for the Advancement of Teaching show that SAT scores are directly proportional to family income. Students from families with incomes under $10,000 score an average of 768 (combined verbal and math scores) out of a possible total of 1,200. Students from families with incomes in the $30,000 to $40,000 range have scores averaging 884. Students from families with incomes over $70,000 have scores averaging 997. Since scholastic aptitude is related to a student's position on the wealth/poverty scale, which has a lot to do with where a family lives (affluent suburb or inner-city slum), alleviating poverty would be one way of improving scholastic aptitude.

Edd Doerr, "Whither Public Education?" *The Humanist* (November/December 1991): 41.

8. So much of the male behavior that puts women at risk—multiple partners, bisexuality, reluctance or refusal to wear condoms—cannot be changed by women alone. And so many of the attitudes that pervade societies about women's worth and

> place and men's rights make effective prevention campaigns extremely difficult to achieve. . . . Even when informed of the risk, women too rarely have the power to protect themselves. In every society, women are subservient to men. Depending on the degree of pressure on her to be submissive in sexual and social matters, a woman who tries to use information to prevent infection may become the target of mockery, rejection, stigmatization, economic reprisal, violence, and death.

Marcia Ann Gillespie, "HIV: The Global Crisis," *MS. Magazine* (January/February, 1991): 17.

Exercise 3 Following is the text of a speech presented by Representative Cliff Stearns in the *Congressional Record.* After reading the entire speech, apply the concepts in this chapter by accomplishing the following objectives:

1. Locate all the claims, reasoning, and evidence in the speech. Draw a line under each one and label it.

2. Apply the standards for the logical, dialectical, and rhetorical perspective.
   a. For the logical perspective, consider whether the evidence offered by the author appears to be accurate, whether his reasoning seems sound, and whether there are links established between his premises and conclusions.
   b. For the dialectical perspective, consider whether all aspects of the questions are thoroughly explored, whether all issues are considered, and whether standards for judgment are provided. Does this article contribute to public discussion about drug use in athletics?
   c. For the rhetorical perspective, consider whether this article adapted to the author's audience and whether it addresses the circumstances and contexts relevant to the topic in our society.

3. How does Stearns try to create a relationship with his audience? What techniques does he use? Do you think they are effective?

4. What critical conclusions can you reach about the argument? Does it seem reasonable? How might Stearns have improved it?

STEROIDS IN SPORTS

I'm a big sports fan. I have had the opportunity to play sports in high school and in an industrial league. I played it in the Boys Club back in 90-pound football. And I think, like most of us, we understand that the vast majority of stars today were a testament to true hard work. . . . Their performances, victories, records, and careers seemed to capture the straightforwardness of honesty, hard work, and integrity that is based upon the heart of sports today, at least in the past, the ideal that sports allow success based upon merit, whether it be on the court, the field, or the track.

Unfortunately . . . the scourge of steroids and performance-enhancing drugs is not simply a footnote in the history of sports in America. Steroid use goes much deeper, to the basic integrity of sports and all of athletics. At the most fundamental level, steroid use is just plain cheating. And . . . it is illegal . . .

Furthermore, steroid use involves significant health risks for all athletes who use them. Studies suggest that use of steroids can lead to stunted growth in adolescents, increased risk of heart and liver disease, as well as cancer and hormonal problems for both men and women. And that is why these and other factors demand that our elite athletic organizations, both professional and amateur, establish uniform, world-class drug-testing standards that are consistent and robust, just as our criminal laws are today.

However, the most worrisome development is that steroids are not only infiltrating their professional and elite amateur leagues, they are finding their way into middle schools and high school sports programs. In fact, according to the most recent Monitoring for the Future survey, funded by the National Institute on Drug Abuse, 3.5 percent of high school seniors have used steroids, with similar percentages for grades 8 through 10. These are alarming numbers that represent just a part of the susceptible youth population that is out there. These estimates suggest that the high school steroid problem is just as great, if not greater, than it is in the professional leagues.

As any parent knows, high school is a trying time for many kids, let alone student athletes. These exceptional kids now face yet another hazard all the way to adulthood that is trying to claim the safe haven of sports as its next growth market. We must take an aggressive stand against this plague before these pressures lead young student athletes to use steroids, its destructive effects on honesty and fair play and ultimately, their very health and well-being. . . .

Richard Pound, the founder and chair of the World Anti-Doping Agency, says, "Do we want our children to be forced to become drug addicts in order to be successful in sports? Like it or not, sports stars are heroes and idols to our kids. Our kids copy their heroes' behavior. That's why we have to encourage the stars to be good role models both on and off the field." Congress must continue to look into the use of illegal steroid and performance-enhancing drug use.

Professional leagues have an obligation to be the gold standard with regard to education, detection, and sanctions for the illicit use of steroids and other performance-enhancing drugs. The recent scandals in baseball, the Olympics, professional wrestling, and in other professional amateur sports have served to highlight the significance of the steroids problem.

Now, sometimes I'm asked back in the district why I care about drugs in sports. Shouldn't the athletes perhaps do whatever they want? They are only hurting themselves, is the reply. The use of steroids and performance-enhancing drugs by athletes today goes beyond just the integrity of the sport. By using illegal drugs, athletes are, in effect, telling our children that the only way to be successful and compete at the highest level is to cheat. That is not the message I want our children to hear.

Representative Cliff Stearns, Congressional Record (February 26, 2008): H1033-H1034.

NOTES

1. More information can be found in "Justice Department covers partially nude statues," *USA Today*, January 29, 2002, http://www.usatoday.com/news/nation/2002/01/29/statues.htm (accessed April 16, 2008).

2. Adapted from Jessica Remitz, The Daily Collegian Online, April 21, 2006, http://www.collegian.psu.edu/archive/2006/04/04-21-06tdc/04-21-06dnews-13.asp (accessed April 15, 2008).

3. For more information about the arts and arts censorship, see PBS, "Culture Shock: Are the arts dangerous?" http://www.pbs.org/wgbh/cultureshock/ (accessed April 16, 2008) and Steven C. Dubin, *Arresting Images: Impolitic Arts and Uncivil Actions* (New York: Routledge, 1992).

4. The Laramie Project is a controversial play written by Moisés Kaufman and members of the Tectonic Theatre project about the 1998 murder of Matthew Shepard. His death is widely believed to be the result of a hate crime motivated by homophobia. The play draws out many themes—religious, political, social—that some find challenging and it has often been protested and in some cases shut down over fears of violence.

5. Frans H. van Eemeren, Rob Grootendorst, and Francisca Shoeck Henkemans, *Fundamentals of Argumentation Theory* (Mahwah, N.J.: Erlbaum, 1996), 33–37.

6. Ray Lynn Anderson and C. David Mortenson, "Logic and Marketplace Argumentation," *Quarterly Journal of Speech* 53 (1967): 143–151.

7. George Ziegelmueller, Jack Kay, and Charles A. Dause, *Argumentation: Inquiry and Advocacy* (Englewood Cliffs, N.J.: Prentice-Hall, 1990), 3.

8. Joseph W. Wenzel, "Three Perspectives on Argument," in Robert Trapp and Janice Schuetz, eds., *Perspectives on Argumentation* (Prospect Heights, Ill.: Waveland Press, 1990), 9–26.

9. Joan Burton, "The Spotted Owl: A Victim of Forest Plans?" *The Mountaineer* 80, no. 7 (July 1986): 8. Used by permission of the author.

10. Chaim Perelman and Lucie Olbrechts-Tyteca, *The New Rhetoric: A Treatise on Argumentation*, trans. J. Wilkinson and P. Weaver (Notre Dame, Ind.: University of Notre Dame Press, 1969), 34.

11. We include here only a brief history of logic in the twentieth century. The origins of formal logic go back to Aristotle's *Prior Analytics* and *Posterior Analytics*, and early accounts of practical reasoning appear in Aristotle's *Topics*, *Rhetoric*, and *Sophistical Refutations*, all written in the fourth century B.C. Historical background for the study of reasoning can be found in Frans H. van Eemeren, Rob Grootendorst, and Francisca Shoeck Henkemans, *Fundamentals of Argumentation Theory: A Handbook of Historical Backgrounds and Contemporary Developments* (Mahwah, N.J.: Erlbaum, 1996).

12. For more information on this subject, consider Aristotle, *Prior Analytics*, trans. Robin Smith (Indianapolis: Hackett, 1989), and Harry J. Gensler, *Introduction to Logic* (New York: Routlege, 2002).

13. A good primer that describes formal logic and explains how it is used can be found at University of California, Davis, on its Web site "Logic Primer." It is located at http://tellerprimer.ucdavis.edu/ (accessed on April 22, 2008).

14. Francis Bacon, *The Great Instauration*, 1620 http://www.constitution.org/bacon/instauration.htm (accessed on April 22, 2008).

15. For excellent accounts of traditional syllogistic logic, see *The Encyclopedia of Philosophy*, s.v. "Logic, Traditional"; Edward P. J. Corbett and Robert J. Connors, *Classical Rhetoric for the Modern Student*, 4th ed. (New York: Oxford University Press, 1999), 38–59; Irving M. Copi and Carl Cohen, *Introduction to Logic*, 12th ed. (New York: Pearson Education, 2005); and James D. Carney and Richard K. Scheer, *Fundamentals of Logic*, 2d ed. (New York: Macmillan, 1974). For a book that applies syllogistic forms and criteria to practical argument, see Gerald M. Nosich, *Reasons and Arguments* (Belmont, Calif.: Wadsworth, 1982).

16. Aristotle, *Rhetoric* 1357a and 1395b.

17. Stephen Toulmin, *The Uses of Argument* (Cambridge: Cambridge University Press, 1969), 94–210.

18. Toulmin, 94.

19. Toulmin, 98.

20. Stephen Toulmin, Richard Rieke, and Allan Janik, *An Introduction to Reasoning*, 2d ed. (New York: Macmillan, 1984), 86.

21. Adapted from *Riggs vs. Palmer*, 115 N.Y. 506 (1889), 22 N.E. 188.

22. Lloyd F. Bitzer, "The Rhetorical Situation," *Philosophy and Rhetoric*, 1 (1968): 1–5.

23. Bitzer, 4.

24. Paul Wattzlawick, Janet Helmick Beavin, and Don D. Jackson, *Pragmatics of Human Communication: A Study of Interactional Patterns, Pathologies, and Paradoxes* (New York: Norton, 1967).

25. Adapted from Robert R. Blake and Jane S. Mouton, *The New Managerial Grid* (Houston: Gulf Publishing, 1994).

CHAPTER THREE

ARGUMENT CULTURES AND ETHICS

Human societies are complex. They develop over generations of experience, symbols, histories, and structures that give us meaning and frameworks for understanding our surroundings. Just as people and their experiences are different from one another, so are our communities different as well. Each has its own identity, its own story, and its own values. Argumentation often takes place among people who may or may not share common sets of experiences, values, or even approaches for creating or understanding arguments. Lack of common approaches for understanding and interpreting arguments may lead to misunderstanding and even violence.

   The long-running debate over whaling illustrated in Box 3.1 is one such example. Some cultures have chosen to hunt whales even though whale hunting has been banned by international agreement. Protestors such as Greenpeace have used nonviolent methods to stop hunters, but other organizations such as Sea Sheppard have admitted to sinking whaling vessels and destroying property.[1] Whereas Sea Sheppard characterizes Greenpeace as "ocean poseurs," Greenpeace claims that Sea Sheppard is

■ ■ ■ ■ ■

BOX 3.1
SHOULD WHALES BE HUNTED FOR FOOD?

People have hunted whales for thousands of years, but in the nineteenth century and with the tools of the industrial revolution, whaling became an important and profitable industry. The growth of cities and mechanization increased demand for lighting and lubrication oils that could be produced from whale blubber. Additionally, whale meat, bones, and other parts of the animal were used to feed people and make a wide array of other goods including corset stays, combs, art, and even buggy whips. But the oil was the most important product and made the industry profitable.[2]

By the end of the nineteenth century and with the development of petroleum-based products, the industry began to decline. However, as new, more efficient hunting technologies were introduced, whaling could be profitable by selling the meat as well as other parts of the animal. Better tracking, hunting, and processing capabilities led to international alarm in the 1960s and 1970s as whale numbers plummeted and many whale species approached extinction. Globally, people began calling for a ban on whaling, and in 1982 the International Whaling Commission (IWC) passed a ban that took effect in 1986.[3] Most, but not all, whaling countries and cultures chose to abide by the ban, and within a few years the whale populations began to rebound.[4]

Both Norway and Japan continued whaling and have been the subject of much international criticism.[5] Some other groups such as the Native American Makah tribe in the northwest United States continue limited whale hunting and claim it is an essential part of its culture. The Makah make the point that "the conduct of a whale hunt requires rituals and ceremonies which are deeply spiritual. They are the subject and inspiration of Makah songs, dances, designs, and basketry."[6] Without whaling, a significant part of the tribe's identity is lost.[7]

As the whale population has increased in recent years, Japan and Norway have called for lifting the ban to allow for regulated hunting. The IWC and most Western nations support continuing the ban. Whaling has been a regular conversation topic among many nature and conservation groups that look for ways to accommodate multiple interests while preserving the species. Consider the following discussion as the question of whale hunting is examined:

Chelsea: I know it's not politically correct, but there is no good reason we don't allow hunting whales for food—especially when people around the world are starving. Whales should be treated just like any other animal. I'm not saying that we hunt them to extinction, but they could be a good resource for food, oil, and many other products. As long as their numbers are healthy, why not?

Alex: That is the kind of thinking that took most whale species to the edge of extinction. There is no good reason to hunt whales. We don't need their oil; we don't need their bones for art or clothes. And, we certainly don't need their meat for food—especially if it means we destroy an important and unique animal.

Chelsea: But whales are no longer near extinction. The whaling ban worked and their numbers are increasing. I'm not saying it should be a free-for-all; whaling

(continued)

BOX 3.1   CONTINUED

<table>
<tr><td></td><td>should be regulated and managed appropriately. My point is, though, that the IWC ban worked, whales are out of danger. It is time to lift the ban and allow hunting to resume.</td></tr>
<tr><td>Alex:</td><td>Check your evidence: There is very little factual material about how many whales are left. The numbers are certainly not as high as pro–whale hunters suggest. When the IWC ban went into effect, whales were nearing extinction. If we don't learn from our history, we could kill off important species—and for no good reason.

Besides, even if you are right and there are many whales out there, we still should not kill them. Whales are special. They are intelligent, they are social, and they have language. We should not butcher intelligent and aware beings. It is morally wrong to hunt and kill species that appear to have so many social and intellectual traits in common with us.</td></tr>
<tr><td>Chelsea:</td><td>There is no good measure of whale intelligence. Most research has been done on dolphins, and it is highly controversial. This view—that whales are somehow uniquely special and deserve special consideration—is not held widely by people outside Western countries. They are not in need of special protection any more than other animals. Who are we to tell other cultures what is right or wrong? If Norway or the Makah want to hunt whales, what gives us the right to say we know better?</td></tr>
<tr><td>Alex:</td><td>Even if you are right, whale hunting techniques are cruel and involve animals suffering a slow death. When a nursing mother is killed, the calf dies too, further depleting the population. If whaling is expanded, more inexperienced hunters with limited skills and technology will increase the suffering of these animals.</td></tr>
<tr><td>Chelsea:</td><td>You are talking about people who hunt whales in a traditional way. Whale hunting is an important aspect of some people's cultural heritage. For the Faroese islanders of the North Atlantic, the Makah in the USA and the Bequia people of St. Vincent in the Grenadines, their cultures are deeply affected through whaling. For them, hunting a few whales each year is important for their economy and their cultural identity. Who are we to take that from them?</td></tr>
</table>

Consider the arguments that emerged in this discussion and consider the following questions:

1. As you read the exchange, do you notice any of your own biases emerging? Where do they come from? Are they cultural? From something you read?
2. What arguments were compelling for you? What arguments didn't work? What do you base your assessment on?
3. Does one culture or one cultural perspective have the right to judge other cultures? For instance, is it appropriate for Western nations to pass judgment about the practices of non-Western societies? Why?
4. If a ban on whaling undermines the cultural identity of a people, does the international community have the right to impose the ban? What basis would you use to make that decision?

nothing more than a group of pirates. In any case, Greenpeace employs a set of values and nonviolent practices that differ greatly from those of the more aggressive and forceful Sea Sheppard. And both organizations oppose the values and practice of whale hunting cultures.

When people engage in arguments, their cultural background provides them with a framework to interpret what is being said as well as how to respond to it. This means that because cultures understand the process of argumentation differently, cultural styles and approaches also vary. Cultural analysts can identify cultural tendencies that use particular reasoning forms, types of evidence, as well as approaches for managing disagreement and conflict. In intercultural settings in which members of different cultures engage in argumentation, the opportunity for misunderstanding is heightened because of potential dissonance among styles, approaches, evaluation standards, values, and symbols used by different groups of people. And, when we evaluate arguments, we draw from cultural values and understandings of what is appropriate and reasonable. Some of these understandings vary considerably across cultures, whereas others remain relatively consistent.

Often, our evaluation of arguments as well as our own approach to creating arguments depend on our understanding of what is right and wrong. For instance, is it right to hunt whales to extinction? At the same time, is it right for Western countries to tell people who have a strong cultural connection to whaling that they can no longer practice those traditions? The power of argumentation and its influence on people are considerable. Arguments influenced the International Whaling Commission to pass a ban, and arguments are now being used to try to persuade the IWC to reverse it. As individual arguers, we should not take our own arguments for granted but should understand their potential effects. Given the context in which arguments are made, we should be able to evaluate whether our arguments are appropriate, reasonable, and ethical. Although these might seem intuitive and obvious considerations for any arguer, the means for making reasonable and ethical arguments are not always apparent.

This chapter focuses on culture and ethics as two variables that shape how arguments are made, interpreted, and evaluated. The importance of these two elements in the argument situation discussed in Chapter 2 was emphasized by Joseph Wenzel, who wrote, "In the course of social life, we pass through innumerable contexts in which arguing may occur. All of these are framed by the general matrix of our sociocultural system as well as the special features of each occasion."[8] This sociocultural system incorporates values and assumptions that play an important role in making arguments and judging argument practices. Cultural and ethical values imply that arguments should be well supported, accurate, and intended to benefit their audience. Culture and ethics are related to each other, and in this chapter we will show how values play a significant role in both.

CULTURE AND ARGUMENTATION

An American woman who was spending a year studying in Greece went to the post office to pick up a package that had been mailed to her from home. The package was addressed to her in care of the Greek friend with whom she was staying. The postal clerk told the woman that he could not release the package to her because it was addressed to her friend and not to her. Her friend was out of town and, because she needed her package immediately, she began to try to persuade the clerk to give it to her. She pointed to her own name on the package label; she showed the clerk her passport to assure him of her identity; she reasoned with him, arguing that the package had her name on it and therefore must be hers. Regardless of what she said, the clerk continued to maintain that he could not give her the package because it was not addressed to her. Finally, he announced that it was his break and slammed the parcel pickup window shut, leaving her to storm out of the post office in disgust.[9]

Here we see a clear case of cross-cultural miscommunication that could be attributed to many causes. Perhaps the clerk felt that the woman was aggressive and insulting; perhaps he did not like Americans; or perhaps the woman did not speak Greek well enough to make her point. It's possible, however, that she used the wrong persuasive strategy. What else could she have done in this situation? She might have attempted to bribe the clerk, or tell him a story about some other person who lost his job because he denied service to people, or she might have returned to the post office later and refused to leave until she was given her package. The fact is that persuasive strategies and argument practices vary across cultures. By "culture" here, we do not necessarily mean some identifiable ethnic group such as a tribal culture or a national culture. Instead of being dependent on demographic or physical characteristics, a culture arises from shared experience, practices, and values. *Cultures are systems of shared meanings that are expressed through different symbolic forms such as rituals, stories, symbols, and myths that hold a group of people together.*[10]

This definition of culture implies that people who share a common culture enact the same communication patterns when they communicate with one another. In one culture, a person may make a point by telling a story, while in another culture, people may convey their views obliquely through third parties or by implication. Realizing this, many argumentation theorists and teachers believe that the view of argument we presented in Chapter 1—that an argument states a viewpoint in a context of disagreement through claims, evidence, and reasoning—is culture bound. It is true that not all members of every culture make arguments in this way.

For example, Japanese speakers prefer to avoid conflict, argument, and making explicit claims for a point of view. When communicating, they consider it a virtue to be able to catch on quickly to another's viewpoint without requiring the other person to openly state his or her position.[11] In a study of African American youth, Patrick McLaurin found that there were "few instances of direct, overt attempts to persuade a peer or significant other to change behavior."[12] McLaurin concluded that the groups he observed "seemed to shun direct, persuasive appeals."[13]

Multicultural Argument

In a multicultural world, what should we do when we seek to influence others who do not share the same assumptions as us? There are many approaches to answering this question. Some theorists maintain that we should argue about the pros and cons of a question because that is the best way to discover the significant issues and to promote critical thinking. This view is commonly held among Western theorists who embrace Aristotle's view that:

We must be able to employ persuasion, just as strict reasoning can be employed, on opposite sides of a question not in order that we may in practice employ it in both ways (for we must not make people believe what is wrong), but in order that we may see clearly what the facts are, and that, if another man argues unfairly, we on our part may be able to confute him.[14]

Those who advocate pro–con argument believe that exploring opposing sides of a case through explicit arguments such as those in political debates and law courts is the best way to weigh opposing sides and reach a good decision.[15]

An alternative view of argument has been put forward by people who believe that exclusive emphasis on confrontation, competition, and pro–con advocacy polarizes the issues and is incompatible with the communication practices of many cultures. For example, Deborah Tannen has said that an issue is often "not composed of two sides but is a crystal of many sides."[16] She has observed that we often think and speak of argument as being very competitive. For example, we regularly speak of "winning" arguments or "beating" a person's position. This sets up a mutually exclusive win–lose outcome, which fails to promote open-mindedness, good listening, and alternative approaches to problem solving.

Both of these points of view have some merit. Competitive debate and pro–con argument can reveal the points at issue and the underlying facts and values in a controversy. On the other hand, splitting a topic or question into two opposing sides dichotomizes the issue and does not align well with the communication values and practices of some cultures. To address this question, we propose an enlarged and inclusive view of argument and advocacy.[17]

When faced with a decision, there are many ways in which parties to a controversy can express their points of view and deliberate about the best outcome. They can begin by identifying the areas where they agree (those that fall below the level of dispute). Rather than immediately dividing the issue into pro and con arguments, the disputants can work collaboratively to entertain all aspects of the issue and to include all the criteria that should be applied to decide the best outcome. By listening carefully to others and showing respect for views that differ from their own, participants can discover new perspectives on the topic. It is often the case, as Irwin Mallin and Karrin Vasby Anderson recently observed, that "the best persuaders not only listen to others, but also incorporate their perspectives into a shared solution."[18] This was the point we discussed in Chapter 2 with collaborative argument styles.

Cultural Argument Patterns

In an increasingly complex and interconnected world, we should consider the various approaches and styles in which people from different cultural backgrounds organize and express their beliefs. A recent study of African American, Asian, Asian American, and European American students found, not surprisingly, that students from different backgrounds and cultures had different ways of stating their viewpoints.[19] Generally, four different patterns of argument were apparent in the way members of different cultures and backgrounds interacted. These are described in Box 3.2 and included the following patterns: deductive, inductive, abductive, and narrative.

■ ■ ■ ■ ■ ■

BOX 3.2

FOUR CULTURAL PATTERNS FOR STATING A VIEWPOINT[20]

Deductive Pattern
- States claim or position explicitly.
- Subsequent statements or support are designed to support the initial claim.
- Disagreement with another position is assumed.
- The reasoning is usually quasilogical and causal.

Inductive Pattern
- One speaker has a viewpoint.
- That speaker uses various examples or statistical generalizations to support that viewpoint.
- The general claim being supported can be stated at either the beginning or the end.
- Additional examples, when added, add cogency to the viewpoint.

Abductive Pattern
- Speakers work collaboratively to reach a conclusion.
- Speakers share reasoning; one person's statement may serve as a premise for the other's claim.
- Hypothetical cases may be used to test the speakers' reasoning.
- The conclusion is not stated at the beginning but emerges from the discussion.

Narrative Pattern
- Narratives are used to make a point.
- Narratives come from the speaker or others' personal experiences.
- Narratives are mini-stories that describe circumstances and involve other characters and in which the narrator plays a role.
- The point, if it is explicitly stated at all, is often stated at the end of the story.

When students made their claims directly and at the beginning of their argument, they used a deductive pattern. An example of this pattern is in Box 3.3. With a deductive approach, arguers provide an explicit and clear claim that is then supported typically using quasilogical or causal reasoning. Arguments of this type are relatively easy to diagram and analyze because they are complete and leave little to individual interpretation.

Inductive arguments, like deductive arguments, are clear, and their claims and support are explicit, but the claim is typically at the end of the argument. The support, generally examples and generalizations, comes first. An illustration can be found in Box 3.4. Abductive arguments do not generally have an explicit claim. Rather, the argument is emergent, as is the proposition. In abductive argument, speakers work

■ ■ ■ ■ ■

BOX 3.3
DEDUCTIVE PATTERN EXAMPLE

[I]t is logical to suggest that the Internet's power to revolutionize the relationship between citizen and government is greater than other traditional media. Most critically, each new technology offering in the past featured only unidirectional communication. . . . While radio and television offered new venues for information dissemination, they did not provide innate mechanisms for interactivity. Listeners or viewers could not respond via these media. Nor could they establish their own means of transmitting, due to excessive cost, government licensing, and the requirement of technical competence. Hence, those who controlled the gates of the media were alone capable of transmitting. Cable had the potential for two-way communication. But such experiments were limited to small communities and inevitably failed to catch on even within those areas.[21]

■ ■ ■ ■ ■

BOX 3.4
INDUCTIVE PATTERN EXAMPLE

Joan:	Do you think that news coverage should be objective?
John:	No, because it is the news media's responsibility to gather information and mobilize public opinion. If their coverage is purely neutral, then they can't do that.
Joan:	What do you mean?
John:	Well, consider the war in Bosnia. Before the United States became involved, there was a lot of media coverage of people behind a barbed wire fence in a concentration camp. After we entered the fighting, someone revealed that the whole picture was posed. The people were on the wrong side of the barbed wire fence, which ended three feet outside the frame of the picture! But if that picture hadn't been run in the newspapers, we would not have intervened, and there was genocide going on over there.
Joan:	But isn't it the news media's responsibility to provide objective reportage?
John:	No. It's their responsibility to arouse public interest, to get people involved. If they were really objective, then nothing would happen. No one would know what's going on.
Joan:	Doesn't that put an interpretation on the news?
John:	Yes, well it *should*. Take the Oklahoma City bombing. Dozens of people, including children and infants, were killed. The media coverage was done in a way as to arouse public outrage, and it should have.

collaboratively to reach a common conclusion. Arguers work together and share reasoning and support and collaboratively develop an outcome. This type of argument is generally considered collaborative and is illustrated by the example in Box 3.5. Finally, narrative argument involves stories and reports to express views. Using this

■ ■ ■ ■ ■

BOX 3.5
ABDUCTIVE PATTERN EXAMPLE

Carmella:	What do you think sexual harassment is?
Jerry:	Anything that makes the other person uncomfortable in, I don't know, . . . a sexual way. What's your take on it?
Carmella:	I guess, just anything that makes the other person uncomfortable, you say? Granted, the person doing the so-called harassing may not think it's uncomfortable to them, but just as long as the receiver thinks it's uncomfortable (and it should be told to the harasser) then it's going too far.
Jerry:	Then it's basically up to the receiver to decide what harassment is?
Carmella:	To a certain extent. It can't be every little thing, you know, that could be considered sexual harassment. Some of the things that have been coming up lately, little things, that can be blown really out of proportion, shouldn't be included.
Jerry:	Yes, I think people have definitely gotten carried away. A long time ago, there were things that would not even be considered harassment, but now it's different.

pattern, arguers use experiences to describe circumstances that help develop the argument. The claims in such arguments are seldom stated explicitly and, if they are, generally occur at the end of the narrative. An example of narrative and experiential argument can be found in Box 3.6.

■ ■ ■ ■ ■

BOX 3.6
NARRATIVE PATTERN EXAMPLE

[When I studied history and political theory in Paris], all foreigners had to take a French composition class. Over the year, the format of this class never varied. A subject was set, everyone had one week to turn in an outline and two or more to write the composition. Then the three-week cycle would begin again with the assignment of a new topic. The format of the composition never varied. Each one had to be written in three parts, with each of these parts further divided into three parts. Although I knew many of my classmates took to this style easily, for me it was a completely alien way of writing. My way had been to read, think, and make notes on little pieces of paper. I would spread these notes out in my room, across my bed, desk, and floor. Then I would immerse myself in their contents, move them around into bits of text, and frequently rewrite sections. . . .

[I wrote in a "soft" style]. . . . Our culture tends to equate the word *soft* with unscientific and undisciplined as well as with the feminine and a lack of power. . . . [But] *soft* is a good word for a flexible, nonhierarchical style, one that allows a close connection with one's objects of study.[22]

These four patterns for expressing a point of view demonstrate that people from different cultures reason and express themselves differently. Researchers who have studied reasoning patterns in international negotiations, for example, have found that European Americans generally favor inductive reasoning in which specific claims are backed by facts, whereas members of other cultures may rely on arguments from tradition or authority.[23] Their findings make it apparent that different cultures use different normative standards to evaluate arguments.

Culture provides us with a framework for understanding and interpreting arguments and helps us evaluate their appropriateness. As people become adjusted to a culture, they learn the basic assumptions of that culture so that they can perform their roles and abide by its rules, values, and morality. When we make an argument, our recipients understand our basic cultural assumptions and use them as a framework for evaluating ideas and arguments.

Using culture as a frame for argument practices can be problematic, however, because cultures in a globalized society are becoming increasingly less differentiated. In North America, for example, one finds residents who belong to many cultural groups—European Americans, Latinos/Latinas, Native Americans, African Americans, Asian Americans, and others. Furthermore, many of these residents belong to more than one cultural group. Even within specific cultural groups, there are differences in values and clusters of values. We should therefore be cautious about making any ready generalizations based only on a given cultural group to which people might belong.

Culture and Values

One important way that cultures differ is in how they assign levels of importance to different values. Some cultures value possessions and others value people. Some cultures value collectivism and relationships, whereas others value individualism. Some value progress and change, whereas others value tradition. Differences such as these imply that arguers from one culture or subculture who seek to influence those from another culture or subculture should be aware of how values of their recipients are prioritized and should not assume that their own values, which may not be shared by the members of their audience, can be used as starting points or premises for arguments.

Intercultural differences in values and argument practices can be illustrated by reference to the civil rights movement of the 1960s and 1970s. Many African Americans during that period shared the belief that they were disadvantaged and discriminated against in housing, education, and individual rights. Differing groups formed around differing views about what was to be done about these conditions. Dr. Martin Luther King Jr. and his followers believed in nonviolent protest and resistance to gain equal rights, while Stokely Carmichael and his followers were more militant.

Carmichael preached violence and separatism. He said:

> It seems to me that the institutions that function in this country are clearly racist, and that they're built upon racism.... How can we begin to build institutions that will allow people to relate with each other as human beings? This country has never done that.... Now several people have been upset because we've said that integration was irrelevant when initiated by blacks and that in fact it was a subterfuge, an insidious

> subterfuge for the maintenance of white supremacy. We maintain that in the past six years or so this country has been feeding us a thalidomide drug of integration, and that some Negroes have been walking down a dream street talking about sitting next to white people. . . . We were never fighting for the right to integrate, we were fighting against white supremacy. . . . We are tired of trying to explain to white people that we're not going to hurt them. We are concerned with getting the things we want, the things that we have to have to be able to function. The question is, can white people allow for that in this country? . . . If that does not happen, brothers and sisters, we have no choice, but to say very clearly, move on over, or we're going to move on over you.[24]

Carmichael appealed here to audience members who apparently believed that white people cannot be trusted, that promises of equality and integration are just a subterfuge, and that nonviolent protest will never succeed in obtaining the things that African Americans want and need to function. He felt that his audience would agree that confrontation and use of aggressive tactics might be the only way to achieve their ends.

Carmichael's statement can be contrasted with that of another African American, Barbara Jordan, who spoke as follows to the 1976 Democratic national convention:

> A lot of years have passed since [the Democratic Party first met], and during that time it would have been most unusual for any national political party to ask that a Barbara Jordan deliver a keynote address . . . but tonight here I am. And I feel that notwithstanding the past that my presence here is one additional bit of evidence that the American Dream need not forever be deferred. . . .
>
> We are a people in a quandary about the present. We are a people in search of our future. We are a people in search of a national community. We are a people trying not to solve the problems of the present—unemployment, inflation—but we are attempting on a larger scale to fulfill the promise of America. We are attempting to fulfill our national purpose: to create and sustain a society in which all of us are equal. . . .
>
> As a first step, we must restore our belief in ourselves. We are a generous people, so why can't we be generous with each other? We need to take to heart the words spoken by Thomas Jefferson: "Let us restore to social intercourse that harmony and affection without which liberty and even life are but dreary things. A nation is formed by the willingness of each of us to share in the responsibility for upholding the common good. A government is invigorated when each of us is willing to participate in shaping the future of this nation."[25]

While Carmichael believed that promises of integration and equality were a hoax perpetrated on African Americans by whites, Jordan believed that real equality between the races was possible, that progress had been made toward this goal, and that she (as a keynote speaker at a national convention) was living proof of that. Whereas Carmichael assumed that confrontation and protest were the only means of achieving basic civil rights for African Americans, Jordan felt that equality could best be achieved if all Americans—white and black—worked together for the common good.

The dramatic contrast between the arguments of these two speakers reveals the influence of two subcultures—one militant and the other nonviolent—within the African American culture at that time. This contrast also reveals the important role that values play in making arguments. As illustrated in Chapter 10, values can fulfill multiple functions whenever someone makes an argument. Some of the values used by Carmichael and Jordan include honesty, social justice, equality, and social harmony, and both speakers assumed a certain level of agreement by their audiences that those values were important and that some values were more important than others. Each speaker, then, used agreement on values as a starting point or form of evidence for his or her arguments.

All cultures develop value systems that indicate acceptable modes of conduct and thus premises, which arguers can use to argue for their claims. When you are talking with a person from a culture different from your own, you should consider whether that person shares your values. If not, you would be well advised to consider what that person *does* consider to be important before you begin making your arguments. Furthermore, not every culture shares Western culture's preference for logical argument and empirical evidence. If you want to influence people from a culture different from your own, you might want to consider using stories or metaphor to communicate your ideas. Although this book will focus on Western modes of argument, we do want to point out that they are not the only ways to effectively present your ideas to others.

Developing Cultural Argument Competence

There is little challenge to the premise that cross-cultural communication competence is increasingly important in a multicultural world. In a world defined by technology and instant access to information and people through the Internet and using a variety of media, it is not surprising that developing competence has become a significant theme in higher education.[26] Developing competence in cross-cultural argumentation has the potential to play a significant role in creating relationships and opportunities for peaceful resolutions to disagreements and open conflict. A particularly important example and model for developing intercultural argument competence can be found in Truth and Reconciliation Commissions. One analyst noted that "throughout the world, truth commissions have been created under the assumption that getting people to understand the past will somehow contribute to reconciliation between those who were enemies under the ancient regime."[27] The point here is simply that effective multicultural argumentation has the potential to shape our world in positive ways.

Developing intercultural competence in argument involves being sensitive to diverse cultural norms and expectations. *Competence in intercultural argument is defined as the ability of an arguer to function in a manner that is perceived to be relatively consistent with the needs, capacities, goals, and expectations of individuals from one cultural environment while satisfying one's own needs, capacities, goals, and expectations.*[28] Intercultural argument competence, then, means that arguers need to have the ability to understand and adapt their arguments to situational requirements of culture. B. D. Ruben wrote that intercultural communication competence could be divided into seven behavioral characteristics: display of respect, argument interaction posture, orientation to knowledge, empathy, role behavior, interaction management, and tolerance of ambiguity. These are described in Box 3.7. Taken together, these seven behavioral characteristics provide a template for understanding and adapting to varied cultural settings.

■ ■ ■ ■ ■

BOX 3.7

INTERCULTURAL COMPETENCE IN ARGUMENT[29]

BEHAVIOR	DESCRIPTION
Display of Respect	Ability to argue with respect and positive regard for other people, including understanding behavioral clues such as eye contact, body posture, voice (tone and pitch), and displays of interest.
Argument Interaction Posture	Ability to respond to others in argument situations in descriptive, nonevaluating, and nonjudgmental ways.
Orientation to Knowledge	Being able to recognize that members of different cultures apply differing field-dependent standards for evaluating evidence, reasoning, and claims. Therefore, what constitutes a valid argument may be variable across cultural situations.
Empathy	Ability to put oneself in another's position or context to try to understand their goals and needs.
Role Behaviors	Ability to be functionally flexible in different settings and situations and to know when it is appropriate to act as an advocate or recipient.
Interaction Management	Ability to take turns in discussion and debate and understanding when to initiate or terminate argument interaction based on reasonably accurate assessments of needs and desires of others.
Tolerance of Ambiguity	Ability to react to new and ambiguous situations with little visible distress or discomfort.

ETHICS AND ARGUMENTATION

Because of their potential to affect people's lives for both good and bad, arguers and recipients have a responsibility to be vigilant about the quality and integrity of arguments they present and receive. In other words, all people involved in arguing share an ethical responsibility. *Ethics is the study of what is morally right or just.* When we create a systematic set of ethical principles, we have generated an *ethical code—a set of interrelated principles of ethics.* Some ethical codes are personal. These codes are our individual prescriptions for appropriate behaviors and decision making. They are what guide each of us in our day-to-day activities. Other codes are more formally adopted by groups of similar people or professional associations. For instance, medical doctors live by the Hippocratic Oath (see Box 3.8) or other medical ethic. Public rela-

BOX 3.8
HIPPOCRATIC OATH

There are several codes of ethics governing medical doctors, and which code applies to which doctors is often dependent on professional association or membership. For example, a physician practicing in the United States will probably be governed by the "American Medical Association Principles of Medical Ethics." Members of the World Medical Association practice the "Physician's Oath." However, the most widely known of all the ethical codes governing the practice of medicine is the Hippocratic Oath. Hippocrates was a Greek physician who practiced medicine in the fifth century B.C. and worked diligently to end the plague in Athens as well as teach young doctors the practice and art of medicine.

I SWEAR by Apollo the physician and Æsculapius, and Hygiea, and Panacea, and all the gods and goddesses, that, according to my ability and judgment, I will keep this Oath and this stipulation—to reckon him who taught me this Art equally dear to me as my parents, to share my substance with him, and relieve his necessities if required; to look upon his offspring in the same footing as my own brothers, and to teach them this Art, if they shall wish to learn it, without fee or stipulation; and that by precept, lecture, and every other mode of instruction, I will impart a knowledge of the Art to my own sons, and those of my teachers, and to disciples bound by a stipulation and oath according to the law of medicine, but to none others. I will follow that system of regimen which, according to my ability and judgment, I consider for the benefit of my patients, and abstain from whatever is deleterious and mischievous. I will give no deadly medicine to any one if asked, nor suggest any such counsel; and in like manner I will not give to a woman a pessary to produce abortion. With purity and with holiness I will pass my life and practice my Art. I will not cut persons laboring under the stone, but will leave this to be done by men who are practitioners of this work. Into whatever houses I enter, I will go into them for the benefit of the sick, and will abstain from every voluntary act of mischief and corruption; and, further, from the seduction of females or males, of freemen and slaves. Whatever, in connection with my professional service, or not in connection with it, I see or hear, in the life of men, which ought not to be spoken of abroad, I will not divulge, as reckoning that all such should be kept secret. While I continue to keep this Oath unviolated, may it be granted to me to enjoy life and the practice of the Art, respected by all men, in all times. But should I trespass and violate this Oath, may the reverse be my lot.[30]

tions professionals use the "Code of Professional Standards for the Practice of Public Relations" generated by the Public Relations Society of America.[31] These are only two among many such ethical codes. Most professional organizations have some code of ethics intended to guide their members toward moral and just actions.

When we abide by the prescriptions of our personal or professional ethical codes—for example, when we do not lie, deceive, or attempt to injure others—our arguments are considered ethical. However, when we use the power inherent in arguments to persuade people based on deception or argumentative trickery, then our arguments are considered unethical. Evasion, deception, and misrepresentation cause public distrust, poor decision making, and, occasionally, outright harm and injury to individuals. For example President Richard Nixon's promise, "I am not a crook," was found to be deceptive, and the public trust in government was damaged. When arguments are constructed either intentionally or unintentionally in such a way as to deceive recipients, they are considered unethical and fallacious. Fallacies and their implications are discussed in Chapter 8.

Too often, poor-quality arguments are unrecognized by recipients, and decisions made using them have the potential to adversely affect recipients and others. As both producers and consumers of argument, we must be aware of the quality of our arguments and knowledgeable about standards that will enable us to distinguish arguments that are ethically or morally right from those that are wrong. The remainder of this chapter, therefore, will consider the question, What is an ethical argument?

Each day we are presented with opportunities to make ethical decisions. For example, what would you do if you found a $100 bill on a sidewalk outside a store? If there is no identification on the money, do you keep it? Do you give it to the clerk in the store? Do you take it to a police station? This can be a difficult choice, and your decision will depend on what you believe to be the correct or just choice. Another ethical issue is raised by the *Mason Country Journal*, a newspaper in Shelton, Washington, that routinely publishes the names of rape suspects and victims alike (including juvenile rape victims). The paper's argument is that its job is to publicize the full record of Shelton, and rapes are a part of that record. However, releasing the names has disrupted the lives of many women and girls. Is that ethical? The answers are not always clear.

The question, then, is how do we know what is the moral or just action? Ethicists have long considered the nature of ethical conduct and how different ethical requirements and rules emerge from a variety of contexts.[32] Although understanding how ethics function in any given context can be difficult, generally arguments are considered ethical and just when they enhance the individual or strengthen the community. Arguers who act to undermine their audiences or weaken community bonds and structures are generally considered unethical.

Strengthening the Individual

Arguments strengthen the individual either when they provide recipients with opportunities to make free, informed, and critical choices, or when they help recipients become better people in their community. Individuals, explained ethicist Thomas Nilsen, should have a right of free choice and free decision making.[33] When arguers educate, offer alternative perspectives, or provide new information, they offer their audiences greater opportunities for free and better decision making. Similarly, when arguers help their audiences self-actualize by moving them toward certain culturally based ideals such as honesty, courage, compassion, generosity, fidelity, integrity, and fairness, among others, they are acting ethically. Arguments should work to create opportunities for their recipients and not limit them. The recipient's right to make free choices should be respected. Arguers should recognize that people are not objects for manipulation, but are equal participants in argumentative interactions.

Whenever a person engages in arguments with another, a relationship is created, and that relationship is an important part of the process of argumentation. Wayne Brockriede explained this fact when he wrote an article called "Arguers as Lovers."[34] Brockriede noted that beyond the content of argument transactions, "the relationship among the people who argue may afford one useful way of classifying argumentative transactions."[35]

Brockriede, as the title of his article suggests, takes the position that arguers, in their attempt to influence and relate to their recipients, should act as lovers toward their audiences; they need to respect and understand the needs of their recipients. The goal or ethically correct choice for the arguer is to approach the audience as a partner rather than to coerce them.

Brockriede wrote that the relationship between arguers and their audiences can be classified as three different types: rapist, seducer, and lover. When arguers rape, they view their relationship with the audience as a unilateral one. The arguer will tend to objectify the audience and seek to manipulate the recipients. As Brockriede claimed, "The rapist wants to gain or to maintain a position of superiority—on the intellectual front of making his case prevail or on the interpersonal front of putting the other person down."[36]

Whether or not we like to admit it, argument rape is a common practice, and many people engage in it without even thinking. But we live in an adversarial society in which one person's success often means another's failure and where success at whatever cost is prized over failure. It can be easy for arguers—who may not even be aware of their actions—to "rape" their recipients. Even our language describing arguments suggests this. We often say:

> I beat their arguments.
> I destroyed their position.
> I demolished the competition.

Yet, each of these examples points to our tendency to objectify and treat people who oppose us as less than human.

A second type of relationship between arguer and recipient is that of the seducer who seeks to win covertly through charm or deceit. As Brockriede noted:

> The seducer's attitude toward co-arguers is similar to that of the rapist. He, too, sees the relationship as unilateral. Although he may not be contemptuous of his prey, he is indifferent to the identity and integrity of the other person. Whereas the intent of the rapist is to force assent, the seducer tries to charm or trick his victim into assent.[37]

There are many ways for arguers to trick their recipients. Different types of fallacies make faulty arguments appear reasonable and believable. When employed by a crafty arguer, fallacies may cause audiences to believe in faulty arguments. Similarly, withholding information, telling half-truths, taking evidence out of context, fabricating evidence, among other deceptions, all provide arguers with the means of fooling audiences.

The third type of relationship between arguer and recipient is that of lover. The arguer as lover seeks to empower the recipient through argument and to expand and enlighten the recipient. The lover, according to Brockriede, wants "power parity" in which arguer and recipient share equally in the exchange of arguments. Brockriede noted, "Whereas the rapist and seducer argue against an adversary or an opponent, the lover argues with his peer and is willing to risk his very self in his attempt to establish a bilateral relationship."[38]

The arguer-as-lover relationship views the process of giving reasons in argument as a person-centered enterprise. Its central tenet was summarized by Thomas Nilsen when he concluded that "whatever develops, enlarges, enhances human personalities is good; whatever restricts, degrades, or injures human personalities is bad."[39] For Nilsen, this meant that arguers should always give their recipients a "significant choice," which means that arguers should provide their audiences with enough information to draw their own conclusions.

Strengthening the Community

Arguers who work to strengthen the community look for opportunities to help groups of people live and work together more effectively. They seek ways of equitably sharing resources and look to provide a means for audiences to make difficult decisions.

In the nineteenth century, two British ethicists, Jeremy Bentham and his student John Stuart Mill, developed a standard that was intended as a guide for legislators to determine which laws were morally best.[40] Their criterion, utilitarianism, holds that the greatest balance of good over evil for a given community is ethical in comparison with other actions. Arguers, then, consider various courses of action and then argue for the approach that derives the greatest benefits and causes the least harm. Ethical arguments are those that balance outcomes and promote the decisions that achieve the greatest good for the greatest number.

However, not all decisions or actions can be reduced into such a simple assessment of good and evil. There is also a question of what is just or fair in the decision-making process. Aristotle took the position that arguers should also consider the issues of what is fair and just for the members of a community.[41] He advocated that the basic moral question an arguer should ask is, "Does the decision treat everyone the same way, or does it show favoritism and discrimination?" Ethical decisions are generally fair, whereas unethical decisions are based on inequality and preferential treatment.

Ultimately, if arguers seek to enhance the integrity of the community, they should balance the needs of the majority with principles of fairness and justice that protect the interests of the minority. This means that advocates appealing to community needs engage in an assessment of the "common good" for a given group of people.

The concept of the common good is grounded in the writings of Plato, Aristotle, and Cicero, among other ancient theorists. More recently, ethicist John Rawls defined the common good as "certain general conditions that are . . . equally to everyone's advantage."[42] Using the common good as an ethical standard, arguers focus on ensuring that social policies, social systems, institutions, and environments on which we depend are equally beneficial to all. Examples of policies and decisions that are based in the common good might include affordable health care, effective public safety, peace among nations, a just legal system, and an unpolluted environment.

Arguers who appeal to the common good urge recipients to view themselves as members of the same community reflecting on broad questions concerning the kind of society we want to become and how we want to achieve that society. While respecting and valuing the freedom of individuals to pursue their own goals within a community, advocates challenge their audience to recognize and further the goals shared in common by all the members of a given community.

DEVELOPING AN ETHICAL CODE

The inherent power of arguments requires each of us to take responsibility in argumentative encounters to ensure the quality and integrity of the arguments presented. This is why arguers should have a clear understanding of arguments, their construction, and their ethical uses. Recipients should have a clear understanding of how arguments can be critically evaluated. Because argumentation involves both arguer and recipient, both share in the ethical responsibility for decision making and the consequences of their actions. Therefore, both arguer and recipient should have a clear sense of their own ethic of argument.[43] This section considers the process involved in creating individual codes of ethics.

Ethics for Arguers

1. Arguers should be accountable and responsible for their arguments. As the producer of argument, the arguer is responsible for developing quality, ethical arguments. If the arguer misleads the recipient or, through poorly constructed arguments, motivates an audience to take wrong actions, then the arguer is ethically accountable. Sometimes arguers may take the position that the responsibility for action rests entirely with the audience, suggesting that the ultimate choice to act or not rests with the recipient. While true, this position ignores the role argument plays in the interaction—it has the potential to function as a catalyst. Without the argument, the recipients may not have acted. Hence, arguers are ethically liable for their arguments. The example in Box 3.9 makes this point clearly. Speakers such as Metzger have a responsibility to their audience for the arguments they make. And, although we have a right to free speech, that right comes with a responsibility to use it well.

2. Arguers should promote significant choice. That is, arguments should provide their recipients with the ability to make voluntary decisions that are free from physical or mental coercion. Arguers should furnish the best available information for their hearers so that they may make well-informed and reasoned decisions. This means that arguers should ensure that audiences are aware of the sources of information, the possible alternatives, and the potential consequences of their decisions. Further, recipients should be aware of the motivations and qualifications of those who seek to influence them, the values they hold, and the goals they seek. If evidence is falsified or misrepresented, if arguers deliberately employ fallacies, or if any action is taken or argument is made that interferes with the ability of others to make a reasonable decision, the arguer is acting unethically.

3. Arguers should promote positive relationships with their audiences. A positive relationship is predicated on the view by the arguer that recipients of argument are partners in the decision-making process. As such, the arguer's job is not to force ideas on the recipients, but rather to provide audience members with the information necessary to produce their own decisions.

■ ■ ■ ■ ■

BOX 3.9
TOM METZGER: NEO-NAZI MESSAGES[44]

In 1988, Mulugeta Seraw, an Ethiopian man who worked as an Avis airport shuttle-bus driver, was murdered in Portland, Oregon. He was attacked while returning from a party close to his home by a man named David Mazzella. Mazzella, vice president of the White Aryan Resistance (WAR), struck the Ethiopian man repeatedly with a baseball bat until Seraw was dead. Mazzella, along with a group of local racists, had been out during the evening looking for black and Hispanic people to attack.

During the following investigation and subsequent trial in which Mazzella was convicted for the murder, evidence was uncovered to suggest that he acted on behalf of Tom Metzger and WAR. In fact, letters produced in court made it appear as though Metzger had ordered Mazzella to go to Portland and show the local skinheads "how we operate." Subsequently, attorney Morris Dees, director of the Southern Poverty Law Center in Montgomery, Alabama, filed a civil lawsuit against Metzger and WAR under the common law principle of "vicarious liability," which is most frequently used against employers for employee negligence. Dees claimed that WAR and Metzger were civilly responsible for the murder because they had incited Mazzella to act as their agent in Portland. Therefore, Metzger and WAR, through their messages, were responsible for the death.

In the civil trial that followed, Dees characterized Metzger as a "racial separatist" who motivated others to act on his behalf. Because Metzger, WAR, Mazzella, and the Oregon Skinheads formed a "civil conspiracy" to murder, Metzger acted recklessly and negligently in his message. Metzger, acting as his own attorney in his trial, argued that he was simply a populist who shared his ideas with others. He murdered no one and did not ask anyone to murder for him. He was not the cause of violence. He only provided the message; what others chose to do with that message was their own business. The people acting violently were the cause of the murder.

The court ruled against Metzger and found him liable for the consequences of his messages. It emphasized the power of the spoken word and the responsibilities for its judicious use. Metzger and WAR were ordered to pay $12.5 million in damages.

Ethics for Recipients

Just as arguers have an ethical responsibility for constructing quality arguments, recipients must also be critically aware and vigilant of the arguments they find compelling. Therefore, recipients have the following responsibilities in an argumentative encounter.

1. Recipients should be aware of attempts to influence them. Each of us is subjected to attempted influences every day. From advertisements to public speeches, arguers attempt to tell us how to vote, spend our money, or design our relationships. If we accept their messages without any clear consideration or understanding of the consequences and implications, we are acting irresponsibly. Argument consumers should constantly ask, "How am I being affected by this message?" They should understand that arguers have biases and viewpoints that are reflected in their arguments. This means, then, that we need to consider the validity and worth of arguments beyond their surface and seek to understand the biases and opinions that motivate the claims. We may then choose to accept the claims or not, but the choice will be a considered one.

2. Receivers should be informed. Although it is impossible to know everything, recipients of argument need to be informed about important topics. If we as audience members rely exclusively on the advocate to provide the necessary information for making the decisions facing us, we are acting naively on the assumption that arguers will always be motivated by our best interests. Although it is much easier to rely on the word of the arguer than to take time to investigate the strength of the message, it is time well spent. We need to ask ourselves, "Is there another answer that makes equal or better sense?" Or, "Are there other possibilities that remain unexplored?" Responsible receivers look for alternatives and are curious about other ways of approaching issues and problems. It is easy for arguers to persuade an uninformed audience; the recipient's best defense against unethical attempts at influence is knowledge.

3. Recipients should be aware of their own biases. Each of us has messages we want to hear, and there are messages we choose to avoid. We like hearing messages that support our positions and affirm our decisions. We tend to avoid those arguments that seem to attack us and fail to affirm our understanding of either our own worldviews or ourselves. We tend to avoid messages that are inconsistent with our own positions, and information that we find unpleasant. Responsible receivers should seek out and be open to many different viewpoints.

4. Recipients should understand how fallacies persuade. Fallacies, as we discussed, have tremendous appeal and capacity to persuade audience members to act erroneously. We should be aware of how arguers employ argumentative devices and fallacies to shape and direct our decisions by constraining or confusing our understanding of issues.

SUMMARY

This chapter examined two concepts that affect argument situations, arguers, and recipients. The first part focused on cultural argument and how it shapes argument interactions. The second part considered how ethics can inform the responsibilities shared by both arguer and recipient.

Culture is important to understanding argument practices because values arise from cultural background. This means, then, that culture affects the ways in which we argue. Whereas the United States tends to emphasize adversarial, two-sided forms of argument, other cultures focus on arguments emphasizing multiple points of view and collaborative outcomes. Four different patterns of argument style are commonly used: deductive (claim followed by proof), inductive (examples followed by general conclusion), narrative (the use of stories to reach a conclusion), and abductive (comparing and contrasting experiences to reach a conclusion). Further, each culture determines the standards by which arguments are understood and evaluated.

The second part of the chapter examined ethics and argumentation. Misleading or deceptive uses of argument can greatly harm society and individuals, and therefore argument practices should be governed by sound ethical principles. Ethics is defined as the study of what is morally right or just, but sometimes this is not easy to determine. This is because the question of what ethical standards should be applied to an argument may depend on the culture or situation in which the argument occurs.

Ethical argument practices are related to both the content of the argument and the relationship between the arguer and his or her audience. Ethicists who have written on argument content believe that content that is ethically sound is content that furthers open inquiry, quotes evidence in context, and makes use of sound reasoning. On the relational level, arguers can attempt to manipulate and objectify their audiences, or charm and trick them, or empower and enlighten them. Only the third of these three approaches further opens inquiry and choice among recipients.

Arguers should keep in mind that in any argument situation, there are many diverse, cultural values at work, many argument styles and strategies available, and many ways to further sound decision making and ethical practices. General guidelines are established, however, to ensure that arguers do not hide their agendas, are collaborative with their listeners, and empower their audience.

GLOSSARY

Cultures (p. 70) are systems of shared meanings that are expressed through different symbolic forms such as rituals, stories, symbols, and myths that hold a group of people together.

Ethical code (p. 78) is a set of interrelated principles of ethics.

Ethics (p. 78) is the study of what is morally right or just.

Intercultural competence (p. 77) is the ability of an arguer to function in a manner that is perceived to be relatively consistent with the needs, capacities, goals, and expectations of individuals from one cultural environment while satisfying one's own needs, capacities, goals, and expectations.

EXERCISES

Exercise 1 Below are some passages by various authors. Each uses one of the four methods for stating a point of view described in Box 3.2. These ways of organizing speech are deductive, inductive, abductive, and narrative. For each passage, identify the pattern used and justify your selection. What is the stated or implied viewpoint of the writer or speaker? How does he or she support it?

✱1. Every society has its rich and poor, and inequality is mainly a matter of degree. In 1974, when the gap between the incomes of the richest and the poorest Americans was at a historic low, the top 10 percent of U.S. households had incomes 31 times those of the poorest 10 percent and four times those of median-income households. By 1994, those numbers were 55 times the poorest and six times the median. Not only is inequality growing, its growth is accelerating. Inequality surged between 1991 and 1993 as the recession lowered incomes for all but the richest Americans. Executives killed jobs in ways that would be illegal in Germany and France—for example, shutting down plants in some regions and relocating them in jurisdictions with right-to-work laws.

Michael Hout and Samuel R. Lucas, "Narrowing the Income Gap between Rich and Poor," *Chronicle of Higher Education* (August 16, 1996): B1.

2. We in the university flee from the encounter with knowledge. We peer at it as though through a telescope. We make it distant and detached, so that whatever knowledge is gained remains always strictly abstract and impersonal; almost sterile. It is remote and removed. The very word *academic* has acquired a derogatory definition: "Scholarly to the point of being unaware of the outside world; theoretical or speculative without a practical purpose or intention."

Benjamin Belint, "Suffering Severe Case of Frosh Disillusionment," *Seattle Post Intelligencer* (October 14, 1995): A9.

3. The worst mistake is to execute someone wholly innocent. Now that executions are approaching 100 per year in the United States, the chances rise that at least one will be the wrong guy. Perhaps. But it has pretty clearly not happened in Washington [State]. This state has executed three men, none who claimed he didn't do it. In 1993, it hanged Westley Alan Dodd, who owned up to raping and murdering little boys and said he'd do it again; in 1994, it hanged Charles Campbell, who came back from prison and murdered the witnesses against him; and in 1998, it executed by lethal injection Jeremy Sagastegui, who murdered two women and a three-year-old boy, and who wanted to die.

Bruce Ramsey, "A Difficult Road to Death," *Seattle Times* (April 16, 2000): B9.

*4. My father was extremely ambitious; he had gone to college and later opened his own business. Because he was having stomach problems, he went to stay with his mother back in Philadelphia; he died of stomach cancer ten days later. I was only six years old when he died, so I didn't know him very well, but he spent a lot of time trying to teach me how to read. My brother, who was one and a half years older than me, would read to me. At one point my parents told him to stop reading to me or else I would never learn to read myself. I cried and cried and thought, "I'll show her," and I learned to read. I've gone through life with that sense of "I'll show them."

Dr. Lorraine Hale, *On Women Turning 50* (San Francisco: Harper, 1993), 199.

5. I am of the opinion that one should read a daily paper every day or listen to or watch the news at least once a day. Nowadays it is very important and necessary that one be familiar with the political and economic as well as other events in the world. Finally it is also very interesting when you begin to understand these problems more or less depending on how interested you are. Furthermore it gives the kind of general knowledge which you after all need in order to "be" somebody in today's society.

Anonymous essay cited in Ulla Connor, "Argumentative Patterns in Student Essays: Cross-Cultural Differences," in Ulla Connor and Robert B. Kaplan, *Writing across Languages: Analysis of L2 Text* (Reading, Mass.: Addison-Wesley, 1987), 69.

6. The mission of the Nature Conservancy is to preserve plants, animals, and natural communities that represent the diversity of life on Earth by protecting the lands and waters they need to survive. The Arizona chapter recently acquired a river-bottom inholding within the Verde River Greenway, to be managed by the Arizona State Parks Department. Transferring the land to the state parks department will add rare cottonwood-willow riparian forest and aquatic habitat to the greenway and extend protection of the Verde River. In Hawaii, two wedge-tailed shearwater nests have been reported at

the Conservancy's Mo'omomi Preserve on the Island of Molokai. This is the first sighting of a seabird nest within the preserve since the Conservancy acquired Mo'omomi from Molokai Ranch in 1988.

Adapted from the magazine *The Nature Conservancy*, vol. 50 (May/June 2000): 2, 26, 27.

7. From a discussion of the Internet's effect on young people:

   Adam: Is the Internet changing the nature of childhood, or are children changing the nature of the Internet? I think both. I grew up with the computer. I've used the computer ever since I was three. When we got a modem, I got CompuServe. I've grown up with the Net and I definitely wouldn't be the person I am without the Net. I also change the Net. I have my own Web page.

   Austin: I think it is a bit of both. Kids are one of the driving forces of the Internet because of our incredible abilities to adapt. If the Internet had come along twenty years down the road, I don't think that I would adapt to it as quickly as I did. Also, the Internet is changing kids in many ways. Penpals are written to through e-mail. Homework assignments are passed around through file attachments.

   Don Tapscott, *Growing Up Digital: The Rise of the Net Generation* (New York: McGraw-Hill, 1998), 77–78.

8. A picture may well be worth a thousand words, but as historical documents, photographs are subject to the same questions as written documents. Despite initial appearances, photographs are not objective. Photographic images were created for specific purposes and for audiences. No photograph can be accepted as "representative" of a way of life without additional documentation. The many factors that influenced what photographs show include the wishes and capabilities of the photographers, and the responses of [their subjects].

   Victoria Wyatt, *Images from the Inside Passage: An Alaskan Portrait by Winter & Pond* (Seattle: University of Washington Press, 1989).

9. More and more of our communication is not face to face, and not with people we know. The proliferation and increasing portability of technology isolate people in a bubble. When I was a child, my family got the first television on our block, and the neighborhood children gathered in our dining room to watch *Howdy Doody*. Before long, every family had its own TV—but each had just one, so, in order to watch it, families came together. Now it is common for families to have more than one television, so adults can watch what they like in one room and the children can watch their choice in another—or maybe each child has a private TV to watch alone.

   Deborah Tannen, *The Argument Culture: Moving from Debate to Dialogue* (New York: Random House, 1998), 240.

Exercise 2 Almost daily we are faced with decisions that have a moral or ethical character. Consider the following example and decide what the most ethical course of action is.

What should we do when bad money supports good causes? If, for instance, organized crime offered the Scouts a million dollars, should the Scouts take the money? Should they publicize it or keep it secret? This scenario may seem far-fetched, but it really isn't. Although tobacco companies are not the same as organized crime, their products contribute to more than 440,000 deaths a year, to say nothing of the suffering inflicted on surviving family members. Yet, tobacco companies support good causes. Consider:

■ Many sporting events are sponsored by tobacco companies and some would argue that women's tennis would never have become a high-profile, high-paying sport were it not for the support of companies such as Virginia Slims.

- Tobacco companies support political candidates and give Democrats and Republicans alike large amounts of money for their campaigns.

- The Partnership for a Drug-Free America receives large financial support from the tobacco industry, enabling it to get its message and programs across.

- Tobacco money also supports the American Civil Liberties Union, the NAACP, the Urban League, the National Women's Political Caucus, and the Poetry Society of America. Beyond that, tobacco money supports many different children's charities, environmental groups, and even some health organizations.

There are many more examples. The problem is that money is tight and budgets are being cut and when the tobacco industry offers to help, then good programs survive and flourish. But is there a larger issue at stake? For instance, the Coalition for the Homeless no longer takes money from the tobacco industry because of its source. Amnesty International USA no longer takes money from the industry. Yet, the ACLU has no difficulty taking money from the industry because it allows the organization to survive and do good work to help people.

And the tobacco industry is only one example. There are many other instances of foreign industries and organizations supporting specific candidates for office in the United States. Is there a problem when bad money allows good organizations to be effective?

Consider the following issues:

1. What are the ethical considerations inherent in bad money supporting good causes?
2. Formulate an argument on both sides of the issue. Why is it all right to take the money, and why should we reject the money?
3. Considering all the information you have been presented, should "good causes" take the money?
4. Do cultural considerations play a role in the decision to take the money or not?
5. In general, are there some basic ethical guidelines that might help us decide when to accept money and when not to? What might these criteria be?

Exercise 3 In 1996, *Playboy Magazine* published an article called *"Playboy's* College Sex Survey." In the article, the magazine reported the sex habits of college students based on a survey that had been given to college students across the United States. *Playboy* distributed the survey to university professors who then distributed them in class. The students were not aware of the source of the survey—they did not know that it came from *Playboy.*

When the article was published, none of the students were named. However, the article did identify student gender, age, and university. Several of the students were upset and believed that it was possible to identify them based on the information in the article. They said they wished they had known who it was for and how the data was going to be used. Many had assumed it was only for a class project and had no idea it would ever be published. *Playboy* countered that it wanted to have as objective a survey as possible and therefore had chosen to keep its name secret as the source of the survey. Besides, none of the students were identified.

Who is ethically right? Who is wrong? Explain.

Exercise 4 In 1998, a journal titled *Lingua Franca* published an article written by Ruth Shalit. The article, titled "The Man Who Knew Too Much," outlined how a successful professor at a small university was terminated from his employment over a controversial assignment that was held to be "inappropriate" by the university administration.

Adam Weisberger was a professor at Maine's Colby College. He was well regarded as a successful teacher who was engaging with his students. His student evaluations were consistently very strong. In his Sociology 215 class, in an effort to make some of the critical theories more interesting, he developed an assignment to have students analyze their families using the material discussed in class. His syllabus read as follows:

> What I am aiming for in the assignment is for you to reflect on the class readings and discussion by means of analyzing an important part of your lives—namely, your family. I am willing to entertain other ideas as written work, but you must make a persuasive case. You may be as personal or impersonal as you wish. . . . The outward form of the papers is less important than your using ideas to investigate the relationships of your family.

Some students became upset by the assignment, criticizing that it asked them to reveal too much about their personal lives. After considerable pressure applied to the administration by some students, Weisberger's employment was terminated.

Do you think this assignment is ethically justifiable? How far can a professor probe into a student's life? Is it ever ethically permissable to ask students about their personal lives?

Exercise 5 An eleven-member committee from the British national parliament traveled to Athens, Greece, to discuss the possible return to Greece of the 2,500-year-old Parthenon sculptures. The sculptures, a 175-yard-long frieze, were stripped from the Parthenon on the Athenian Acropolis early in the nineteenth century. They are currently displayed in the British Museum in London.

The sculptures, known as the Elgin Marbles, were legally given to Lord Elgin, the British ambassador to the Ottoman Empire. Since then, Greece became an independent nation, and the sculptures have become a significant point of national pride and identity. Greece would like the sculptures returned. Great Britain, however, maintains that they were acquired legally and are a central display in the British Museum.

What do you think is the most ethical action for the British? Should the Elgin Marbles be returned? Support your answer with appropriate references to the issues discussed in the chapter.

Exercise 6 Consider the following two scenarios. How would you act given the ethical considerations of the chapter?

SITUATION 1

You are an employee for ChemCon, a corporation that makes various chemical products. You have recently been asked to appear on a local news program to discuss the economic growth stimulated by your company's presence in that area. You are to make a two-minute presentation about the company. This will be followed by a question-and-answer session.

Two hours before you are to be interviewed on television, one of ChemCon's tanker trucks overturns and spills hundreds of gallons of toxins into a rural riverbed. You are told about the spill by an executive officer of the company who asks you to refrain from discussing the issue and indicates that the situation is under control—there is no need to cause a scare. You recognize the spilled chemical as one of the deadliest made by your company. You know that the chemical does not break down quickly or easily (so it will dissipate or dissolve), and you know that it is virtually impossible to "clean up" because it spreads rapidly in water flow. You also know that farmers graze cattle and grow crops using that river as a primary water source.

It is time to give your speech. What does your ethical code compel you to say?

SITUATION 2

You are an employee for PlayCorp, a corporation that makes various sporting goods. Your job includes many aspects of marketing, management, and production. However, you have been primarily responsible for tracking information regarding overseas production. Informally, you happen to know that the executives of PlayCorp have motivated others to generate a high return on their overseas investments (those who significantly improve the company's profit margin receive a substantial annual bonus). You also know that many approaches were used to generate that profit, including cutting necessary overhead costs.

Your company has been discussed and challenged in the press lately. The main focus of the media is PlayCorp's overseas practices. The media has discussed everything from poor wages to toxic working conditions to the economic support for dictatorships. Simultaneously to the media coverage, the Multi-National Corporation Investigation Team (MNCIT) has made formal allegations that PlayCorp is engaged in illegal practices overseas. The allegations have led to a formal congressional hearing. Depending on the committee's finding, a formal hearing may follow.

As the individual responsible for tracking information regarding overseas production, you have been called to speak before the congressional hearing. The first question you are asked is open-ended: "Please tell us, what do you know about your company's overseas operations?"

What does your ethical code compel you to say?

NOTES

1. "Activists Disagree on Whaling Protests," *Sydney Morning Herald*, http://www.smh.com.au/news/whale-watch/activists-disagree-on-whaling-protests/2008/01/31/1201714116250.html (accessed on May 2, 2008).

2. Whaling Past to Present," ThinkQuest, http://library.thinkquest.org/05aug/00504/Sea_pages/historyofwhaling.htm (accessed on May 30, 2008).

3. The IWC main Web site provides information about the Commission and offers reports and documents related to whaling. Its addresses are http://www.iwcoffice.org/ index.htm and http://ourworld.compuserve.com/homepages/iwcoffice/.

4. More information can be found at "Saving the Whales," http://www.ypte.org.uk/docs/factsheets/env_facts/saving_the_whales.html (accessed on May 30, 2008).

5. Encyclopaedia Britannica's Advocacy for Animals, "Hunting the Whales," June 4, 2007, http://advocacy.britannica.com/blog/advocacy/2007/06/hunting-the-whales/ (access on May 29, 2008).

6. Makah Whaling Tradition, Makah.com, http://www.makah.com/whalingtradition.html (accessed on April 30, 2008).

7. A discussion of the controversy can be found in Richard Blow, "The Great American Whale Hunt," Mother Jones September/October 1998, http://www.motherjones.com/news/feature/1998/09/blow.html (accessed on May 30, 2008).

8. Joseph Wenzel, "On Fields of Argument as Propositional Systems," *Journal of the American Forensic Association* 18 (1982): 204.

9. This example was taken from Barbara Johnstone, "Linguistic Strategies and Cultural Styles for Persuasive Discourse" in *Language, Communication, and Culture: Current Directions*, Stella Ting-Toomey and Felipe Korzenny, eds. (Newbury Park, Calif.: Sage, 1980), 144.

10. Charles Conrad, *Strategic Organizational Communication*, 2d ed. (Fort Worth: Holt, Rinehart, & Winston, 1989), 4.

11. William B. Gudykunst and Tsukasa Nishida, *Bridging Japanese/North American Differences* (Thousand Oaks, Calif.: Sage, 1994), 30.

12. Patrick McLaurin, "An Examination of the Effect of Culture on Pro-Social Messages Directed at African-American At-risk Youth," *Communication Monographs* 62 (1995): 312.

13. McLaurin, 320.

14. Aristotle, *Rhetoric*, 1355a.

15. Thomas O. Sloane, *On the Contrary: The Protocol of Traditional Rhetoric* (Washington, D.C.: Catholic University of American Press, 1997).

16. Deborah Tannen, *The Culture of Argument: Moving from Debate to Dialogue* (New York: Random House, 1998), 10.

17. We agree with the view stated by David E. Williams and Brian R. McGee in a recent special issue of *Argumentation and Advocacy*, "Revisioning Argumentation Education": "We believe that the traditional argumentation course may overemphasize competition, but we are not convinced that the idea of competitive argument should be banished from the classroom." [See their essay in vol. 36 (Winter 2000): 109.]

18. Irwin Mallin and Karrin Vasby Anderson, "Inviting Constructive Argument," *Argumentation & Advocacy* 36 (2000): 131.

19. Barbara Warnick and Valerie Manusov, "The Organization of Justificatory Discourse in Interaction: A Comparison Within and Across Cultures," *Argumentation* 14 (2000): 381–404.

20. Adapted from Barbara Warnick and Valerie Manusov, "The Organization of Justificatory Discourse in Interaction: A Comparison within and across Cultures," *Argumentation* 14 (2000): 381–404.

21. Richard Davis, *The Web of Politics: The Internet's Impact on the American Political System* (New York: Oxford University Press, 1999), 36.

22. Sherry Turkle, *Life on the Screen: Identity in the Age of the Internet* (New York: Simon & Schuster, 1995), 50, 56.

23. E. S. Glenn, D. Wittmeyer, and K. A. Stevenson, "Cultural Styles of Persuasion," *International Journal of Intercultural Relations* 1 (1977): 52–66.

24. Stokely Carmichael, "Black Power," in *Black Protest: History, Documents and Analysis*, Joanne Grant, ed. (New York: Fawcett Premier, 1968), 459.

25. Barbara Jordan, "Democratic Convention Keynote Address," in *Contemporary American Speeches*, 7th ed., Richard L. Johannesen, R. R. Allen, and Wil A. Linkugel, eds. (Dubuque, Iowa: Kendall/Hunt, 1992), 371, 373.

26. Much has been written on the importance of developing intercultural communication competencies. For examples, see Betty Leask, "Bridging the Gap: Internationalizing University Curricula," *Journal of Studies in International Education* 5(2), 2001: 100; Johann Le Roux, "Effective educators are culturally competent communicators," *Intercultural Education* 13(1), 2002: 37–48.

27. James L. Gibson, "Does Truth Lead to Reconciliation? Testing the Causal Assumptions of the South African Truth and Reconciliation Process," *American Journal of Political Science* 48(2), 2004: 201.

28. B. D. Ruben, "Human Communication and Cross-Cultural Effectiveness," in *Intercultural Communi-*

nication: A Reader, 3d ed., L. A. Samovar and R. E. Porter, eds. (Belmont, Calif.: Wadsworth, 1982): 336.

29. Adapted from B. D. Ruben, "Cross-Cultural Communication Competence: Traditions and Issues for the Future," *International Journal of Intercultural Relations* 13(3) (1989) and B. D. Ruben, "Human Communication and Cross-Cultural Effectiveness," in *Intercultural Communication: A Reader*, 3rd ed. L. A. Samovar and R. E. Porter, eds. (Belmont, Calif.: Wadsworth, 1982): 331–339.

30. The Gersten Institute. "The Oath of Hippocrates," www.imagerynet.com/hippo.orig.html (accessed February 1, 2001).

31. Public Relations Society of America, *Code of Professional Standards for the Practice of Public Relations*, 4 April 2000, www.prsa.org/profstd.html (accessed February 1, 2001). Additionally, there are many different codes of ethics from many varied organizations. Some of the more interesting include *American Medical Association Principles of Medical Ethics*, www.ama-assn.org/ama/pub/category/2512.html (accessed February 1, 2001). *American Psychological Association Ethical Principles of Psychologists and Code of Conduct*, www.apa.org/ethics/code.html (accessed February 1, 2001).

32. Manuel Velasquez, Clare Andre, Thomas Shanks, S. J., and Michael J. Meyer, "Thinking Ethically: A Framework for Moral Decision Making," *Issues in Ethics* 7 (1996): 1–3; see also Robert B. Ashmore, *Building a Moral System* (Englewood Cliffs, N.J.: Prentice-Hall 1987); William K. Frankena, *Ethics*, 2d ed. (Englewood Cliffs, N.J.: Prentice Hall, 1978); and Tom Regan, ed., *Matters of Life and Death: New Introductory Essays in Moral Philosophy* (New York: Random House, 1980).

33. Thomas R. Nilsen, *Ethics of Speech Communication*, 2d ed. (Indianapolis: Bobbs-Merrill Publishing Co., 1974), 45.

34. Wayne Brockriede, "Arguers as Lovers," *Philosophy and Rhetoric* 5 (1972): 1–11.

35. Brockriede, 2.

36. Brockriede, 3.

37. Brockriede, 4.

38. Brockriede, 5.

39. Nilsen, 1974.

40. Velasquez et al., 1.

41. Velasquez et al., 1.

42. Velasquez et al., 2.

43. Sarah Trenholm, *Persuasion and Social Influence* (Englewood Cliffs, N.J.: Prentice Hall, 1987), 18–20.

44. Adapted from Morris Dees, "Hate Crimes: Our Nation Is Greater Because of Our Diversity," *Vital Speeches of the Day* 66 (2000): 247–253; and J. Willwerth, "Making War on WAR," *Time* 136 (1990): 60–62.

THE PARTS OF AN ARGUMENT

CLAIMS AND PROPOSITIONS

When disputes arise, arguers make arguments. As we noted in Chapter 1, arguments consist of claims, evidence, and reasoning. When we parse arguments, we break them up into their components, which allow us to examine, understand, and evaluate each of the parts that compose the argument. Consider the arguments for and against peer-to-peer file sharing developed in Box 4.1. As you read the arguments, you can see how the speakers developed each of the parts of the argument. There are claims about legality and ethics; there is evidence about laws and the impact of illegal downloads; and there is reasoning that helps develop the claims and illustrate each speaker's point of view.

An in-depth understanding of each of these parts both improves our ability to present arguments to recipients and allows for meaningful criticism of their appropriateness and effectiveness. This chapter focuses on developing claims and propositions. As we discussed in Chapter 1, a claim is the end point of an argument; it is "an expressed opinion or a conclusion that the arguer wants accepted." As discussions unfold, arguers make decisions about their positions and create claims to support that position. With the case of file sharing, Nick's position is simply that illegal activity is bad and should be banned. His claims all support that larger point of view. Eva, on the other hand, takes a less legal point of view and creates claims that support what is in the best interests of the consumer as well as the producers. As recipients of this discussion or any other set of arguments, we must be able to identify an arguer's claim and distinguish it from the evidence and reasoning used to support it. Doing so enables us to analyze and competently criticize arguments made by others.

■ ■ ■ ■ ■

BOX 4.1
SHOULD PEER-TO-PEER FILE SHARING BE STOPPED?

By some estimates, more than 8 million people are logged into file-sharing networks around the world at any one time. With more than 900 million illegal music files available on these networks, along with movies, texts, and images, illegal file sharing is one of the single largest uses of the Internet.[1] College and university students represent some of the most active participants in these networks that share illegally copied and distributed files. In response to calls from recording artists and movie studios, the U.S. Congress has begun developing legislation to strengthen existing copyright laws and increase penalties for violators. Higher-education leaders are being asked to move quickly and aggressively to eliminate illegal peer-to-peer (P2P) sharing on their campuses.[2] Senator Lamar Alexander, for instance, demanded that colleges and universities immediately "adopt policies and educational programs on their campuses to help deter and eliminate illicit copyright infringement occurring on, and encourage educational uses of, their computer systems and networks."[3] Despite their efforts, campuses have found it difficult to control because of the ease of access to the Internet and inexpensive technology.

The core of the controversy is copyright law. Copyright laws state that if a work is going to be used, the original producer must give permission for its use and, generally, the author should be compensated for it. When a song is sold on iTunes, for instance, the original recording artist receives a royalty payment for the sale. When a college or university stages a play, typically, it pays fees to the copyright holder for the use of the script.[4] But technologies that provide easy ways of reproducing and distributing original

(continued)

BOX 4.1   CONTINUED

works have made circumventing copyright simple. Although governments have worked to adapt laws to meet these threats, almost anyone with a computer and access to the Net has the ability to illegally share files with others. This is why the Internet has been described as the biggest threat to copyright since the invention of the printing press.

In response, recording artists and studios have worked aggressively to stop illegal file sharing, and many copyright violators have been taken to court. Their focus has been individual users and the result has been that hundreds of people, mostly college students, have been prosecuted for sharing files without proper permission or paying royalties. File sharing has been a widely discussed and debated issue on college campuses; included in the debate is whether or not a college or university should turn over student file-sharing records. Following is a discussion between two students about whether file sharing should be banned on college campuses.

Nick: File sharing is wrong and unethical. An honest person would never swap music, movies, games, or any other file without paying for them. File sharing has completely destroyed the music industry and that hurts all of us who want to purchase quality music. People no longer buy music, they rip it off. Artists have been hurt, music stores have gone bankrupt. Pretty soon, there will be no new music because artists won't be able to afford to live. File sharing is illegal and we should not tolerate it. Anyone caught doing it on campus should be expelled.

Eva: The fact that people share files without paying for them is the fault of the music industry. Record producers pack albums full of tracks that no one wants and they force you to pay excessive amounts of money for one good song buried in the middle of ten bad songs. Sites like iTunes have made it better, but even so, the music is too expensive. Besides, file sharing gives people more choices and people discover artists they didn't know existed. I am not saying we should rip off artists, but file sharing lets us discover new bands and it gives young artists an opportunity to be heard—and that doesn't happen on commercial radio or television where big labels pay high premiums to get songs played over and over. File sharing gives people a choice and provides a level playing field for new artists. Expelling a student for sharing files is a little extreme, don't you think?

Nick: Your argument doesn't make any sense. You are saying that new artists will be better off giving their music away so that they can be heard. But if they never make any money, how will they produce the songs in the first place? I understand that MP3 files could help promote new artists, but that is not what people download. I have read that only ten songs in a thousand were from relatively unknown artists. Besides, even if everything you say is true, nothing prevents new artists from putting up content for free. My only point is that sharing should be done with permission. We should not allow stealing, especially when there are legal, low-cost alternatives.

Eva: Copyright laws need serious updating. Sharing is not stealing. Whenever anything is released to the public, it has been shared, and once someone has paid for a book, song, movie, or anything else, why can't they share it with whomever they choose? Libraries pay for a book once and then allow anyone to check it out. If I buy a DVD, don't I have the right to show it to my friends? I'm allowed to record my favorite song off the radio. What makes sharing MP3s so different? Our copyright laws need to adapt to new technologies.

(continued)

BOX 4.1   CONTINUED

Nick: Maybe the laws should change and maybe they are outdated. But that doesn't matter. File sharing is illegal. People who do it without permission are breaking the law. While the Digital Millennium Copyright Act has a fair-use provision for personal purposes, it does not allow those copies to be traded. You and I can rip a CD we bought, but when we give it away to someone else, we have broken the law. There is no difference between sharing the track with someone else and stealing it from the store.

Eva: The law needs to change. File sharing helps artists. When people have a chance to preview tracks, new artists get discovered. No one has demonstrated a negative effect on artists. Musicians were worried when blank, recordable cassettes were introduced. The movie industry opposed recordable VHS and Beta tapes. Yet, at the end of the day, music and movie sales went up.[5] With more download opportunities, companies have new markets. Television and movie studios have found new audiences for vintage programs. Copying files has been going on a long time, and I don't see any evidence it has harmed anyone.

Nick: You are wrong. Illegal file downloads have decreased legal sales, and that is why so many stores are getting out of the music sales business. To make a profit, producers will have to raise prices, and that hurts people who buy music and movies legally. The industry will figure out a way to make a profit, and ultimately illegal downloads will result in increased costs for people who follow the law. The recording industry cannot compete against illegal downloads, and everyone will end up paying the price.

Consider the arguments that emerged in this discussion and answer the following questions:

1. Should sharing illegal files stop? What arguments persuade you that this conclusion is correct?
2. Which arguer was stronger in terms of developing quality arguments? Why do you think so?
3. If file sharing is illegal, why do people do it? If you represented a recording studio, what would you do?
4. Take a close look at the claims made by each speaker. Were they strong or weak? What makes a claim strong?

THE NATURE OF CLAIMS AND PROPOSITIONS

Whenever we argue, we use claims and propositions. Both serve an important function in arguments because they help define and focus the direction of a discussion or debate. At this point, it is useful to distinguish clearly between claims and propositions. Argument claims, as they were defined in Chapter 1, are the end points of an individual argument. They are supported by reasoning and evidence and focus on a single issue or idea. When we argue, we may develop many different arguments, and each of those arguments has a claim. For instance, when Eva says that "copyright laws need serious updating," she is making an argument. But it is only one of many arguments she makes, and each of those other arguments also has a claim. Taken together, she develops a set of arguments that take a position on the main discussion topic: "Should peer-to-peer file sharing be stopped?"

Propositions

Beyond the claims of individual arguments, however, lie propositions. *Propositions are overarching or main claims that serve as the principal claim of an extended argument.* Extended arguments occur whenever a group of individual arguments are collected together to prove a larger point or proposition. Propositions in an extended argument function like the thesis in an essay. This means first that propositions are a type of claim. They are the primary point made by an arguer. Second, propositions focus the field of discussion. They define and limit the issues that are available to arguers in a dispute. For instance, when Nick and Eva talk about P2P file sharing, the topic area serves as a proposition. It includes some issues—what is legal, what protections exist, whether artists are harmed—and it excludes other issues—should Nick and Eva go out for pizza? Propositions, by their nature, include some issues and exclude others.

Propositional Arenas

Issues are important to the process of developing arguments, and they were introduced in Chapter 1 as things to consider when engaged in critical thinking and reflection. *Issues are the various points of potential disagreement related to a proposition.* As main claims, propositions set the boundary of acceptable and reasonable issues relevant to a particular topic. In other words, they create a propositional arena that defines what issues are appropriate for discussion. *A propositional arena is the ground for dispute and includes all the issues for controversy within a given proposition.* Propositions are supported by individual arguments that are developed from the issues within the propositional arena. These individual arguments are all related in some way to the proposition and may either support or deny it. Propositions thus provide a framework for understanding the relevance of individual arguments.

Figure 4.1 provides a good illustration of how propositions serve to limit the issues in a discussion. In this figure, potential and relevant issues for debate are contained within the field. These include A, B, C, D, E, F, G, and H. With this model, the file-sharing example could be looked at as a collection of the following issues:

A = Is it legal?
B = Does it harm new artists?
C = Did it destroy record stores?

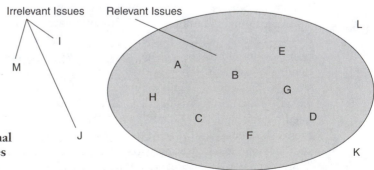

FIGURE 4.1   The Propositional Arena Includes Relevant Issues and Excludes Irrelevant Ones

D = Is it immoral and unethical?

E = Does it open new markets?

F = Does illegal sharing actually increase legal sales?

G = Is the consumer harmed?

H = Will artists and studios go bankrupt?

These issues, among many others, can be found in the propositional arena. Irrelevant issues are excluded by the proposition's boundary. In the figure, these issues are represented as I, J, K, L, and M. Examples of irrelevant issues that should be excluded from the discussion might be:

I = Should we go out for pizza?

J = There is no good music being produced anyway.

K = This is a dumb topic for a debate.

L = Should we have health care reform?

M = What do you want to do tomorrow?

It is important for arguers and recipients to be clear about the meaning of a proposition because it determines what is included and excluded from the discussion. And, if irrelevant issues are allowed to become part of an argument, discussions and debates can be sidetracked to the point that the proposition may not be addressed at all.

Using Claims and Propositions

Every proposition contains within its field more issues than an arguer can reasonably address—and it is not important that an arguer address every potential issue. The relevant question is, "What issues must be argued so that the advocate can make the point with the recipients?" Arguers select from the available issues and construct extended argument cases supporting or denying the proposition. Some issues may never be addressed. The choice rests with the advocate who decides what is appropriate for a given audience, situation, and level of dispute.

Often, claims and propositions are stated explicitly, but not always. Occasionally, someone will ask the arguer, "What point are you getting at?" because the claims are implicit or unclear. Arguers who want to be understood should respond by clearly and explicitly stating their claim or proposition. Consider the following example:

Lisa: You know the Webers are coming over tonight?

Nigel: Of course I know! Why do you think I got out the grill and cleaned it?

Lisa: It's too bad Perry's gone this week.

Nigel: Why? I'm enjoying the peace and quiet.

Lisa: Yes, but I miss having him around to do certain chores.

Nigel: Like what, for instance?

Lisa: Like mowing the lawn, for instance.

Nigel: Oh, you want me to mow the lawn, is that it?

Lisa wanted Nigel to mow the lawn for two reasons: They had guests coming over for a cookout, and the regular lawn mower was out of town. But her statements made no sense to Nigel until he discovered that her claim was, "I think you should mow the lawn."[6]

In essays, speeches, and other forms of one-way communication, claims are usually stated at the beginning or at the end of the argument. This placement occurs because arguers like to either state their position and then support it or present evidence or reasoning followed by a conclusion. Where are the claims in the following paragraphs?

Dogs can teach us a lot about gift-giving and generosity. They can also teach us about our most basic experiences of grace and mutual responsibility. Gilda Radner once observed, "I think that dogs are the most amazing creatures; they give unconditional love. For me they are the role model for being alive." In fact, dogs are a part of an "anti-economy." They give without requiring payment. They care without stipulation or reservation. These characteristics of dogs led Agnes Repplier to comment: "Our dogs will love and admire the meanest of us, and feed our colossal vanity with their uncritical homage." If all people modeled their behavior after dogs, we would live in a much happier world.[7]

The labels we use affect how others perceive us and how we see ourselves; they shape how we see others and how we want to be seen by them; they are used by those in power to define the rest even as they struggle to define themselves. They shape who we are.[8]

The beginning sentence in the first paragraph put forward the claim that the remainder of the paragraph supported, and the final sentence in the second paragraph did the same. Someone wanting to identify the central claim in a paragraph can also watch for terms like *therefore*, *then*, and *so* that show the conclusion is coming.[9]

On the other hand, informally developed arguments—such as arguments developed among friends in a conversation—may not have clearly placed claims. This is because claims often emerge and develop as we argue. We tend not to begin discussions with a claim and then proceed in some strict, rational order.

Propositions often emerge and are formulated over time. Initially, they are tentatively stated and then honed and refined as participants become knowledgeable about vital issues in a dispute. For example, prosecutors study the particulars of a case before bringing charges; legislators study and revise bills before they are introduced; doctors study a patient's symptoms before issuing a diagnosis; and most of us think and read about social and political problems before we venture to express opinions about them.

Networks of Claims

Long essays, speeches, extended discussions, and lengthy conversations in which efforts to argue and influence are taking place frequently contain a network of related claims that are combined to support a proposition. Figure 4.2 illustrates this.

Figure 4.2 displays a network of claims supporting the proposition "The lack of a clear policy for treating patients in irreversible comas is a problem in our society."[10] The proposition is supported by a hierarchy of subsidiary claims—principal subclaims, secondary subclaims, and sub-subclaims. The principal subclaims state four major problem areas: lack of a definition of "death," rapid technological advancement, physical liability, and inconsistent procedures for decision making. Each of these four

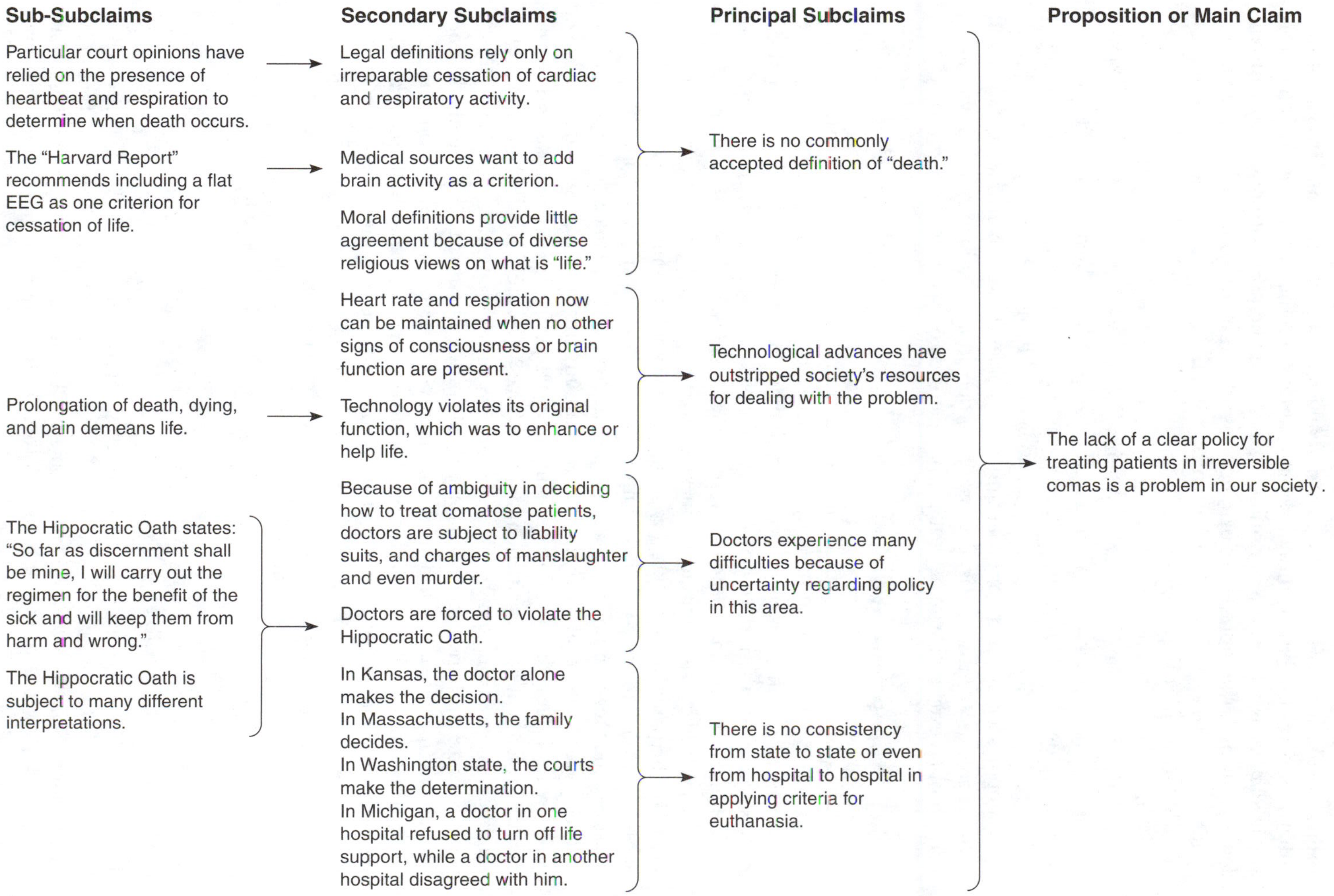

Proposition or Main Claim

Principal Subclaims

Secondary Subclaims

Sub-Subclaims

The lack of a clear policy for treating patients in irreversible comas is a problem in our society.

There is no commonly accepted definition of "death."

Technological advances have outstripped society's resources for dealing with the problem.

Doctors experience many difficulties because of uncertainty regarding policy in this area.

There is no consistency from state to state or even from hospital to hospital in applying criteria for euthanasia.

Legal definitions rely only on irreparable cessation of cardiac and respiratory activity.

Medical sources want to add brain activity as a criterion.

Moral definitions provide little agreement because of diverse religious views on what is "life."

Heart rate and respiration now can be maintained when no other signs of consciousness or brain function are present.

Technology violates its original function, which was to enhance or help life.

Because of ambiguity in deciding how to treat comatose patients, doctors are subject to liability suits, and charges of manslaughter and even murder.

Doctors are forced to violate the Hippocratic Oath.

In Kansas, the doctor alone makes the decision.
In Massachusetts, the family decides.
In Washington state, the courts make the determination.
In Michigan, a doctor in one hospital refused to turn off life support, while a doctor in another hospital disagreed with him.

Particular court opinions have relied on the presence of heartbeat and respiration to determine when death occurs.

The "Harvard Report" recommends including a flat EEG as one criterion for cessation of life.

Prolongation of death, dying, and pain demeans life.

The Hippocratic Oath states: "So far as discernment shall be mine, I will carry out the regimen for the benefit of the sick and will keep them from harm and wrong."

The Hippocratic Oath is subject to many different interpretations.

FIGURE 4.2   In a Network of Related Claims, Sub-Subclaims Support Secondary Subclaims, Which Support Principal Subclaims, Which Support the Proposition, or Main Claim

principal subclaims is in turn supported by clusters of secondary subclaims and sub-subclaims. Taken together, the subclaims form an argument chain that reaches from the level of dispute to the proposition. The further the proposition is away from the level of dispute, the more layers of subclaims are necessary to prove the proposition. The more complex and controversial a proposition, the longer the chain of arguments required to support the proposition.

In extended arguments such as the one illustrated in Figure 4.2, argument claims begin with assumptions or factual statements (see the two leftmost columns) that function as evidence because they are accepted by all parties to the discussion. They therefore fall below the level of dispute and act as starting points linked together through reasoning and evidence to support further claims. The network of claims as a whole in turn supports a main claim or proposition that possesses certain characteristics arising from its role as a central thesis. Because the proposition functions as it does within the context of an extended argument, it can be identified only within that context.

Fields, Propositions, and Claims

Depending on the field in which they occur, extended arguments supporting a main claim or proposition appear in many forms. In journalistic circles, they may appear as editorials; in criminal law, as cases constructed by the prosecution or defense; in business, as recommendations to management; in religious settings, as sermons and theological discussions; and in academic research, as articles in scholarly journals.

The field of argument determines the form of proposition for an extended argument. In a parliamentary setting, propositions may appear as motions ("I move that we abolish the university's core curriculum in general education"). In argumentative discussions, they may be expressed as an opinion ("MTV is a menace to the morality of today's youth"). In legal cases, they appear as indictments ("The state charges John Smith with reckless driving"). In medicine, they take the form of diagnosis and recommended treatment ("The patient appears to have a uterine fibroid tumor; surgery to remove it is recommended").

Because a proposition provides the focal point for issues in a dispute, the absence of a clearly formulated statement of the main claim to be argued is problematic. In some situations in which you will argue, the proposition will be formulated by another party to the dispute or by some agent authorized to state it in advance. At other times, however, you yourself will be able to state the proposition to be supported. Such an opportunity might arise in interpersonal argument when no one has clearly formulated the central question to be discussed. You may also need to formulate a proposition for an essay or speech you plan to make. The next section, therefore, discusses the criteria for clear, precise propositions.

FORMULATING A PROPOSITION

People who engage in argument expect certain things to happen. Their expectations grow out of the conventions, or implicit "rules," for conducting arguments that influence argumentative discussions in our society.[11] Because people expect that arguments are made for specific purposes and are directed toward specific goals, arguers need to formulate their propositions and statements of opinion to meet others' expectations. This section will consider the basic requirements for expressing well-developed propositions and claims. Individual claims and propositions need to be both controversial and clear.

Controversiality

All claims and propositions should be controversial. *If a claim or proposition is controversial, it states a position that is not currently accepted or adhered to by the audience.* As we noted in Chapter 1, argumentative theses are concerned with matters that are controversial. After all, if everyone agrees about an issue, what need is there to argue? In fact, statements that are not controversial probably serve the function of evidence rather than claims. As main claims for extended arguments, propositions also need to be balanced and to challenge the status quo to ensure an overall discussion of the topic that is both fair and provocative. People do not argue about things such as whether the earth is round or whether murder is wrong. Instead, they use their understanding of these accepted claims as evidence to ground other claims. In selecting a topic, advocates should choose something that will be important and controversial to their audience. For example, advocates defending the proposition "Education is beneficial to society" or "Freedom is important in a democracy" might be met with ambivalence or disinterest from their readers or listeners. They might wonder why such a thesis needs to be defended since everyone already agrees with it.

When issues require the recipients to have specialized knowledge or background, the arguer has two responsibilities. First, the arguer should provide the recipients with sufficient information about issues to make them aware of the controversy. And second, the arguer should provide sufficient depth to the issues to develop the recipients' capabilities to make reasoned judgments about the arguers. For example, if the arguer were going to discuss means for resolving conflicts in the Middle East, the arguer would have to provide the recipients with sufficient history and cultural knowledge to be able to make a reasonable interpretation of the arguments.

In deciding on a proposition for discussion or debate, it is wise to canvass newspapers and other current periodicals. What is controversial and the subject of public attention at one time may be of little interest later because the matter has been settled or because other issues seem more pressing. Questions of what to do about the polio epidemic or whether we should have mandatory seat belt laws were very controversial at one time. However, a vaccine was found for polio, and the passage of seat belt laws has successfully reduced the number of highway fatalities. The controversiality of a proposition may depend on what issues are timely and of significant public interest.

Clarity

When people engage in argument, they expect to know the argument's goal and how to determine when the issue has been resolved. As we observed in the last section of this chapter, ambiguous, unclear, muddled claims and propositions generally lead to muddled argumentation. *Clarity refers to how well a claim focuses arguments on a particular set of issues.* People need to know where they are starting in order to decide when

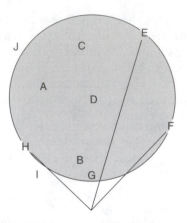

FIGURE 4.3   Ambiguously Worded Claims—The Issues on or near the Edge of the Propositional Area Not Clearly Included or Excluded

they have finished. If, through ambiguous wording, the claim allows multiple interpretations or fosters misunderstanding, then it is not clear. Consider Figure 4.3. If a proposition is stated clearly, it is easier to decide which issues are relevant and which are not. But if a proposition is ambiguous, the relevant issues are less apparent, and arguers may find themselves discussing extraneous matters or tangential issues.

Ambiguous Terms

One major source of confusion in stating propositions is the use of ambiguous terms that are interpreted one way by one party to the dispute and another way by the other. Since each party is interpreting the proposition differently, each arguer has a different starting point and is probably going in a direction unanticipated by the other. For example, consider a dispute between two professors discussing the merits of non-graded credit options for students. Both are unaware that there are actually *two* such options at their university. One option (Credit/No credit) is offered on a classwide basis. (All students take the class on a Credit/No credit basis.) The second option is Satisfactory/Nonsatisfactory, which can be elected by individual students in courses where other students take the course for a grade. Professor Jones, who teaches a Credit/No credit course, is talking with Professor Smith.

> **Prof. Smith:**   I think the pass/fail grading system is just a way of letting students goof off.
>
> **Prof. Jones:**   That's not true! The students in my class work just as hard as they would for a grade!
>
> **Prof. S.:**   Oh, come on! They just use pass/fail grading to make life easier for themselves. It's the easy route to accumulating credits.
>
> **Prof. J.:**   That would only be true if students worked only for grades. Some are motivated more by the subject matter and the pleasure of learning.
>
> **Prof. S.:**   You surely are an idealist. Everyone knows that it's the concrete pay-offs that allow students to get ahead that really motivate them.
>
> **Prof. J.:**   All I can speak from is my own experience.

This discussion is not going in a profitable direction, primarily because of the ambiguity of the phrase "pass/fail grading system." For example, if Professor Jones made it clear that he was speaking of the Credit/No credit designation that is mainly used for activity-based and performance courses (internships, readers' theatre, orchestra, etc.), his statements about motivation and the pleasure of learning might be more readily accepted by Professor Smith. Here are two more examples of ambiguous terms in propositions:

Euthanasia should be allowed when the patient and family consent to it.

Does "euthanasia" in this claim refer to removal of life support systems (passive euthanasia) or to administering drugs or other means to induce death (active euthanasia, or "mercy killing")?

Grades are not an efficient means of determining a student's intelligence.

Does "determine" here mean "to obtain knowledge of" or "to bring about as a result"? Both are accepted dictionary definitions, yet they lend very different interpretations to the claim. Examples such as these show the desirability of using precise and exact terms when stating claims.

Double-Barreled Statements

A second source of confusion and lack of clarity in stating claims is the "double-barreled" statement. *Double-barreled claims advance two or more claims simultaneously and, as with ambiguous terms, often lead arguers in separate directions because the relevant issues for each part of the claim are different.* Because double-barreled claims and propositions include issues from two or more propositional arenas, arguers often find it difficult to focus on and define the arena under dispute. If a proposition or claim has two different objectives, it is best divided by the arguer. Figure 4.4 illustrates the problems of double-barreled claims. In this diagram, the double-barreled claims encompass issues that support one idea and not the other. The result is that an arguer is faced with confusion regarding which issues are relevant and which issues are not.

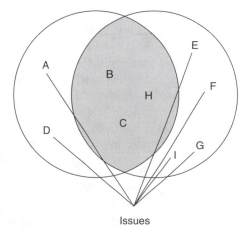

**FIGURE 4.4   Double-Barreled Claims—
The Unshaded Areas Contain Issues
That Do Not Fit Clearly within a Single
Propositional Arena**

Confusion because of double-barreled claims has occurred in the example of the discussion between Professors Smith and Jones. Smith's claim really is that "opportunistic students exploit the pass/fail grading system." Consequently, Smith and Jones are actually discussing two issues simultaneously—whether nongraded options have an effect on student learning and performance, and whether students are likely to take the "easy way out." If Smith had more clearly stated his claim and if Jones and Smith had agreed on what the main claim was to be, their discussion might have been less diffuse and more profitable. Here are two additional examples of double-barreled claims broken into two separate claims:

> **Double-barreled claim:**   The U.S. federal government should cut the income tax rate to stimulate the economy.

> **Claim 1:**   The U.S. federal government should cut the income tax rate.
> **Claim 2:**   Cutting the income tax rate will stimulate the economy.

> **Double-barreled claim:**   If corporations test employees for drugs, they should also test for alcohol, which is the biggest drug of all.

> **Claim 1:**   Alcohol is the "biggest" (most frequently used) drug of all.
> **Claim 2:**   Drug testing should be combined with alcohol testing by corporations that test for substance abuse.

The desirability of breaking double-barreled claims into separate claims is illustrated by the rules of parliamentary procedure. *Robert's Rules of Order* state that only one proposal or claim can be considered at a time. If someone proposes a motion with a dual idea, the motion should be divided into separate motions that can be debated separately.[12] Dividing related but separate ideas allows participants in a discussion to recognize their starting point and to know when they have reached their goal. Stating individual ideas separately enables arguers to recognize the points on which they agree and the points on which they disagree, thereby conforming to the conventions of argument and promoting productive, orderly discussions.

Balance

A productive, fair discussion of the issues in a dispute can result only when the topic of discussion is stated in a form with which both parties feel comfortable. Recipients can be drawn into a discussion and persuaded by the evidence an arguer offers only when they are convinced that the arguer has a balanced perspective on the topic. *Balance is the requirement that the issues for and against a proposition be included equally in the propositional field.* When the topic is specifically and clearly stated in neutral language, the field is left open for both its proponents and its opponents to discuss it freely. In fact, a neutral, dispassionate statement of the proposition is a convention in many forums of argument. In law, the charges brought against a defendant are stated neutrally and are agreed upon before the trial can begin (Ms. Jones committed libel against Ms. Davis; Mr. Smith is charged with driving while intoxicated). In business management, decision makers usually discuss a specific policy or course of action that has been recommended (Should we acquire the Widget Company as a subsidiary of our operation?

Does the preliminary information we have on this product line indicate that it should be heavily promoted?).

When a proposition for discussion is stated in connotative or prejudicial language, however, the deck is stacked against the viewpoint that opposes the proposition because the issues available to the opposing arguers have been limited or tainted by the emotionally loaded language. Furthermore, speakers and writers who state their theses in ways that reveal personal biases cause their audiences to become suspicious. Consider, for example, the following propositions:

> The space race is the world's biggest money waster.
> Unprincipled recidivists should be put away for life.

Propositions such as these overstate one's case and close off rather than promote open discussion because extraneous language serves to limit the issues available to the arguers. Propositions that avoid connotative language, superlatives, and stereotypes encourage all parties to the dispute to consider all available options and decision proposals. The propositions given above could be rephrased to be more neutral. As a general rule of thumb, the wording of the proposition should be agreeable to all parties of a dispute.

> Funds invested in space exploration should be significantly reduced.
> Repeat offenders should receive life imprisonment.

Challenge

One of the characteristics of an argument that we discussed in Chapter 1 is that it is an attempt to influence someone else. *Challenge means that an arguer's claim confronts recipients' existing values, beliefs, or behaviors.* Generally, the arguer who initiates the dispute by stating the initial claim expresses dissatisfaction with a prevailing belief or state of affairs. The arguer tries to change the other's attitudes or behavior to something different from what the attitudes or behavior would be if no argumentation took place.

A proposition for argument or debate should, therefore, challenge what people already believe or do. This is more than the requirement of being controversial. Whereas controversy refers to how ready a recipient is to agree to or believe in a proposition or claim, challenge focuses on changing the recipient in some way. This convention is based on the principle that there is no reason to defend an already accepted practice or belief unless it is questioned or criticized. Richard Whately, a nineteenth-century educator and clergyman, described this convention and its implications for argument.[13] He observed that in most argumentation there was a *presumption* and a *burden of proof.* The presumption favors the position that, because it is already accepted, "preoccupies the ground" in a controversy until some challenge is made against it. The person initiating the dispute therefore has the burden of proof entailed in making such a challenge.

The metaphor of preoccupying ground that Whately uses is carried through in the associations we make when we hear the word *claim.* A land claim is a claim to a parcel of land owned or possessed by someone else. The agency or the institution against which the claim is made enjoys no other advantage than the prerogative to retain the land if the claim is not upheld and accepted.

Therefore, the implication of Whately's concepts is that arguers who advance claims should challenge existing beliefs, policies, and states of affairs. Those who put forward proposals or advocate new ideas assume the *burden of proof*, which *obligates arguers to provide good and sufficient reasons for changing what is already accepted.* Those who defend existing beliefs and practices enjoy the *presumption,* that is, *the predisposition to favor an existing practice or belief until some good reason for changing it is offered.* The following claims do not challenge existing beliefs and practices and thus do not fulfill the burden-of-proof requirement:

> School desegregation is desirable.
>
> Washington State should continue to rely on sales and property taxes for revenue.
>
> The legal drinking age should be twenty-one.

Propositions such as these do not advocate change, and if arguments supporting them were not made, the policies and conditions they advocate would continue anyway. The following propositions, on the other hand, assume a burden of proof for the person who defends them because they challenge beliefs and policies that are presently accepted.

> A nationwide system of magnet schools is desirable.
>
> Washington State should implement an income tax.
>
> The legal drinking age should be set at fifteen nationwide.

Because they raise the possibility of innovations and new policies, such propositions challenge the present system and fulfill our expectation that attempts at influence be necessary and justified.

CLASSIFICATION OF CLAIMS

Generally, claims can be classified using three continua. These are illustrated in Figure 4.5 and include type, expression, and emergence. The concept of a continuum is useful here because it suggests that claims are interconnected—they "fit" into ways of thinking and knowing, they carry assumptions about the types of issues an arguer needs to address, and they help us understand an arguer's goals and direction. Knowing how a claim functions using each continuum in any given argument or situation can help the arguer decide what issues or questions need to be addressed.

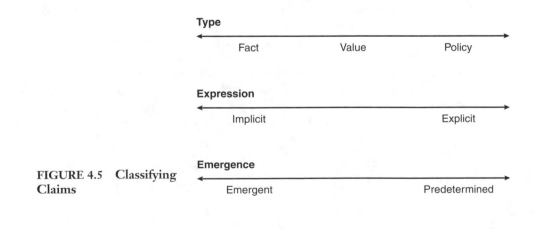

FIGURE 4.5   Classifying Claims

Some claims are stated expressly and refer to sources or conditions that can be readily checked for verification. Yet, other claims and propositions may not be stated directly and depend on the recipient to consider the supporting material and then draw the conclusion the arguer sought. Advertising often uses this form of argument. Abercrombie and Fitch ads, for instance, have been criticized for sexual images and no clear message about what the company expects the consumer to purchase. Of course, there is a clear message—it is implicit in the ad, but there is a message.

Sometimes arguers do not know what the proposition is until the end of the argument is reached. Other claims, such as those involving social values or policies, require more complex forms of support. For example, in Figure 4.2, the claim restating the Hippocratic Oath can be verified merely by referring to the text of the oath itself. If the group discussing euthanasia were to question whether "prolongation of death, dying, and pain demeans life," however, it would have to spend some time defining the terms of the claim and generating criteria to decide whether certain practices "demean life." This section will explore each of the three continua of claim classification and examine how these concepts influence the way we argue.

Types of Claims

Many category schemes for classifying claims have been proposed.[14] Some are very complex and suggest dozens of types, whereas others are much simpler and argue that it is impossible to divide claims into subtypes. However, the simplest and most frequently used scheme divides claims into the categories of fact, value, and policy. We will use this scheme here because it includes the major recognized types of claims used as subjects of argument and because the sets of issues each type generates can be distinguished from the sets of issues generated by the other two.[15]

Factual Claims

Factual claims make inferences about past, present, or future conditions or relationships. They are described in Box 4.2. If a statement is about a condition or relationship that is already known and readily apparent to participants in the argumentation, it functions as *evidence*, or, in a network of claims, as a sub-subclaim used as a starting point for argument. (Remember from Chapter 1 that previously established claims can be used as evidence in new arguments that build on them.)

Some statements of fact are straightforward and easily established, therefore not disputable. For example:

Mary weighs more than John.
The flight cannot leave because of heavy fog.
Central Airlines has the worst record for losing baggage in the United States.

Such statements are unlikely to serve as propositions for extended arguments because they are relatively easy to verify or prove. On the other hand, propositions of fact as discussed in Chapter 9 are much more difficult to prove because the information we need to establish them is not available or because such information is subject to varying interpretations. Such claims could function as propositions and be supported and attacked in extensive argument.

■ ■ ■ ■ ■

BOX 4.2
FACTUAL CLAIMS

Definition: *Factual claims make inferences about past, present, or future conditions or relationships.*

- Factual claims are relatively easy to prove because the needed information is generally available and clear. Example: Mary weighs more than John.
- Some factual claims require clear definitions and strong supporting material because they include terms that may be ambiguous. Example: Capital punishment deters crime.
- Factual claims are generally one of three types: relational, predictive, and historical.

Definition: *Relational claims attempt to establish a causal relation between one condition or event and another.*

Example: A diet high in fat will harm your health.

Definition: *Predictive claims are based on the assumption that past relationships and conditions will be repeated in the future.*

Example: Every home in the United States and Canada will have an Internet connection by 2015.

Definition: *Claims of historical fact rest on the strength of probable evidence to which we have access.*

Example: There was no evidence of weapons of mass destruction in Iraq.

One type of factual claim that states a controversial position is the relational claim. *A relational claim attempts to establish a causal relation between one condition or event and another.*

Capital punishment deters crime.
Smoking marijuana harms your health.
Violence on television affects children's behavior.

Researchers have completed many studies on each of these topics, and their results do not agree. Sifting through and comparing information on such topics is worthwhile because the inferences made in the claims are so controversial. In Chapter 8, we will discuss procedures for analyzing and supporting such claims.

A second type of factual claim that makes an argumentative statement about what will happen is the predictive claim. *A predictive claim is based on the assumption that past relationships and conditions will be repeated in the future.* Because information that might prove such claims is often not available, predictive claims often serve as the subject of argumentation. For example:

A staffed space mission will reach Mars by 2015.
Our economy is headed for a massive depression.
A severe shortage of teachers will occur by the year 2020.

Such claims are usually supported by descriptions of long-term trends and statistically based projections; they also involve studying causal relationships that may be affected by unanticipated developments and events.

A third type of controversial factual claim is the *claim of historical fact*, which *rests on the strength of probable evidence to which we have access.* Because historical records and artifacts are damaged, destroyed, or lost as time passes, evidence supporting historical claims may be as unavailable as that supporting predictive claims. Extensive controversy has surrounded the following claims:

> The Shroud of Turin was worn by Jesus in the tomb.
>
> The author of *On the Sublime* was not Longinus.
>
> Lee Harvey Oswald was the sole assassin of John F. Kennedy.

Supporters of such claims collect and describe as much circumstantial evidence as possible to convince skeptics that their claims are true. Historical claims cannot be positively proven because direct evidence to support them is unavailable.

Three types of factual claims that can serve as the subject of argument, then, are relational claims, predictive claims, and historical claims. Relational claims connect two conditions and infer that one of them has brought about or will bring about another. Predictive claims are grounded in the assumption that past events will be repeated in the future and make a claim about some future occurrence. Historical claims are descriptive and informational and are usually based on a preponderance of evidence that a particular account or interpretation of past events is the correct one. All three deal with matters that are disputable because the information we would need to establish them conclusively is insufficient or unavailable. They describe how or why something has come about or will come about in ways that are controversial and subject to argument.

Value Claims

Value claims assess the worth or merit of an idea, object, or practice according to standards or criteria supplied by the arguer. They are described in Box 4.3. The focus of argumentation about values is the values held by participants in a dispute. *Values are fundamental positive or negative attitudes toward certain end states of existence or broad modes of conduct.*[16] Such fundamental attitudes influence our conceptions of what is desirable or undesirable in a given situation. Joseph W. Wenzel has noted that "values exist in an intersubjective realm of agreements that are the fabric of a community; they exist in the actions and discourse of persons constructing, sustaining, testing, and revising the rules by which we will live and act together."[17] Examples of values expressing fundamental conceptions of desirable end states are equality, salvation, self-fulfillment, and freedom; those regarding models of conduct are courage, honesty, and loyalty.

Values govern our choice-making and indicate to us what we ought to believe and do. When we make value claims by assigning a value to an object, practice, or idea, we are actually making recommendations to others. Following are examples of value claims:

> Capital punishment is beneficial to society.
>
> Private schools provide better elementary and secondary education than public schools.
>
> Edgar Degas's paintings are ethereally beautiful.

■ ■ ■ ■ ■

BOX 4.3

VALUE CLAIMS

Definition: *Value claims assess the worth or merit of an idea, object, or practice according to criteria supplied by the arguer.*

■ Values are fundamental positive or negative attitudes toward certain end states of existence or broad modes of conduct such as equality (end state) and honesty (mode of conduct).
■ Value claims focus on the values held by the participants in a dispute.
■ Values govern our choices and indicate what we *ought* to do.

Examples:

Stem-cell research is beneficial to society.
Grading undermines the quality of education.
Censorship of Internet pornography is justified.

In each of these claims, a value judgment is made. The first deals with social benefit, the second with quality, and the third with aesthetic merit. The claims also involve an object of evaluation that may be an idea, a practice, a person, or a thing. Analysis of value claims must be located within some field or framework that implies the standards or criteria for the value judgment. For example, judging capital punishment according to its social benefits might involve a utilitarian standard whereby we try to determine whether capital punishment provides the greatest good for the greatest number of citizens. Criteria suggested by a utilitarian standard might include the following:

■ Does capital punishment actually prevent capital crimes?
■ Does implementing capital punishment save more lives than it takes?
■ Does capital punishment discriminate against minorities?

More will be said about the analysis of issues in value claims in Chapter 8.

Policy Claims

Policy claims call for a specific course of action and focus on whether a change in policy or behavior should take place. These are illustrated in Box 4.4. Policy claims frequently deal with complex social, political, or economic problems, but they may also deal with actions on a much smaller scale. In the conversation between Nigel and Lisa near the beginning of this chapter, Lisa's implication that Nigel should mow the lawn must be considered a policy claim. Other examples of policy claims are the following:

The King County government should legalize prostitution.
Sales of handguns to private citizens in the United States should be banned.
You should not smoke cigarettes in public places.

When making policy claims, arguers express either a dissatisfaction with present practices or a belief that a change in practices or behavior would be an improvement.

■ ■ ■ ■ ■

BOX 4.4
POLICY CLAIMS

Definition: *Policy claims call for a specific course of action and focus on whether a change in poli-cy or behavior should take place.*

- The claims focus on action and/or policies.
- They frequently deal with complex social, political, and economic problems that rely on an understanding of values and facts.
- Policy claims imply dissatisfaction with the status quo or a belief that a change in behavior would be beneficial.

Examples:

Pierce County should legalize prostitution.
Washington State should pass a 1 percent sales tax to fund schools.
We should rent this apartment.

The types of issues generated in policy claims and methods for analyzing them will be explained in Chapter 11.

Interconnection of Claims

Having divided propositions and claims into the three types just discussed, we must make one important observation. The three categories are not discrete and unrelated to one another, but are instead interconnected. Fact claims serve as the foundation for both value and policy claims. We are not inclined to make value or policy claims in the absence of fact claims. For example, to argue the value claim "Restricting access to the Internet for children is desirable," we must also understand and accept certain fact-based arguments. These might include the following:

There are pornographic sites on the Internet that might harm children.
There is language on the Web that is not suitable for children.
There are topics on the Internet that children are not developmentally ready to understand.

Fact claims are the basis for making most of our value and policy claims. They provide arguers with a foundation for the claims that follow.

Similarly, value claims assume the existence of certain facts and serve as the basis for making policy claims. We might make the claim, for instance, that "censoring pornographic material is desirable." This value claim assumes the existence of certain facts (the existence of pornographic material) and at the same time provides a justifica-tion for a policy action (pornography should be banned). All three types of claims, therefore, are linked together by networks of subsidiary or foundational claims: fact claims supporting value claims, value claims supporting policy claims, and policy claims assuming facts and values.

Such a network could be seen if we were to discuss the policy claim "Sales of handguns to private citizens in the United States should be banned." In this case, we might consider one or all of the following claims:

The number of handgun deaths and injuries in our country is appalling. (value claim)

The licensing and regulation of handgun sales is inconsistent from state to state. (fact claim)

Eliminating handguns will decrease the number of unpremeditated and accidental gun injuries. (predictive fact claim)

The "right to bear arms" is not as important as the public's right to safety and freedom from harm. (value claim)

An examination of the network of claims supporting policy propositions will always reveal subsidiary claims of fact and value. Furthermore, a value proposition such as "compulsory national service for all U.S. citizens is desirable" will involve decisions about policy (What is to be done to provide the needed service? Does "compulsory national service" mean a universal draft, required public service, or some other practice?).

Arguers need to keep in mind that because different types of claims are interdependent, they are not always easily distinguished from one another. For example, if an arguer claimed that "driving above the speed limit is harmful," the claim seems to come to rest somewhere on the continuum between fact and value. The term *harmful* implies a value. What is meant by harm? How do we evaluate harm? At the same time, we can assume that excessive speed results in a fact of harm.

Between each classification (fact, value, policy) there is a "gray zone" in which claims may hold both fact and value elements or value and policy elements. Furthermore, no claim exists independently. Because certain facts are true, we tend to value things. Because certain values are important, we tend to make policies. Similarly, our policies reflect our values, which in turn reflect our understanding of how the world works (facts). Claims of various types often occur in conjunction with each other and are interdependent. If arguers can identify and distinguish them, however, they will be able to focus on the issues and vital questions that the claims imply.

Expression of Claims

Some claims are expressed explicitly, whereas others remain implicit and rely on recipients to reach the conclusion on their own. *Explicit claims are stated clearly and publicly such that both the arguer and recipient are equally aware of their meaning.* In Chapter 3 we discussed how different cultures approach argument. Explicit claims are typically found in Western traditional arguments, whereas implicit claims are more often found in Asian or some African cultures. *Implicit claims are not stated publicly and are understood by the participants engaged in the argument.* These claims rely on the arguers having sufficient contextual knowledge of the argument situation to be able to clearly understand and argue about the topic. Because implicit claims are open to interpretation, they are seen as less confrontational than explicit claims that can polarize an argument.

Consider the following explicit claims:

Schools should expel students who bring any weapon to school—even toy weapons.

The United States should pass an amendment to eliminate the Electoral College.

The drinking age should be reduced to eighteen.

Marijuana should be decriminalized.

Each of these claims is clear and can be understood even if the recipient did not know the history or context that generated the claim. Each one clearly divides the argument field and provides an advocate with a clear propositional arena. Contrast these explicit claims with the following conversation between a married couple:

Kyle: I can't believe you are home late again. This is ridiculous!

Minerva: Work has been really busy this month. I can't help it.

Kyle: Work should not define your life. You are already putting in a sixty-hour week.

Minerva: I'll try to do better, but I need a little patience right now.

It is difficult to know exactly what the proposition is in this exchange because unless we know the context that created the exchange, it is difficult to interpret its meaning. The implicit claims could be:

We need to spend more time together.

Because you are not working, I need to work harder to make ends meet.

You are ignoring your family.

Depending on the argument situation, the relationship among arguers, and the culture, claims can be both explicitly stated or implicitly understood. An argument critic trying to examine an argument needs to be aware of how implicit claims function and should be able to examine the larger context to find the underlying assumptions, relationships, and cultural connections.

Emergence of Claims

When a court convenes, it examines a proposition. It might consider the guilt of someone, whether legislation was constitutional or not, or if the process was appropriately conducted. In any case, courts decide on propositions that are determined in advance. Examples might include:

John Doe is guilty of murder.

The Broadcast Decency Act is unconstitutional.

An appeal should be granted because the evidence was tainted.

Legislatures and governing assemblies are similar. They meet to discuss whether a particular action should be taken or if a decision should be made. These are all examples of predetermined claims. *Predetermined claims are claims that precede and guide an extended argument.* In other words, these are claims and propositions that initiate arguments. When a claim is predetermined, the propositional arena, sets of issues, and direction for the arguments are all fairly well defined. The advocates know in advance what the focus of the discussion or exchange will be.

However, in many conversational arguments, claims and propositions emerge from the discussion—they are not predetermined. These types of claims are referred to as emergent claims. *Emergent claims are claims and propositions that develop within an exchange among advocates; they are not agreed to in advance.* In these cases, people focus and develop the propositional arena through the course of the exchange as the conversation unfolds. The arguers might have had an idea about a direction for a discussion, but the specific proposition was not stated or agreed on by the participants in advance. Consider the following exchange between two friends:

> **Donna:**   I'm thinking about going to a movie.
>
> **Amanda:**   Me, too. Is there anything good playing now?
>
> **Donna:**   I don't know. I heard that the *I Am Legend* sequel was pretty good. It's playing at the Grand. I also heard that *Rainbow 6* was pretty good.
>
> **Amanda:**   I think I would rather see *Rainbow 6* than *I Am Legend*.
>
> **Donna:**   That works for me. Let's go.

The proposition that emerges from this conversation is "Let's go to see *Rainbow 6*," but it did not exist as a proposition before Donna and Amanda began talking.

When critics examine arguments, the proposition and structure of claims can be deceiving if the analyst fails to consider how propositions and claims function in the complete argument. Is it a fact or value or policy claim? Is it implicit or is it clearly stated? Figure 4.6 illustrates some questions to ask in trying to analyze the claims and

Type of Claim

Fact ←————————————→ Policy

What is the propositional arena?
Are the definitions in the proposition clearly understood?
Is the focus of the proposition clear?
What issues are included and excluded in the proposition?

Expression of Claim

Implicit ←————————————→ Explicit

Do the parties understand what the proposition is?
What assumptions guide the discussion?
Are the assumptions shared?
What context must be understood to understand the argument?

Emergence of a Claim

Emergent ←————————————→ Predetermined

Who created the proposition?
Do the participants understand and agree to the proposition?
What issues and underlying assumptions guided the development of the proposition?
What issues were included and excluded by the way the proposition emerged?
How was the decision made to shape the proposition?

FIGURE 4.6   Questions for Claim Analysis

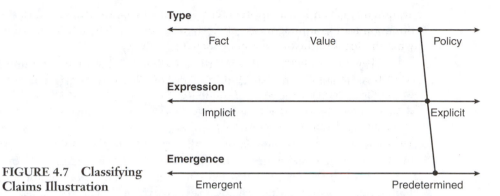

FIGURE 4.7   Classifying Claims Illustration

argument. Do the arguers really know what the proposition is that they are discussing? One way of examining the role of propositions in any extended argument is simply to chart it. Figure 4.7 provides an example of this for the proposition: "The United States Congress should amend the 1982 Nuclear Waste Policy Act to allow for research of non-geological nuclear waste storage sites." This is a predetermined, expressed policy proposition. If, however, it were an implicit, emergent policy proposition, an analyst would need to consider the assumptions of the advocates, the situation for the exchange, and the issues involved in reaching the conclusions.

SUMMARY

Claims and propositions serve important argument functions. They focus arguers' attention on the purpose of the argument and imply the issues that need to be decided before a dispute can be resolved. Extended arguments, whether they are in the form of conversations, discussions, speeches, or essays, include a network of claims that combine to support a proposition, or main claim. Skillful arguers should be able to identify the main claims and principal subclaims in the arguments of others. They should also be able to phrase their own claims so that they conform to others' expectations. By phrasing their claims appropriately, arguers will be more successful in constructing extended arguments.

People who participate in arguments expect the subject to be controversial or open to dispute. Anyone who advances a claim should be able to explain why it needs to be justified and supported. Arguers should therefore advance claims about which there is likely to be disagreement. People participating in arguments also expect them to be clear; that is, they want to know what the issues are and what is required to resolve them. Arguers stating claims should therefore avoid ambiguous terms, statements with multiple meanings, and statements that introduce multiple issues simultaneously. Furthermore, stating claims in a biased or prejudiced way forestalls open discussion of the options to be considered. Claims should therefore be stated objectively, and stereotypes and connotative terms should be avoided. Finally, people expect arguers to take issue with prevailing attitudes and practices. If an arguer attempts to influence someone, he or she must make a claim that would change what would continue to be done or believed had the argument not taken place. In presenting an argument for change, the arguer assumes the burden of proving there is good reason for the change to be made.

Claims can be classified using three continua. The first continuum is type; the second continuum is expression; and the final one is emergence. There are three major types of claims that are made in arguments. Each type of claim calls for a different type of analysis to identify the issues that the claim implies. Claims of fact make inferences about the past, present, or future conditions or relationships. Sometimes factual claims are readily verifiable and agreed on by all parties to the dispute, or come to be agreed on as the argument progresses. At other times, factual claims cannot be conclusively established because the needed information is unavailable, in conflict, or subject to conflicting interpretations. Value claims assess the worth or merit of something according to standards supplied by the arguer. The focus of disputes on value claims is on the fundamental attitudes (values) of participants in the argumentation. Value disputes may involve ethical, aesthetic, or moral judgments. Policy claims call for a course of action or change in the beliefs of others. They usually express dissatisfaction with present practices or a belief that a change in policy or behavior will bring improvement. It is important to remember that claims are not separate and discrete. Rather, each of the three types of claims may often rely on other types of claims for its support.

Depending on the relationship among the arguers and the context for the discussion, claims may be explicit or implicit. Explicit claims are those that are stated publicly and are understood by the arguers. Other claims may be implicit and not stated publicly, but rather they are understood and exist as part of the web of assumptions that underlie the relationship or history of the advocates.

Finally, some claims are predetermined, whereas others are emergent. Predetermined claims and propositions are those that exist and are understood prior to the arguers beginning their discussion. Emergent claims stem from the conversation and are understood as a result of a discussion.

GLOSSARY

Balance (p. 106) is the requirement that the issues for and against a proposition be included equally in the propositional field.

Burden of proof (p. 108) obligates arguers to provide good and sufficient reasons for changing what is already accepted.

Challenge (p. 107) means that an arguer's claim confronts recipients' existing values, beliefs, or behaviors.

Claim of historical fact (p. 111) rests on the strength of probable evidence to which we have access.

Clarity (p. 103) refers to how well a claim focuses arguments on a particular set of issues.

Controversiality (p. 103) means that a claim or proposition states a position that is not currently accepted or adhered to by the audience.

Double-barreled claims (p. 105) advance two or more claims simultaneously and, as with ambiguous terms, often lead arguers in separate directions because the relevant issues for each part of the claim are different.

Emergent claims (p. 116) are claims and propositions that develop within an exchange among advocates; they are not agreed to in advance.

Explicit claims (p. 114) are stated clearly and publicly such that both the arguer and the recipient are equally aware of their meaning.

Factual claims (p. 109) make inferences about past, present, or future conditions or relationships.

Implicit claims (p. 114) are not stated publicly and are understood by the participants engaged in the argument.

Issues (p. 98) are the various points of potential disagreement related to a proposition.

Policy claims (p. 112) call for a specific course of action and focus on whether a change in policy or behavior should take place.

Predetermined claims (p. 115) are claims that precede and guide an extended argument.

Predictive claim (p. 110) is based on the assumption that past relationships and conditions will be repeated in the future.

Presumption (p. 108) is the predisposition to favor an existing practice or belief until some good reason for changing it is offered.

Propositional arena (p. 98) is the ground for dispute and includes all the issues for controversy within a given proposition.

Propositions (p. 98) are overarching or main claims that serve as the principal claim of an extended argument.

Relational claim (p. 110) attempts to establish a causal relation between one condition or event and another.

Value claims (p. 111) assess the worth or merit of an idea, object, or practice according to standards or criteria supplied by the arguer.

Values (p. 111) are fundamental positive or negative attitudes toward certain end states of existence or broad modes of conduct.

EXERCISES

Exercise 1 In this chapter, four criteria were described that enable you to decide whether a proposition is well formulated. They are as follows:

- *Controversiality.* The proposition should state a thesis that is potentially disputable rather than one about which most people would agree.
- *Clarity.* The proposition should be clearly and precisely stated; ambiguous terms and double-barreled claims should be avoided.
- *Balance.* The claim should be stated in objective, neutral language rather than in a way that reveals the personal biases or prejudices of the person making the claim.
- *Challenge.* The proposition should confront an audience's prevailing beliefs, values, or state of affairs.

Using these criteria, criticize the following propositions. Are they well formulated? If not, why not? How could they be reformulated to function more effectively?

 *1. Exercise is good for one's health.

  2. Pirating music through the Internet is justified.

  3. The United Nations is ineffective.

  4. Plea bargaining is a good and essential means of case disposal.

 *5. Euthanasia is a desirable and necessary medical practice.

  6. Suing McDonald's for contributing to obesity is a frivolous law suit.

  7. The U.S. government should adopt broadcast decency laws.

  8. People who are HIV-positive should not be allowed to teach in public schools.

  9. The United States should reduce its deficit by cutting wasteful social programs.

 10. All schools should adopt school uniforms for their dress code.

 11. Schools should become more rigorous.

 12. Degenerate and perverted pornographic material should be pulled from every bookstore and magazine stand in America.

 13. Good salespeople are effective.

 *14. Women should have access to abortion on demand.

 15. Legalization of casino gambling has made the rich richer and the poor poorer.

 16. Education is good.

 17. America's industries need to invest in manufacturing if the United States is to be internationally competitive in the twenty-first century.

 18. People who own large cars with big engines are wasteful, stupid, and trying to destroy our environment.

 19. Dams are destructive to the environment and should be removed.

 20. Parties are a way of life in college.

Exercise 2 This chapter discussed a continuum of claims within which three types of claims could be identified: fact, value, and policy. Fact claims make inferences about past, present, or future conditions or relationships; they can be explanatory, predictive, or historical. Value claims judge an idea, object, person, or practice by some value standard or set of criteria. Policy claims advocate a course of action that is not currently followed. Where would you place each of the following criteria on the continuum of claims?

 *1. Extraterrestrial beings visited Earth during prehistoric times.

  2. Every state should require that all teachers pass a proficiency examination.

  3. All nations should destroy their biological weapons.

  4. Illegal immigrants generally take jobs U.S. citizens do not want.

  5. Discrimination is never justified.

  6. Marijuana should be legalized in all fifty states.

  7. Mandatory seat belt laws violate our constitutional rights.

  8. Polygraph evidence is better than eyewitness testimony in criminal trials.

  9. Pornography causes sex crimes.

10. Required automotive emissions tests are an inefficient means of ensuring clean air.

11. The U.S. welfare system has abandoned the poor.

12. The United States should not interfere in the social, political, and economic affairs of other nations.

13. Movies made today in America have more graphic violence and gratuitous sex than they did ten years ago.

14. Higher education in America is the best in the world.

15. Colleges and universities should stress technical and applied subjects over the liberal arts.

Exercise 3 Select three topics on which you would like to develop an argumentative case. A list of suggested topics is given, but you may choose some other topic area. What is important is that you already know enough about the topic to construct claims related to it. Within each topic area, construct a proposition of fact, a proposition of value, and a proposition of policy. Be sure that the propositions you supply adhere to all the guidelines for working propositions supplied in this chapter and listed in Exercise 1. Here is an example:

Topic area: Alcohol abuse
Proposition of fact: Alcohol-related accidents bring about more deaths than any other cause in the United States.
Proposition of value: Alcohol is a more dangerous substance than marijuana.
Proposition of policy: The allowable BAC (blood alcohol content) in drivers should be significantly reduced across the nation.

Suggested topics (or select three of your own):

abortion	endangered species	legalized gambling
AIDS	environment	political campaigns
animal rights	financial aid	poverty
capital punishment	foreign policy	religion
censorship	gun control	restricting drivers
consumer protection	illegal drugs	trade barriers
crime	inner cities	

NOTES

1. Helen Nugent, staff writer, "File sharing takes up to 95% of net use at night," TimesOnline, http://business.timesonline.co.uk/tol/business/industry_sectors/technology/article3353372.ece, February 12, 2008 (accessed May 3, 2008).

2. Katherine S. Mangan, "College Could Face Lawsuits Over Illegal File-Sharing," The Chronicle of Higher Education, October 4, 2002, http://chronicle.com/free/2002/10/2002101401t.htm (accessed on May 4, 2008).

3. Steve Tally, "Senate, industry target illegal file sharing across campus networks," Purdue News Service, July 10, 2006, http://news.uns.purdue.edu/html3month/2006/060710.Tally.sharing.html (accessed May 3, 2008).

4. Copyright laws can be complex and they vary by country. There are, however, some good guides. For instance, "Know Your Copy Rights," produced by the Association of Research Libraries, can be found at http://www.knowyourcopyrights.org/bm%7Edoc/kycrbrochurebw.pdf (accessed May 3, 2008) and provides guidelines for educational use of protected material. There is also a good guide to peer-to-peer file sharing written by Fred von Lohmann, "Peer-to-Peer File Sharing and Copyright Law: A primer for Developers," http://iptps03.cs.berkeley.edu/final-papers/copyright.pdf, February 2003 (accessed May 2, 2008).

5. Eva is referencing a study reported on the BBC that suggested illegal downloading can increase legal sales. More information can be found at "Downloading

'myths' challenged," BBC News Channel, July 27, 2005, http://news.bbc.co.uk/1/hi/technology/4718249.stm (accessed May 4, 2008).

6. Lisa's original "claim" was actually a veiled request to mow the lawn. When requests are supported by reasons, they function as arguments. Study of such argument forms occurs in Sally Jackson and Scott Jacobs, "Structure of Conversational Argument: Pragmatic Bases for the Enthymeme," *Quarterly Journal of Speech* 66 (1980): 251–265; and Frans H. van Eemeren, Rob Grootendorst, Sally Jackson, and Scott Jacobs, *Reconstructing Argumentative Discourse* (Tuscaloosa: University of Alabama Press, 1993).

7. Adapted from Stephen H. Webb, "It's a Dog's Love," *UTNE Reader* (January/February, 1996): 61.

8. Kevin P. Phillips, "Is the Party Over?" *Seattle Times* (July 20, 1986): A16.

9. More techniques for identifying claims and conclusions on the bases of contextual cues were discussed in Chapter 3.

10. These claims are drawn from a group discussion of the topic "What policy should be enacted in regard to patients in potentially irreversible medical situations?" The discussion occurred at the University of Washington on May 8, 1983. Student participants were Steven McCornack, Ann Hurd, Leigh Chang, Anne Bigelow, Carrie O'Connor, Liza Thomas, and Margo Welshons. This discussion predated a significant Supreme Court decision that ruled that patients have the right to refuse medical treatment and to write living wills precluding extraordinary measures to prevent death.

11. A good deal of work has been done in elaborating the conventions or "rules" of argument. By a rule, we mean "a regularity (formalized . . . written, understood, or tacitly observed) that defines an activity." See Gary Cronkhite, "Conventional Postulates of Interpersonal Argument," in *Argument in Transition*, David Zarefsky, Malcolm O. Sillars, and Jack Rhodes, eds. (Annandale, Va.: Speech Communication Association/American Forensic Association, 1983), 697. See also Frans van Eemeren and Rob Grootendorst, *Speech Acts in Argumentative Discussions* (Dordrecht, The Netherlands: Foris Publications, 1984).

12. General Henry M. Robert, "Division of a Question," *Robert's Rules of Order Revised*, 1915 version, April 11, 2000, www.constitution.org/cs_refer.htm (accessed May 5, 2000).

13. Richard Whately, *Elements of Rhetoric*, Douglas Ehninger, ed. (Carbondale: Southern Illinois University Press, 1963), 112–113.

14. For example, some authors break down proposition types into fact/value (including descriptive, predictive, or evaluative statements that assert the existence or worth of something) and policy, which advocates a course of action. See George Ziegelmueller, Jack Kay, and Charles Dause, *Argumentation: Inquiry and Advocacy*, 2d ed. (Englewood Cliffs, N.J.: Prentice Hall, 1990), 14–15. Church and Wilbanks describe another unique category scheme that divides propositions into those of inference, value, and policy, with the category of inference subdivided into trait, relational, historical, and predictive inferences. See Russell T. Church and Charles Wilbanks, *Values and Policies in Controversy* (Scottsdale, Ariz.: Gorsuch Scarisbrick, 1986), 35–42.

15. A fourth type of claim is the claim of definition, or classification. Examples would be "This is an act of burglary" and "By 'euthanasia,' I mean the removal of life support from terminally ill patients." To support claims such as these, the arguer justifies the definition or classification by referring to a source that others find acceptable. The arguer may also have to show that the chosen definition is applicable. Only rarely do definitive claims serve as central theses in argumentation; they more frequently function as subsidiary claims when participants disagree about how to define a term in the main claim or proposition.

16. Daryl J. Bem, *Beliefs, Attitudes and Human Affairs* (Belmont, Calif.: Brooks/Cole, 1970), 16.

17. Joseph W. Wenzel, "Toward a Rationale for Value-Centered Argument," *Journal of the American Forensic Association* 13 (1977): 153.

CHAPTER FIVE

EVIDENCE

CHAPTER OUTLINE

THE NATURE OF EVIDENCE

TYPES OF EVIDENCE
Fact Evidence
Reports and Descriptions
Statistics
Artifacts
Opinion as to Fact Evidence

EVALUATING EVIDENCE
Reliability
Expertise
Objectivity
Consistency
Recency
Relevance
Access

EVALUATING STATISTICAL EVIDENCE
Pseudostatistics
Comparing Noncomparable Units
Unrepresentative Samples
Poor Methodology

PRESENTING EVIDENCE
Omitting Words
Identifying Secondary Sources
Qualifying Sources
Plagiarism

SUMMARY

GLOSSARY

EXERCISES

KEY CONCEPTS

Reports and descriptions (p. 130)
Statistics (p. 130)
Artifacts (p. 130)
Reliable source (p. 132)
Expertise (p. 133)
Objectivity (p. 133-134)
Bias (p. 134)
External consistency (p. 134)

Internal consistency (p. 135)
Relevance (p. 136)
Access (p. 136)
Sample (p. 138)
Representative sample (p. 138)
Primary source (p. 140)
Secondary source (p. 140)
Plagiarism (p. 142)

Evidence plays a vital role in argumentation and decision making. Russel R. Windes and Arthur Hastings suggest that the acceptance of conclusions and decisions in the absence of evidence "has resulted in decisions and actions which have led to indescribable human suffering and misery—to wars and material destruction, to political inequities and the suppression of human rights, to economic catastrophes, to unjust persecutions, to mob violence, and to superstition and prejudice."[1] World history has witnessed countless examples of suffering and aggression based on evidence that was faulty, erroneous, or used unethically. Nazi Germany and the extermination of millions of Jewish people is certainly an example. So are the war crimes committed as the former Yugoslavia broke into independent republics. And, according to many analysts, the U.S. invasion of Iraq was based on faulty evidence. In each of these cases, one lesson that became increasingly clear was that if recipients hear something enough times, they will begin to accept it as true.[2]

Not only do we need to be aware of the absence or misuse of evidence in arguments we hear and read, but we also should be mindful of the need to use evidence in arguments we make. In numerous studies of the effects of evidence on persuasiveness, researchers have found that audiences are nearly always more influenced by arguments supported with evidence than those that are not.[3] Particularly in situations in which an arguer is unknown to an audience or does not have an established reputation with them, evidence is vital in establishing the credibility of claims and arguments the arguer makes. Researchers who have studied the effect of evidence on the persuasiveness of arguments have found that speakers unknown to or only moderately respected by an audience will be more successful if they use evidence to support their claims.[4] As recipients, critics, and producers of arguments, then, it is important for us to be aware of the vital role played by evidence.

In Chapter 1, we defined evidence as "facts or conditions objectively observable, beliefs or premises generally accepted as true by the audience, or conclusions previously established." Evidence is what we produce whenever we are asked to prove something or when someone asks us, "How do you know?" or "What have you got to go on?"

Box 5.1 provides a good illustration of how evidence is used in everyday conversational arguments. The advocates in this case are students, and most people would not assume that they are credible sources to talk about a "fat" tax based on their experience or background. They are not scientists or economists. They have not personally conducted any studies of how obesity affects health or how taxes affect consumption. However, throughout their arguments, the speakers ground their claims in statements that are accepted by the other advocate. Those statements serve as evidence. For instance:

> Junk-food restaurants are popping up everywhere.
> Some hamburgers have more than 1,000 calories.
> Overweight and obesity have reached epidemic proportions.
> Some cultures hold overweight and obesity in high esteem.
> Lack of exercise is a contributing problem.
> A study from Great Britain shows that taxes decrease consumption.

During the discussion, the speakers provide evidence to support their claims. In this case, the evidence is relatively informal. The speakers do not provide specific sources for their evidence nor do they reference the qualifications or credentials of any experts who produced the evidence. If challenged, the speaker would need to provide the source and qualifications for the evidence to be acceptable. The argument field, as we discussed in Chapter 1, determines the level of formality as well as the rules for

■ ■ ■ ■ ■

BOX 5.1

SHOULD THERE BE A "TWINKIE" TAX?

In 1994, Dr. Kelly Brownell of Yale University published an op-ed piece in the *New York Times* that advocated taxing unhealthy foods.[5] The suggestion was met with much ridicule, and opponents quickly dubbed it the "Fat Tax," "Twinkie Tax," and "Snack Tax." Yet, in some circles, it gained attention and support as a means to help alleviate the consequences of overweight and obesity. A tax, some said, in addition to potentially decreasing unhealthy food consumption, might also help pay for nutrition education and physical exercise programs.

Overweight and obesity are a worldwide epidemic. The World Health Organization (WHO) reported that globally there are more than a 1.6 billion overweight adults, with at least 300 million classified as obese.[6] These numbers are expected to grow by 40 percent in the next ten years as more people in more countries increase their consumption of energy-dense, nutrient-poor foods that have high levels of sugar and saturated fat. Many rich and poor countries work to manage the problems brought on by overweight and obesity. For instance, the five countries with the most overweight adults are Nauru, Federated States of Micronesia, Cook Island, Niue, and Tonga. Ninety percent or more of their adult population are overweight or obese.[7] The United States ranks as the ninth heaviest country in the world, with 74.1% of its adult population classified as overweight.[8] Almost 30 percent of American children under the age of nineteen are overweight or obese, as are nearly 1 in 5 Chinese adults.[9]

The implications for health and health care are significant. Obese and overweight people experience higher frequencies of cardiovascular disease, diabetes, musculoskeletal disorders, as well as some cancers. The Centers for Disease Control, for instance, claimed that for the United States, overweight and obesity cost as much as $92.6 billion annually in 2002, representing approximately 9.1 percent of total U.S. medical expenditures. Half of these costs were paid for by government assistance programs including Medicare and Medicaid, making overweight and obesity a significant taxpayer obligation.[10]

The WHO also offered many approaches that nations could use to reduce junk-food consumption. Among them were age restrictions, education campaigns, and zoning strategies for fast-food restaurants.[11] To pay for some of these efforts, the WHO suggested that nations might use a "fat" tax to promote healthy living, balanced eating, and exercise. Just as alcohol and cigarette taxes have been correlated with a decline in consumption, many argue the same would happen if snack foods were taxed. A study in the *British Medical Journal* found that a "fat" tax, properly developed, could help prevent up to one thousand deaths each year from heart disease in Great Britain.[12]

However, just as many people rallied in support of "fat" taxes, many have been skeptical. Some argue that a "fat" tax would be regressive because it targets the least educated and the least financially able. And, there is a great deal of discussion about the validity of studies linking taxation to positive health outcomes.[13] But even if the tax resulted in decreased junk-food consumption, some claim that governments have no right to interfere with individual liberties and freedom of choice.

Consider the following debate in which these issues are developed and pay attention to how evidence is used in support of claims:

(continued)

BOX 5.1   CONTINUED

Leah: The world needs to get a handle on obesity. Even in my hometown in Colorado, there is a huge increase in the number of junk-food restaurants popping up everywhere—full of people all the time. People like high-calorie, high-fat foods that have no nutritional value. Some fast-food hamburgers have more than 1,000 calories. That's ridiculous. This kind of eating leads to obesity and contributes to a worldwide epidemic. Children model our behavior, and they learn from their parents. Not only are we increasing our own risk of disease, but we are passing it down the generations. There is absolutely no reason to allow this kind of behavior. I really support taxing junk food to get people to stop eating it. A tax makes sense; we use tax policies all the time to help people make good choices. We tax cigarettes and alcohol. We give tax breaks to people who save for retirement. We give tax breaks to companies that decide to go "green." Using our tax policies to save lives is reasonable and important. Besides, being fit and healthy is a desirable personal goal that we should support. People who take care of themselves perform better at work and in their private lives. Because this is a global problem that affects many people, governments are justified in creating incentives and taxes to improve lives.

Kyle: I understand what you are saying about being healthy, but in many parts of the world, being fat represents prosperity and fertility—we shouldn't apply a U.S. standard to other cultures. In many places, larger people are viewed as stable and self-sufficient. Besides, a "fat" tax makes it seem as though being overweight is bad. Everybody is different—a weight chart or some standard of being overweight doesn't take into account genetics or what is healthiest for each individual. What message does that send to kids who struggle with bulimia and anorexia? Doesn't a tax threaten to increase eating disorders? Weight and health issues may not be related to junk food. Eating disorders are often driven by the impression that society demands skinny, and a government policy that taxes junk food may reinforce that perception. We should not assume that being overweight automatically says someone is unhealthy.

Leah: Being overweight or obese causes severe medical problems including high blood pressure, cancer, heart disease, and diabetes. It doesn't matter if fat is attractive or not; people die from it. If a "fat" tax is introduced, junk-food consumption will drop. People will eat healthier—and if they don't, then the tax revenue can help support education, nutritional alternatives, and exercise programs. A recent study in Great Britain showed that a "Twinkie" tax could prevent hundreds of premature deaths each year and cut heart disease by 10 percent. If we tax cigarettes and alcohol to promote health, it seems to me this is the same thing. Why shouldn't we tax unhealthy food? We know it contributes to obesity. It seems to me that we have an opportunity to fix a serious problem.

Kyle: We can make a decision to tax or not tax, but these just gloss over the real problem. Regardless of the decisions we might make about a "fat" tax, the larger health-related issues are caused by socioeconomic factors, exercise, and education. Health is at least as much about exercise as it is about diet, and this is a bigger problem with lifestyle that is not recognized. A "fat" tax makes it sounds as though we have solved something when we haven't.

(continued)

BOX 5.1   CONTINUED

Consider the arguments that emerged in this discussion and consider the following questions:

1. As you read through the case study, how is evidence used? Is it done effectively?
2. What kinds of arguments are most convincing? In those arguments, what evidence was used? Why did you find it believable?
3. If you were researching to find support for each side, where would you look? What kind of evidence would you hope to find?

introducing evidence. Conversations among friends are fairly informal. If this argument were occurring in a court of law, the field would require expert witnesses and credible testimony that could be produced in the courtroom. If this argument were occurring in a legislature considering a "fat" tax, statements could be read, experts could be called to testify, and personal experience could support the arguments. In each case, the rules of the field determine how evidence can be introduced and what evidence is credible.

When evidence is used effectively, it can enhance an arguer's credibility even about subjects with which the advocate might have little direct experience or expertise. The students drew upon their research and observations to support their claims and enhance their credibility. Evidence serves to ground the argument and support its believability. The introduction to Box 5.1 also provides evidence from credible sources that is introduced in a more formal, explicit way.

This chapter will discuss the nature and types of evidence, ways to evaluate the quality of evidence, procedures for locating evidence in libraries and resource materials, and guidelines for using evidence to support your arguments. After reading this chapter, you should be able to recognize various types of evidence and evaluate the quality of evidence used in your own and others' arguments.

THE NATURE OF EVIDENCE

Our definition of evidence from Chapter 1 indicates that evidence is not simply concrete facts or observable behavior. Rather, the defining characteristic of evidence is that it is accepted by the audience and can be used to support statements (claims) that are not accepted. The three ways in which evidential statements can function will be discussed in this section so as to reveal the nature of various forms of evidence.

First, evidence can stem from objectively observable conditions in the world. For most people, this is what evidence is. Evidence is simply what we can see and hear, feel, touch, and smell. For instance, your desk can serve as evidence that is objectively observable; so can the color of the sky or the number of people in your argumentation class. These are things that can be seen or discovered by anyone looking for them.

Second, beliefs or premises generally accepted as true by the audience can function as evidence (as long as they do not clearly disagree with directly observable evidence). This view of evidence can be problematic for some people because it means that evidence is not always concrete. However, the concept of level of dispute introduced in Chapter 2 can provide a useful means for understanding this view of evidence. Evidence can be used as support because it lies below the level of dispute. If evidence fell above the line, then it would become a focal point for argument instead of support for a claim.

For instance, in Box 5.1, Leah claimed that a study conducted in Great Britain demonstrated that a properly designed tax could save hundreds of people who die prematurely each year in Britain. Her argument is that if a "Twinkie" tax existed, there would be less consumption. With less consumption, there would be less disease. As long as Kyle accepts these statements, they can serve as evidence in the argument. However, if Kyle discovered that the British study was inaccurate or used inappropriate methodologies for collecting its results, then the statements about the research could not be used as evidence. They would become the subject of argument regarding whether taxes can actually improve health.

As long as an argument's recipients find the statements acceptable and reasonable, the statements can function as evidence. If, however, the recipients believe—either correctly or incorrectly—that the statements are flawed or false, then an argument would need further support, and instead of functioning as evidence, the controversial statements become claims. Kyle, therefore, could have challenged the evidence and asked Leah to provide better support from credible sources. Then, Leah would have had to make the claim that the British study was a good study and provide evidence and reasons supporting that claim. But if Kyle does not challenge the statements, they can function as evidence. Provided a statement falls below the level of dispute, it functions as evidence.

Third, conclusions that have been previously established can serve as evidence. In the argument developed in Box 5.1, if Kyle accepts Leah's claims regarding the dangers of fast food, then her argument that we should do something to reduce the consumption of fast food can be based on the accepted claim. Once the first claim that fast food causes illness is accepted, then it can be used as evidence to support the next argument because—once accepted—it falls below the level of dispute. By doing this, Leah is creating an argument chain built on her experience and research, which leads to claims about the dangers of junk food as well as possible approaches for managing the obesity epidemic. At each step, once the claim was proved, she was able to use it as evidence to support the next claim.

A prospective car buyer can provide a useful example of how people might commonly use evidence. There are many publications to help car buyers choose from hundreds of makes and models. One of the most prominent of these is *Consumer Reports*, which tests dozens of automobiles each year. These tests and surveys can provide the prospective buyer with a wealth of evidence: the price of the car and options, predicted reliability, comfort and convenience, ease of service, drivability, and performance. With the information from *Consumer Reports*, John, a prospective car buyer, goes looking for a new car. He drives many makes and models and notes the features in each of the cars he tests. With all of this information, he selects the car he wants and sits down to bargain with the dealer.

The *Consumer Reports* evidence is useful to John in making an argument with the dealer for a better price. He can tell the dealer that he likes the car but the $20,000 price is too high because the consumer magazines claimed that the dealer paid only $12,000 for the car in the first place. He can also claim that the car was not quite as comfortable, reliable, or gas-efficient as he had hoped, and perhaps he should look elsewhere for another car. In each case, John appeals to evidence to support his claims about the car.

Suppose, however, that the dealer rejected John's $12,000 figure and asserted that the particular car with its options cost him a good deal more. John's original evidence would then become a claim because it would be disputed and the subject of argument.

This illustration points to the nature of evidence. Evidence is not always concrete nor is it always certain. In fact, evidence can be placed on a continuum from concrete, objectively observable, certain evidence to evidence that is probably true. For instance, John knew the car existed. He could make an argument for the car's existence and have little difficulty getting people to agree with him. John could use any of the car's physical features as evidence without much fear of contradiction. On the other hand, suppose John argued that *Consumer Reports* conducted a reliability study on the car. Evidence from such a study is not directly experienced by the participants in an argument, and because neither party had a concrete experience with the evidence, there is room for dispute. It could be that no such study was conducted, or that John's interpretation of the study is wrong, or that the study was biased. The results of the study and John's interpretation of them are probable but not certain. Sometimes evidence functions as fact; at other times it functions as opinions or premises accepted by the audience.

TYPES OF EVIDENCE

Evidence can be divided into two broad classifications—fact and opinion as to fact.[14] Facts may be thought of as things people believe to be the case, either because they have experienced them firsthand or because they regard them as the truthfully reported experiences of others. Many times, however, we do not have the expertise to directly observe and interpret events. For example, none of us observed the fall of the Roman Empire. But we have knowledge of the events surrounding the fall as well as historical analyses of why it fell that have been given to us by scholars from multiple disciplines. These people examined the historical records and, based on their expertise, rendered an opinion about the causes and implications of the fall of the empire. This type of evidence, evidence that depends on the expert and credible interpretation of facts, is referred to as opinion as to fact.

Fact Evidence

As we noted in the preceding section of this chapter, one way that people come to believe that something is a fact is through the perception of their senses. Another is through common experience. We can talk about the history of the United States and the Civil War. Although none of us have directly experienced the Civil War, it is part of our common heritage. We do not question it because we accept it as a fact, a historical occurrence well substantiated in many sources. Factual evidence can be further divided into three types that vary in the form in which they occur.

Reports and Descriptions

Reports and descriptions are nonnumerical or narrative accounts of some object or occurrence. They often occur in arguments as examples and illustrations and may make a passing reference to something or describe it at some length. Here are two examples of this type of evidence:

> Tombstone, Arizona, a Wild-West town known for mock gunfights, plank sidewalks, hitching posts, and Western atmosphere, passed a measure requiring horses to wear diapers or dung bags to help keep the streets clean. People thought it looked pretty silly, but it is having an effect on keeping the streets clean.[15]

> Parson had pleaded not guilty after his arrest last August, but told U.S. District Judge Marsha Pechman on Wednesday, "I downloaded the original Blaster worm, modified it and sent it back out on the Internet." Different versions of the Blaster worm, also known as the LovSan virus, crippled computer networks worldwide last summer. Parson's variant launched and distributed a denial-of-service attack against Microsoft Windows Update Web site as well as personal computers. The government estimates his version inundated more than 48,000 computers.[16]

Reports and factual descriptions such as these lend immediacy and vividness to many arguments. They help recipients identify with the characters and relate to the situations described. And they bring home or dramatize situations or conditions that might otherwise seem remote and unimportant.

Statistics

Statistics are facts and figures that have been systematically collected and ordered so as to convey information. Generally, statistics provide a quantitative summary of the characteristics of a population or sample (selectively chosen instances) of a population. Statistics may take the form of averages, numerical comparisons, percentages, totals, or estimates, for example. Following are some examples of statistics:

> "This is a tragic case, but you need to look at the overall risk-benefit of the surgery," said Dr. Harvey Sugerman, president of the American Society for Bariatric Surgery, an educational group for obesity surgeons. Sugerman estimated that more than 11,000 gastric bypasses will be done in the United States this year. Complications strike as many as 1 in 5 patients, and it is believed that for every 200 patients, 1 to 4 will die.[17]

> In the 2000 census, 4 million Americans described themselves as Indian American or Alaska Native. Of these, nearly 70 percent lived in urban areas and 25 percent lived in counties served by health-care agencies that receive federal funding for Indians.[18]

Statistics lend credence to arguments by showing that problems and conditions are not limited to isolated instances but instead affect many people in many different types of situations. Statistics are useful in showing the breadth of a problem, and reports and descriptions are used often to show its depth or human consequence.

Artifacts

Artifacts are physical evidence that helps to prove an argument. An artifact is simply a physical object that a speaker might use to prove a point. For example, exhibits in a trial are artifacts. X-ray films showing the damage caused by smoking are also artifacts. Artifacts may also take the form of demonstrations. Often a trial lawyer will demonstrate how a piece of evidence works in order to make a point. Teachers will have students do an exercise or science experiment to illustrate a concept. These are artifacts that help support claims. Since we are influenced more strongly by what we see and experience than by what we hear or read, artifacts can be a very effective form of factual evidence because they involve the recipients of argument in multidimensional ways.

Opinion as to Fact Evidence

When advocates make arguments that are based on their own firsthand knowledge and understanding of the facts, then they are making arguments grounded in fact-based evidence. However, sometimes the facts surrounding an issue are excessively complex or large, such that an advocate cannot reasonably review all the factual material. In such cases, arguers turn to others who have examined the factual evidence and distilled it into meaningful compilations or opinions.

The second broad type of evidence, then, is opinion as to fact. Opinion evidence is someone's interpretation of the meaning of factual evidence. Whereas facts are based on direct or indirect experience, opinions are judgments about how an event or state of affairs is to be understood, evaluated, or dealt with. In using opinion evidence, the advocate uses the statements of others' judgments and estimations to support his or her own claims. Consider the following opinion statement and the claim it might support:

> Recently, psychologists presented at the annual American Psychological Association convention in Toronto an in-depth examination of the American Presidents. Opinions from more than 100 experts were sought and the raters designed and completed a battery of standardized tests designed to evaluate each of the Presidents. Several of these tests included more than 100 questions. Their goal was to develop a personality profile of each of the past US Presidents and develop a rating system to help guide voters in future elections. The psychologists looked at many dimensions including their: level of neuroses, openness to the experience of others, intelligence, extroversion, agreeableness, among others. Their conclusions included the following.
>
> Ronald Reagan was the least neurotic of all the Presidents. Richard Nixon was the most. Thomas Jefferson was the most intelligent and Theodore Roosevelt was second. Warren G. Harding was the least open to the experience of others and he was the least conscientious. Bill Clinton was the second least conscientious. George Washington was rated as the most conscientious. James Madison and Abraham Lincoln were rated among the most agreeable. Theodore and Franklin Roosevelt were among the most extroverted; Bill Clinton was third.[19]

The factual data compiled by the psychologists are extensive and overwhelming. It would take a single arguer weeks to read through it all and, assuming the advocate had the appropriate education, she or he might be in a position to use it as factual evidence in support of a claim. However, for most people, the quantity of factual evidence and the expertise required to understand it means that arguers often rely on the opinions of others in developing their own arguments. Using this study as opinion evidence, an arguer might be able to make the following argument:

Claim: George Washington was the best president we have had.

> **Evidence:**   Psychologists presented a paper at the American Psychology Association Convention in Toronto that concluded he was the most conscientious of all our presidents, in the upper third in intelligence, open to the opinions of others, and an agreeable president.
>
> **Reasoning:**   These elements, taken together, make Washington the most balanced of all our presidents because he exhibited far above average abilities in each of the areas studied by the psychologists.

Just as arguers can draw on factual evidence in the form of reports, statistics, and artifacts, arguers can also draw on the opinions of others about what reports, statistics, and artifacts mean. In other words, just as there are three types of factual evidence, there are three parallel types of opinion evidence. These include opinion as to reports and descriptions, opinion as to statistics, and opinion as to artifacts.

EVALUATING EVIDENCE

Just as a house or any structure is only as strong as the foundation on which it is built, so is an argument only as strong as the evidence used to support it. As arguers and as recipients of argument, we need to be aware of the quality of evidence so that we can judge others' arguments and select strong evidence to support our own arguments.

The remainder of this section will list and describe criteria to be applied to various types of evidence. Applying criteria such as reliability, expertise, objectivity, consistency, recency, and relevance to our own and others' evidence supplies us with a system for judging the quality of support provided for claims. The result can only be to make us better critics and users of argument.

Reliability

One question many audiences ask about a source is whether or not the source is reliable. *A reliable source is one that has proven to be correct many times in the past.* An excellent example of a reliable source is cited by Robert P. Newman and Dale R. Newman in their book on evidence:

> [Senator J. William] Fulbright's overall record of prophecy is pretty good. He warned President Truman that unless atomic energy were put under international control, there would be a monstrous arms race and proliferation. . . . He told Secretary [of State John Foster] Dulles that arms shipments to India and Pakistan would lead to war between the two. He . . . warned President Kennedy the Bay of Pigs would be a fiasco.[20]

Given Senator Fulbright's accuracy record for predictions, political leaders would have done well to listen to his opinions. People naturally trust sources and other people who have been proven right in the past. Thus we are likely to put our confidence in a Wall Street newsletter that accurately predicts stock market fluctuations or in *Consumer Reports*, whose product assessments have repeatedly proven to be correct.

Expertise

Studies on factors affecting whether a source is believed have indicated that the most important factor is the recipients' perception of the source's competence.[21] *Expertise is the possession of a background of knowledge and information relevant to the subject matter under discussion.* Generally, we determine whether or not someone is an expert in a subject area by examining or considering the nature and extent of his or her experience with the topic. Education and formal training in a subject are one index as to whether a person is qualified. Experience may be gained in other ways, however. Any given senator would not necessarily be considered an expert on the conduct of Pentagon business, whereas a senator who had chaired the Senate Armed Services Committee for a number of terms would probably be considered an expert on the status of American armed forces. Any person who has published favorably reviewed books or articles on a subject is generally accepted as an expert on that subject. Furthermore, people who hold elective offices in professional organizations are highly regarded because it is assumed that they are respected by their peers.

However, professors, elected officials, and other people who tend to be viewed as credible sources are not necessarily experts on all issues. Expertise in one area does not extend to areas outside the individual's particular area of knowledge. A professor of communication who has written extensively on Internet campaign strategies has the expertise to comment on the Web-based campaign strategies of candidates in an election, but probably does not have the expertise to assess the potential economic benefits of each candidate's tax plan. In the case of the latter, an expert in economics would likely be a better source.

Because of the importance of expertise in establishing the acceptability of evidence with most audiences, it is vital for arguers to fully cite their source's qualifications and experience with the topic. Instead of saying "John Smith concluded that performance-enhancing drugs may cause health risks such as heart disease and high blood pressure," an advocate should say "Dr. John Smith, a professor of sports medicine at the University of Oregon, reported in the May 2003 issue of the *New England Journal of Medicine* after seven years of investigation that . . ." Unless the source's qualifications and experience with the topic are fully reported to recipients, they will have no way of making any judgment about the source's expertise. An exception lies with sources whose qualifications are known by or are generally accepted by the audience. If it is generally known and accepted that the president holds certain qualifications and expertise in particular aspects of U.S. policy, you need not state her or his qualifications explicitly. That said, because you can never be sure of the audience's knowledge of certain sources, it is better to fully cite your source's qualifications, even if the audience knows them, than to risk your audience not knowing or accepting your source as credible. Emphasizing the source's credentials can enhance the argument's persuasiveness by showing that evidence is taken from someone whose knowledge and expertise can be trusted.

Objectivity

Recipients feel confident in trusting sources they believe are objective about the topic of the argument. *Objectivity refers to a source's tendency to hold a fair and undistorted view on a question or an issue.* An objective source does not have views strongly colored by a personal emotional investment in one ideological viewpoint on the topic. We can hardly expect a member of the People for the Ethical Treatment of Animals (PETA) to provide a well-balanced discussion of the pros and cons of animal testing in the medical field. Nor can we expect a representative from the Focus on the Family (a conservative organization devoted to preserving family values) to provide a complete account of the state of family values in the United States. In both of these cases, the sources would not be considered objective because they hold a clear set of views on those issues.

We should not expect all sources to be completely impartial in their analyses of issues. After all, if they did not have a viewpoint to argue, they would not be making a claim of supporting a point of view. We should, however, expect sources to be unbiased. *A bias is an unreasoned distortion of judgment or a prejudice on a topic.* A biased source usually has a personal stake in the outcome of an argument and is thus unlikely to provide a fair account of differing points of view, as the examples of PETA and Focus on the Family demonstrate. This is not to suggest that either PETA or Focus on the Family cannot be used for source material in an argument. Rather, an advocate should look for alternative points of view that can help balance or counter any accusation of bias. If an arguer fails to balance the potential bias of source material, the objectivity of the evidence could be called into question and thereby the evidence would fall above the level of dispute.

Bias can also overwhelm or influence reasoning, choice of supporting material, or design of statistical measures to ensure a certain outcome. For example, if PETA decided to run a poll of public opinion about animal rights, it is possible that the sample would be drawn from those visiting the PETA Web site instead of a random sample and that the questions might be designed to increase the likelihood of answers that support PETA's cause. Biased sources are not objective. Arguers who draw from such sources are likely to discover that their audiences are aware of the biases of such groups and, as such, are suspicious of information taken from them. Nonobjective sources can weaken your argument and hurt your credibility as a speaker. You should always strive to find objective, nonbiased sources for your arguments.

Consistency

Recipients of an argument expect evidence used to be consistent with other information and with itself. Consistency with other information is called external consistency. *External consistency is the agreement of evidence with sources of information other than the source being used.* A piece of evidence that runs counter to what is already believed or known about a topic is not necessarily wrong, but the arguer using it has the burden of proving that the evidence is correct and can be reconciled with other seemingly incompatible facts the audience already believes or accepts. After all, the mainstream of opinion, or even of what is thought to be "knowledge," is not always correct. For example, Galileo argued that the Earth revolved around the sun at a time when most people believed the sun revolved around the Earth. Columbus believed that one could reach Asia by sailing west at a time when most people thought someone attempting such a voyage would fall off the edge of the Earth. However, when evidence fails to agree with other credible facts and sources, it can be detrimental to acceptance of an argument.

Advocates can increase the acceptability and believability of their arguments by using a sufficient amount of evidence from different sources to show that their support is externally consistent. Recipients of arguments can assure themselves that evidence is externally consistent by comparing it with facts they already know or information to which they have access.

Evidence should also be internally consistent. *Internal consistency is the absence of self-contradiction within the information provided by a source.* When political leaders and other public figures contradict themselves, the media and the public take great delight in pointing it out. For instance, in a student presentation about a presidential election, Betty argued that one of the candidates was inconsistent in his policies. She noted that the candidate, as a senator, voted against increased funding for national security in 2000, but that same candidate called for increased national security spending in his 2004 campaign. Betty claimed that this and other similar examples of internal inconsistency were reasons that the candidate would make a poor president.

Few things are more damaging to an arguer's credibility than the appearance of inconsistency or self-contradictions in statements. Although it is cliché to charge politicians with this offense, consistent internal contradictions or broken promises make people wary of politicians. When arguers contradict themselves, they diminish the level of trust and credibility they have with their audiences.

Keep in mind that the appearance of internal inconsistency may reveal that there is more to the story than what is presented. Recall Betty's argument about the inconsistency of a presidential candidate. Betty's classmate Amanda responded to this argument in Betty's presentation by stating that the reason for the inconsistency was that times have changed between 2000 and the time of the election. Amanda argued that terrorist attacks on the country in 2001 may have changed the candidate's mind on an issue. This brings up an important point with regard to internal consistency. People can change their minds over time as new evidence is discovered and as they have new experiences. It is also possible that people change their minds by being persuaded by other arguers.

Recency

As a general rule, arguers should be aware of whether their evidence is sufficiently current on the topic of their argument. The extent to which evidence must be recent varies with the topic of discussion. Advocates examining Internet technologies, cancer research, or international terrorism should rely on the most recent evidence available because our knowledge about such topics changes frequently, perhaps daily. Evidence about the world, objects, people, or anything else that changes needs to be current.

Other topics may be less affected by the comparative recency of evidence. Evidence relating to human rights or capital punishment, for example, may be of more enduring usefulness because conditions and values relating to these topics are less subject to change. Consequently, speakers appealing to values such as "life, liberty, and the pursuit of happiness" are arguing from safe ground because such values are an enduring part of American political life regardless of when the appeal was made.

Relevance

It is not uncommon for an arguer to present something that sounds like evidence and to connect it with a given claim, when in fact, the evidence is unrelated to the claim as made. *Relevance refers to whether the evidence as stated is topically and sufficiently related to the claim as made.* Consider the following example of an ad for pain-relief medication:

Evidence: Nine out of ten doctors recommend aspirin for headaches.

Claim: Aspirin is a powerful all-purpose medication.

A close examination of these two statements quickly reveals that the claim goes well beyond what is warranted by the evidence. First, the doctors stipulated a specific purpose for aspirin use and did not say it was "all-purpose." Second, the doctors made no statement about the aspirin's potency. So the evidence as stated does not relate to the claim as made.

One might think that irrelevant or unrelated evidence would be obvious, but often it isn't. The evidence is frequently somewhat related but does not directly support the claim because of the way it is worded or qualified. To detect this problem, we should be aware of the way the language and focus of the claim relate to the language and focus of the evidence. The following excerpt from a student's paper will illustrate how irrelevant evidence might appear to support a claim when, in fact, it does not.

> A 1982 Safe Schools study showed that 36% of all secondary schools paddle children in a typical month. For junior high schools the figure jumps to 61%. Children all across the United States are being legally beaten under our laws.

The arguer uses a very connotative term—"beaten"—in her claim. Is this term, normally associated with child abuse, which is illegal, to be equated with paddling? Furthermore, do the arguer's statistics show that this is happening "all across the country"? The answer to both of these questions is, probably not. The study makes no mention of geographical location, and punishment deemed legal by the courts should not be equated with abuse. Therefore, the claim departs from and exaggerates the evidence given to support it.

Access

When an arguer cites opinion as to fact about a situation or event, recipients should expect the source of that opinion to have been in a position to observe directly the matter in question. *Access depends on whether someone offering an opinion is or has been in a position to observe firsthand the matter being disputed.* A person who has not directly experienced something must rely on reports or summaries provided by others or on impressions based on limited information. But anytime we hear or read something secondhand, certain features and aspects are filtered out by the perspective and viewpoint of the person who reports it to us. The features identified and reported may not at all be the ones we would notice if we had an opportunity to observe the situation ourselves firsthand. The further we move from the original situation as directly observed by eyewitnesses, the greater the possibility for misinterpretation or error.

Consider the following example about evidence of war crimes in the Congo:

> While the 65-page U.N. Report to the Security Council, released Monday, does not mention the investigation, it provides details of many massacres and other abuses

committed during attacks on villages in Ituri and information about political killings, rapes, and the use of children by all armed groups. The report was prepared by human rights and child welfare experts in the U.N.'s peacekeeping mission in the Congo and is based on more than 1600 interviews.[22]

In this example, the report was based on the experts who were involved in the peace-keeping mission and personally interviewed individuals involved in the mission. Because of direct observation of the conditions in the Congo during the peacekeeping mission, their testimony had greater credibility than that of someone who had heard about it second- or thirdhand. In addition, the interviewees also have credibility because they are speaking to events that they directly observed.

EVALUATING STATISTICAL EVIDENCE

One should keep in mind the adage "Figures lie and liars figure." All of the standards we have just proposed for fact and opinion evidence apply equally well to statistics. Statistics are the end result of a process subject to human bias and human error. Questions on a survey can be loaded; the people surveyed can be subjectively chosen; comparisons may be made of noncomparable units; and reports of findings can be slanted. Actually, statistics are often no more reliable than other forms of evidence, yet people often think statistics are true. As Newman and Newman laconically observed:

> If you would not believe a man who testifies that he has seen a flying saucer, do not believe him when he claims to have seen fourteen flying saucers each measuring twenty-two feet in diameter and weighing eleven tons.[23]

Gathering, using, and assessing statistics nevertheless present problems and challenges different than in other forms of evidence. This section will alert you to difficulties that frequently arise when arguers use statistics to support their claims. Advocates should take care to avoid these pitfalls in conducting research. Recipients should scrutinize the statistics they hear and read and be alert to some of these practices and mistakes.

Pseudostatistics

Sometimes we hear statistics applied to phenomena and situations in which it is difficult if not impossible to imagine how the statistics could have been compiled using good statistical methods. Here are three examples:

> According to *Esquire* magazine, February, 1964, Judy Garland sang "Over the Rainbow" 1,476 times.
>
> Seven out of every ten Americans cheat on their income taxes.
>
> *Mega Foods* has developed a revolutionary line of *Food* Vitamins and *Food* Minerals that are up to sixteen times more effective than the so-called "natural" vitamins and we can prove that with scientific research.

Although the first case appears innocent enough, a closer look invites criticism. Specifically, how does anyone know precisely how many times Garland sang "Over the Rainbow"? Did someone count every time the song was sung in rehearsal, on stage, and in the shower? It is unreasonable to assume that this statistic could be accurate because there is almost no way it could have been collected. Similarly, the second piece of evidence would be difficult to arrive at reasonably. In order to collect the figure seven out of ten, what would a researcher have to do? Ask a group of people which one of them cheats? How would each of the respondents interpret what is meant by "cheat"? Given people's concern about tax audits, how many would honestly say they cheat? And how would "scientific research" determine that a certain brand of vitamins and food supplements is precisely sixteen times more effective than the natural alternative? Would respondents have to feel sixteen times better? Would they need to be sixteen times more resistant to disease? Was the study based on the self-reports of people taking the vitamins and supplements, or on some other measure? We don't know.

Comparing Noncomparable Units

In essence, this practice, which emerges most frequently when longitudinal trends are reported, involves comparing dissimilar items while assuming they are the same. For example, due to inflation, the value of the dollar has declined. The 2008 dollar does not have the same value that the 1971 dollar did. This is why salary comparisons and commodity prices are always "corrected for inflation" when across-time comparisons are made. A similar problem arises when advocates use the federal government's crime statistics. The definition of what constitutes a felony or a misdemeanor varies from one time or location to another. When new types of crimes are included in the class of felonies, the felony rates appear to increase simply because the method of classification has changed.

Unrepresentative Samples

A sample is a population or group of people or objects that researchers survey when a study is conducted. Most researchers do not have the time, money, or ability to survey or study every individual in a given state or the country. Consequently, researchers must draw upon a group or sample of people small enough to work with. Conclusions about the sample are then generalized to a broader group. One example is the studies of college students that conclude that seventy percent will graduate after four years and find employment in their chosen field. This statistic was arrived at by surveying a group of students and then generalizing the conclusions to all other students. Certain questions need to be answered before such evidence should be used or accepted. Was the sample representative? Was the sample too small? Was the sample randomly selected?

A representative sample is one that possesses all the characteristics of the larger group from which it is drawn. For example, if the general population of college students on which a study is done is 35 percent college freshmen, 20 percent college sophomores, 10 percent juniors, and 35 percent seniors, then a representative sample is one made up of approximately the same proportion of individuals. In this sense, a representative sample is a group drawn from a larger group that shares most of the larger group's characteristics. As another example, one survey on Web use gathered its data from Internet users who were promised a chance at prizes for answering the survey questions.[24] Critics of the survey argued that this was not a representative sample of Web users but only those who were motivated to compete for prizes. More recently, other surveys of Internet use have begun with random telephone samples of the U.S. population.[25] Yet these surveys exclude people on the national Do Not Call list.

Poor Methodology

Sound methods for gathering statistical information should guard against redundancy and bias when responses are counted. For example, surveys that count some of the respondents twice or those that count only people who are highly motivated to respond are using poor statistical methods.

One example is the compiling of casualty statistics during the Vietnam War. Officers in the various services frequently sought totals of the number of enemy dead after battles. Various platoons were dispersed to conduct body counts, but there was no way to ensure that one platoon would not duplicate another's count. Furthermore, it was difficult to distinguish civilians from soldiers because many Vietnamese soldiers did not wear uniforms. Combat conditions also made counts very difficult to conduct. Nevertheless, casualty totals, however inaccurate, were reported.[26]

PRESENTING EVIDENCE

When we make a decision on the basis of someone else's argument, we generally have certain expectations about the evidence presented to us. We hope it has been fully reported, is of the best possible quality, and is not misrepresented or intentionally distorted. Information that is second rate or distorted does not provide reliable grounds for decision making. Arguers and recipients of argument should be aware of the ethical obligation to cite accurately the sources used to support arguments. There are many ways to interpret and communicate evidence so as to mislead recipients about its nature or quality, and not all involve deliberate falsification. Everyone would agree that adding to or altering a source's words is unethical, but often selectively omitting words or sentences is also ethically questionable.

In Chapter 1, we discussed the role of argument spheres and argument fields. Determining how to use evidence and what rules or standards apply to that evidence is largely contingent on these two variables. The arguments developed in Box 5.1 were between two friends exploring issues related to "fat" taxes. The arguments occurred in a personal sphere where there was an ongoing relationships and knowledge of the other. If, however, those arguments appeared in a technical sphere—a courtroom or legislative assembly—the evidence presented would have been inadequate because it would not have met the minimum field-specific standards for technical arguments in those arenas. And, if the arguments were presented to a public sphere, the audience would have expected much more detailed evidence and source citation. The standards for evaluating arguments depend on their contexts.

The overarching question is, "Does the manner in which an arguer uses evidence give recipients an accurate and faithful picture of the nature and intent of the source?" As discussed in Chapter 3, the central ethical issue is whether or not the recipients had a reasonable and significant choice. To clarify the implications of these issues, we will consider some of the practices to be avoided.

Omitting Words

Omitting words to make the evidence more favorable to the arguer's claim is unethical. Quotations from sources should be faithful to the context from which they are taken. If the citer of the source omits qualifying words or phrases or otherwise alters the meaning of the original, the practice is unethical. It is not difficult to completely reverse the meaning of a quotation by leaving part of it out. For example, an arguer once claimed that:

> For a man who is supposed to be a champion of democracy, it is odd that Lincoln said: "You can fool all of the people some of the time." This doesn't show much faith in the judgment of the people.

While this claim uses Lincoln's words, its interpretation was flawed because it does not include the remainder of Lincoln's statement, which was:

> You can fool some of the people all the time and all the people some of the time, but you can't fool all the people all the time.

Omitting statements from quotations to make them support one's point is easy to do, but it is wrong because it misleads and deceives the audience.

Identifying Secondary Sources

When arguers fail to distinguish between primary and secondary sources, they can potentially deceive the recipients. *A primary source is the original source of the evidence.* This means that *the primary source is the source in which the evidence first appeared.* Eyewitness accounts, original documents (letters, diaries, personal notebooks), and transcripts of speeches as originally delivered are examples of primary sources. Primary sources provide the most immediate possible account of what was said by the source at the moment it was uttered.

Secondary sources are those that compile, analyze, or summarize primary sources. Secondary sources often provide an interpretation or a restatement of what was originally said. For example, Thomas Jefferson's own correspondence about events leading to the Declaration of Independence is a primary source; an account of the Revolutionary War period in a history book is a secondary source. An original editorial is a primary source; a reprinting or summary of that editorial is a secondary source.

Arguers should use primary sources whenever possible because they are authentic and there is less possibility for error when they are used. When original or primary evidence is unavailable, arguers may use secondary sources, but they should always report that the information was cited in a secondary source and give credit to the secondary source. Information in a secondary source may have been shortened, changed, or edited. For example, *Reader's Digest* often changes and alters the articles it republishes. It is therefore important for recipients to know that the arguer is not citing the original source.

Qualifying Sources

Advocates should give all relevant information about the source from which the evidence was taken. When sources are cited, arguers should provide complete information about where the evidence was found, and the qualifications of the sources should be given. This includes the name of the author (if available), his or her qualifications or expertise, the date the statement was made, and the publication information. The arguer should provide enough information so that recipients could track down and find the information if they wanted. Fully disclosing source information makes the argument appear more credible and the arguer more trustworthy.

It is important to note that there are differences between oral and written citations. In written arguments, arguers follow reference style guides that provide rules for how to cite sources in essays, term papers, or research projects. Most style guides, such as the Modern Language Association (MLA) or the American Psychological Association (APA) manuals or the *Chicago Manual of Style*, provide guidelines for citing sources in the text of an essay and in a full bibliography at the end of the paper. Generally, arguers should include the qualifications or expertise of a source either in the text of the paper or in the notes attached to the essay. For example, a written source citation should look something like this:

> Dr. James Brilhart, professor of anthropology at the University of California at Berkeley, argued, "there is no such thing as a primitive language" ("Primitive Languages," *Time*, November 26, 1980, p. 25).

A full source citation, in this case including the article title, the magazine in which the article was published, and the full date, should be given in a way that follows the rules of the style guide used.

In the case of oral arguments, recipients generally will not have access to written versions of the full source citations. It is important, therefore, that arguers provide enough of the citation information orally so that the recipients have the opportunity to locate the material if they wish. For example, an oral presentation might cite the source as follows:

> Dr. James Brilhart, professor of anthropology at the University of California at Berkeley, argued in the November 26, 1980, issue of *Time* that "there is no such thing as a primitive language."

Alluding to one's sources vaguely ("according to several articles that have appeared recently") is unacceptable. Not openly dating the information is deceptive. What if an arguer decided to leave out the date in the preceding statement about primitive language? A good deal of research has been done on language behavior recently, and, if the recipients thought the comment was current, they would be deceived.

Ethical requirements for using evidence, then, include citing the words of the author so that the citation conforms to his or her intentions and to the context; distinguishing between primary and secondary sources; and providing recipients with complete information about the source's qualifications and where the evidence was found. Omission or addition of words or information to make the evidence appear more favorable to one's claim is unacceptable.

Plagiarism

Engaging in plagiarism not only undermines an arguer's credibility but it is an unethical practice that undermines academic and personal integrity. *Plagiarism is the use of another person's ideas or words without proper attribution.* Different fields, as discussed in Chapter 1, apply different standards for what constitutes plagiarism. For instance, in a corporate environment, it is not uncommon to have project proposals drafted that draw on the contributions of many people who may or may not be cited. Personal arguments among friends may not require complete source citations. However, most technical and public sphere arguments rely on credible and accurate attributions of source material. It is important for an advocate to be clear about the sphere and field rules that apply to their arguments.

In the academic field, plagiarism can take several forms, including:

- Failure to include or have available an accurate source citation sufficient to allow recipients to find the information.
- Using another person's ideas without citation.
- Using another person's words without citation.
- Borrowing part or all of another's work without proper citation.
- Using a paper-writing service.[27]

Knowingly submitting work that is plagiarized is unethical. To avoid plagiarism, it is important that arguers cite sources and take steps to avoid it. These steps include:

- When researching, take careful notes that include quotation marks when you use someone else's words and complete citation information.
- When writing or presenting a speech, give citation information every time you use someone else's words or ideas.
- When in doubt, cite your source.

As we have discussed, using evidence from well-qualified sources to support your arguments makes them stronger. Plagiarism is not only unethical, but failure to cite your sources weakens your own credibility.

SUMMARY

It is vital to be aware of the absence or misuse of evidence in arguments we hear and read and to avoid these problems in the arguments we make. As defined in Chapter 1, evidence includes objectively observable facts and conditions, generally accepted beliefs or premises, and previously established conclusions. The purpose of this chapter was to discuss the nature and types of evidence and to provide guidelines for using evidence.

Evidence functions as such because it is accepted by recipients and can be used to support other statements. If participants in an argument dispute a statement, it cannot function as evidence because it is not agreed on. Generally, evidence falls into two broad classifications—fact and opinion as to fact.

Factual evidence comes from our observations and experience. It includes reports and descriptions of events or phenomena, statistics, and artifacts that are actual objects used to support an argument. Factual evidence is expected to mirror physical reality.

Opinion evidence is someone's interpretation of the meaning of factual evidence. When an arguer uses opinion evidence, he or she uses the statement of someone else to support a claim. Opinion evidence from experts is useful when an arguer does not have a great deal of personal experience with the subject of the argument.

We should be aware of the quality of evidence so that we can judge the quality of support for our own and others' arguments. Evidence should come from reliable sources who have been proven correct many times in the past. Sources for evidence should have expertise in the subject matter of the argument, and it is important that audiences be informed of sources' qualifications when evidence is given. Sources should be objective, offering an undistorted and fair view of the question or issue. Evidence should be consistent, both with itself and with evidence from other sources. It should also be recent, particularly on topics in which conditions change over time. Evidence offered to support a claim should be directly relevant to the claim as stated, rather than tangential or irrelevant. People who testify about a situation should have had access to it and an opportunity to observe it firsthand. Otherwise, the evidence is hearsay and less reliable. Finally, arguers who cite the statements of others should be accurate. They should not violate the context or intended meaning behind a quotation by omitting crucial words, making secondary sources seem to be primary, or omitting information about the source's qualifications or where the information was found.

Like other forms of evidence, statistics are often subject to bias and human error as well as errors by the people who use them. There are certain problems unique to the discovery and use of evidence, however. First, we should be aware of pseudostatistics, those that are applied to phenomena and situations in which it is difficult to imagine how they could have been compiled using good statistical methods. Second, we should be cautious about comparing noncomparable units that seem to be of the same class but that are actually different. Third, we should use a representative sample, one that includes all the important characteristics of the group from which it was drawn.

GLOSSARY

Access (p. 136) depends on whether someone offering an opinion is or has been in a position to observe firsthand the matter being disputed.

Artifacts (p. 130) are physical evidence that helps to prove an argument. An artifact is simply a physical object that a speaker might use to prove a point.

Bias (p. 134) is an unreasoned distortion of judgment or a prejudice on a topic.

Expertise (p. 133) is the possession of a background of knowledge and information relevant to the subject matter under discussion.

External consistency (p. 134) is the agreement of evidence with sources of information other than the source being used.

Internal consistency (p. 135) is the absence of self-contradiction within the information provided by a source.

Objectivity (p. 133-134) refers to a source's tendency to hold a fair and undistorted view on a question or an issue.

Plagiarism (p. 142) is the use of another person's ideas or words without proper attribution.

Primary source (p. 140) is the original source of the evidence. The primary source is the source in which the evidence first appeared.

Relevance (p. 136) refers to whether the evidence as stated is topically and sufficiently related to the claim as made.

Reliable source (p. 132) is one that has proven to be correct many times in the past.

Reports and descriptions (p. 130) are nonnumerical or narrative accounts of some object or occurrence.

Representative sample (p. 138) is one that possesses all the characteristics of the larger group from which it is drawn.

Sample (p. 138) is a population or group of people or objects that researchers survey when a study is conducted.

Secondary sources (p. 140) are those that compile, analyze, or summarize primary sources.

Statistics (p. 130) are facts and figures that have been systematically collected and ordered so as to convey information.

EXERCISES

Exercise 1 The following passages help illustrate correct and incorrect uses of evidence. For each passage, try to identify the primary weaknesses by applying the following criteria as discussed in this chapter.

Tests of Evidence. Apply each of the following tests to the passages:

Reliability	Evidence should be drawn from sources that have proven to be correct many times in the past.
Expertise	Evidence should be drawn from sources having a background of knowledge in relevant information.
Objectivity	Evidence should be taken from sources who hold a fair and undistorted view on a question or issue.
Consistency	Evidence should agree with other sources and should be consistent with itself.
Recency	Evidence should be based on the most current information available.
Relevance	The facts and evidence presented should be relevant to the claim that is made.
Access	Evidence should be drawn from sources who have observed firsthand the matter being disputed.

Now, here is the evidence to be evaluated.

∗1. Mr. Herbert Kause convincingly argued last month that pregnant women should restrict their intake of caffeine. According to studies he conducted over the past six years, he has found strong evidence that supports the conclusion that caffeine is dangerous to unborn children.

2. Recently, at the University of Wisconsin, a study was conducted on listening and study patterns of freshmen students in a Speech 101 course. This study found that students in this course exhibited a lack of concentration in their studies and note-taking. Therefore, we can conclude that college students have poor study skills.

3. In a special advertisement on Zenith Data Systems, Enrico Pesatori, Zenith Data Systems president and chief executive officer, said, "We have taken many major steps over the past 18 months to respond to our customers' needs for innovative, aggressively priced products, and to adapt to the upheaval in the PC industry. The product lines we have developed will clearly distinguish Zenith Data Systems in the marketplace."

4. But, in actuality, almost 25,000 people are involved in fatal alcohol-related accidents per year. Of these 25,000 people, over 25 percent are under the age of 21. This means we are losing over 6,000 young people per year because of alcohol. There are several reasons a nationwide drinking age should be enforced. Statistics show that raising the age would save over 750 young lives per year nationwide.

∗5. We should reinstitute the military draft in this country. After all, we should recall John F. Kennedy's famous words, "Ask not what your country can do for you, ask what you can do for your country." Our country is currently in a military force crisis, and a military draft is something we can do for our country.

6. As the National Rifle Association has argued, if handguns were made illegal, then only those people who abide by the law would be barred from obtaining handguns. The criminals and the smugglers and racketeers would still have them.

7. A nationwide survey of college freshmen by Alexander W. Astin in 1991 revealed that 85.5 percent of those polled agreed that the government is not doing enough to control pollution. Water and air pollution controls should definitely be increased.

8. According to the Environmental Policy Institute and the Health and Energy Institute, "The Food and Drug Administration allowed irradiation of canned bacon in 1963 based on Army research. Five years later the FDA rescinded the approval, saying that the tests had been improperly structured and sloppily conducted."

9. A cosmetics company conducted a study of prospective customers for a new skin lotion. They sent 10,000 questionnaires to these customers, asking them to compare the new product with a variety of other products. Ninety percent of those responding favored the new skin lotion; therefore, the cosmetics company should proceed with production of the new lotion.

∗10. Dr. Harvey Brenner concluded a study of unemployment in 1975. He argued that for each 1 percent increase in the unemployment rate, the death rate increases by 36,667 lives. Therefore, the federal government should take immediate action to decrease the levels of unemployment in this country.

11. People like high-calorie, high-fat foods that have no nutritional value. Some fast-food hamburgers have more than 1,000 calories. That's ridiculous. This kind of eating leads to obesity and contributes to a worldwide epidemic. Children model our behavior, and they learn from their parents. Not only are we increasing our risk of disease, but we are passing it down the generations.

12. Cheating in school has reached epidemic proportions. In a study conducted at a large eastern university, researchers discovered that 88.3 percent of the students cheated at some point in their academic careers.

13. In an advertisement signed by Bill Gates, chairman of Microsoft Corporation, and his CEO, Steve Ballmer, the two men early in the year 2000 predicted that appellate courts considering a court order to break up their company "will reaffirm the well-established legal precedent that antitrust law should encourage—not discourage—firms to improve their products rapidly to meet customer needs." Therefore, the antitrust decision against Microsoft should be overturned.

14. On March 3, 2000, the National Rifle Association's Institute for Legislative Action criticized President Bill Clinton's claim that "13 children are killed by guns every day." The NRA pointed out that to reach the "13 children" figure, President Clinton and antigun groups counted anyone under the age of twenty as a child. Since there are relatively few handgun deaths among children under fourteen but a much greater number among young adults age fifteen to nineteen, adding both groups together increases the number of deaths among "children" by 569 percent.

15. The *Cecil Textbook of Medicine* reported in its fifth edition on page 1,031 that "in a series of patients studied post-mortem more than 90 percent complained of shortness of breath."—From the *Journal of Irreproducible Results*, 40(2), (1995): 15.

Exercise 2 Find an editorial in a local newspaper or magazine and analyze the evidence in it. When you are done, you should be able to answer the following:

1. What types of evidence did you discover?
2. What were the strengths and weaknesses of the evidence?

Exercise 3 Below are a number of pieces of information that could be relevant as evidence for certain claims in argumentative speeches or essays. To complete this exercise, divide the class into groups of three or four. Within each group, each individual should decide which *types* of resources (e.g., the Internet, books, periodicals, newspapers, etc.) should be examined for the answers to these questions and then inform the other group members of where she or he plans to look. When everyone has had an opportunity to locate the information in question, reconvene your group. Then consider the following questions:

1. Did everyone find the same answer to the question? What was it?
2. If different sources differed in the answer, how can the discrepancy be resolved?
3. How long did it take to find the answers to the questions in the various sources available? (That is, which sources were the easiest to use and the most efficient?)
4. How credible and in-depth is the information provided in the various sources?
5. Based on your experience, develop a "position statement" to share with the class about your group's views on the best strategies and venues for conducting research to locate evidence.

Now here are the questions to answer:

1. What are the demographics (age, income, profession, etc.) of Internet users?
2. What has happened to the hole in the ozone layer?

3. What major instances of terrorism have occurred against U.S. citizens (at home or abroad) during the past twelve months?

4. What is the most effective form of birth control currently available?

5. What bills related to gun control are currently being considered by the U.S. Congress?

6. What are said to be the major causes of domestic violence (spousal and child abuse) in the United States?

7. What are the most promising treatments presently available for AIDS?

8. What are the gun-control laws in four nations, not including the United States?

9. How promising is solar power as a major energy resource?

10. What is the current status of the deforestation of rain forests? Who benefits from clearing the forests?

Exercise 4. Plagiarism is a serious issue on college and university campuses, especially in an era when information is easily accessible over the Internet. This exercise asks you to analyze plagiarism policies in the following ways:

1. What is the policy at your home institution? How is it organized? What are the sanctions?

2. Find the plagiarism policies of two other colleges or universities. How are they similar? How are they different?

3. If you found differences, why do you think they exist?

Exercise 5. Read the following persuasive appeal by the National Highway Transportation Safety Administration. The evidence presented in this document provides support for banning mobile telephone use in vehicles. Read the argument and do the following:

1. Identify the types of evidence used.

2. Assess the quality of the evidence.

USING A CELL PHONE WHILE DRIVING IS DANGEROUS

A growing body of research suggests that using a cell phone while driving is a serious safety problem—even if a driver's hands are on the steering wheel. . . .

With 2,600 highway deaths and 330,000 injuries per year linked to cell phone use, according to a recent Harvard University study, the search for ways to mitigate distracted driving is becoming urgent. . . .

Automakers are loading up vehicles with ever-more sophisticated technologies—such as screen-based navigation systems, dashboard entertainment consoles, and MP3 players—challenging engineers with how to continue the business boom without further compromising safety.

Automakers have made a huge bet that hands-free technology would be the answer. Services such as OnStar from General Motors Corp. let customers make calls over a voice-activated in-car cell phone, talk to an operator to get directions, or even consult with a concierge for shopping or restaurant recommendations. . . .

But the latest research shows people talking on cell phones are distracted even if their hands remain on the steering wheel. The National Highway Traffic Safety Administration is currently conducting in-depth research at its National Advanced

Driving Simulator, run jointly with the University of Iowa. Preliminary research released last month indicates clear trade-offs with hands-free technology. Even though their hands remained on the wheel, study subjects using voice-activated systems take longer to dial—a potentially dangerous distraction. . . .

"The distraction risks associated with cell phone use do not diminish with hands-free devices," said Rae Tyson, spokesman for NHTSA.

To the extent that hands-free technology gives drivers a false sense of security and prods them to engage in longer phone conversations, it may even exacerbate the safety problem, Tyson said. . . .

Despite the safety concerns, customers' desire to stay connected to the outside world is only expected to increase. With some 163 million cell phone subscribers in the United States, NHTSA estimates that 3 percent of U.S. drivers are talking on cell phones at any given time.

A 2003 study by the Harvard Center for Risk Analysis suggested a very real safety problem exists when drivers are paired with cell phones.

The study found an estimated 2,600 deaths a year could be linked to cell phone use. Cell phone use also is connected to approximately 330,000 moderate to critical injuries annually and 1.5 million instances of property damage a year, the study found.

But the Harvard researchers wanted to quantify the potential cost, measured in lost productivity, of banning cell phone use in cars. They concluded that taking cell phones away from drivers would cost $43 billion a year in lost economic activity—about the same economic value of the lost lives and injuries.

"It's like cars themselves," said Joshua Cohen, co-author of the study. "Cars kill 40,000 people a year. That translates into a one in a 100 chance that a child born today will eventually die in a car crash. Yet we still have cars. Why? Because they are very useful. . . ."

Adapted from National Highway Transportation Safety Administration, "An Investigation of the Safety Implications of Wireless Communications in Vehicles," November 1997, www.nhtsa.dot.gov/people/injury/research/wireless (accessed December 1, 2004 and American Automobile Association Web site, "Drive Safer, Talk Later: The AAA *Guide* to Cell Phones and Driving," www.aaawa.com/traffic_safety/ cell_phones.html (accessed December 14, 2004).

NOTES

1. Russel R. Windes and Arthur Hastings, *Argumentation and Advocacy* (New York: Random House, 1965), 95.

2. For an account of Nazi propaganda efforts, see Randall L. Bytwerk, *Julius Streicher* (New York: Stein & Day, 1983).

3. John C. Reinard, "The Empirical Study of the Persuasive Effects of Evidence: The Status after Fifty Years of Research." *Human Organization Research*, 15 (1988): 3–59; E. James Baesler and Judee K. Burgoon, "The Temporal Effects of Story and Statistical Evidence on Belief Change," *Communication Research* 21 (1994): 582–602.

4. Reinard, 41–42.

5. A very good discussion of these issues can be found in Paul Fieldhouse, "Taxing Food," Current Issues: The Inside Story, http://politiquespubliques.inspq.qc.ca/fichier.php/146/DCTaxingFood.pdf (accessed May 10, 2008).

6. World Health Organization, "Global Strategy on Diet, Physical Activity, and Health," http://www.who.int/dietphysicalactivity/publications/facts/obesity/en/ (accessed May 6, 2008) and World Health Organization, "Obesity and Overweight," http://www.who.int/mediacentre/factsheets/fs311/en/index.html (access on May 9, 2008).

7. Lauren Streib, "World's Fattest Countries," *Forbes*, http://www.forbes.com/2007/02/07/worlds-

fattest-countries-forbeslife-cx_ls_0208worldfat.html (accessed May 9, 2008).

8. Streib, "World's Fattest Countries."

9. MSNBC, "Nearly 1 in 5 Chinese overweight or obese," http://www.msnbc.msn.com/id/14407969/ (accessed May 9, 2008) and "Overweight and Obesity," KidsHealth for Parents, http://www.kidshealth.org/parent/nutrition_fit/nutrition/overweight_obesity.html (accessed on May 9, 2008).

10. Centers for Disease Control and Prevention, "Overweight and Obesity: Economic Consequences," http://www.cdc.gov/nccdphp/dnpa/obesity/economic_consequences.htm (accessed May 9, 2008).

11. Center for Consumer Freedom, "WHO Wants a Fat Tax?" http://www.consumerfreedom.com/news_detail.cfm/headline/2336 (accessed May 10, 2008).

12. David Charter and Sam Lister, "Junk food under attack by fat tax," *The Times* (London), February 19, 2004.

13. Gary Becker and Richard Posner, "The Fat Tax—Posner's Comment," The Becker-Posner Blog, http://www.becker-posner-blog.com/archives/2006/10/the_fat_taxposn.html (accessed on May 10, 2008).

14. A discussion of this division and the types of evidence is presented in George W. Ziegelmueller and Charles A. Dause, *Argumentation: Inquiry and Advocacy* (Englewood Cliffs, N.J.: Prentice-Hall, 1975), 49–82. See also a discussion of the types of evidence in J. Vernon Jensen, *Argumentation: Reasoning in Communication* (New York: Van Nostrand, 1981), 107–137.

15. Mark Shaffer, "Raising a Stink over Horse Diapers," *Tacoma News Tribune* (September 25, 1995): A4.

16. John Cook, "Blaster worm sender bound for prison," *Seattle Post-Intelligencer* (August 12, 2004), http://seattlepi.nwsource.com/business/185885_blaster12.html (accessed December 5, 2004).

17. Linda A. Johnson, "Deaths Raise Fears over Stomach Stapling," *Seattle Post-Intelligencer* (August 11, 2004), http://seattlepi.nwsource.com/national/apscience_story.asp?category=1500&slug=FIT%20Stomach%20Stapling (accessed August 11, 2004).

18. Lornet Turnbull, "Study: Urban Indians Face Health Disparities," *Seattle Times* (March 18, 2004): B1.

19. Shari Roan, "Psychologists Rate Presidents' Personalities," *Tacoma News Tribune* (August 14, 1996): SL 13.

20. Robert P. Newman and Dale R. Newman, *Evidence* (New York: Houghton Mifflin, 1969), 95–96.

21. This research is summarized in Robert N. Bostrom, *Persuasion* (Englewood Cliffs, N.J.: Prentice-Hall, 1983), 79–81.

22. Edith M. Lederer, "Armed Congo Groups Accused of War Crimes," *Seattle Post-Intelligencer* (August 9, 2004), http://seattlepi.nwsource.com/national/apafrica_story.asp?category=1105&slug=UN%20Congo (accessed August 11, 2004).

23. Newman and Newman, 223–24.

24. Colleen Kehoe, et al. "Results of GVU's Tenth World Wide Web User Survey," Graphics Visualization and Usability Center, May 14, 1999, www.gvu.gatech.edu/user_surveys/survey-1998-10/tenthreport.html (accessed June 21, 2000).

25. The Pew Research Center for the People and the Press, "Online Newcomers More Middle-Brow, Less Work-Oriented," 1998, www.people-press.org/tech98que.htm (accessed Feb. 6, 2001); and The George Washington University Graduate School of Political Management. "Democracy Online Survey," Dec. 6, 1999, www.gwu.edu/~media/pressreleases/11-06-00-GoldenDot.cfm (accessed on March 30, 2005).

26. Newman and Newman, 211–213.

27. UW Committee on Academic Conduct in the College of Arts and Sciences, *UW's Faculty Resource on Grading*, http://depts.washington.edu/grading/issue1/honesty.htm (accessed March 29, 2005).

CHAPTER SIX

REASONING

CHAPTER OUTLINE

KEY CONCEPTS

This chapter considers the reasoning process used in argument. As you may recall from Chapter 1, reasoning is the rational link between the evidence and the claim in the argument; it authorizes the step arguers make when they connect an argument's evidence to its claim. This is the point of the violent video game discussion in Box 6.1. In the discussion, both JP and Spencer had researched and formulated opinions about whether violent games such as "*Doom*" or "*Mortal Kombat*" should be sold. Based on the evidence Spencer found, he reasoned that such games posed a significant risk to public safety. JP, on the other hand, found evidence that suggested Spencer's reasoning was flawed. He reasoned that in the absence of conclusive evidence demonstrating a risk, we should not allow government to censor expression or entertainment. Based on their research and consideration of the subject, each advocate reasoned to his conclusions and shared those reasons with the other.

When we reason, we make connections, distinctions, and predictions; we use what is known or familiar to reach conclusions about the unknown or unfamiliar. In reasoning, we might break a whole into its component parts, consider the precise ways in which the parts are connected, extrapolate from a situation we can see to some underlying condition, or in some other way think about the world and how it operates.

Within the framework of perspectives on argument we introduced in Chapter 2, a focus on reasoning emphasizes the *logical* perspective on argument (as opposed to the rhetorical or dialectical perspectives). The logical dimension of argument is primarily concerned with whether the links or connections the arguer makes in reaching a conclusion are sound and make sense to recipients. Good critical thinking involves good reasoning that meets certain tests for the particular kind of reasoning being used. In this chapter, we will describe six forms of reasoning frequently used in everyday discussions and consider the tests for those six types of reasoning.

■ ■ ■ ■ ■ ■

BOX 6.1
SHOULD VIOLENT VIDEO GAMES BE BANNED?[1]

On April 20, 1999, two students, Eric Harris and Dylan Klebold, killed twelve students and a teacher. Twenty-three others were wounded before Harris and Klebold killed themselves at Columbine High School in Colorado. With no apparent triggering event or cause behind the massacre, investigators looked for some motivation to explain their behavior. Some blamed the parents; others blamed the school and cliques of students. Michael Moore's documentary film *Bowling for Columbine* linked the tragedy to a culture of violence in the United States. Other observers noted the teens' obsession with the violent video game "Doom" and argued that it and others of its genre, such as "*Mortal Kombat*" and "*Wofenstein 3D*," lead to violent outbursts among some individuals and might have served as one cause of the Columbine massacre.[2]

There has been an ongoing controversy over violent media almost since the beginning of television. Studies have examined media violence in efforts to demonstrate conclusively that exposure to certain types of stimuli can have harmful and even tragic effects. Although media violence has been studied for years, as of yet there remains division in the scientific field regarding the exact relationship between exposure to violent images and violent outcomes.[3] Looking for clear answers and in response to growing public pressure to regulate or ban violent media content, the U.S. Senate passed a bill in 2006 requiring the Centers for Disease Control and Prevention (CDC) to investigate how electronic media affect children.[4]

The video game industry, in an effort to self-regulate and eliminate the need for government action, established the Entertainment Software Rating Board (ESRB) in 1994. The ESRB moved quickly to pass and implement a global labeling system that has now rated almost 10,000 games along a continuum from "EC" for "early childhood" players through "AO" for "adults only."[5] The European Union is working on a stronger rating system with possible bans for certain violent video games.[6]

(continued)

BOX 6.1   CONTINUED

Yet, there remains a great deal of controversy over what the research demonstrates. Are violent games the cause of violent behavior? Or, do violent people act out through violent media? Are these games simply a symptom of potential problems? Does a ban or increased regulation increase safety and diminish violent behavior? Consider the discussion between two students, Spencer and JP, and analyze how their argument develops—especially the connections each makes that link claims to evidence.

Spencer: It is time to ban violent video games. I've read about this all year, and it seems to me that there is a very clear link between violent games and violent behaviors. Last week, I read an article by Amanda Schaffer that surveyed existing research, and she is pretty clear about three conclusions in the research. First, the more children are immersed in violent video games, the more likely they will get into fights and act aggressively. Second, there is longitudinal evidence that shows that, over time, the more children play violent video games the more they become physically and verbally aggressive. And, third, the bulk of experimental studies reach the same conclusions.[7] There are hundreds of studies that support these conclusions, but even if the studies are not absolutely definitive, the preponderance of evidence is clear. One of the best articles I read was by psychologist Craig Anderson, who reviewed the myths and facts in the scientific literature.[8] He shows there are problems with letting children play violent games. Violent video games teach violence, and they teach violence as a way to solve problems. When people are placed in violent role-playing games, they learn and practice how to find aggressive solutions to conflict. We need to ban these games; there is no good reason for them to be sold.

JP: Wait a minute. The research isn't as clear as you might think. Even if you just go online and search using Google or Ask, you find thousands of entries showing all kinds of explanations and conclusions, many of which don't agree. I've read the material that says there is a link between violent media and violent behaviors, but I have also read many studies that show there is no causal link. For instance, take a look at a really interesting article by Dmitri Williams and Marko Skoric published in *Communication Monographs*.[9] They concluded that there is no conclusive support showing that violent video games contribute significantly to increased violent behavior in the "real world." And, some people such as Dr. Cheryl Olson have noted in interviews that experimental data are mostly from studies of college students with study designs that *assumed* a link between violent games and violent behavior.[10] It is not surprising, because of the way the study was set up, to find an association between violent games and violent behavior. My only point is that the data are not clear. You and I have played violent video games, we might get frustrated and angry if we lose, but we don't act out beyond the game. Increased aggression inside the game does not necessarily translate to violence outside. I think it is more likely that violent people like violence and choose entertainment that supports their predisposition. Because they are already violent, they watch violent TV shows and movies and they play violent games. In fact, violent video games may actually be beneficial for these

(continued)

BOX 6.1   CONTINUED

people. A recent study by Unsworth, Devilly, and Ward makes the point that perhaps violent video games actually play a cathartic role—which could be a positive outlet for otherwise violent behaviors.[11]

Spencer: Even if what you are saying is true, violent video games still pose a significant risk because *some* people may act out on the basis of a game. Several authors have made the point that the interactive nature of video games blurs the lines that separate reality from fantasy, meaning that people who have a violent predisposition may be more likely to act out aggressive fantasies. It seems to me that these games—whether they are the cause of violence or make violence more acceptable—should not be allowed if there is any level of risk associated with them.[12] And, there is a risk that players who are already disturbed may become even further agitated by these games and that they will act out the fantasies.

JP: The evidence is not sufficiently clear to support what you are saying. But even if it were, you cannot ask government to restrict every possible risk. There is no clear, causal connection that shows playing violent games results in aggressive behavior. Government restrictions on the possible risk undermine our rights to free expression, allow government censorship, and place someone in charge of what we do for entertainment. This is a very dangerous path that we should not follow.

Questions to consider:

1. How was reasoning used in the preceding discussion? Did you find it effective? Why?
2. Which arguments seemed to have the best reasoning? What made the reasoning persuasive?
3. Which arguments had the weakest reasoning? Why did they appear weak?
4. If you were Spencer and you were going to reply to JP's last comment, what would you say? What reasons would you use?
5. Why do you think some members of the scientific community conclude that violent video games are harmful, but other scientists say they are not? What does this tell you about field theory that was developed in Chapter 1?

THE ROLE OF THE ADVOCATE

Competent arguers can evaluate their own and others' reasoning, construct good arguments, and identify the unstated assumptions and connections people make in their arguments. They can also analyze other people's arguments to discover strengths and weaknesses. As we noted in Chapter 1, reasoning, along with claims and evidence, is one of the three basic components of any argument. Claims, as you will recall, are the end points of arguments, and evidence is the beginning or grounding for an argument. Reasoning serves as the process that connects evidence with claims.

In moving from what is known and acceptable (the evidence) to what is unknown or controversial (the claim), arguers often state their reasoning in an inference. *An inference states the step one has made in linking the evidence to the claim.* Inferences can be explicit or implicit in an argument. For example, we might explicitly say, "Don't play in the street because a car might hit you." On the other hand, we might simply say, "Don't play in the street. You might get hurt." In this case, the inference, "because a car might hit you," is unstated or implicit. In studying and analyzing the arguments of others and in detecting possible weaknesses in reasoning, it is important to be able to identify the type of reasoning used in the argument, even if the arguer does not state it.

When people argue, they use various inference patterns that they may not always be able to identify and explain. Sometimes you can "flush out" a person's reasoning by way of a challenge ("Wait a minute, how did you reach that conclusion, based on the information you just gave me?"). Often, the unstated inference is the weak point in the person's argument. If you can identify how the arguer connected the claim to the evidence, you will know what type of reasoning was employed. Each kind of reasoning suggests a set of tests or questions that function as standards to evaluate its quality. Knowing what type of reasoning was used and what tests to apply will improve your critical-thinking skills as you become better able to analyze and critique others' arguments.

Knowing the various reasoning forms will not only make you a better argument critic, it will make you a better arguer. Knowing how reasoning functions and the tests and standards for judging it will help you monitor the effectiveness and quality of your own reasoning, which, in turn, is another important critical-thinking skill. Argument theorist Stephen Toulmin observed that a "sound" argument is "one that will stand up to criticism."[13] Each of the inference types discussed in this chapter—quasilogical, analogy, generalization, cause, coexistence, and dissociation—must meet certain standards to be judged as sound.[14] Knowing these types and the applicable tests will enable you to foresee possible weaknesses in your arguments and anticipate objections others might raise to them.

FORMAL LOGIC AND PRACTICAL REASONING

In Chapter 2, we discussed how the Toulmin model helped evolve our way of understanding arguments from the formal construction of the syllogism to the practical and informal understanding of arguments in conversations and everyday interaction. Although many philosophers were at first understandably cool toward Toulmin's approach, teachers and scholars in the fields of speech and English were more enthusiastic about it. They had been teaching students for some time how to construct and critique arguments expressed in everyday language designed for real audiences, and they thought that Toulmin's model for analyzing arguments and his view that arguments were constructed and supported by principles in specific fields were very useful.

At about the same time that Toulmin's book appeared, two European scholars, Chaim Perelman and Lucie Olbrechts-Tyteca, published the English translation of *The New Rhetoric: A Treatise on Argumentation.*[15] Like Toulmin, these two authors argued that sole reliance on formal logic to study practical arguments was inadvisable. Their approach was different from, yet complementary to, Toulmin's.

Unlike Toulmin, who was primarily concerned with a *logical* perspective on argument, Perelman and Olbrechts-Tyteca were interested in a *rhetorical* perspective. They began their work by observing how all sorts of arguers—public speakers, essayists, and even philosophers—constructed their arguments with an audience in mind. Arguers who wish their arguments to succeed, they said, will select the various elements that make up their arguments with an eye to their audience. They will use premises they know their audience agrees with, values they believe them to hold, examples with which they are familiar, and language they will understand. Perelman and Olbrechts-Tyteca also believed that arguers make use of reasoning forms recognizable to their audiences.[16]

Perelman and Olbrechts-Tyteca worked by studying arguments in use—in speeches, essays, books, and articles. They described the reasoning forms they found in these sources and, after ten years of studying arguments, they identified thirteen categories of argument forms used in practical argument.[17] In this chapter, we will adopt their category scheme. In particular, we will describe six categories of reasoning—quasilogical, analogy, generalization, causal, coexistential, and dissociation. We selected these six of the thirteen categories because they are probably the ones most frequently used by arguers.[18]

REASONING AS INFERENCE MAKING

Of the six inference types we will discuss in this section, the first five—quasilogical, analogy, generalization, cause, and coexistential—are *associative* schemes; they bring together elements and evaluate or organize them in terms of one another. They may bring together the elements in terms of equivalence, comparison, contrast, sequence, or some other connection, but the reasoning works because each part of the argument is viewed in terms of the other. The sixth form is *dissociative;* it aims to disengage or disunite elements originally considered as a unity. Dissociation is unique from the other five types, but equally important.

Before we begin our discussion of the argument types, we want to remind you that some arguments may fall into more than one type. This is because real arguments as used in daily life do not possess the neatness and clarity of the forms of mathematics and formal logic. An argument might make a causal claim based on a comparison (analogy), or it might use examples to show that a causal relationship exists. This will be a problem only when you are identifying arguments by type, as in some of the examples in the exercises at the end of this chapter. In these cases, more than one correct classification of an argument may be possible. What is important is to correctly identify at least one of the reasoning forms occurring in an argument, and not to be too troubled by some overlap among the forms.

Quasilogical Arguments

Quasilogical arguments are labeled "quasi" because they appear *similar* to the syllogistic structures of formal logic. Their similarity to the formal reasoning of logic or mathematics gives quasilogical arguments a compelling air, and people often find them persuasive because of their simplicity and clarity. *Quasilogical arguments place two or three elements in a relation to one another so as to make the connections between them similar to the connections in formal logic.* It would be fair to say that quasilogical arguments can be reduced to formulas because of their simplicity and clarity.

For example, one could make the argument:

If the Seattle Mariners can beat the Texas Rangers, and if the Texas Rangers can beat the Oakland Athletics, then it only makes sense that Seattle should be able to beat Oakland.

This is simply stated and formulaic, but the statement is probable and not certain like the statements in formal logic. In the following section, we will emphasize three types of quasilogical arguments that are quite common—transitivity, incompatibility, and reciprocity. These arguments are rhetorical and co-orientational, which means they are based in the recipients' willingness to accept the probability that the conclusion will come true.

Transitivity

Transitivity arguments are structured like categorical syllogisms discussed in Chapter 2. They have three terms that are associated with one another through a process of classification, but the relationships among the terms are probable and not certain, as in the syllogism. Nevertheless, the relationships established among the terms by the arguer are so clear and simple that they seem compelling—just as with formal logic. Consider the following example:

As a student at Big Time Private University, Mary is paying high tuition.

This could be reconstructed in the form of a categorical syllogism, as:

Major Premise: All students at ivy league universities pay high tuition.
Minor Premise: Mary is a student at an ivy league university.
Conclusion: So, Mary pays high tuition.

Notice that the middle term (students at ivy league universities) appears in both the major and the minor premises. The middle term functions like an equal sign; it enables the arguer to associate the remaining two terms ("pay high tuition" and "Mary") in the conclusion of the argument.

Transitivity arguments have to meet certain tests in order to be considered cogent, and these tests generally are related to their form. First, they must contain three and only three terms. If they have four or more terms, they do not have the simple infrastructure of the categorical syllogism and thus cannot be classified as transitivity arguments. Second, their premises must be true. Because the conclusion of a transitivity argument simply combines the substance of the two premises, those premises must be true, or the conclusion will be just as false as the premise with which one starts. Third, all three of the statements must be stated (or restatable) as simple classifications. If the relations are too complex ("is greater than," "leads to," "is comparable to," "represents," and so forth), then the inference is not a simple categorical inference, and the argument is not a transitivity argument. Fourth, the middle term must occur in both of the premises so it can fulfill its "equals" function and make it possible to connect the remaining two terms in the conclusion.

Incompatibility

The next type of quasilogical arguments are incompatibilities. Incompatibilities are similar to the contradiction in that they imply two alternatives between which a choice must be made. (That is, one must choose one or the other, not both.) The problematic nature of the incompatibility results because both alternatives are stated at the same time. Because the two alternatives are opposite each other and are being stated simultaneously, their combination is "incompatible" and implies a situation that should be resolved. Here are two examples:

> I hate all people who generalize.
> Wait a minute, if I want people to trust me, you're saying I have to deceive them into thinking I'm something I'm not!

Of course, the first person is making a generalization while claiming to hate everyone who generalizes. The second person observes that in order to obtain trust, he has to deceive others. Both are affirming mutually incompatible and conflicting ideas together. Incompatibilities, then, contain two alternatives that are incompatible and show a conceptual conflict or a conflict of interests.

Incompatibilities can be tested in much the same way as disjunctive syllogisms. First, the two terms must indeed be mutually exclusive; if they can be maintained together, then no contradiction exists. Second, they must be viewed as necessarily relevant to each other. If one of the terms can be defined as irrelevant, then the incompatibility can be resolved.

Reciprocity

The third form of quasilogical argument to be considered in this section is argument from reciprocity. Reciprocal relations are reflected in the if–then relation of the conditional syllogism:

Major premise:	If you expect your superiors to treat you well, then you should treat your own subordinates well.
Minor premise:	Your superiors do treat you well.
Conclusion:	So, you should treat your subordinates well.

Reciprocal relations assert a hypothetical relationship between two situations or conditions and imply a mutual dependence between them: "You should treat your own subordinates as you want your superiors to treat you." Reciprocity implies symmetry; the two parts of the argument are related to each other, and their equivalence is emphasized.

Reciprocity is based on our belief that individuals and situations that can be put into the same category should be treated in the same way. It emphasizes the characteristics that make situations or persons equivalent to each other. How can supervisors who treat their employees badly complain when they are mistreated by their own bosses? Employees, supervisors, and their bosses are all workers in the same company; they all likewise deserve fair and equal treatment.

Reciprocity arguments may be stated in various ways:

> What is honorable to learn is also honorable to teach.
> Do unto others as you would have them do unto you.

In both cases, what is valid or acceptable in one situation is considered equivalent to what is valid or acceptable in another.

Arguments from reciprocity generally should meet two tests. They should equate two situations, individuals, or phenomena with each other. If more than two are implied, then the argument falls into some other classification. Furthermore, the arguer should use the symmetry between the two to argue that they should be treated reciprocally. Since the claim of reciprocity arguments is that the two elements should be treated together and equivalently, the arguer must highlight the similarity between them.

Quasilogical arguments occur frequently and are commonly used in ordinary speech. People using quasilogical arguments generally attempt to simplify a situation by reducing it to a very limited number of component parts and then set those components into clear and unequivocal relations. The clarity and simplicity of these relations thereby give their arguments the same compelling nature that we find in formal logic and in mathematics. For additional examples of quasilogical arguments, see Box 6.2.

BOX 6.2
QUASILOGICAL ARGUMENTS

- Sort of logical; resembles formal logic; limited to two or three terms
- Views two elements as equal to, incompatible with, or dependent on each other
- Relationship between the elements appears simple and clear

EXAMPLES

Transitivity:	Bill's friends are my friends, and you're a friend of Bill's, so you are a friend of mine.
As syllogism:	Bill's friends are my friends. You are Bill's friend. So, you are my friend.
Incompatibility:	The candidate says he's opposed to nepotism, but he appointed his cousin as director of the White House Travel Office. (Nepotism is hiring or appointing relatives.)
As syllogism:	No opponents of nepotism appoint their relatives. This candidate appointed his relative. So, this candidate is not really opposed to nepotism. (And his words and actions are incompatible.)
Reciprocity:	Meeting our responsibilities means doing a better job.
As syllogism:	If we do a better job, we will meet our responsibilities. We are doing a better job. So, we are meeting our responsibilities.

Analogy

Like reciprocity, analogy emphasizes the similarity between two elements. *An analogy reasons that because two objects resemble each other in certain known respects, they will also resemble each other in respects that are unknown.* Analogy differs from reciprocity, however, because its purpose is different. A reciprocity argument claims that two situations should be treated alike; an analogy makes an attribution about something that is unknown. Most of our early learning occurs by means of analogy. The child who discovers that the flame of a candle is hot and can burn fingers will avoid other fires in the future. We come to expect that what has happened in the past will happen in the future, that similar situations will have similar outcomes, and that similar objects will exhibit the same characteristics. Such regularities give order and uniformity to our experience and interpretation of the world.

Literal

There are two forms of analogy. The first is the literal analogy and the second is figurative analogy. *A literal analogy compares two objects of the same class that share many characteristics and concludes that a known characteristic that one possesses is shared by the other.* The inference made in a literal analogy can be represented by Figure 6.1, and it can be stated as follows:

Object X has attributes A, B, C, and D.
Object Y has attributes A, B, and C.
Therefore, Object Y will probably possess attribute D as well.

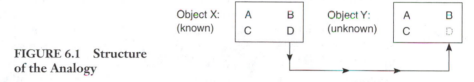

FIGURE 6.1   Structure of the Analogy

For example, if one were to argue that a ban on nonreturnable bottles and cans should be instituted in Washington State because a similar ban in Oregon worked to decrease container litter, the argument would be a literal analogy. The arguer would probably support the analogy by pointing out similarities between the two states and conclude that what worked in one state would work in the other.

> The state of Oregon has moderate beverage consumption, limited revenues for collecting and disposing of container waste, demographic characteristics similar to Washington state, and a ban on returnable bottles and cans that effectively reduced container waste.

> The state of Washington also has moderate beverage consumption, limited revenues for collecting and disposing of container waste, and demographics similar to Oregon's.

> Therefore, Washington state's proposed ban on nonreturnable beverage containers will reduce container waste.

In this analogy, the *evidence* consists of all the statements of similarity between the two states; the *claim* draws the conclusion that the ban (the unknown characteristic) will work; and the *inference* is that the two states resemble each other in all relevant respects.

Literal analogies are subject to tests of at least three different kinds. The first has to do with the *quality of the comparison*. To have probative value, literal analogies must compare two objects that belong to the same class. In the preceding example, Washington and Oregon are clearly in the same class: Not only are both states, but they are also similar in size and demographics and located in the same region of the United

States. To the extent that the compared objects are not alike in respects relevant to the conclusion of the analogy, the comparison is undermined.

The similarities cited must also be relevant to the comparison and to the claim to which it leads. In the example comparing Washington and Oregon, some aspects (patterns of beverage consumption, facilities for waste disposal, amount of litter) are relevant to the claim about whether a bottle bill will work. Other aspects, such as the climate and natural features of the two states, could be considered irrelevant.

A second test for the literal analogy has to do with *quantity;* is there a sufficient number of similarities to support the comparison? How many are enough? Obviously, there is no unequivocal answer to this question. The larger the number of relevant similarities, the more probable the conclusion. For example, if the support of the bottle bill could demonstrate that more bottles would be returned if purchasers had to pay a deposit than would be returned through increased recycling, the analogy would be strengthened. Or, if Washington and Oregon are virtually identical in all relevant demographic details, the comparison would be stronger.

The third test for a literal analogy is related to *opposition;* are there any significant dissimilarities that would undermine the comparison? For example, in Washington state at present, citizens generally recycle container litter. They are motivated to do so by the high cost of garbage disposal and because recycling is free. Oregon does not have the same costs and the same recycling program. Since so many containers are presently recycled in Washington, the benefit from a bottle bill might be minimal. This example illustrates the importance of considering possible significant differences when one advances a literal analogy or comparison to prove a claim. For additional examples of literal analogies, see Box 6.3.

■ ■ ■ ■ ■ ■

BOX 6.3
ANALOGY ARGUMENTS

- Assume two objects, situations, or events are similar.
- One is known; the other is less known.
- Assume that if the two are similar in ways that are known, they will also be similar in other ways.
- Make an attribution to a comparatively unknown object, situation, or event.

EXAMPLES

As it becomes easier and easier to obtain images and documents online in the home, it is possible that people will download and copy these somewhat indiscriminately. The advent of the photocopy machine led researchers to become less discriminating and to copy articles of only marginal interest. . . . In a similar way, online access to full-text documents and digital images may lead people to accumulate items of only marginal interest.[19]

Evidence: Photocopy machine led to indiscriminate copying of articles.

Inference: Online access to full text and images may lead to accumulation of marginal items.

(continued)

BOX 6.3   CONTINUED

In this fiftieth anniversary of the end of World War II, Germans remain understandably nervous about the staying power of fascism, which was largely a product of the interwar years. How much more cautious, then, should Americans be about assuming that racism and sexism—much older and more pervasive problems—have been defeated by a mere thirty years of legal and social initiatives?[20]

Evidence: Germans are still concerned about fascism fifty years after the Holocaust.

Inference: Americans today cannot assume racism and sexism are no longer problems.

Figurative

The second type of analogy is the figurative analogy. From a logical point of view, figurative analogies do not have probative value but can be used to illustrate a point or to get listeners to see things in a different light. *The figurative analogy is a comparison between two objects of different classes in which a relation or quality within one is said to be similar to a relation or quality within the other.* Since the two objects in a figurative analogy are not truly similar, the comparison is metaphorical and illustrative rather than concrete and literal. Figurative analogies function primarily to make what is remote or poorly understood immediate and comprehensible. Speakers and public figures often use figurative analogies to focus the public's attention on the features of a situation that they want to emphasize.[21] President Reagan repeatedly referred to the Strategic Defense Initiative as a "shield," thereby causing the American public to see it as a passive barrier to be used only for defense. President Franklin Roosevelt compared the Lend Lease Act by which we supplied Great Britain with weapons and equipment to fight the Germans in World War II to the act of lending a garden hose to a neighbor to put out a house fire. Figurative analogies can be tested for their rhetorical effectiveness: Do they cause audiences to reshape their attitudes in the direction desired by the arguer? These analogies cannot be tested on logical grounds, however, because they compared items and objects from different classes.

Generalization and Argument from Example

In a generalization, one reasons that what is true of certain members of a class will also be true of other members of the same class or of the class as a whole. As in the analogy, one begins with what is known or familiar (the examples that have been observed) and moves to what is less well known or less familiar. Furthermore, since reasoning is usually on the basis of characteristics that are known, the same type of inference is made in the generalization as is made in the analogy. The generalization, however, involves more than two instances and often makes claims about a whole class of objects.

Generalizations move from some to all members of a class. For example:

Because the rabbits I have seen have short tails, all rabbits must have short tails.

We've had a dry spell during July and August for the last three years, so there must be one every summer.

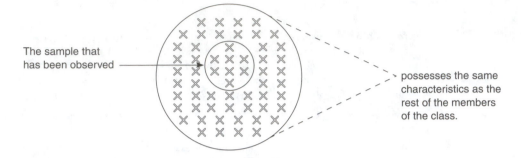

FIGURE 6.2   Structure of the Generalization

The characteristics (short tails, dry spell) that have been observed are generalized and applied to the class as a whole (rabbits, summer seasons). This sort of inference is illustrated in Figure 6.2.

Generalizations occur very frequently, and we use them to make conclusions about groups of people or experiences. We also see professionally produced generalizations in the form of Gallup polls, Nielsen ratings, market surveys, clinical experimentation, and other forms of statistical sampling where the population sampled is considered to represent the general population. Generalizations are also used when an arguer has been able to observe some but not all the members of a class and wishes to make a claim about the class in general. For example, Doris explains why she monitors her child's television viewing by referring to the programs she has seen:

> **Doris:**   I never let Heather watch Saturday morning cartoons. I try to find something else to occupy her time.
>
> **Ann:**   Why? I surely do appreciate their babysitting potential.
>
> **Doris:**   Listen, have you ever watched that stuff? Crass commercialism and violence, that's all it is.
>
> **Ann:**   Oh, come on. You're exaggerating.
>
> **Doris:**   No, I'm not. I watched *She-Ra* and *Hercules* and two other adventure cartoons one morning. Over one-third of the time was devoted to commercials for candy and toys. And I counted thirty-two violent acts in two hours of programming. I can think of better ways for my child to spend her time!

In her argument, Doris makes an inference about the programs she has not watched based on the programs she has watched. Her *evidence* is that one-third of the time was devoted to commercials and that she saw thirty-two violent acts. Her *claim* is that these programs display "crass commercialism and violence." Her *inference* is that *She-Ra*, *Hercules*, and two other programs are typical of all Saturday morning cartoons.

Another form of generalization is reasoning from example. Whereas a generalization will make a general statement based on observation of a number of examples, an argument from example will make a general statement based on observation of just

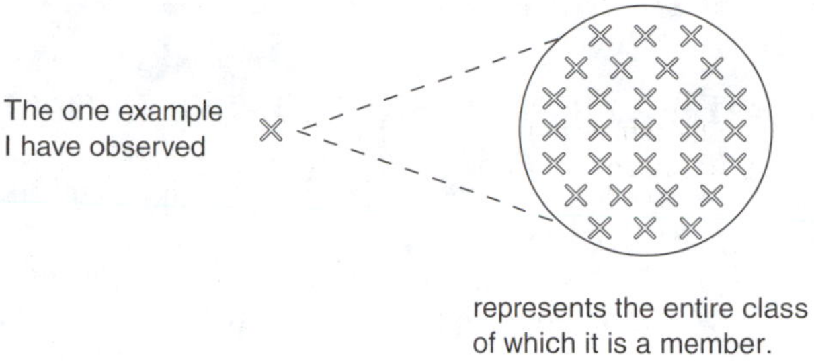

FIGURE 6.3   Structure of Reasoning from Example

one example. *Argument from example seeks acceptance for some general rule or principle by offering a concrete, particular case.* Suppose Doris had said, "In one of the programs I watched, there were eight fights in twenty minutes. The characters used swords, knives, and their fists to resolve every problem. Every disagreement led to a confrontation, and every confrontation led to a fight. This program shows how continuously violent these cartoons can be." As in the discussion between Doris and Ann, Doris is trying to establish a general trend. She does this by describing in detail a single program she has seen. The form of reasoning is illustrated in Figure 6.3.

Like the analogy, arguments from generalization and example are subject to tests of *quality*, *quantity*, and *general opposition*. First, the example or examples cited must be *relevant* to the general claim. If the programs Doris cited were not cartoons, or if they were cartoons intended for older or adult viewers, her generalization would not be relevant to a claim about children's cartoons. Furthermore, the example or examples cited must be *typical* of the class in question. If no other Saturday cartoon has as many as eight acts of violence in a single showing, then the one Doris watched could not be considered representative of the rest of the cartoons, and her generalization would be open to question.

Second, the criterion of *quantity* (applicable only to the generalization) can be met only when Doris has cited a sufficient number of examples. There are nearly three dozen children's cartoons aired on commercial networks and cable channels on most Saturday mornings.[22] Are Doris's four examples enough to support her general claim? The cogency and persuasiveness of her claim will surely depend on the number of examples she can cite. This raises the question of how many examples are sufficient to support a generalization. There is no clear-cut answer because the requisite number of examples depends on the particular argument and the size of the available sample. There should be enough examples to satisfy the audience and to be weighed against possible counterexamples.

Third, the existence of counterexamples provides the test of *opposition* to both generalization and argument from example. Cartoons such as *Arthur*, *Dragon Tales*, and *The Magic School Bus* contain very few or no acts of violence and portray characters who cooperate peacefully with one another and have a good time. If Ann listed or described programs such as these, Doris would have to reconsider whether the characteristics of violence and commercialism really apply to all children's cartoons. For additional examples of generalization and reasoning from example, see Box 6.4.

BOX 6.4

GENERALIZATION AND REASONING FROM EXAMPLE

- Assume that what is true of one or some members of a class will also be true of others or of the whole class.
- The evidence is the presentation of specific instances.
- The inference is that these are representative of others.

EXAMPLES

Along with reducing tax rates, we must also aggressively reduce tax rules and regulations. It's estimated that last year alone, American taxpayers spent 1.8 billion hours filling out their tax forms. Businesses spent twice as much time sending the IRS over 1 million reports.[23]

Evidence: 1.8 billion hours, over 1 million business tax forms

Inference: Represent complicated tax rules and regulations

When one teaches about Marco Polo, or William of Normandy, or Goethe, or Joan of Arc, one is essentially engaging in the process of transmitting information about a cultural heritage and legacy. The names of the Africans, Ibn Battuta, or King Sundiata of Mali, or Ahmed Baba, or Yenenga, are never spoken in high school classes, and under the current curricular structure, if they were heard, would lack credibility even though they are by world standards certainly the equal of the Europeans I have mentioned in contrast.[24]

Evidence: Marco Polo, William of Normandy, Goethe, Joan of Arc

Inference: These represent the exclusion of African figures from American classrooms

---

Cause

Arguments from cause claim that one condition or event contributes to or brings about another condition or event. Causal arguments are also arguments from succession; one event must happen before the other. Furthermore, the causal event must produce or bring about the effect. Some general examples of causal argument are presented in Box 6.5.

There are two forms of causal argument. The first, or weaker form, is the necessary condition. *A necessary condition is one that must be present for the effect to occur.* To remain alive, people must consume both fluids and food. If either of these two necessary conditions is lacking, death from dehydration or starvation will result. In order to communicate, two people must speak the same language or at least understand the same nonverbal code. Reasoning from necessary condition is a relatively weak form because the effect is not guaranteed by the cause. For example, food does not *cause* life; it is simply *necessary* for life to continue.

The second form of causal argument is the sufficient condition. *A sufficient condition for an event or effect is a circumstance in whose presence the event or effect must occur.* In other words, the presence of a sufficient condition guarantees that the subsequent effect will occur. A broken fan belt on an automobile guarantees that the engine will overheat. If lightning strikes overdry timber, a fire will result. Furthermore, a number

■ ■ ■ ■ ■

BOX 6.5
CAUSAL ARGUMENTS

- Assert that one condition or event brings about another condition or event.
- "Weak" cause: first condition must be present for effect to occur.
- "Strong" cause: first condition guarantees effect will occur.
- Evidence is the physical presence of causes and effects.
- Inference is that one condition or event brings about the other.

EXAMPLES

The new beltways and interstates offered cheap access to farmland on the fringe, and the result was suburban sprawl and disinvestment in existing business districts. People are waking up to the fact that low density, auto dependent sprawl has profound consequences on our quality of life and our individual and collective pocketbooks. The Chicago region grew 4 percent in population and 40 percent in land area from 1970 to 1990.[25]

Cause:	beltways and interstates
Effect:	suburban sprawl, disinvestment in existing business districts
Cause:	low density, auto dependent sprawl
Effect:	consequences for quality of life, pocketbooks

A great deal of effort has gone into discovering and analyzing the ways in which humans could be exposed to radioactive materials from a [nuclear] waste repository. Dozens of scenarios have been offered. In the one that has received the most attention, waste canisters corrode, and water leaches radioactive elements . . . out of the spent fuel or vitrified high-level waste, then carries them into groundwater. People would be exposed if they used the water for any of the usual purposes: drinking, washing, or irrigation.[26]

Cause:	stored radioactive materials leakage into groundwater
Effect:	people exposed to radioactivity

of necessary conditions, taken together, may guarantee an effect. The presence of oxygen, combustible material, and temperatures in a certain range, taken together, constitute a sufficient condition for fire.

Causal influences are complex and frequently difficult to sort out and identify. The preceding examples of causes as necessary and sufficient were supported with examples of physical, natural, or mechanical phenomena in which causal sequences are clear and inevitable. In everyday affairs, however, causal sequences are often embedded in sets of necessary and sufficient conditions that mutually influence one another in complex relationships. Consider the following argument for increased state support of public education:

We should increase our support for public education in our state. Rather than being a drain on our revenues, such an increase is actually a long-term investment. Increased funding will lead to a small class size, better facilities, and improved materials for use in the classroom. Students will complete their education with better skills than they now have and be more productive contributors to the workforce.

This, and the new industry which an improved educational system will attract to our state, will, in the long run, increase our tax base, which will result in improved revenues for state government.

An arguer advancing such claims would have available data on the effects of increased state support on student–teacher ratios, capital improvements, and educational resources. These would serve as *evidence*. The arguer's *claim* would be, "We should increase our support for public education in our state." The arguer's inferences are a series of causal claims: first, increased funding will lead to improved education; second, better-educated students will become more productive workers; third, increased productivity will improve the tax base and thus increase state revenues in the future. This network of causal claims is represented in Figure 6.4.

Like the other forms of reasoning, causal argument has tests to gauge its adequacy. The *quality* test deals with whether the cause is a necessary or sufficient condition for the claimed effect. The fact that the necessary (as opposed to sufficient) condition does not *guarantee* the effect suggests weaknesses in the argument. Increased funding for education might be spent hiring more administrators and bureaucrats rather than on items that directly affect students; thus, education might not necessarily be improved. Furthermore, if a desired effect can be attained in the absence of the purported cause, that cause is not necessary. If the schools could be improved by being reorganized, or if teachers could be trained differently without spending more money, then increased funding could not be said to be a necessary cause.

The test of *quantity* is applied to a causal argument when one considers whether the cause is sufficient to produce the effect. If increased funding alone will not measurably improve the quality of education, then funding improvement alone is not enough. Other measures, such as improvement in teacher training programs and enhanced counseling to prevent student dropouts, may also be needed.

Finally, the test of *opposition* suggests that first, the effect may have been produced by some other cause; second, the effect may be the cumulative result of many causes working together; or third, there may be some other, unanticipated cause

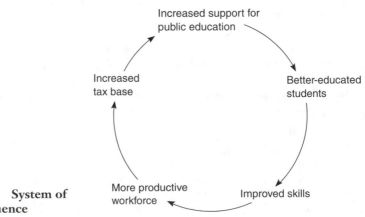

FIGURE 6.4   System of Causal Influence

working counter to the cause the arguer has cited. For example, increased funding for schools may not lead to improved learning because of other forces in society, such as poverty and drug use, that undermine formal education. Factors such as broken families, child abuse, and racism might cause the failure of education even when large sums of money are spent to improve the schools.

Many times, although two events are related to each other, the relationship is neither necessary nor sufficient. For an argument to meet the tests for causal reasoning, it must be fairly rigorous. Because of the many causes that can contribute to a particular effect, and because of the possibility that alternative causes can intervene and reduce or eliminate the expected effect, reasoning that relies only on linear, one-to-one cause–effect relationships is risky.

A method that has proved useful in discussing the relationships among phenomena is correlation. *A correlation claims that two events or phenomena vary together; an increase or decrease in one is accompanied by an increase or decrease in the other.* For example, if a market analyst observed that improvements in the economy would be bad for bond values (because higher interest rates devalue existing bonds carrying lower rates), the analyst would be correlating economic health, higher interest rates, and bond values with one another. The arguer who wishes to show a causal relationship among phenomena is often well advised to show that a variation in one will probably contribute to a variation in the other—an argument more modest than direct causal argument, but also less risky because it acknowledges the possibility of alternative and counteracting causes.

Coexistential Arguments

An argument from coexistence reasons from something that can be observed (a sign) to a condition or feature that cannot be observed. The sign or indication functions as the evidence; the existence of the condition or essence it indicates is the claim; and inferring from what we can observe to something we cannot observe constitutes the inference. Coexistential reasoning is illustrated in Figure 6.5. As in analogy and generalization arguments, the inference moves from what is known (the sign) to what is unknown or less known (the condition or essence).

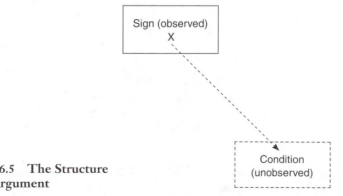

FIGURE 6.5   The Structure of Sign Argument

We frequently use signs that we can observe to infer conditions we cannot observe directly. A sore throat and runny nose are symptoms or signs of a cold. Buds on vegetation are a sign that spring is on the way. Or, consider the inference in the following conversation, for example:

Jill: You need to put oil in your car before you drive it today.

John: Why? Is the oil low?

Jill: Well, the oil light was on when I came home last night.

In this conversation, Jill's *evidence* is that the oil light came on. Her *claim* is that the oil is low. And her *inference* is that the light is a reliable indicator of the amount of oil in the car.

This example illustrates an important distinction between two forms of argument that are often confused—sign and cause. In a sign argument, the arguer intends to claim that a condition exists; in a causal argument, the arguer intends to explain *why* a condition exists or how it came about. Jill's intent is to claim that the oil is low in the car, not why or how it came to be that way. There could be an oil leak, the engine could be burning oil, or oil could have been consumed through normal wear and tear: If Jill had proposed one of these factors as leading to the low oil, she would have been making a causal argument.

Sometimes the distinction between coexistential and causal reasoning is subtle and depends on how the argument is worded. Consider the following examples:

> The merchants downtown are beginning to close early and have installed iron grillwork on their windows. Crime must be becoming a serious problem in the community.

> Discrimination has existed in this country for a long time. This is shown by the Civil Rights Act, the Voting Rights Act, and the equal-opportunity laws, all of which would have been unnecessary if discrimination did not exist.

Both of these are coexistential arguments that claim an unobserved condition—crime or discrimination—exists. In both of these examples, the arguer's intent was to show that certain underlying conditions existed, *not* to show their cause or how subsequent events came about. They could be viewed as causal arguments if the arguer had claimed that crime had caused the merchants to put up the grillwork or that discrimination brought about antidiscriminatory legislation, but these would be claims of a different type from the one in the preceding example.

In coexistential arguments, both the sign and the condition it indicates coexist or occur at the same time. Two varieties of coexistential argument are person/act argument and argument from authority. *Person/act argument reasons from a person's actions to his or her character or essence.* The act is taken as the sign; the person's character is taken as the essence.

> John turned in his last two papers late, hasn't washed his dishes in a week, and has a month's worth of dirty laundry piled up. He must be a procrastinator.

Unlike other forms of coexistential argument, person/act inferences often occur in the other direction; we reason that a person's essence or character will result in certain acts. ("Don't expect John to turn in his paper on time; he's a real procrastinator, and everybody knows it.")

Another variant of coexistential argument is argument from authority. *Argument from authority reasons that statements by someone presumed knowledgeable about a particular issue can be taken as evidence sufficient to justify a claim.* In argument from authority, the actual quote or statement functions as the evidence (sign); the claim is that whatever the quote attests is true (unobserved condition); and the reasoning is that the authority is qualified and accurate on the matter in question. Consider the following example:

> A team of researchers, led by John A. Ruben of Oregon State University, has conclud-ed that birds descended from reptiles, not dinosaurs, as has long been claimed. Their claim is based on observation of the most complete fossil of the reptile *Longisquama* ever found, which has about eight pairs of long appendages resembling feathers.[27]

The presumed feathers on the fossil and the research team's conclusion function as *evidence* in this argument; the *claim* is that birds descended from reptiles; and the *inference* is that the research team is a qualified authority to speak on the subject.

Like many other forms of reasoning, coexistential arguments must meet the tests of quality, quantity, and opposition. Sign, person/act, and authority arguments meet the test of *quality* when the relationship between the indication and the condi-tion it indicates is constant and reciprocal. If the relation is only sporadic or intermit-tent, then the inference is unreliable. If a car's electrical system is shorting out, its oil light may come on even when the oil level is fine. One might see occasional grillwork on a building in an area because it is used for decoration, not protection. Making person/act ascriptions is usually a little risky because people do not invariably behave the same way all the time. (John might surprise you and actually get his paper written by the due date!) And authorities are often wrong on an issue, however compelling their credentials might be. The quality of authoritative arguments also depends on the quality of the source itself. Is the person cited truly an expert with current firsthand information relevant to the claim? The tests for authoritative opinion evidence, such as expertise, objectivity, consistency, and access, were discussed in Chapter 5.

The test of *quantity* is met when there are enough signs of the condition in ques-tion. We could be surer that crime was a problem in an area if there were further indi-cations of it—a greater police presence and a higher incidence of arrests and convictions. We are more confident of claims based on authoritative statements when an arguer can cite multiple authorities with credible credentials on the issue.

Coexistential arguments meet the test of *opposition* when there are no counter-signs that work against the arguer's claim. Frequently, the presence of a condition might be disputed because there are as many signs indicating that it does not exist as there are signs indicating that it does. A common example of this is speculation about the health of the economy. In a given fiscal quarter, durable goods orders and housing starts may increase, causing some economists to announce that the country is entering a period of economic growth. Meanwhile, unemployment may rise and productivity decline, causing other experts to point to these as countersigns that indicate economic decline. This same standard may, of course, be applied to arguments from authority;

we are more likely to believe authoritative arguments when there are no other equally credible authorities testifying on the side of the issue opposite the one in question. For additional examples of coexistential argument, see Box 6.6.

■ ■ ■ ■ ■

BOX 6.6
COEXISTENTIAL ARGUMENTS

- Claim that two things coexist.
- Reason from something that can be observed (a sign) to a condition that cannot be observed.
- What is known is the concrete sign; what is unknown (or claimed) is the condition.
- Could reason from a person's acts to his or her character, or from an authoritative statement to an unobservable condition.

EXAMPLES

One of the central criticisms of the World Trade Organization (WTO) is that it is a fundamentally undemocratic body. . . . Consider its dispute resolution system: The WTO's dispute panels are its most undemocratic features. These panels are composed of three trade lawyers that are not bound by "conflict of interest" rules. All proceedings are closed to the public and the press. All documents are kept secret. There is no outside review or appeal after a decision has been made.[28]

Signs:	Three-member panels, closed proceedings, secret documents, no outside review
Condition:	WTO is undemocratic

Federal assistance to parochial schools . . . is a very legitimate issue actually before Congress. I am opposed to it. I believe it is unconstitutional. I've voted against it on the Senate floor this year.[29]

Sign:	I voted against it
Condition:	I believe it is unconstitutional; I am opposed to it.

Dissociation

The last type of inference to consider is dissociation. Unlike arguments from quasi-logic, analogy, generalization, example, cause, and coexistence—which bring together or associate ideas—dissociation disengages, or differentiates, between two ideas. Furthermore, arguers using dissociation seek to assign a positive value to one of the ideas and a lesser or negative value to the other. *Dissociation arguments disengage one idea from another and seek a new evaluation of both ideas.* Most dissociations are based on the distinction between appearance and reality, with reality being what is valued. Consider the following dissociation used by Dr. Martin Luther King Jr. in his speech "I Have a Dream":

> I have a dream that my four little children will one day live in a nation where they will
> be judged not by the color of their skin but by the content of their character.[30]

Here the external appearance—the color of one's skin—is dissociated from the internal substance—the content of one's character—and greater value is placed on the second concept. The claims in dissociative arguments are usually implied. Here, King's claim was that "[people should not] be judged by the color of their skin but by the content of their character." The success of King's argument is based on society's recognition that substance is more important and more to be valued than surface appearances. In a sense, this commonly recognized and accepted distinction functions as the basis or grounds for King's argument.

Dissociations are based on value hierarchies. *A value hierarchy places one value or values above another value or values.* There are many value hierarchies that are recognized and accepted in American society: The objective is valued over the subjective, the end over the means, the unique over what is common, and the permanent over the transitory.[31] Dissociative arguments make use of these hierarchies and especially of the appearance/reality hierarchy to dissociate concepts.

To clarify how value hierarchies are used in dissociative arguments, we will consider two more examples. In the first, a frustrated voter complains:

> I'm tired of all the rhetoric in this presidential campaign. I want to see the candidates
> engage in some substantive debate on the real issues.

This arguer dissociates "substantive debate" (real) from the candidates' "rhetoric" (appearance). Her use of *substantive* and *real* makes it clear that it is the second idea—engaging on the real issues—that she values. Or, consider another example from a discussion on corporate takeovers.

> I don't see a takeover plan here that's going to be beneficial to the corporation. It's a
> one-time hit, where we get a spike in the share price, and we cash out a corporation
> instead of operating it as a viable entity sometime into the future.

The value hierarchy behind this dissociation is the permanent as opposed to the transitory. The "beneficial" plan, the corporation as a "viable entity" (permanent), is dissociated from the "cash out," the "one-time hit" (transitory). For additional examples of dissociation, see Box 6.7.

BOX 6.7
DISSOCIATION

- Disengages two ideas.
- Assigns a positive value to one of the two ideas and a lesser value to the other.
- Can usually be stated in a "not this . . . but that" form.
- Based on accepted value hierarchies (evidence).
- Link is to a less accepted or unrecognized value hierarchy.

(continued)

BOX 6.7   CONTINUED

EXAMPLES

Ask not what your country can do for you—ask what you can do for your country.[32]

Accepted hierarchy:	altruism over selfishness (not stated explicitly)
Claimed hierarchy:	what you can do for your country over what your country can do for you

Real objectivity does NOT mean the reporter has no opinion. Anyone with a pulse has an opinion. The reporter's JOB is to have an opinion, to aggressively dig up the facts, and apply his or her carefully honed opinion to sort it all out. . . . Objectivity means the reporter is ultimately alone with the facts, and must make a SUBJECTIVE decision what to write. They must be independent of organized agendas and interest groups, not independent of their own judgment.[33]

Accepted hierarchy:	objectivity over subjectivity
Claimed hierarchy:	a reporter's "objective" (that is, considered) opinion versus a reporter with a bias who is not objective

The tests for dissociation arguments are much more appropriately applied from the rhetorical rather than the logical perspective. Dissociation arguments rest on hierarchies accepted by the arguer's audience. The *quality* of a dissociation depends on the pervasiveness and strength of the value hierarchy used by the arguer. For example, during the 1992 presidential campaign, Vice President Dan Quayle repeatedly appealed to "family values" over other "lifestyle choices." He sought to dissociate family units made up of single parents and homosexual couples from the traditional two-parent family. His argument appealed to those audiences who believed the nuclear family unit should be valued over other kinds of families because the dissociations he sought to make depended on that hierarchy. A dissociation can meet the test of *opposition* when there are no hierarchies more pervasive and more accepted than the one the arguer is using. Quayle's dissociation was questioned by the segment of the American public that values freedom of choice over the more traditional lifestyle options.

SUMMARY

This chapter defines and describes the types of reasoning used in arguments. The reasoning an arguer uses is expressed in an inference statement that links the argument's evidence with its claim. Often, arguers do not expressly state their reasoning in an inference statement. The ability to determine the nature of an unexpressed inference and its workings is an important critical-thinking skill. Therefore, this chapter explains the various reasoning forms and the standards for judging them.

The first form of reasoning is quasilogical, which is based on formal logic and the syllogism. Quasilogical arguments are composed of a limited number of statements (three or less), and state relationships between a limited number of terms (three or less).

The simplicity and clarity of quasilogical arguments make them seem compelling and persuasive. This chapter describes three kinds of quasilogical arguments—transitivity, incompatibilities, and reciprocity. Transitivity arguments are based on the categorical syllogism and link terms together through a middle term that functions like an equal sign. Incompatibilities are based on the disjunctive syllogism and state two incompatible alternatives at the same time, thus implying a contradiction. Reciprocity arguments state two mutually dependent alternatives and imply that they should be treated equivalently.

The second reasoning form is analogy. Analogies claim that because two objects resemble each other in certain known respects, they will also resemble each other in respects that are unknown. Literal analogies compare objects in the same class, whereas figurative analogies compare relations or qualities of objects in different classes. The probability or cogency of analogies depends on the number of similarities shared by the compared objects, the relevance of those similarities to the argument's claim, and the number of dissimilarities between the compared objects.

The third form of reasoning includes generalization and reasoning from example. A generalization attributes characteristics shared by certain members of a class to the class as a whole, whereas argument from example reasons from a concrete, particular case to a general tendency, rule, or principle. The strength of reasoning from generalization or example depends on how typical the example or examples are of the class, whether there are counterexamples, and, in the case of generalization, whether there are sufficient examples to represent the class as a whole.

Causal reasoning is the fourth reasoning form. Arguments from cause claim that one condition or event contributes to or brings about another condition or event. Causal relations take two forms: the necessary condition for an effect is one that must be present for the effect to occur, and the sufficient condition is a circumstance whose presence guarantees the effect will occur. The cogency of causal arguments depends on whether the cited cause alone is sufficient to guarantee the effect and whether there are countercauses working against the claimed cause–effect relationship. Furthermore, relations among phenomena are rarely as linear and rigorous as causal reasoning implies. For that reason, arguers wishing to show that variations are related often use correlation rather than causation.

Coexistential arguments are the fifth form of reasoning. An inference based on coexistence reasons from something that can be observed (a sign) to a condition or feature that cannot be observed. Two of the most common types of coexistential arguments are person/act inference and reasoning from authority. In order for coexistential arguments to be cogent, the relation between the sign and the condition it indicates must be reciprocal, the number of signs indicating the condition must be sufficient, and there should be no significant countersigns.

The sixth and last form of reasoning is dissociation. Dissociation distinguishes between ideas rather than bringing them together, as do other forms of reasoning. Dissociative arguments disengage one idea from another and seek a new evaluation of both ideas. Dissociations connect the first idea with what the audience most values (reality) and the other idea with what is less valued (appearance). They thereby break the links between the ideas and cause the dissociated idea to be more valued. The tests for dissociation arguments depend on how strongly the audience actually holds the values relevant to the argument.

GLOSSARY

Analogy (p. 158) reasons that because two objects resemble each other in certain known respects, they will also resemble each other in respects that are unknown.

Argument from authority (p. 169) reasons that statements by someone presumed knowledgeable about a particular issue can be taken as evidence sufficient to justify a claim.

Argument from cause (p. 164) claims that one condition or event contributes to or brings about another condition or event.

Argument from Coexistence (p. 167) reasons from something that can be observed (a sign) to a condition or feature that cannot be observed.

Argument from example (p. 163) seeks acceptance for some general rule or principle by offering a concrete, particular case.

Correlation (p. 167) claims that two events or phenomena vary together; an increase or decrease in one is accompanied by an increase or decrease in the other.

Dissociation (p. 170) disengages one idea from another and seeks a new evaluation of both ideas.

Figurative analogy (p. 161) is a comparison between two objects of different classes in which a relation or quality within one is said to be similar to a relation or quality within the other.

Generalization (p. 161) is reasoning that what is true of certain members of a class will also be true of other members of the same class or of the class as a whole.

Inference (p. 153) states the step one has made in linking the evidence to the claim.

Literal analogy (p. 159) compares two objects of the same class that share many characteristics and concludes that a known characteristic that one possesses is shared by the other.

Necessary condition (p. 164) is one that must be present for the effect to occur.

Person/act argument (p. 168) reasons from a person's actions to his or her character or essence.

Quasilogical argument (p. 155) places two or three elements in a relation to one another so as to make the connections between them similar to the connections in formal logic.

Sufficient condition (p. 164) is a circumstance in whose presence the event or effect must occur.

Value hierarchy (p. 171) places one value or values above another value or values.

EXERCISES

For each of the following arguments,

   A. Identify what type of argument it is: quasilogical, analogy, generalization or example, cause, coexistential, or dissociation.

   B. Identify the evidence, claim, and inference. (Remember that the inference is often implicit. If it is not explicitly stated, supply it.)

C. Provide two questions that you might use to test the argument.

Note: It is important to remember that sometimes an argument can fall into more than one classification. The nonreturnable bottle argument in this chapter, for example, was cause and analogy. Note, too, that you will find some of these arguments quite controversial. They should be interpreted as sympathetically as possible, i.e., in line with what the author intended.

The three steps described are demonstrated in regard to the following argument:

> About 35 years ago, the presidents of Harvard, Johns Hopkins, Stanford, Brown, and other colleges issued a manifesto warning against federal aid to education. Their point was that federal aid inevitably meant federal control, and of course they were correct. Federal aid now means that colleges . . . have to swear up and down that they do not discriminate against women. . . . And of course there is the whole business of affirmative action and record-keeping that, one major college has complained, takes about $1 million worth of clerical time to complete.
>
> William F. Buckley Jr., "The Feds and College Aid," *National Review* (August 1, 1986): 46.

A. This is an argument from *cause.*
B. Evidence: Thirty-five years ago, the presidents issued a warning. Colleges must swear they do not discriminate. One million dollars' worth of clerical time is spent in affirmative-action record keeping.

  Claim: Federal aid means federal control.

  Inference: Federal aid and involvement cause the federal government to try to control education.

C. Might the effects of federal aid have desirable as well as undesirable consequences? Are the actions opposing discrimination the result of causes other than federal aid?

∗1. The listener should often be shown the conclusion contained in the principle. From this principle, as from the center, light shines on all parts of the work. In much the same way, a painter plans his painting so that light emanates naturally from a single source to each object. The whole work is unified and reduced to a single proposition enlightened in various ways.

François Fénelon, *Letter to the French Academy*, Barbara Warnick, trans. (Lanham, Md.: University Press of America, 1984), 68.

2. Many of the stories depicting sexual harassment as a severe problem spring from "consultants" whose livelihoods depend upon exaggerating its extent.... Susan Webb, president of Pacific Resources Development Group, a Seattle consultant, says she spends 95 percent of her time advising on sexual harassment. Like most consultants, Miss Webb acts as an expert witness in harassment cases, conducts investigations for companies and municipalities, and teaches seminars. She charges clients $1,500 for her 35-minute sexual harassment video program and handbooks.

Gretchen Margenson, "May I Have the Pleasure . . .," *National Review* (November 18, 1991): 37.

3. It is said by those who have examined the matter closely that the largest number of divorces is now found in communities where the advocates of female suffrage are most numerous, and where the individuality of woman as related to her husband, which such a doctrine inculcates, is increased to the greatest extent. If this be true, it is a strong plea . . . against granting the petition of the advocates of woman suffrage.

Joseph Emerson Brown, "Against the Woman Suffrage Amendment," in *American Forum*, Ernest J. Wrage and Barnet Baskerville, eds. (Seattle: University of Washington Press, 1960), 341.

4. Any Presidential candidate who would take a holiday on a remote Caribbean island with a woman to whom he is not married and with whom he plans to spend a nonworking vacation is the biggest idiot who walked the face of the earth and for that reason alone is unqualified to be president of the United States.

   Adapted from a statement by Jeff Greenfield, "Politics, Privacy, and the Press" in *Ethics in America* television series (Corporation for Public Broadcasting, 1989).

＊5. If we burn the forests of the Amazon, we are told, our planet's lungs will give out, and we will slowly asphyxiate. Surely we have better, more practical reasons for not burning them than to stave off universal catastrophe. I can easily imagine similar arguments that would have required the interior of North America to remain empty of cities—and yet I don't think this continent is a poorer place now than it was 20,000 years ago.

   Thomas Palmer, "The Case for Human Beings," *The Atlantic Monthly* (January, 1992): 88.

6. We observe here today not a victory of party but a celebration of freedom—symbolizing an end, as well as a beginning—signifying renewal, as well as change.

   John Fitzgerald Kennedy, "Inaugural Address, 1961," *Speech Criticism: Methods and Materials*, William A. Linsley, ed. (Dubuque, Iowa: William C. Brown, 1968), 376.

7. Carla Kiiskila, a resident of a section of north Wallingford that seems pretty tranquil until you try to cross the street, wrote to the Engineering Department to complain about the hazards of N. 50th Street at Sunnyside Avenue. . . . Kiiskila complains that she has several times narrowly escaped being hit and had to run for the curb to get across 50th.

   So the Engineering Department's van Gelder came out to examine the intersection. No doubt there's a danger and a problem there, he admits. [One citizen] got the Engineering folks to try crossing at the speed of an 85-year-old, and proved it was impossible. She unwittingly proved her point afterward, when she went to cross back (at normal speed) and very nearly got hit by a speeding car that spun broadside to avoid hitting her.

   Eric Scigliano, "How Can a Citizen Cross the Road?" *The Weekly* (August 27–September 2, 1986), 22.

8. 1991 statistics from the Carnegie Foundation for the Advancement of Teaching show that SAT scores are directly proportional to family income. Students from families with incomes under $10,000 score an average of 768 (combined verbal and math scores) out of a possible total of 1,200. Students from families with incomes in the $30,000 to $40,000 range have scores averaging 884. Students from families with incomes over $70,000 have scores averaging 997. Since scholastic aptitude is related to a student's position on the wealth/poverty scale, which has a lot to do with where a family lives (affluent suburb or inner-city slum), alleviating poverty would be one way of improving scholastic aptitude.

   Edd Doerr, "Whither Public Education?," *The Humanist* (November/December 1991): 41.

9. Scandal has been part of the American system from the beginning. There were allegations of sexual misconduct during the Washington presidency. The Washington cabinet almost broke up over Hamilton and Jefferson fighting with each other. These are the problems that happen in a democratic government subject to public information.

   Adapted from a statement by Rudolph W. Giulani, "Public Trust, Private Interests" in *Ethics in America* television series (Corporation for Public Broadcasting, 1989).

10. Mass culture is in some senses lonely and individualistic. The reasons for this can be summed up, as usual, in a single word: television. More and more, entertainment is about observing and absorbing, not about participation. It is a matter of millions of

atomized individuals, each on a solitary couch, clutching a solitary beer, with the set turned on and the zoom lenses beamed at singers or players or stars.

Lawrence Friedman, *The Horizontal Society* (New Haven, CT: Yale University Press, 1999), 25.

∗11. Let us not seek to satisfy our thirst for freedom by drinking from the cup of bitterness and hatred. We must forever conduct our struggle on the high plane of dignity and discipline. We must not allow our creative protest to degenerate into physical violence. Again and again we must rise to the majestic heights of meeting physical force with soul force.

Martin Luther King Jr., "I Have a Dream," in *Speech Criticism*, 381.

12. Video games work just like the operant conditioning used by modern armies to train soldiers. . . . Whereas soldiers in World War II were taught to shoot (calmly, at stationary targets), soldiers sent to Vietnam were taught to kill—as a conditioned response. They were trained, in full combat garb, to shoot instantly at human-shaped figures that suddenly popped up in front of them. This is very much like the training many children receive playing video games in which lifelike figures pop up and the player has to respond automatically by aiming and pulling a trigger—and gets instant reward if the target is hit.

Deborah Tannen, *The Argument Culture: Moving from Debate to Dialogue* (New York: Random House), 248–249.

13. The awesome power of government needs to be constantly checked by defense lawyers so that mere accusations don't inevitably turn into guilt. As Justice Brandeis said, "In order to promote liberty, we need eternal vigilance."

Adapted from a statement by Jack Litman, "To Defend a Killer" in *Ethics in America* television series (Corporation for Public Broadcasting, 1989).

14. The deficit is a hard problem, but we know that it is not the wallet Washington lacks, it is the will! We know Washington . . . will find $500 billion to bail out banks and bankers that stole people's money. Think about it; $5 billion would allow us to reach nearly every child eligible for *head start*, and yet, we're told we don't have the resources. But when it comes to S and L's, we are ready to commit 100 times that amount. How does that make sense? Are savings and loans 100 times more important?

Mario Cuomo, "Is Government Working?," in *Contemporary American Speeches*, 7th ed., Richard L. Johannesen, R. R. Allen, and Wil A. Linkugel, eds. (Dubuque, Iowa: Kendall/Hunt, 1992), 320.

15. The [Supreme] Court's description of the place of *Roe [v. Wade]* in the social history of the United States is unrecognizable. Not only did Roe not, as the Court suggests, *resolve* the deeply divisive issue of abortion, it did more than anything else to nourish it by elevating it to the national level where it is infinitely more difficult to resolve.

National politics were not plagued by abortion protests, national abortion lobbying, or abortion marches on Congress, before *Roe v. Wade* was decided. Profound disagreement existed among our citizens over the issue—as it does over other issues, such as the death penalty—but that disagreement was being worked out at the state level.

Justice Scalia, dissenting, *Planned Parenthood v. Casey*, 505 US 995. Supreme Court 1992.

16. We are much too intelligent; much too victimized by racism, sexism, militarism, and anti-Semitism; much too threatened as historical scapegoats to go on divided from one another. We must turn from finger pointing to clasped hands. We must share our burdens and our joys with each other once again. We must turn to each other and not on each other and choose higher ground.

Jesse Jackson, "The Rainbow Coalition," given to the Democratic National Convention, July 17, 1984, in *Contemporary American Speeches*, 385.

17. A campaign for president or prime minister looks a lot like show business, or the selling of show business, with its live appearances and TV interviews, its spot advertisements on TV, its market research and focus groups. When Bill Clinton campaigned for the American presidency in 1992, there was "little to distinguish" his appearance in San Francisco's Mission District "from a movie premiere," as one author put it.

Lawrence Friedman, *The Horizontal Society* (New Haven, CT: Yale University Press, 1999), 35.

18. [T]he first amendment to the Constitution does not protect only nice speech or only attractive speech, or only popular speech. We would not need a Constitution for that purpose. The great thing about the United States of America is that our Constitution protects any crackpot who wants to stand on his soapbox and express any oddball point of view that pops into his mind.

John Danforth, "Against a Constitutional Amendment Banning Flag Burning," in *Contemporary American Speeches*, 334.

19. Stricter control over pesticides that affect the female hormone estrogen will be necessary if alarming findings are borne out regarding their potential harmful effects on humans and wildlife.

Scientists from Tulane University have published findings in the journal *Science* that show worrisome effects when pesticides that have been linked to breast cancer and male birth defects are combined. . . .

The Tulane findings came days after an international group of experts, the Work Session on Environmental Endocrine Disrupting Chemicals, warned of threats to intelligence, development, and reproductive health posed by chemicals such as dioxin and PCBs found in pesticides and plastics.

Those chemicals, which mimic natural human and animal hormones, can "change the character of human societies or destabilize wildlife populations," they said.

"Pesticides, Estrogen Link," editorial, *Seattle Post-Intelligencer* (July 12, 1996): A14. Used by permission.

∗20. Even uglier has been the growing number of cases where affirmative action for qualified minorities has turned into affirmative discrimination against qualified majorities and minorities. Asian Americans are denied entrance to the University of California system because of their ethnicity; white males face an almost impossible job market in academia. People with one-eighth Indian blood seek favored treatment as disadvantaged Native Americans. The misnamed Equal Opportunity Commission fined a Chicago firm for hiring too many Hispanics and too few blacks. A high school in Piscataway, New Jersey, fired one teacher because she was white in order to make room for a black teacher. And on it goes.

Doug Bandow, "A Vision Betrayed: Discrimination Is No Answer to Discrimination," *Books and Culture: A Christian Review* (September/October 1995): 13.

21. Under the World Trade Organization, instead of democracy regulating capitalism, capitalism regulates democracy. . . . Instead of a voluntary, humanistic, culturally diverse and ecologically sensitive globalization driven by people's desire to know and learn from each other, we are force-fed an unregulated capitalist homogenized globalization that tantalizes our individual desires while it impoverishes our community and environmental needs. . . . Our challenge is to go beyond the narrow economic and technological globalization that is atomizing people and homogenizing culture, and forge a broad globalization that meets our material needs without compromising our human or ecological diversity.

"World Trade Organization—*Whose Trade Organization?*" *Ruckus* (student newspaper) (October, 1999): 2.

22. Let the skeptics of this peace recall what once existed among these people. There was a time when the traffic of ideas and commerce and pilgrims flowed uninterrupted among the cities of the fertile crescent. In Spain, in the Middle East, Muslims and Jews once worked together to write brilliant chapters in the history of literature and science. All this can come to pass again.

President Bill Clinton, "Statements by Leaders at the Signing of the Middle East Pact," *New York Times* (September 14, 1993, International Edition): A6.

23. President Reagan says the nation is in recovery. Those 90,000 corporations that made a profit last year but paid no federal taxes are recovering. The 37,000 military contractors who have benefited from Reagan's more than doubling the military budget in peacetime, surely, they are recovering. The big corporations and rich individuals who received the bulk of the three-year multibillion tax cut from Mr. Reagan are recovering. But no such recovery is under way for the least of these. Rising tides don't lift all the boats, particularly those stuck on the bottom.

Jesse Jackson, "The Rainbow Coalition," in *Contemporary American Speeches*, 386.

24. The states [of the United States] are pitted against each other in the kind of destructive competition that we sought to move away from 200 years ago when we tore up the Articles of Confederation. Ironically, this is occurring just as Europe moves toward *consolidation*—uniting—in order to make themselves *stronger*. In 1992, the European Economic Community will fuse itself into the largest economy . . . in the world. They, getting *stronger* by uniting, *we* growing weaker—by *fragmentation*.

Mario Cuomo, "Is Government Working?" in *Contemporary American Speeches*, 318.

25. The evidence is clear, cumulative, and robust enough to rule out dismissal or denial. And it has been accumulating for over two decades. . . . What it points to is this: Information technology, upon which we are now very dependent, has occasioned an epidemic of chronic, often crippling, workplace injuries and layoffs. It has also failed remarkably to reduce workloads or, in most cases, to boost productivity. As a result, computers have significantly raised the cost of doing business and intensified the pace of work without delivering on many of the benefits presumed, promised, or imagined to have accompanied the information age.

R. Dennis Hayes, "Digital Palsy: RSI and Restructuring Capital," in *Resisting the Virtual Life*, James Brook and Iain A. Boal, eds. (San Francisco: City Lights, 1995), 173.

NOTES

1. The topics for this discussion were drawn from Debatepedia, which can be found at http://wiki.idebate.org/index.php/Welcome_to_Debatepedia%21.

2. Sean Swint, "Violent Video Games Linked to Aggressive Behavior," WebMD, http://www.webmd.com/news/20000424/children-violence-video-games (accessed on May 12, 2008).

3. A very clear discussion of current research and the relationship of violent video games to violence can be found in Craig A. Anderson, "Violent Video Games: Myths, Facts, and Unanswered Questions," *APA Online*, http://www.apa.org/science/psa/sb-anderson.html (accessed on May 12, 2008).

4. Eric Bangeman, "Senate bill mandates CDC investigation into video game violence," *Ars Technica*, http://arstechnica.com/news.ars/post/20060918-7771.html (accessed on May 17, 2008).

5. The video-game rating system is described on the ESRB Web site, which can be found at http://www.esrb.org/ratings/ratings_guide.jsp (accessed May 18, 2008).

6. Tom Samiljan, "Should Violent Video Games be Banned?" Yahoo! Tech, http://tech.yahoo.com/blogs/samiljan/4146 (accessed on May 18, 2008).

7. Amanda Schaffer, "Don't Shoot: Why Video Games Really Are Linked to Violence," Slate, http://www.slate.com/id/2164065/ (accessed on May 18, 2008). See also Craig A. Anderson, Douglas A. Gentile, and Katherine E. Buckley, Violent Video Game Effects on Children and Adolescents: Theory, Research, and

Public Policy (New York: Oxford University Press, 2006).

8. Anderson, "Violent Video Games," *APA Online*, 2003.

9. Dmitri Williams and Marko Skoric, "Internet Fantasy Violence: A Test of Aggression in an Online Game," *Communication Monographs* 72 (June 2005): 217–33.

10. "New Book Cuts through Violent Video Game Myths," Slashdot, March 7, 2008, http://interviews.slashdot.org/article.pl?sid=08/03/07/226235 (accessed on May 21, 2008).

11. G. Unsworth, G. J. Devilly, and T. Ward, "The effects of Playing Violent Video Games on Adolescents: Should Parents Be Quaking in Their Books?" *Psychology, Crime and Law* 13 (2007): 383–94.

12. John Borland, CNET New.com, "Blurring the line between games and life," February 28, 2005, http://ecoustics-cnet.com.com/Blurring+the+line+between+games+and+life/2100-1024_3-5590956.html (accessed May 21, 2008) and Julie Hilden, "The Attacks on 'Violent' Video Games and 'Torture Porn' Films: Two Different Strategies To Try to Get around First Amendment Protections," FindLaw: Legal News and Commentary, September 17, 2007, http://writ.news.findlaw.com/hilden/20070917.html (accessed on May 21, 2008).

13. Stephen Toulmin, *The Uses of Argument* (Cambridge: Cambridge University Press, 1958), 8.

14. Our typology of inferences is taken from Chaim Perelman, *The Realm of Rhetoric*, W. Kluback, trans. (Notre Dame, Ind.: University of Notre Dame Press, 1982), 53–137.

15. Perelman and Olbrechts-Tyteca, *The New Rhetoric: A Treatise on Argumentation*, John Wilkinson and Purcell Weaver, trans. (Notre Dame, Ind.: University of Notre Dame Press, 1969).

16. This point is emphasized in Barbara Warnick and Susan L. Kline, "*The New Rhetoric*'s Argument Schemes: A Rhetorical View of Practical Reasoning," *Argumentation and Advocacy* 29 (1992): 1–15.

17. Perelman explains their method of research in "The New Rhetoric: A Theory of Practical Reasoning," in *The Rhetorical Tradition*, Patricia Bizzell and Bruce Herzberg, eds. (Boston: St. Martin's, 2001), 1384–1409.

18. In a study of 622 arguments in five televised panel discussions, Warnick and Kline found that 37 percent of the arguments were quasilogical; 22 percent were causal; 12 percent were coexistential; 5 percent were generalization or example; 6 percent were analogical; and 4 percent were dissociative. In considering these percentages, it is important to note that many arguments were classified into two or more of these categories.

19. Howard Besser, "From Internet to Information Superhighway," in *Resisting the Virtual Life*, James Brook and Iain A. Boal, eds. (San Francisco: City Lights, 1995), 9.

20. Mary Steward van Leeuwen, "The Affirmative Action Glass: Half-Full or Half-Empty?" *Books and Culture* (September/October 1995): 15.

21. Perelman and Olbrechts-Tyteca, 385.

22. *TV Times* (supplement to *Seattle Times*), August 26, 2000.

23. Bob Dole, "Weekly Radio Address," July 13, 1996. Online, CNN Time, Allpolitics, http://allpolitics.com/news/9607/13/gop.radio/transcript/shtml (accessed July 15, 1996).

24. Molefi Kete Asanti, "Imperatives of an Afrocentric Curriculum," in *Contemporary American Speeches*, 7th ed., Richard L. Johannesen, R. R. Allen, Wil A. Linkugel, eds. (Dubuque, Iowa: Kendall/Hunt, 1992), 265.

25. Preston Shiller and Hank Dittmar, "Nation of Highways Paved with Opportunities and High Costs," *Seattle Post-Intelligencer* (July 23, 1996): A9.

26. Chris G. Whipple, "Can Nuclear Waste Be Stored Safely at Yucca Mountain?" *Scientific American* (June 1996): 76.

27. Adapted from "Down with Dino Birds?" *Scientific American*, 283 (September, 2000): 32.

28. "The WTO History, Record, and Agenda," *Ruckus* (student newspaper) (October, 1999): 6.

29. John F. Kennedy, "The Responsibility of the Press," in *"Let the Word Go Forth": The Speeches, Statements, and Writings of John F. Kennedy*, Theodore Sorenson, ed. (New York: Delacorte Press, 1988), 126.

30. Martin Luther King Jr., "I Have a Dream," in William A. Lindsay, *Speech Criticism: Methods and Materials* (Dubuque, Iowa: William C. Brown, 1968), 382.

31. For a description of hierarchies accepted in Western society, see Gregg B. Walker and Malcolm O. Sillars, "Where is Argument? Perelman's Theory of Values," in *Perspectives on Argumentation*, Robert Trapp and Janice Schuetz, eds. (Prospect Heights, Ill.: Waveland, 1990), 134–150.

32. John F. Kennedy, "Inaugural Address," in *Contemporary American Speeches*, 7th ed., Richard L. Johannesen, R. R. Allen, Wil A. Linkugel, eds. (Dubuque, Iowa: Kendall/Hunt, 1992), 350.

33. Real People for Real Change PAC, "What's Wrong with the Entertainment and New Media?," 1996, www.realchange/org/why.htm (accessed July 15, 1996)

PRESENTING AND CRITICALLY EVALUATING ARGUMENTS

COMMUNICATING ARGUMENTS

CHAPTER OUTLINE

KEY CONCEPTS

Box 7.1 provides a good illustration of the challenges speakers face when presenting arguments. In this case, Nick and Eva had done many things correctly, especially when compared to opponents who did not present the same quality or depth of background and research. They debated on a topic about which they were well-informed. But they failed to consider fundamental questions about the recipients and their attitudes that were vital in getting the message accepted. These included the following: How much does this audience already know about the topic? What are the audience's present values and beliefs about file sharing and online piracy? What sources are they likely to accept as credible? How should the presentation be organized so that the arguments will have the greatest impact? How many arguments can be developed in the time available? What are the audience's attitudes toward the arguers? What can the arguers do to appear credible, especially about a topic that most of the audience may disagree with?

■ ■ ■ ■ ■

BOX 7.1
FILE SHARING

In Chapter 4, Box 4.1, we reviewed the challenges facing the music recording industry because of illegal file sharing. In that case study, Nick and Eva argued over the ethics and illegality of file sharing and whether universities should intervene more aggressively to prevent it. Their discussion was in preparation for a public debate focusing on the proposition that "students caught illegally sharing files should be immediately expelled from campus."

Because the debate developed a policy proposition, Nick and Eva decided to convince their listeners that all forms of peer-to-peer music sharing and downloading are illegal and that students caught engaged in any illegal activity should be expelled. They reviewed the evidence they had found earlier and gathered additional information from their university's computer science library and business library as well as reports from the music industry. Well equipped with strong evidence, Nick and Eva carefully designed their arguments and organized their presentation. They practiced multiple times, and when the day for the presentation arrived, they were confident in their level of preparation.

In a technical but succinct analysis, Nick and Eva described the way peer-to-peer technology is used for unauthorized copying of music, and they argued that strong penalties against illegal file sharing would provide economic benefits for society, preserve the rights of musicians and the music industry, and help prevent future abuses of online computer technologies. Their opponents, Dan and Dan, did not present the same depth of evidence, and their reasoning focused more on emotional arguments than on the legal and technical aspects of the issue.

When the debate was finished, Nick and Eva were certain they had impressed the audience and that they had convinced the recipients by virtue of their strong research, clear legal analysis, complete information, and carefully constructed arguments. However, in the question-and-answer session that followed, they were surprised and dismayed that the audience reacted negatively to the presentation. In fact, the audience responded much more favorably to Dan and Dan's weaker and more emotional arguments that supported illegal file sharing because students didn't have much money to spend on overpriced CDs. Members of the audience also commented that although Nick and Eva had

(continued)

BOX 7.1   CONTINUED

good information, it was boring and overly complex because of their use of jargon-laden descriptions of peer-to-peer technology and too many quotations from legal analysts.

Whereas audience members commended Dan and Dan for being clear and "connecting" their arguments to the recipients' experiences, they said that Nick and Eva had failed to make their arguments clear and did not address the views and attitudes of the majority of the people in the room who believed that music downloading was a justifiable response to the music industry's price gouging.

Recipients commented that Nick and Eva used biased evidence from the music industry, which stood to gain from their policy position, and that they ignored the perspectives of those who chose to share and download music. Nick and Eva were also criticized for failing to include members of the music industry who supported file sharing. Audience members stated that their policy position of completely expelling students for file sharing was unrealistic and that they should have focused on alternatives that seek a compromise among the parties, including the possibility of having the university implement a flat fee paid to the music industry for downloading.

Nick and Eva left the auditorium discouraged. They didn't understand what went wrong with such a carefully researched and well-crafted presentation. Consider the following questions:

1. How is it possible that well-crafted and thoroughly researched arguments fail when presented to an audience?
2. Beyond the evidence, claims, and reasoning, what other factors determine whether recipients accept or reject arguments?
3. Under what conditions do technically weaker arguments such as those presented by Dan and Dan become more persuasive for audiences?
4. In Chapter 2 we explored how an arguer's relationship with the audience is important. What role did that relationship play here?
5. What could or should Nick and Eva have done differently?

Nick and Eva had good, well-substantiated, and carefully reasoned arguments. But they forgot that the audience is an integral and important part of argumentation. In this case, although the arguments were timely, ethically presented, and appropriate, they placed the arguments in the wrong sphere. They combined a focus on the technicalities of music sharing and downloading technologies with technical explanations of the economic repercussions of unauthorized downloading. Their audience, university students, was unprepared to evaluate arguments originated and presented from this sphere. Many of the recipients had personal experience with music downloading and were more likely to be prepared to evaluate arguments presented from the public sphere.

The concept of argument spheres and fields was developed in Chapter 1 and is particularly important here because, by placing their arguments in the wrong sphere, Nick and Eva had little hope of successfully convincing their audience of the proposition. In other words, Nick and Eva had presented good arguments that were lost on the audience because the presentation was not appropriately designed or presented for a public-sphere discussion.

In Chapter 2, we developed a co-orientational approach for understanding how arguments function in the relationship between arguer and recipient. As you may recall, we made the point that argument recipients represent a significant part of argument situations. They do not function as blank slates or logic machines responding only to the validity of an arguer's reasoning or evidence. They are influenced by the relationships they have with one another and with the speaker, by the subject matter, and by their own knowledge, experience, and attitudes (among many other variables). The best evidence, strongest arguments, and most clearly designed presentations are irrelevant if recipients reject or fail to understand them.

In this chapter, we will examine how arguers can enhance and develop strong relationships with and messages for their listeners. First, we will focus on issues related to arguers and how they build relationships and interact with their recipients. Second, we will consider issues related to audiences and how audience members come to believe or reject arguments. And, finally, we will examine strategies for how arguers can work to enhance their relationship with recipients and become more persuasive while speaking.

ARGUER AS COMMUNICATOR

The primary role of an advocate is to ethically and persuasively communicate arguments that recipients can understand and choose to accept or not. This is the premise behind the co-orientational approach developed in Chapter 2. Co-orientation assumes that arguers and recipients work together in a relationship to share argument content and achieve mutually beneficial outcomes. Argumentation theorists Perelman and Olbrechts-Tyteca suggest that advocates consider argumentation as a collaborative process toward problem solution.[1] We should attend to multiple points of view and seek solutions that embrace alternatives.

Theodore Newcomb's A-B-X model in Figure 7.1 illustrates this objective.[2] In Newcomb's model, "A" and "B" represent arguer and recipient. "X" represents the arguer's goal or objective, which may change and develop as issues are explored and ideas shared. Arguers are successful when a mutually beneficial "X" is developed to the satisfaction of the participants. This means, then, that "A" is interdependent with "B" because their success is contingent on each other. Consider the case in Box 7.1. Nick and Eva, "A," might have had superior arguments supporting a superior point of view, but if their recipients, "B," did not understand or were bored or uninterested, their objective, "X," could not be met, and no mutually beneficial outcomes was achieved.

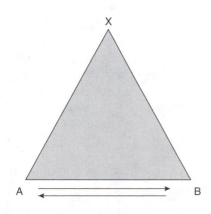

FIGURE 7.1   Co-Orientation Model of Argument

Adapted from Theodore Newcomb, "An Approach to the Study of Communicative Acts," *Psychological Review* 60 (1953): 393–404.

No matter how significant and compelling their arguments were, if Nick and Eva could not arrive at an acceptable outcome with their recipients, they would be unsuccessful.

How Arguers Influence

Social psychologists who have studied persuasion and compliance gaining have identified three major ways that people get others to comply or agree with their requests or claims: compliance, identification, and internalization.[3] The first two forms depend heavily on nonlogical responses to messages and are independent of many of the reasoning processes described in this book. The third, however, is closely related to the quality of argument in a message and will be carefully considered later in this section.

Compliance

Compliance is the use of rewards and punishments by a powerful source to get recipients to believe or act in a certain manner. A familiar example is demonstrated by the way students undertake an academic assignment. They recognize that the teacher possesses the means to reward them in the form of a favorable grade, so they carefully structure their work to conform to the teacher's expectations. For a person to gain acceptance of a position through rewards and punishments, other people must believe that person has the resources to reward or punish them and cares whether or not they comply.[4] Argumentation, however, is not a necessary condition for compliance. A teacher may attempt to justify an assignment; a supervisor may explain a work order. But such actions are not required to produce the outcome they desire. The power they possess causes others to do as they say. This form of influence is therefore relatively unimportant for our purposes because it is independent of argumentation.

Identification

Identification is influence that occurs because people find a source attractive and wish to enhance their own self-concept by establishing a relationship with the source. People identify with other people whom they like and admire. People often want to be like someone who possesses traits similar or complementary to their own. Advertising often uses this principle. Because we want to be attractive and sexy like the models in the ads, we buy Calvin Klein or Diesel jeans even if they cost more than others. Because we admire the athletic prowess of Alex Rodriguez or Tom Brady, we are persuaded to buy the athletic shoes and products they endorse. Soccer star David Beckham was signed to a $10 million deal with Gillette to endorse their products.

R. Glen Hass has observed that attitudes changed through identification "are not incorporated into the individual's system of beliefs and values; nor are they maintained independent of the message source."[5] In other words, people's acceptance of an argument because of identification is not related to message content but rather to the identity of its source. If the source loses his or her attractiveness or changes the claim in the message, then the recipients will change their own positions as well. For instance, when Atlanta Falcons quarterback Michael Vick was accused of participating in illegal dog fighting, sponsors such as Nike, Reebok, and Upper Deck distanced themselves from him and his tainted image.

Researchers demonstrated this principle in an interesting and revealing experiment that showed the influence of attractiveness. Experimenters designed a questionnaire, and a female confederate volunteered to assist by contributing to the group discussions led by the experimenters. She responded the same way in both discussions, and the same people participated in both groups. For one discussion, she looked very attractive, with a stylish haircut, chic clothing, and becoming makeup. In the other, she appeared unattractive, with ugly clothing, messy hair, and a trace of a mustache on her upper lip. The results showed that as an attractive woman, she was much more effective in influencing the group.[6] The group's reactions were based on her attractiveness and not on cognitive processes. They had not thought about her message or about its quality.

Internalization

Unlike compliance and identification, internalization is based on the thought that recipients give to the content of a message. *Internalization is a process in which people accept an argument by thinking about it and by integrating it into their cognitive systems.* Whereas attitudes and beliefs acquired because of compliance or identification usually fade or disappear when the message source loses power or attractiveness, attitudes and beliefs that are internalized often persist and are maintained.

Before continuing our discussion of internalization and the form of source credibility connected with it, we should pause to stress that, like all category schemes, this three-part division of source influence by means of compliance, identification, and internalization is somewhat oversimplified. Power, attractiveness, and content-related credibility often are closely related in any given argumentative situation. If a confident, attractive, highly respected supervisor explains a new marketing plan to subordinates and details a strategy for implementing the plan, that supervisor has clearly influenced the subordinates in all three ways simultaneously. Furthermore, one study of attractiveness revealed that attractive persuaders also tended to be perceived as better communicators, more highly educated, and better informed.[7] In many situations, it would be difficult, if not impossible, to separate any one of these three forms from the other two.

Nevertheless, researchers have linked internalization most closely to what is actually said in the message. People who believe an argument because of its content are most affected by two aspects of the arguer's credibility: expertise and trustworthiness. *Expertise is the possession of a background of knowledge and information relevant to the argument.* It depends on whether people believe an arguer knows the correct position on a topic. *Trustworthiness depends on whether people believe the arguer is motivated to tell them the truth.*[8] Although expertise and trustworthiness are often established partly by initial credibility (the arguer's reputation for being knowledgeable, sincere, and honest), what the arguer actually says and does while presenting the argument is even more vital.

Expertise and Trustworthiness

There are five situational factors that determine the importance of expertise and trustworthiness in judging an arguer's credibility. First, expertise and trustworthiness are especially influential when the question being discussed appears to have a right or wrong answer. For example, if the question is whether violence on television causes violent behavior in children, we are more likely to accept the claims of a media scholar who has studied the relationship over the claims of the "average" parent. However, if the question relates to values and preferences, such as what television programs are most enjoyable and entertaining, we may be heavily influenced by persons we find attractive.[9]

Second, the less involved people are in a message and the less knowledge they have of the topic, the more influenced they will be by the credibility of the source. Presumably, people with low levels of knowledge and interest are unprepared or disinclined to think about the content of arguments or to weigh the merit of claims and evidence advanced in their support. Arguers with low credibility who must address uninformed and disinterested recipients face a greater challenge than that encountered by arguers with high credibility.

Third, people who hear and read arguments from arguers with varying degrees of credibility will tend to forget who made the argument and remember only its content. So people who are initially influenced by an arguer's credibility will later forget the source and remember only the arguments. Researchers call this the "sleeper effect." Although research experiments showing this phenomenon have been somewhat inconsistent, they do indicate that people often forget the identity of a message's source and remember only what was said.[10]

Fourth, expertise seems particularly important when recipients disagree strongly with the position an arguer favors. In a situation in which the position advanced is extremely controversial and in basic disagreement with the recipients' position, a highly credible source will be more persuasive than one who has less credibility. In an experiment reported by Richard E. Petty and John T. Cacioppo, the argument concerned how many hours of sleep were necessary per night. It was attributed to either a Nobel Prize–winning physiologist or a YMCA director. The highly credible source influenced recipients even when advocating extreme positions (such as two or three hours of sleep per night). When the less expert source advocated the same extreme position, however, recipients were much less likely to believe it.[11] The researchers concluded that the more extreme the discrepancy between an arguer and the audience, the more pronounced will be the influence of credibility in producing attitude change.

Fifth, it is vital that recipients perceive a source as being free of bias and vested interest and concerned primarily with their welfare. Researchers have found that subjects were more influenced by a message when they thought arguers were unaware they were being overheard and thus did not intend to persuade them.[12] Research has also shown that when arguers are expected to have a personal interest in one side of an issue but in fact favor the other side, they have high credibility. For example, a union officer who opposes a strike is more likely to be believed than one who advocates a strike simply because he would be expected to do so. These results and others indicate that recipients' perception of arguers' objectivity, fairness, sincerity, and disinterestedness all contribute to both their trustworthiness and their credibility.

CHARACTERISTICS OF RECIPIENTS

Two of the questions an advocate needs to ask first are: "Who am I addressing and what do they need?" Although these questions are relatively simple, finding and developing the answers are challenging. Argument recipients are complex and varied. They have different needs, interests, backgrounds, and enthusiasm, depending on the topic.

Additionally, their role as recipients changes depending on the situation. A common perception of argumentation places two speakers in opposition over an issue. An audience listens to arguments and then decides what to do with them. But this is only one type of audience that judges arguments in a competitive style, which was introduced in Chapter 2. In fact, much argumentation theory and practice is based on this competitive and adversarial style of argumentation, which places recipients in the role of objective decision-makers, much like a judge or jury. This model has been the traditional one for teaching argument and debate.[13]

Adversarial Argumentation

Adversarial argumentation focuses on a clash between two points of view. With this style, the advocates develop persuasive presentations and refute the opposing points of view. It is a fight that is often characterized by warlike metaphors: "I beat their arguments," "My case won," "I tore down my opposition," or "I crushed my opponent." In most formal and institutional argument forums, such as law, politics, or journalism, advocates argue only one side. Politicians are often referred to as "flip-floppers" if they try to adapt and evolve their positions as new information and ideas develop. The same is true in other situations as well. In academic debate, students argue for or against a particular position. In courts of law, attorneys will prosecute or defend the guilt or innocence of a person. And, in legislative assemblies, two sides will debate for or against a particular bill or amendment. In these cases, we proceed from the assumption that there are two sides, and one will win while the other will lose.

When we focus on argument as an adversarial exchange between two combatants, we tend to rely on external audiences to decide which side is right. For example, when a prosecutor argues to convict an accused criminal, the lawyer is seeking to persuade a jury, not the defense counsel. The jury is supposed to be an unbiased, external entity. When legislators debate over the merits of a bill, the bill's author is usually not the audience. Rather, the legislators who will vote on the bill are the audience. Adversarial argumentation assumes there will be a winner and a loser and that the arguers' role is to persuade an external audience of the merits of the case. Adversarial argumentation is appropriate and effective in the proper situation, but it is not the only style and is not always appropriate.

Co-Orientational Argumentation

The perception that argumentation and debate are simply a clash between two sides is limited, and many theorists have been critical of teaching methods that focus on argumentation as competitive, in which one side wins while the other loses.[14] Rather, in some situations, argument and debate are a partnership or collaboration among the participants, and multiple sides are expressed and developed. In Chapter 2, we referred to this approach as co-orientational—arguer and recipient participate together to create arguments. The collaborative argumentation style allows for the participants to achieve common goals, enhance their relationship, and create common solutions to significant issues. Generally, this style is regarded as a preferred approach for managing disputes because it allows for more points of view and fosters a collaborative decision-making environment.[15]

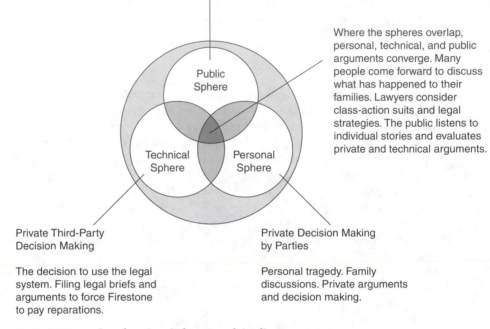

Public Third-Party
Decision Making

Providing the media with information. Taking the
arguments public and asking Firestone to answer
for the alleged product liability.

Where the spheres overlap,
personal, technical, and public
arguments converge. Many
people come forward to discuss
what has happened to their
families. Lawyers consider
class-action suits and legal
strategies. The public listens to
individual stories and evaluates
private and technical arguments.

Public
Sphere

Technical
Sphere

Personal
Sphere

Private Third-Party
Decision Making

The decision to use the legal
system. Filing legal briefs and
arguments to force Firestone
to pay reparations.

Private Decision Making
by Parties

Personal tragedy. Family
discussions. Private arguments
and decision making.

FIGURE 7.2   Overlapping Spheres and Audiences

Once disputes rise to a level that involves third-party decision-makers, collaborative problem solving is more difficult to achieve because those arguments tend to result in a winner and a loser. Court cases, contract disputes, and formal grievances are all examples of this type of argumentation. However, in the sphere of private argumentation, partnership and collaboration can guide arguers.[16] Figure 7.2 illustrates how overlapping audiences can result from overlapping spheres, and Box 7.2 provides an example of how different spheres and audiences can intersect.

Box 7.3 demonstrates how arguments function at different levels for different recipients; it further shows how arguers use different strategies within each of those levels. Some of the claims against Firestone were handled privately, whereas others used third parties. In the end, accusations were made public and became the subject of legislation and public court cases. When developing arguments, arguers must carefully consider the recipients they wish to target. Understanding the argument situation, who the decision-makers are, and the kind of decision the arguer wants is central to adapting and developing persuasive presentations.

BOX 7.2
FIRESTONE TIRES[17]

On October 16, 1998, fourteen-year-old Jessica LeAnn Taylor, a junior-high-school cheerleader, died in a car accident on her way to the homecoming football game in Mexia, Texas. That day, the tread of the Firestone ATX tire on the left rear of the Ford Explorer she was traveling in separated from the tire. The vehicle veered to the left and flipped over.

As noted in Chapter 2, difficult situations and tragedies such as this invite argument. Jessica's parents were faced with the decision how to proceed against a large tire manufacturer. They had choices about the appropriate venue and recipients for argument. They could have chosen to talk directly to Firestone and ask for compensation—private decision making. Instead, they sought help from Randy Roberts, an attorney who specialized in product liability cases. Roberts filed a lawsuit against Firestone and asked the judge to force the company to make its records available to him. Although Firestone resisted the request, the judge, as an administrative decision-maker, compelled the tire manufacturer under the rules of discovery to provide Roberts with the necessary records.

In those documents, Roberts discovered more than 1,100 incident reports and 57 lawsuits accusing Firestone of making a defective product. Most of those victims had settled with Firestone privately, using private decision making. Others had reached a court settlement for an undisclosed amount—private third-party decision making. Roberts, however, decided to make the records public by inviting the National Highway Traffic Safety Association to examine the reports. This decision shifted the audience and discussion toward the public sphere. Once the reports were made public, Firestone became the subject of public scrutiny and debate, which resulted in the largest tire recall in U.S. history.

BOX 7.3
AUDIENCES AND ARGUMENTS

AUDIENCE TYPE	STRATEGY	DEFINITION
Private audience	Argument avoidance	Arguers choose not to say anything. They may wait for another advocate to initiate the argument, or they may wait for the situation to end before making the choice to argue. For example, consider two roommates: one smokes in the dorm room, and the other is a nonsmoker. If the nonsmoker chooses to say nothing, then avoidance has been used.
	Informal discussion	Arguers work in partnership to collaborate over a collection of issues. Argumentation tends to be freeform and will evolve as arguments and responses are made by the participants. For example, if roommates sit down to talk about smoking in the room and try to collaborate to find a way to accommodate the needs of both the smoker and the nonsmoker, then an informal discussion has taken place.

(continued)

BOX 7.3   CONTINUED

AUDIENCE TYPE	STRATEGY	DEFINITION
	Negotiation	Arguers advocate positions and work together to collaborate and compromise toward a mutually agreeable outcome. With the roommates, if the smoker wants to be able to smoke and the nonsmoker does not want any smoke in the room, they may work to agree on times when smoking can happen in the room or try to find an alternative place for the smoker to smoke.
	Mediation	When tension, hostility, or other barriers inhibit arguers from talking with one another, the arguers may invite a facilitator to help manage the exchange of arguments. Mediators do not make the decision; rather they assist the participants in developing arguments, ideas, and alternatives toward a mutually agreeable conclusion. Mediation is often referred to as facilitated negotiation. For example, if both roommates are so angry about smoking and the others' attitudes that they can no longer talk with each other, they may invite a mutual friend or the dormitory resident aid to help them reach a mutual agreement.
Private third-party audience	Administrative decision	Administrative decisions are made by a neutral third party. The third party is private in the sense that it is typically a member of the organization or field. Most often the arguers seek out and mutually agree upon the third party, and the third party is typically an expert in the area of the dispute. In the case of the roommate conflict, a residence-hall staff member or director might reach an administrative decision. A university grievance committee could also make an administrative decision. In any case, an administrative decision is made by considering the rules of the field and the arguments presented, and by looking for alternative solutions or methods for resolving the problem.
	Arbitration	Arbitration is the use of an external third party to listen to both sides of the issue and then render a decision. Whereas an administrative decision may seek some middle ground between the advocates, an arbiter will typically decide for one or the other but not offer alternatives. In the case of the smoking roommate, the arbiter may decide that since smoking is banned in residence halls, the smoker will have to leave the building to smoke.
Public third-party audiences	Judicial decision	Once the authority for a decision leaves the private and technical spheres and enters the public arena, public decisions are made. Judicial decisions occur when advocates seek legal recourse to resolve a dispute. Judicial decisions are typically public, apply publicly accepted

(continued)

BOX 7.3   CONTINUED

AUDIENCE TYPE	STRATEGY	DEFINITION
		standards (such as the application of the Constitution or other laws), and make decisions that are binding to the advocates. If, hypothetically, the case of the smoking roommate arrived in court because the smoker was expelled for refusing to obey the law and smoke outside, the court may fine the student or force the university to reinstate the student. In any case, the proceedings and decision become a matter of public record.
	Legislative decision	Legislative decisions occur when public, third-party audiences use the legislative process to change law, policy, or legal processes. Typically, a legislative agenda becomes the subject of political debate, campaigns, or debate on the floor of the legislative assembly. If, for example, the smoking student was expelled for smoking, that student may seek legislative recourse by working to have the laws governing smoking changed to allow greater freedom for smokers.
Extralegal audiences	Nonviolent direct action	Extralegal decisions occur when audiences turn to means outside the legal process, often because they view the legal system as an illegitimate means through which to resolve conflict. Nonviolent direct action involves collective protest. In the case of the student, if the university administration decided in favor of the smoking roommate and other students' rights to smoke in the dorms, the nonsmoking roommates might organize a demonstration to communicate the dangers of secondhand smoke and attempt to persuade the university to change its decision.
	Violent direct action	Violent direct action occurs when audiences attempt to change minds through violence and coercion. Violence is not a form of argumentation and may be used when groups believe that argumentation will not be effective.

Recipients and Situations

Chapter 2 explored how argument situations are shaped by several factors. For every argument and persuasive case presented, arguers must work to adapt their style and approach to the recipients and the situation. Some situations call for a collaborative style, whereas others require competing, compromising, or any of the other styles discussed. Consider Figure 7.3, which represents a continuum of audience relationships. In this figure, four types of argument audiences are detailed: private decision-makers, private third-party decision-makers, public third-party decision-makers, and extralegal decision-makers. For each audience type, the arguers employ different strategies of persuasion, ranging from avoidance and discussion through legislative

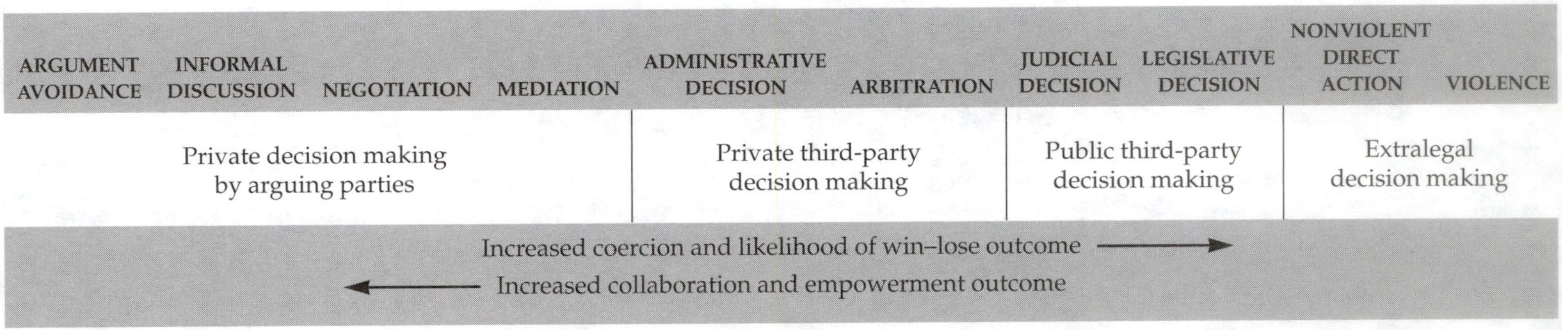

FIGURE 7.3 Continuum of Audience Relationships

Adapted from Christopher W. Moore, *The Mediation Process: Practical Strategies for Resolving Conflict* (San Francisco: Jossey-Bass, 1986).

action. Each recipient type is dependent on the role the recipient plays in the argument situation.

When arguers and recipients work together to develop issues and reach decisions, they are engaged in private decision making. *Private decision-makers argue in the private sphere and use rules and conventions that are decided among the participants.* The advocates function as both arguer and recipient because all sides work to find agreement. Private decision making arguments tend to be more collaborative and informal than other types. For instance, when Nick and Eva argued over the ethics and legality of music file sharing, they were arguing for their own benefit in preparation for a public debate. They explored issues and made decisions using their own criteria. Because the advocates used their own rules and norms and then made their own decisions about which arguments to use, they were functioning in the private sphere as private decision-makers.

Private third-party decision-making audiences add an external audience. Arguments aimed at third-party audiences tend to be technical-sphere arguments to specialized audiences. The decision-makers are no longer the arguers but are instead a third party. The conventions and issues for argument come from within the technical sphere and are decided by those who understand the rules and norms of a particular field. Third-party audiences remove the power of decision making from the individual advocates. Nick and Eva understood this fact—to a point. They argued as though the recipients had sufficient legal and technical expertise to properly evaluate the arguments. Had they spoken in front of members of the music industry, musicians, or owners and operators of file-sharing Web sites, they might have been more successful. However, they spoke to an audience that lacked the field-specific background to process and evaluate the arguments effectively.

Public third-party audiences largely apply the norms and conventions of the public sphere. Arguers speak to these audiences in the larger context of public debate and use public rules and expectations to govern arguments and decisions. Such arguments rely on the public audience, rather than the arguers, to make the decision. This type was the primary audience that Nick and Eva were addressing. Instead of focusing on the technical issues related to file sharing, they would have been more successful in developing a common understanding of the issues and arguments if they had adapted to the expectations of the public sphere and the public audience.

Extralegal decision-makers are groups that use nonviolence, direct action, or violence to influence decision processes. Nonviolent protest may include sit-ins, boycotts, picketing, or other means to disrupt social control. Direct action might include other extralegal means, such as computer hacking or verbal protest. Extralegal protest is not truly a form of argument because violating the law and becoming violent are not rhetorical strategies. They use force as opposed to argument to compel a decision. If, however, Nick and Eva became frustrated with their lack of success in the public sphere, they might decide to take extralegal action. They might construct and deploy a virus to attack file-sharing servers. They could send anonymous letters to musicians that reveal the names and addresses of people who are illegally downloading files.

It is important to note from Figure 7.2, however, that as we move from private, collaborative argument toward external, third-party decision-makers, we have a tendency to assume that argument becomes a win-lose situation between two opposing groups. Box 7.3 illustrates how different strategies are used for various audience types.

COMMUNICATION STRATEGIES, TECHNIQUES, AND PRINCIPLES

Arguers should select strategies and styles that are appropriate for the recipients. They may change and adapt arguments and presentations to meet the needs of each audience.

Listening

The single most important skill an arguer must master is the art of listening carefully to what others say—both in preparation and in presentation of arguments. Arguers should listen actively before developing and presenting a response. *Active listening means to hear for meaning.* Arguers should listen to *how* something is said as much as to *what* is said. They should endeavor to understand the meaning of the message as the speaker intended it.[18] Active listening is different from other types of listening.[19] It is not an easy skill to master and involves careful concentration and reflective questions, but it is important.

Competitive listening is characterized by advocates who are more interested in winning an argument or a particular position rather than understanding other viewpoints. Academic debate, legislative assemblies, and political debates are all contexts in which competitive listening can dominate. *Passive listening involves hearing other points of view but does not verify or affirm understanding.* This means that arguers and recipients hear arguments and then respond to what they heard, assuming that they correctly understood the intentions and meaning behind what was said. Active listening focuses on hearing *and* verifying the meaning so that there is a common understanding of the argument.

Active and accurate listening to arguments is essential. The tone, strength, and emotions behind arguments can reveal agendas, needs, or fears. Constructive argument moves speakers beyond exclusive reliance on understanding logical arguments and toward adaptive and flexible understandings that allow arguers to be sensitive to the issues of culture, ethics, occasion, and situation. Constructive argumentation assumes that the feelings and contexts behind arguments can be as important as the arguments themselves.

Reframing

Often, advocates focus on a particular position or point of view and create arguments that support only that idea. Nick and Eva focused exclusively on expelling from campus students caught downloading files illegally. Yet different approaches may exist that achieve the same goals. This is the process of reframing.

Reframing means to analyze arguments and argument outcomes using alternative points of view. Instead of accepting an advocate's conclusions, arguers and recipients should consider alternatives that fit the evidence and situation equally well. By paying careful attention to the interests, feelings, and needs that motivate another's arguments, arguers have the opportunity to reframe the issue to find mutually acceptable solutions to seemingly insurmountable problems. Arguments can be adapted if the arguers are sensitive to ways of reframing an issue that meet the needs of other arguers.

Organizing

Students of argument frequently ponder the order in which to organize the arguments they have constructed. They often ask themselves the following questions: "Should I openly state my conclusion or thesis, or leave it implicit?" "Where should I place my strongest arguments so that they will have the greatest possible impact on the audience?" "Should I organize my argument around possible objections to my position?" "Should I use all my arguments, even the weaker ones?" "Should I present both sides of the question or only one side?" Arguers who ask such questions want to organize their arguments so that audiences will respond to them favorably. Although their decisions will probably be affected by the requirements of the topic being discussed and the nature of the situation, some information based on research about audience reaction to various patterns of organization may be helpful.

Stating Conclusions

Should one openly state one's conclusion when making a controversial argument? Researchers have compared the use of explicit conclusions with conclusions that were implied or left unstated and have found that explicitly stated conclusions were generally more effective.[20] One researcher speculated that when claims are not explicitly stated, audiences fill in the gaps with claims and arguments of their own—ones that frequently go against what the arguer had intended.[21] The arguers in such cases can lose control of the argument. If the audience is intelligent and the argument is very clearly organized, the audience may be favorably influenced even if the conclusion is not stated. Otherwise, arguers who fail to state their claim clearly may lose the concurrence of their audience.

Presenting Both Sides

Should one present one side or multiple sides of an issue when making extended arguments? In answering this question, one should consider at least two additional factors besides the audience. First, consider the nature of the topic itself. When multiple courses of action are available, it is desirable to consider them. That is especially important when one considers the ethical responsibility of empowering the audience. Of course the arguer may prefer one alternative over the others, but audiences should be given sufficient information to help them understand why one direction is superior to the others. Second, consider the context for the argument. Is another speaker responsible for alternative arguments? For example, in a court of law, a prosecutor does not need to present both sides of the case because another speaker, the defense attorney, has that responsibility.

Research into the characteristics of audiences has revealed that when the audiences are favorably predisposed to the message, a one-sided message is better: The audience responds more favorably to one-sided presentations.[22] However, these are not argumentative contexts since the audience and the arguer are in agreement. The claims do not rise above the level of dispute, and arguments do not occur.

When the audience is well-informed or disagrees with the arguer's position, a two-sided analysis is more effective. People who know both sides of the argument or who oppose the arguer's position will rehearse counterarguments as they listen or read, and they will not necessarily concentrate on the argument while it is being presented. Furthermore, they will view a two-sided argument as more credible because it appears fair and well-informed. Finally, hearing both sides causes audience members to be more resistant to opponents' later efforts to argue against the arguer's position.

Presenting Weak Arguments

Sometimes advocates wonder how selective they should be about the arguments they use. Usually, they have a large number of potential arguments. Should they use them all? Or should they be selective, using only the best and most cogent in support of their thesis? Generally, selective application of only the strongest arguments is the better course of action. Ruth Anne Clark, a persuasion theorist, explains why:

> There is a major danger in this policy [of using weak arguments]. Members of the audience who are predisposed to disagree with the advocate will look for some justification for discounting the validity of the entire message. Although it seems reasonable that such individuals would simply ignore arguments they do not agree with, often this is not the case. If an argument seems invalid or insignificant, they will concentrate on it, frequently ignoring all other arguments. A week later, if someone asks them what the message was about, they may recall only the argument they found invalid.[23]

Clark's observation reminds us of why we should not use weak arguments indiscriminately. Not only do they undermine our credibility, but they also give those who are opposed to our proposal a reason not to accept it.

Presenting Strong Arguments

The recognition that the arguments available for construction of a message have various degrees of strength implies another question about the relationship between the audience and the organization of the message: Where should the stronger arguments be placed? People interested in this question have studied the cognitive processes and recall patterns people use when responding to arguments. *They have found that audiences are most likely to remember what comes at the beginning and end of messages.[24] This is called the primacy–recency effect.* Whether placement of a strong argument at the beginning or at the end of a message is more effective depends on situational and other factors, but arguers are generally well advised to place their strongest arguments at either of these two positions.

Selecting Starting Points

In Chapter 2 we observed that, to function as evidence in an argument, a statement must fall below the level of dispute—that is, audience members must agree with it. If a statement is uncontroversial and accepted by the people to whom the argument is made, then the arguers can get started on the right track and proceed to build an argument chain. Otherwise, the arguer will run into trouble and may be derailed. This is why having a clear understanding of audience type and context for argument is particularly important. Arguers must have some knowledge of the audience's values and attitudes to be assured that premises will be accepted and not challenged or rejected. What are the recipients' needs and interests? What are their priorities? In the topic area in which the argument is made, what do they value? Finding out the answers to such questions will ensure that the process of making the argument goes smoothly.

In selecting starting points, it is also important to consider the sphere of argument and the type of audience with which you are engaging in argumentation. The sphere of argumentation—private, public, or technical—will help determine the choice of starting points. Moreover, the type of audience—private, private third-party, public third-party, or extralegal—will also affect the starting points for argument. Consider the following example:

> **Car Salesperson:**   This is a wonderful example of a 1965 Triumph TR4A. You will never see such a good example of British engineering. In fact, this one happens to have the dual Stromberg setup and the all-synchro 4-speed with the 3.91 differential. Tough to find that in this kind of vehicle. That, with the 87-mm sleeves, makes this quite a collectible classic.
>
> **Buyer:**   What is a Stromberg, and why is that important? How many miles are on this car?

To help the buyer understand the product, the salesperson needed to explain how the car met the buyer's needs and expectations, and the arguments should have been adapted to the buyer's level of understanding. As presented, the salesperson relied too much on technical argument for a buyer making a personal decision. The same thing happened with Nick and Eva. They began their presentation with a technical discussion within a legal sphere. It did not meet the recipients' needs or expectations.

The arguer is responsible for creating a connection with the recipients by adapting arguments to their background, situation, needs, and values. Regardless of the quality of the organization, reasoning, and presentation, if speakers do not begin with accepted points, the recipients may reject what is said. Of course, many audiences are heterogeneous, and it is sometimes hard to discover the values, assumptions, and facts on which all audience members would agree. Advocates should recognize these audiences and design a presentation that creates a connection with them.

Supporting Reasoning

In Chapter 1, we noted that an argument's reasoning constructs a link between its evidence, or starting point, and the claim that the arguer wants the audience to accept. Selecting reasoning recognizable to the audience is just as important as selecting a starting point acceptable to them. Arguers should use reasoning acceptable to the recipients. If arguers use an analogy to make a comparison, for example, the two things that are compared should be viewed as similar by the audience. If a speaker makes a causal connection (e.g., between legalizing software duplication and economic benefit), then the audience should clearly understand the reasoning being used.

Consider the following argument made by a defense attorney attempting to persuade a jury not to convict a defendant based on circumstantial evidence:

> **Defense Attorney:**   Just because the defendant was seen leaving the victim's home the evening of the murder, owned a .22-caliber gun of the type used in the crime, and had recently quarreled with the victim, we cannot conclude he is guilty. His guilt must be proven beyond a reasonable doubt.

The attorney's *claim* is, "You should not vote for a conviction." His *evidence* is that the defendant was *only* seen leaving the home, owned a .22-caliber gun, and had quarreled with the victim. His *reasoning* is unstated but is probably that the signs shown in the evidence are circumstantial and insufficient to support a conviction. Why? Because in our judicial system an accused person is assumed innocent until proven guilty beyond a reasonable doubt. If challenged, the defense attorney would further support his reasoning by stating this principle, which he knows is recognized and accepted by the members of the jury.

As a second example, consider a student making a classroom speech opposing capital punishment. Here she attempts to refute an argument often put forward by supporters of capital punishment:

> Some people have argued that capital punishment saves taxpayers money because it costs society $35,000 per year to keep an inmate in prison. Over a lifetime, that amounts to hundreds of thousands of dollars. I would argue that this expense does not mean we should put a person to death. How can we put a monetary value on human life, particularly when there is a chance that the accused may be proven innocent?

Here, the arguer's *evidence* consists of her opponent's cost argument; her *claim* is that cost is an insufficient reason for putting a person to death; and her *reasoning* comes from the prioritization of human life in our culture. Her reasoning, then, is based culturally in the sanctity of human life—a value not all cultures share. Her argument is likely to succeed in a Western culture that orders values in the same way as she does because she has adapted her reasoning to the reasoning habits of her audience.

Knowledge about the audience, therefore, can provide materials useful for supporting reasoning. Principles, conventions, rules, laws, value hierarchies, and other cultural artifacts act as resources arguers can call on in constructing arguments. These resources can be related to the argument field and sphere as well as to the audience type. Certain conventions and rules that guide the use of supporting reasoning in the legal system may hold true in the private sphere as well. For example, argumentation in the private sphere with a private audience may rely upon relational hierarchies and cultural beliefs that may influence the choice of supporting reasoning. Arguers preparing their arguments should ask questions about their audiences, such as, What principles and laws are recognized by my audience? How do audience members order their values and priorities? What rules or conventions do they accept and follow? By determining the answers to such questions, an arguer can locate a foundation for the reasoning and inferences drawn in the argument as a whole.

Using Evidence

An arguer who knows how audiences are likely to respond to evidence will generally be more effective than one who does not. A good deal of experimental research has been undertaken on the use and effectiveness of evidence in speeches and arguments. The results of this research have at least three implications for the planning and presentation of arguments.

Authoritative Evidence and Persuasiveness

Arguments are more effective if you use authoritative evidence. Researchers who study the persuasive effects of messages have found that arguers who use evidence are more influential with their audiences.[25] Unless you are a widely recognized expert on a topic, you should use evidence from authorities accepted by your audience. No matter how thoroughly you have prepared or how much you know about your topic, the audience is unlikely to take your word alone as sufficient support for your claims.

Evidence Credibility and Audience

Arguers should identify authorities of their particular topic that the audience is likely to perceive as credible and unbiased. Calling upon the statements and observations of individuals perceived as credible enhances your own credibility. For example, Martin Luther King Jr. is widely recognized as a civil rights leader who modeled the principles of nonviolent resistance. Bill Gates of Microsoft and Phil Knight of Nike are both good examples of business leaders who serve as role models of the values and ideals in their respective fields. For this reason, they are considered credible when the state of American business and economics are discussed, especially as related to their respective industries. In addition, although both of these authorities have an interest in the success of their businesses, their agendas are clear and not hidden.

Perceptions of Bias

Advocates should also be aware of the audience's perceptions of bias in authoritative statements. In Chapter 5, we saw that a biased source is one who has personal, political, or economic reasons for supporting a particular point of view. A biased source has a "hidden agenda"—a vested interest in the outcome of the matter being discussed. Audiences are suspicious of biased sources and are likely to reject arguments based on their opinions.[26] Before citing the American Tobacco Institute's claims that there is no causal link between smoking and cancer, or the National Rifle Association's arguments against gun control, the arguer should consider the effect of these authorities on the audience. Even if the facts or opinions of such authorities are well founded, their content may be rejected by an audience because of suspicion over their motives.

Novel Evidence

Arguers should introduce facts and information that are "news" to the audience rather than relying on information already well-known. When people initially encounter evidence that shocks or disturbs them, they make an effort to reconcile or cope with it. Once the evidence has entered their cognitive systems and they have dealt with it, they are much less impressed or disturbed by it when they encounter it again. Research on the effects of evidence shows that people are more influenced by novel information than by information they have heard before.[27] Therefore, before preparing your argument, you should have some idea of your audience's prior exposure to your topic. Facts already known to your audience will not be as effective as new information gleaned from current in-depth research, as described in Chapter 5. New information that dramatizes the nature and extent of a problem or value discrepancy will be more likely to change or influence the attitudes and values of your audience.

In summary, persuasion research on the use of evidence shows that you should use and cite external evidence, draw from authorities that your audience views as credible, and use novel information and statistics. Your use of evidence is one of the most important factors in your argument. If you have done your research and gain a sense of the information your audience will understand and accept, you will be more likely to produce an effective argument.

Credibility

In the 1968 presidential campaign, opponents of Richard Nixon mass-produced a button portraying a picture of a shifty-eyed Nixon above the question, "Would you buy a used car from this man?" The button's producers were attempting to impugn Nixon's source credibility. *Source credibility refers to an arguer's ability to be believed and trusted by recipients.* The buttons functioned as an argument with an implied claim: "If you wouldn't trust this man enough to buy a used car from him, you should not elect him president." The buttonmakers counted on the public's recollection of charges that Nixon had illegally used campaign funds in 1952, that he had used questionable campaign tactics in the past, and that he had been an ill-humored bad sport after losing a campaign for governor of California in 1962. The button was intended to make voters once again question Nixon's trustworthiness and integrity. Factors such as expertise, trustworthiness, and integrity cause people to accept claims because they have confidence in the character of the person making them. Such factors also contribute to an arguer's source credibility.

Credibility Characteristics

The importance of credibility as a factor in persuasion has been recognized at least since the time of Aristotle's *Rhetoric*, written more than two thousand years ago. Aristotle identified the personal character of the speaker as one of the three modes of persuasion and called it *ethos*. (The other two modes are *pathos*, the way the audience's emotions put them in a certain frame of mind, and *logos*, the rational proof offered within the message.) Of *ethos*, Aristotle said:

> Persuasion is achieved by the speaker's personal character where the speech is so spoken as to make us think him credible. We believe good men more fully and more readily than others: this is true generally whatever the question is, and absolutely true where exact certainty is impossible and opinions are divided. This kind of persuasion, like the others, should be achieved by what the speaker says, not by what people think of his character before he begins to speak.[28]

Aristotle's statements about credibility bring out four points that should be kept in mind when we consider its relationship to argumentation. First, credibility is not a characteristic that the arguer possesses, but one that is attributed to the arguer by the recipients. When Aristotle said that the "speech is spoken so as to make us think [the speaker is] credible," he emphasized the fact that how the speaker appears and what he or she does lead recipients to form certain impressions and beliefs, both about the speaker and about the claims being made. These impressions and beliefs then influence the recipients and cause them to accept or reject the speaker's message.

A second and related point is that credibility is a field- and context-dependent phenomenon. If credibility results from what recipients perceive about the arguer rather than from intrinsic characteristics of the arguer, then it will vary from one time and situation to another, depending on what an arguer does or says. For example, once elected, Nixon found his credibility rising after foreign policy successes, such as his trips to China and Russia and the settlement of the Vietnam war; it dropped sharply once the revelations about Watergate became public.[29] Even within a speech or during reception of a message, the credibility of an arguer may increase or decrease depending on how recipients perceive and react to the points made by the arguer.[30]

The third point Aristotle made is that we value credibility most "where certainty is impossible and opinions are divided." If we cannot verify facts to learn whether a claim is true, or if the claim is value-based rather than fact-based, we will rely heavily upon credibility as a source of our belief. Four decades of research in social psychology and communication have confirmed the importance of credibility.[31] Having reviewed this research, R. Glen Hass concluded, "Few areas of research have produced results as consistent as the findings that sources high in expertise and/or trustworthiness are more persuasive than those low in these qualities."[32] The implications for argument, of course, are that you should design your arguments to enhance your audience's perceptions of your expertise and trustworthiness.

The fourth point Aristotle made is to distinguish between credibility "achieved by what the speaker says" and that attributed to the speaker based on prior reputation. This latter form is called initial credibility. *Initial credibility is based on an arguer's credentials, status, and reputation as known to recipients before they hear or read the message.* Although initial credibility is an important factor in persuasion, its role is based largely on the extent to which a speaker's audience finds the speaker to be attractive or influential. *Derived credibility results from what is said in the message—the quality of the claims and evidence used and the ways arguers employ their own expertise to get their claims accepted.* Compared with initial credibility, derived credibility depends much more on what the audience thinks about the arguer's claims, the extent to which they produce counterarguments, and their assessment of the quality of an arguer's evidence.

An arguer with low credibility, such as a student or entry-level worker, faces a challenge every time he or she produces a persuasive message. That challenge is to enhance credibility through and by means of the message itself. This sort of derived credibility comes from features of the message and depends on the arguer's ability to incite listeners to believe that the arguer has their best interests at heart.

Enhancing Credibility

As an arguer, you will usually have three goals to establishing your credibility: (1) to focus the attention of the audience on the content of your message; (2) to make an initial favorable impression on the audience; and (3) to cause the audience to form a favorable impression of your expertise and trustworthiness. The first two are preliminary but necessary conditions for the development of the third. Initial impressions are based on your attractiveness and self-presentation. Although those impressions are superficial, they are important. Arguers who cause negative perceptions because of careless appearance or an offhand or grating manner create a deficit against which they must work to get their message fairly considered. If the argument is orally presented, such matters as appearance, delivery, and vocal mannerisms will be significant. If it is in written form, poor style, misspellings, and other visual cues will adversely affect the reader.

Once you have made a favorable personal impression, you must win a favorable consideration of your claims and evidence by holding your audience's attention and keeping them engaged in your argument. This task is essential to the process of internalization by which audiences integrate new beliefs and attitudes into their cognitive systems through an active consideration of your claims. Useful strategies for maintaining attention include use of examples close to the recipients' experiences, concrete information, good style, personal narrative, new and unknown facts, and other materials that contribute to the immediacy of the message. As noted in the last section, people who have low involvement in and little prior knowledge of the arguer's topic will attend more to the credibility of the source than to the content of the message. The arguer with low to moderate credibility, therefore, should expend effort in getting recipients to actively listen to and consider the message.

Credibility-Enhancing Strategies

The next item an arguer should have on the agenda is to enhance recipients' perceptions of his or her expertise and trustworthiness. Expertise is enhanced by showing that the position advocated is well supported and thus "correct." Trustworthiness is developed when arguers show that they have no biases or vested interests they are trying to hide from their recipients. Below are seven specific strategies for enhancing your credibility. The first four relate to expertise and the last three to trustworthiness.

1. *Show that you or the sources you use have experience with the topic.* Before seriously considering your position, audiences must be reassured that you have studied the matter. Therefore, when you present an argument, it is important not only to reference the appropriate sources but to provide their source qualifications as well. If you are the authority on a subject, it is equally important to establish your qualifications or experience with the argument.

2. *Use as many qualified sources as possible.* Qualified and respected sources have a halo effect. They endow those who cite them with their own credibility. If a well-intentioned and earnest, but inexperienced and unqualified, arguer assures us of something, we may be equally likely to believe her as not to believe her. But if the same speaker cites several respected authorities in support of her claim, the claim gains cogency.

3. *Use sources the recipients are likely to respect.* Sources that one audience might perceive as highly respectable may not be respected by another audience. For example, a labor union officer might be highly credible with union members but have very low credibility with management on the subject of working conditions and employee benefits.

4. *Use sound reasoning and avoid fallacies.* Recipients of an arguer's message who are being persuaded through the process of internalization will often detect weaknesses in the inferences an advocate makes, and they will think of counterarguments. Well-educated or intelligent recipients often have native reasoning skills and can criticize the arguments of others. A weak and easily rejected argument will often do more harm to one's case than no argument at all because it will raise doubts in recipients' minds about the arguer's credibility on all the other issues in the message.

5. *Demonstrate fairness.* Recall that audiences often become suspicious when they believe an arguer is presenting a one-sided or biased treatment of an issue. Directing attacks at opponents and not their arguments, ignoring or superficially citing their points of view, twisting or misconstruing their position, or engaging in similar practices are not only unethical but also have a boomerang effect, causing audiences to suspect an arguer of unfairness and to distrust his or her overall trustworthiness.

6. *Use reluctant testimony. Reluctant testimony is testimony made by sources who speak against their own vested interest.* Anyone who furnishes evidence against his or her own interests or prejudices is likely to be highly credible to most audiences. The student who argues that tuition should be increased to maintain quality in education, the teacher who maintains that competency tests for teachers are necessary, and the lawyer who supports no-fault divorce laws are all likely to be believed. That is because they are advocating positions opposite to ones they would be expected to advocate.

7. *Avoid inconsistency.* People who take a strong position on an issue and then reverse it lose considerable credibility in the eyes of the public. Such sudden reversals give people the impression that the arguer has not thought through his or her position and lacks a sense of principle.

USING LANGUAGE

The previous section detailed how arguers develop credible, collaborative relationships with recipients that can facilitate mutually agreeable outcomes. Part of this process involves selecting appropriate language to communicate effectively and provide the appropriate strength and credibility in an argument situation. This section examines the nature and functions of language in general and then makes specific recommendations regarding its use in argument. Perhaps one of the most famous passages in U.S. history that illustrates this point comes from a speech delivered by President Abraham Lincoln in his Gettysburg Address on November 19, 1863. It began:

> Four score and seven years ago our fathers brought forth on this continent a new nation, conceived in liberty, and dedicated to the proposition that all men are created equal.[33]

Is there any significance to Lincoln's words? The speech itself certainly carried with it an importance and elegance suitable not only for 1863 but for the twenty-first century as well. But do the actual words used to convey the message carry with them any particular significance? Lincoln's opening could just as easily have begun:

> Eighty-seven years ago those who came before us established in this country a new system of government created in freedom and based on the idea that all people are created equal.

Is there a difference? The content remains the same, but the words are now simpler and perhaps more contemporary. But the change in language seems to change more than just the words; some of the force and spirit of the original version are gone.

The language Lincoln used to express his message was not chosen randomly—nor is the language used to express everyday arguments. Even if we are not aware of our language choices, we adhere to the rules of grammar and vocabulary inherent in our language. The stronger our command of language, the better able we are to select which words to use. As you will see later in this chapter, the eloquent language Lincoln used contributed not only to the beauty of his address, but also to its persuasiveness. Harold Zyskind, in his study of Lincoln's address, noted that, although the occasion was ceremonial (dedication of the cemetery at Gettysburg), the address itself was argumentative and was designed by Lincoln to persuade members of his audience to rededicate themselves to the reunification and continuance of the federal government after the Civil War.[34] Gilbert Highet, writing of Lincoln's address, observed:

> No one thinks that when he was drafting the Gettysburg Address, Lincoln deliberately looked up these quotations and consciously chose these particular patterns of thought. No, he chose the theme. From its development and from the emotional tone of the entire occasion, all the rest followed, or grew—by the marvelous process of choice and rejection which is essential to artistic creation.[35]

In the course of devising and framing arguments, we select the words by which our arguments are expressed. These words have a profound impact on the use and interpretation of arguments because their significance lies not in the words themselves, but in what they come to mean for the people who use them. The effects of language depend upon the degree of concreteness and emotive significance of the words themselves.

George Orwell once lamented about the decline of the English language. He argued that when people use language inaccurately or sloppily, they cloud the ability of others to think clearly. They make the language unclear such that their thinking becomes unclear. He said:

> A man may take to drink because he feels himself to be a failure, and then fail all the more completely because he drinks. It is rather the same thing that is happening to the English language. It becomes ugly and inaccurate because our thoughts are foolish, but the slovenliness of our language makes it easier for us to have foolish thoughts. The point is that the process is reversible.[36]

As we discussed in Chapter 1, the ability to think critically about arguments is important for both arguers and analysts. When language is used inaccurately and sloppily, it becomes a barrier to our ability to think critically and argue intelligently about problems. The importance of understanding how language is used and misused was highlighted by Howard Kahane when he commented, "It is quite useful for students to gain insight into how language, the medium through which they obtain information from others, can be and often is used to obfuscate and otherwise deceive the unwary."[37]

Too often arguers obscure their true meanings by using words that are ambiguous. Just as often, arguers decide to use words that may sound complex and intelligent but have the effect of unintentionally obscuring their meaning. For example, consider the language of computers. Jargon words such as *RAM, ROM, byte, BPS 128 bit slot,* and the like may be clear to those involved with computers but confusing to those without common frames of reference or a common understanding of the language.

Orwell's argument is important. If we communicate our ideas clearly, we are able to engage our audiences' minds in more complex and accurate ways. If we are not clear, then our ideas may become lost in our audiences' confusion. We need to be careful with our language choices, and we need to avoid patterns of confusing language choices. Orwell said, "If one gets rid of these habits once can think more clearly, and to think clearly is a necessary first step towards political regeneration. . . ."[38]

Language and Meaning

Words by themselves have no intrinsic meaning. They acquire meaning only insofar as people use them to describe their world. This is the point made by C. K. Ogden and I. A. Richards in their book *The Meaning of Meaning*.[39] Their argument was that humans are symbol users who, develop symbols to stand for thoughts and ideas in their minds. The mental image, also known as a representation, is the result of direct experience or imagination. For example, if John Smith sees a green pine tree, he develops a representation of the tree through direct experience. John is also able to imagine a green pine tree that he has never seen—based on his past experience with pine trees.

Communication involves the process of transforming such representations into symbols. Therefore, the user's mental image of a tree is translated into the word *tree*, and the language provides the tool for sharing representations, or meanings, with other language users. Ogden and Richard's model is illustrated in Figure 7.4.

The referent is the actual material object referred to in language. The symbol is the word used to refer to the referent. The reference is the association the language user makes between the symbol *tree* and the material object that the user has experienced.

The major point this model makes is that the symbol is connected with the referent only by way of an association made by the language user. In other words, the meaning of the word rests in the people using the word. Therefore, the connection is indirect and represented by a broken line. What is the implication of this for communication? Because there is no direct relation between symbol and referent, there is

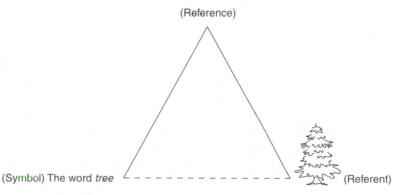

FIGURE 7.4   Symbol, Reference, and Referent

room for misunderstanding. Two language users could make the connection differently and therefore have two diverse understandings of what is meant by *pine tree*. Language user 1 may think of a giant evergreen tree, while language user 2 may think of a dwarf pine. It is not difficult to imagine the misunderstandings in language use that arise when symbols are ambiguous or when language users have widely discrepant experiences with some set of referents. Because of this, the level of abstraction and concreteness of words and symbols in the language system affects the precision and accuracy of communication.

Language and Abstraction

Because the relationship between the symbol and the referent is subject to variation, communication is not 100 percent efficient. Variations occur for many reasons. Members of different cultures may have different meanings for symbols. Members within the same culture may not always share the same frame of reference. In either case, complex meanings can become lost or changed because communication is not completely efficient.

For communication to be entirely efficient, the representation in the recipient's mind should be identical to the representation in the speaker's mind. In other words, if Sue says, "There is a tree outside my window," a hearer would have to be able to know exactly to which tree Sue is referring. This is not possible, because the symbol used is not the referent. It is only indirectly related to the referent through the user's mind.

Language serves as a vehicle for conveying meaning between a source and a receiver. When we speak, we not only select words and gestures we think will effectively communicate our thoughts and intentions, but we also select those we think will have some meaning for the recipient. For example, this book could have been written for high school students. Although the language used would convey meaning for everyone reading the book, a college student would probably find it simple and boring. Similarly, the book could have been targeted toward a graduate-level course. It would convey meaning, but high school students would find it very difficult to understand.

The difference in each case is the knowledge and experience the recipient is able to use in understanding the language. If the recipient has a great deal of knowledge about argumentation, the book would not need to dwell on aspects of definition or concrete examples. Instead, it could develop more abstract and theoretical discussions, and the language used could be more complex. The complexity of the connection between the referent and the symbol is measured by the relative abstractness of the symbol. *Abstraction refers to the degree to which relevant characteristics are omitted in language.* As a recipient's knowledge of a subject increases, the language used to convey the subject can be more abstract. Consider the following:

Kari: Would you go to my car and get my book?

Mark: Sure, but what book in what car?

Kari: My car is the white Nissan Altima license plate KARl-I. I need my argumentation textbook.

Mark: Sure, no problem.

In the first part of the conversation, Kari assumed that Mark knew which car was hers and what book she wanted. Her language choices were relatively vague and abstract because she assumed he had a level of knowledge that would supply the missing details. After it became apparent that Mark was unsure about which car and book, Kari added more information to help make the request clearer and less ambiguous.

When we argue, we use language that we assume the recipients can understand. We develop examples and speak with a level of abstraction and ambiguity appropriate for the given audience. It is important, however, to recognize that not all recipients have the necessary background and experience to understand abstract language. Based on the advocate's understanding of the particular recipients being addressed, relatively more or less ambiguous language and examples may be used to convey the argument.

S. I. Hayakawa was noted for his work in the area of language abstractness and the development of the abstraction ladder.[40] He argued that when we use language, we choose to make it more or less abstract as the situation warrants. His abstraction ladder looks much like the one in Figure 7.5.

The bottom of the ladder represents the most concrete—and least abstract—form of language. It uses symbols that represent the referent as specifically as possible. The top of the ladder, however, is the least specific. A manufactured item can be

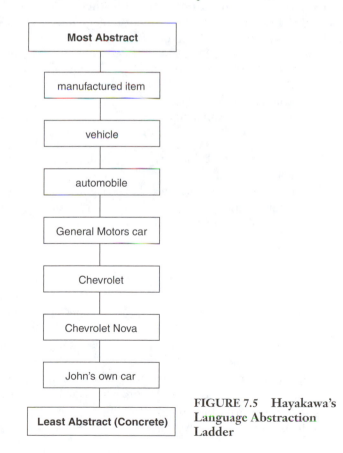

FIGURE 7.5   Hayakawa's Language Abstraction Ladder

almost any human-made product. A listener hearing more specific language would be better able to develop a mental representation of the referent than a listener hearing the more abstract language.

Abstract language is, by its nature, ambiguous. Arguers selecting ambiguous language run the risk of being misunderstood. Why, then, would a speaker choose to use abstract language? The answer can be found in the nature of the audience. For instance, most people have never seen John's car. If he refers to it and wants to persuade his listeners to buy it, they would be unable to create an accurate mental image if the language he uses is too specific for them to understand. Therefore, as a speaker, he needs to orient the recipients with language they can understand by using more abstract, commonly understood language. He might say:

> Come buy my car. It is a Chevrolet Nova built in one of the General Motors plants in California.

By blending the concrete with the abstract, arguers are able to orient their recipients to the reference and then move to more concrete symbols. We do this often because it is important that recipients understand the context, or orientation, of the argument. Even the process of giving directions involves a careful blend of the concrete with the abstract. If a speaker invites someone to her home and says, "I live at 4111 North 37th Street," she assumes that the recipient understands what city and how to get there. The address alone is very concrete. But if the recipient was from another city or country, the speaker would need to be more concrete until the recipient was oriented. For instance she might have to say:

> I live in the United States.
> I live in Seattle, Washington.
> If you take Interstate 5, take Exit 165.

In this case, the speaker begins by providing directions with a common frame of reference, which may be relatively abstract, and then provides greater focus and concreteness as the discussion moves forward. The significance of appropriately placing words on the ladder of abstraction when making arguments will be explored further in the last section of this chapter.

Connotations and Denotations

The triangle of meaning and abstraction has several important implications for arguers. If one recognizes that people may interpret words differently depending on the degree of abstraction, then an arguer should be able to consciously select words that affect people in the way the arguer intends.

The process to be used in selecting words can best be understood by considering the two poles of meaning in language use. Each word when used has a denotative meaning and also a connotative meaning. *The denotative meaning is the objective meaning held by language users in general.* A word's denotative meaning is usually found in dictionaries. Dictionaries record the meanings of words generally agreed on and established in the culture as a whole. Denotative meanings are relatively stable and are agreed on by most language users at any given point in time. *Connotative meanings, however, are the subjective meanings a given individual holds of symbols used in a particular situation.* Connotative meanings have emotive significance and are unique for the individual. Words used by language users, therefore, have both denotative and connotative significance.

For example, consider the word *fag. Webster's New Collegiate Dictionary* defines *fag* as "toil or drudgery."[41] Yet, if you were to call someone a fag, referring to the nature of that person's work, odds are that person would respond impolitely. This is because the meaning of the word *fag* is found not in the word itself, but in the person to whom the word is addressed. Similarly, in the seventeenth century, the word *good-bye* was seen as blasphemous because it contracted the Lord's name. The correct phrase to use when parting was "God be with you," and the shortened form, "God b'ye," was seen as inappropriate and disrespectful. Over time, the meanings of words change and adapt as the culture changes and as words become used and acquire new or different meanings. (Box 7.4, for example, lists some rather obscure words that are so dated or infrequently used that they may disappear from the English language entirely.)

Our language is full of words that have been replaced by other words carrying less negative or more positive connotations. This is the function of euphemisms. *Euphemism is a linguistic device for replacing words and phrases that carry a negative connotation with those that carry a positive connotation.* (Of course a speaker intending to convey a negative feeling might also substitute negative words for positive words.) For example:

POSITIVE TERM	NEGATIVE TERM
collateral damage	unavoidable innocent deaths
daytime drama	soap opera
indiscretion	moral wrong
inappropriate	illegal
air support	bombing
terminated	fired
destabilize	overthrow
intelligence gathering	spying
sanitation engineer	garbage collector
correctional facility	prison
low-income	poor
freedom fighters	revolutionary guerrillas
passed away	died
differently abled	disabled

There are many other possible examples, but in each case words with the same denotative meaning may be substituted, for one another with the objective of changing the connotative meanings.

This section has illustrated three characteristics of language. First, the meaning of language depends on language users because symbols by themselves have no intrinsic meaning. Second, language can be abstract or concrete, and arguers must decide

---

BOX 7.4
LOST SYMBOLS

Symbols are important to our thinking and communicating processes. Without them, the communication becomes nearly impossible, and the ability to share complex thoughts is remote at best. Language symbolizes the importance of things by naming them or giving them a symbol. People, for example, are important because we have names. Some symbols, however, are almost lost in the huge collection of English symbols. For example:

Aglet—the covering on the end of a shoelace.
Duff—the decaying organic matter found on a forest floor.
Harp—the small metal hoop that supports a lampshade.
Phosphenes—the lights you see when you close your eyes hard.
Piggin—a small wooden pail with one long stave used as a handle.
Quarrel—a small, diamond-shaped pane of glass, like that used in lattice glass.
Solidus—the oblique stroke (/) used between words or in fractions such as 7/8.
Zarf—a holder for a handleless coffee cup.

---

what degree of abstraction is appropriate for a given situation and audience. And third, because language allows room for variable interpretations of the meanings of symbols by both the speaker and the listener, meanings of symbols may vary. Whereas denotative meanings are the objective meanings of words agreed on by the language users, connotative meanings are the subjective interpretations of words that depend on the individual symbol user. Arguers should be sensitive to the fact that the words they use have both denotative and connotative meanings when they are interpreted.

Using Language in Argument

Understanding the functions of argument can help you better construct effective arguments. Because language is used referentially, artistically, and persuasively in arguments, to be effective it must be understood, adhered to, and remembered. Certain strategies for the choice of language and phrasing in your arguments will make them clearer, more vivid, and more persuasive. In his essay "Politics and the English Language," George Orwell, warned that if we allow our language to become imprecise and ambiguous, each of us contributes to the decline of our society. To avoid such decline, he offered the following six guidelines that all communicators should use in the presentation of ideas:

1. Never use a metaphor, simile, or other figure of speech which you are used to seeing in print.
2. Never use a long word where a short one will do.
3. If it is possible to cut a word out, always cut it out.
4. Never use the passive where you can use the active.
5. Never use a foreign phrase, a scientific word, or a jargon word if you can think of an everyday English equivalent.
6. Break any of these rules sooner than say anything outright barbarous.[42]

Orwell's point was simply that we need to be vigilant when comes to our communication skills and language use. Our ideas and arguments should be clear. We should work to minimize confusion and maximize common understandings and shared meanings. What follows are general guidelines and principles for language use, not hard-and-fast rules. As you recall from previous sections, the use of language in argument depends as much on the situation and the listeners as it does on the argument itself; however, these guidelines will help to ensure that you make the best possible use of the resources language has to offer.

1. *Use clear language.* Clarity is composed of two factors: selecting language at the appropriate level of abstraction for the recipient, and avoiding convoluted or ambiguous language. Matching the concreteness of the word choice to the experience of the arguee and expressing oneself simply and directly ensure that the argument will be understood as the arguer intended.

As we noted earlier in the chapter, the appropriate use of abstraction/concreteness depends on the relationship between the arguer and arguee. If the arguee does not know of or understand very concrete references made by the arguer, the language is too concrete. Likewise, if the arguer and arguee understand each other's personal references or the background to the argument, then more concrete terms can be used.

The second requirement of clarity is simplicity. Often people use convoluted and ambiguous language to convey their argument when simpler language might be just as effective. But such practices as circumlocution (using an unnecessarily large number of words to express an idea) and obfuscation (using words confusingly) are not always intentional. Their unintentional use often muddles arguments and interferes with their effectiveness.

Because the objective of the arguer is to get the audience to understand the argument, the language should be as simple and concise as possible:

> In my well-considered interpretation of the events preceding this encounter and considering what others have said to me as well as my own background, I think we should increase the expenditures for the bus fare by 10 cents.

A simpler way of conveying the same message is:

> I think we should raise the bus fare by 10 cents.

If the argument is not understood or if there is confusion about what the arguer is claiming, the argument will not be effective.

2. *Define terms when necessary.* If an arguer's argument hinges on a particular term, and if there's a chance that an arguee might not understand the term in the way the arguer intended, then the term should be defined. By providing clear definitions, the arguer can help reduce unwanted connotations or ambiguities that might otherwise develop. For example:

> I think that regardless of the politics in any given country, we should provide the people with support—by support I don't mean military aid; I do mean economic and food assistance.

By defining "support," the arguer avoided possible pitfalls from a misinterpretation of what "support" is used to mean. The definition helps shed the connotation of military assistance and makes the claim more concrete.

3. *Express arguments vividly.* An important dimension of an argument's persuasiveness is the vividness with which it is expressed. We can select words and modes of expression that depersonalize what we say and make it seem distant and remote from the audience. Using the passive voice, the antecedentless "it," and complex formal language makes what we say less vivid, compare the following two arguments (which say essentially the same thing):

> Sometimes the debate over abortion asks the wrong question. What is truly at issue is not a balancing of the rights of one person against the rights of another. Rights are not zero sum, and they do not shrink when they are extended to someone else.[43]

> Sometimes the abortion controversy is directed at incorrect issues. It is believed that one person's prerogatives are counterbalanced against another's. Individuals' rights are not differentially assigned so that rights accorded to some individuals are removed from others.

The second passage uses the passive voice and such formal words as:

> prerogatives
> counterbalanced
> differentially assigned
> accorded

The original version uses active voice and everyday language. In addition, it employs colorful terms and metaphor to engage readers and enliven their interest, such as:

> asks the wrong question
> truly at issue
> balancing . . . against
> zero sum
> shrink

When we make a problem or a description come alive for the arguee, we endow it with what one theorist calls "presence."[44] *Presence is a quality of argument that moves things near to us in space and time so they act directly on our sensibility.* This quality is best demonstrated by the following story:

> A kings sees an ox on its way to sacrifice. He is moved to pity for it and orders that a sheep be used in its place. He confesses that he did so because he could see the ox, but not the sheep.[45]

We care much more about what is immediate to us than about what is distant. Vivid language increases the immediacy of the arguer's subject and point of view.[46] By engaging his or her audience's care and concern, the arguer can use vividness to make arguments more effective.

4. *Avoid sexist and racist language.* Our earlier discussion of George Orwell and language use made the point that language can limit and shape the way its users think and act. Women, minorities, and economically and culturally oppressed groups have become increasingly sensitive to language that labels and disparages or devalues them. Many language users are unaware how their conscious forms of expression reflect unconscious assumptions about groups that may be a part of their audience. When those assumptions are negative and are negatively reflected in the claims an arguer makes, the argument's effectiveness is undermined.

Sexist use of language occurs in many of our habits. When we are referring to a group of mixed gender, we often use the masculine pronoun. The structure of our language typically gives men first priority.

> The men and women in this room . . .
> The men and women of this university . . .
> Mr. and Mrs. Smith

Women traditionally abandon part of their identity or definition upon marriage by giving up their "maiden" names. Furthermore, women are often equated with children. The expression "women and children first" testifies to the linguistic equality women share with children. There are many terms used to define women as children or subhuman people. For instance, a woman may be called a "babe," "chick," "doll," or "fox."[47] Likewise, women are referred to as girls—even when they are twenty, thirty, forty, fifty, and even sixty years old ("The office girls got this for you").

In framing arguments, arguers often allow sexism to creep into their expression in very subtle ways. Consider the following paragraph:

> The standards of achievement in this profession are set by the men who have been most productive. The exceptional manager should recognize that his productivity depends upon his sales team and the women in his office staff.

Several sexist uses of language are embedded in this passage. In the first sentence, *men* is used to refer generically to all practitioners of the profession (and they are productive). Again, in the second sentence, the manager is, referred to by the masculine possessive pronoun *his.* Furthermore, supervisors are characterized as male, while clericals ("the office staff") are assumed to be female. Slips such as these should be avoided.[48] Although nonsexist language rarely, if ever, alienates recipients, sexist language is almost certain to do so.

Unconscious racism in language use is also highly problematic. In the century following the Civil War, America became increasingly committed to equality among races and ethnic origins. In such Supreme Court cases as *Brown v. Board of Education* in 1954, in the Civil Rights Act of 1964, and in affirmative action measures, efforts have been systematically made to eliminate discrimination against minority groups.

These measures were important, but failed to provide for equality because, at least in part, they did nothing to override the attitudes of the people opposed to racial and ethnic equality. The laws changed, but the language did not, and because language helps to shape a culture's reality, the attitudes were fostered by the language.

Civil rights leader Stokely Carmichael recognized the power of language as a barrier to racial equality when he spoke in 1967:

> The need of a free people is to be able to define their own terms and have those terms recognized by their oppressors . . . for white people to be allowed to define us by calling us Negroes, which means apathetic, lazy, stupid, and all those other things, is for us to accept those definitions. We must define what we are and move from our definitions and tell them to recognize what we are.[49]

African Americans and other minorities have objected to labels and terms of reference having negative connotations. The key terms to keep in mind when discussing minorities and minority, issues are "respect" and "equality." Minorities should not be set apart unless there is good reason to do so and if they are, they should be referred to in nonoppressive ways. At one school, a discussion was held concerning salary differentials related to people's ethnic origin. Caucasians discussing the issue continually referred to themselves as "majority faculty." This self-reference reasserted their status within the system. When reminded that a term such as "nonminority faculty' might be more neutral, one officer responded that he was not about to make that concession. Evidently, he was well aware of the role language plays in reasserting power relations between Caucasians and minority groups in this country.

In framing arguments in language, arguers should make every possible effort to engage, befriend, and appeal to the recipients through the medium of their expression. Conversely, they should systematically avoid sexist and racist language along with obscenity or other inappropriate word choices. Nothing is to be gained by insulting or alienating recipients. It is in the arguer's best interest to word arguments with care, taste, and sensitivity for those to whom the argument is directed.

SUMMARY

This chapter emphasized a co-orientational perspective on argument—a concern with working with audiences to develop strong and clear arguments by adapting messages to recipients and using language that enhances the meaning of the argument. The chapter considered how arguments are designed and constructed to be suited to particular argument situations.

The primary role of an arguer is to ethically and persuasively communicate arguments to recipients in ways that are clear, easily understood, and ethical. Arguers strive to have recipients understand and act on their message. For this reason, arguers must have some knowledge of the recipients and the argument situation.

Arguers have many potential ways of influencing an audience. Social psychologists have identified three major ways. Compliance uses rewards or punishments. Identification is based on the recipients' desire to be more like or close to the arguer. And internalization is the integration of new information and ideas into recipients' cognitive systems.

Internalization occurs when a source is perceived to possess expertise and trustworthiness. Expertise depends on whether an arguer is viewed as knowing the correct position on a topic. Trustworthiness is the extent to which recipients believe the arguer is willing to communicate that position for their benefit. Other research findings indicate that over time people tend to remember the content of a message more than the source from which it came. Also, people who are disinterested and uninformed about a topic will rely more on whether its source appears credible than on what they think of the message content.

Arguers, therefore, must have a clear understanding of the recipients. First, we stressed that arguers should strive for a co-orientational view of the relationship with the audience as opposed to using adversarial argumentation strategies. And second we noted the importance of understanding, clearly, the characteristics of the argument situation. Specifically, we looked at the role of recipient in a variety of situations including private decision-making, private third-party decision-making, public third-party audiences, and extralegal actors.

We offered several strategies for improving presentations. First, arguers need to be effective, active listeners who understand and verify meaning. Second, advocates should be able to reframe arguments and ideas to look at them from different perspectives. Third, speakers should employ organizational strategies that are adapted to the audience. Fourth, they should select starting points appropriate to the situation and the recipients' knowledge. Fifth, selecting acceptable reasoning is vital if arguers and recipients are to effectively connect evidence through claims. Sixth, evidence needs to be appropriate for the situation and acceptable for the audience. Seventh, arguers should work to enhance their credibility to provide a stronger connection with the audience.

The second half of the chapter considered the role language plays in argument. Language should not be used unconsciously or without concern; rather, speakers should deliberately adapt language to their audience. Arguers, in particular, can enhance their effectiveness through their use of language.

Words used to refer to objects or experiences have certain characteristics that influence their use in language. They are abstract (having general reference to broad classes of objects) or concrete (referring to specific or particular objects or experiences). They are also used denotatively as symbols with objective, generally agreed-upon meanings, or connotatively as symbols with subjective or emotive meaning for each individual. People manipulate words by replacing negative connotations with positive ones. These result in euphemisms such as "daytime drama" for soap operas, "projects" for slums, and "correctional facility" for prison.

Understanding how language functions can assist arguers in getting their arguments understood, remembered, and adhered to by recipients. Four guidelines for using language can assist in this process. First, arguers should be clear. They should employ language that is sufficiently concrete to keep their messages interesting. They should also speak or write simply, avoiding convoluted or ambiguous language. Second, arguers should define any terms that their recipients might misunderstand. This is particularly true when the terms have an important role in the argument, and the arguers' usage of the terms departs from ordinary usage. Third, arguers should express their arguments vividly. Using active rather than passive voice, personalized constructions, and nonformal language along with colorful terms and metaphors will engage recipients and cause them to be more likely to accept an arguer's claim. Fourth, arguers should avoid sexist or racist language. Although few arguers intentionally try to offend recipients, many do so inadvertently by expressing their ideas in ways that set women and minorities apart as having less status in society than men and European Americans. Concerted efforts to eliminate discriminatory forms of reference and ways of speaking will ensure that no recipients are inadvertently alienated by the way an argument is expressed.

GLOSSARY

Abstraction (p. 208) refers to the degree to which relevant characteristics are omitted in language.

Active listening (p. 196) means to hear for meaning.

Competitive listening (p. 196) is characterized by advocates who are more interested in winning an argument or a particular position rather than understanding other viewpoints.

Compliance (p. 186) is the use of rewards and punishments by a powerful source to get recipients to believe or act in a certain manner.

Connotative meaning (p. 211) is the subjective meaning a given individual holds of symbols used in a particular situation.

Denotative meaning (p. 210) is the objective meaning held by language users in general.

Derived credibility (p. 203) results from what is said in the message—the quality of the claims and evidence used and the ways arguers employ their own expertise to get their claims accepted.

Euphemism (p. 211) is a linguistic device for replacing words and phrases that carry a negative connotation with those that carry a positive connotation.

Expertise (p. 187) is the possession of a background of knowledge and information relevant to the argument being made.

Extralegal decision-makers (p. 195) are groups that use nonviolence, direct action, or violence to influence decision processes.

Identification (p. 186) is the influence that occurs because people find a source attractive and wish to enhance their own self-concept by establishing a relationship with the source.

Initial credibility (p. 203) is based on an arguer's credentials, status, and reputation as known to recipients before they hear or read the message.

Internalization (p. 187) is a process in which people accept an argument by thinking about it and by integrating it into their cognitive systems.

Passive listening (p. 196) involves hearing other points of view but does not verify or affirm understanding.

Presence (p. 214) is a quality of argument that moves things near to us in space and time so they act directly on our sensibility.

Primacy-recency effect (p. 198) means that audiences are more likely to remember what comes at the beginning and end of messages.

Private decision-makers (p. 195) argue in the private sphere and use rules and conventions that are decided among the participants.

Private third-party decision-makers (p. 195) add an external audience.

Public third-party audiences (p. 195) largely apply the norms and conventions of the public sphere.

Reframing (p. 196) means to analyze arguments and argument outcomes using alternative points of view.

Reluctant testimony (p. 205) is a testimony made by sources who speak against their own vested interest.

Source credibility (p. 202) is an arguer's ability to be believed and trusted by recipients.

Trustworthiness (p. 187) depends on whether people believe the arguer is motivated to tell them the truth.

EXERCISES

Exercise 1 Select a situation in which you have recently made or will soon make an argument to a particular recipient or group of recipients.

1. Think of at least three strategies you could use to find out information about your audience's values and attitudes.

2. How could you incorporate the information you would gather into the planning of your message? Specifically, what changes or adjustments could you make in your argument to design it for this particular audience?

3. What strategies could you use to appear credible to this audience? How could you enhance the credibility of your arguments so they would be accepted?

Exercise 2 This chapter provided a number of strategies arguers could use to relate their arguments to the orientations of their audiences and to enhance their own credibility. These included the following:

A. Use premises the audience accepts.
B. Use audience values and principles for supporting your reasoning.
C. Cite authorities the audience is likely to respect.
D. Use novel evidence.
E. Keep the audience interested and involved in the argument.
F. Focus on issues the audience is likely to be concerned about.
G. Be aware of possible audience objections and reservations.
H. Appear attractive, and emphasize similarities you share with the audience.
I. Emphasize your own and your source's experience with the topic.
J. Use unbiased and reluctant testimony.
K. Avoid inconsistency.

Examine each of the arguments below in which the speaker or writer adheres to or violates one or more of these strategies. Decide whether the audience would respond more or less favorably to the argument because of what is said. Also, decide which of the strategies the arguer uses or violates. Some information about the audience is provided.

∗1. From Martha D. Lamkin, manager of the Indianapolis Office for the U.S. Department of Housing and Urban Development, "Power: How to Get It, Keep It, and Use It Wisely," a speech delivered to Women in Communications, Inc., Indianapolis, Ind., October 24, 1986. Reprinted in *Vital Speeches of the Day* 53 (1986): 153.

> I mentioned at the outset that Machiavelli's essay, "The Prince," gave power a bad name. Perhaps it's up, to a woman, Rosabeth Moss Kanter, to reverse this perception, Her book, entitled *The Changemasters*, makes the point that organizational

genius is 10 percent inspiration and 90 percent acquisition—acquisition of power (that is, information, resources, and support) to move beyond the formal job charter to influence others to accomplish organizational objectives.

2. Senator John McCain, *Congressional Record* (April 8, 2004): S3996–S3999. This speech was delivered to the U.S. Senate:

> The sport of baseball is America's pastime and an institution inextricably interwoven into the fabric of our culture. If Major League Baseball and its players fail to act to preserve and protect the sport by adopting a drug-testing policy that effectively deters the players from using anabolic steroids or any other similar performance-enhancing substances, this important part of our culture will remain tarnished. The resolution we are introducing today would call on Major League Baseball and its players to restore legitimacy to professional baseball and make the welfare of the sport more important than the self-serving interests that have a chokehold on America's game.

3. Steve, a student, to other college students about whether a school should be allowed to censor a play:

> People's rights should not be limited or eliminated unless there is a very, very clear and present threat to the safety of others. With art—and with this play [*The Laramie Project*]—no one has proved a clear danger to our campus or our community. [Who cares if people threaten to protest?] Protests don't hurt anyone—the opposite is true. Protests could highlight the dangers of homophobia and discrimination. And, if this play might offend someone, they don't have to see it. As long as people have a choice to see it or not, there should be no problem and no limitation on expression. My only point here is that all art forms—this play, music, art exhibitions—can have significant and important messages that combat hate and stereotypes and that serve to bring us to a better understanding of one another. Before it is censored, the school, the government, or whoever has a burden to prove there would be some harm.

4. Representative Bart Stupak, *Congressional Record* (November 18, 2004): H9992. This speech was delivered to the U.S. House of Representatives:

> I come tonight to put people first, to put our children first as I continue to speak out against the acne drug Accutane. As a legislator, I have called for more restrictions on the distribution and use of this drug, which is known to cause severe birth defects and a form of impulsive behavior and depression in young people taking this drug. This drug has devastated my family with the loss of our son BJ and more than 250 other families who have lost their young son or daughter across this nation while they were taking Accutane.
>
> As we were flying back from Little Rock, Arkansas, CBS news ran a story tonight, and I quote an FDA safety reviewer, Dr. David Graham, when he spoke to the Senate Finance Committee. Dr. Graham said, "I would argue that the FDA as currently configured is incapable of protecting America against another Vioxx." He told the Senate Finance Committee that "there are at least five other drugs on the market today that should be looked at seriously to see whether they should remain on the market." He cited the acne drug Accutane.

*5. From Glenna M. Crooks, director of the policy division of the American Pharmaceutical Association, "How to Make a Difference: Shaping Public Policy," a speech delivered to the First Annual National Conference on Women's Health, Washington, D.C., June 18, 1986. Reprinted in *Vital Speeches of the Day* 52 (1986): 756.

> When I first began to work on this topic I was a government official assigned to attend an international meeting of policymakers, theologians, philosophers and scientists to discuss the ways in which the religious values and cultural ethics of a nation affected the ways in which health policy was made . . . .
>
> They assigned me a title, "Policymaking in America," and I set out to explore how I made my living in the public policy arena. My social science perspective shifted into high gear. I read the Declaration of Independence and the Constitution and observed the actions of my contemporaries in government, associations and as individuals in a new light. My observations impressed and awed me. I saw a process that I have come to passionately believe in and promote; one that in my opinion truly capitalizes on the great strengths of the nation.
>
> Some of my friends and colleagues here today know that I have just returned from the Soviet Union where I led a group of health professionals in an international professional exchange. As a result of that experience and my observations of such an oppressive society, my views about the strengths and value of our consensus-building passions as Americans are even stronger. It is one of our greatest national treasures.

6. R.L. Crandall, chair and president, American Airlines, Inc., "The Volatile Airline Industry," a speech before the Economic Club of Detroit, February 23, 1987. Reprinted in *Vital Speeches of the Day* 53 (1987): 468.

> It's a pleasure to address such a distinguished audience as the Economic club of Detroit, for two reasons: First, because I suspect many of you are frequent flyers on American, and I always like to be among our best customers. Second, because, for a long time, the name Detroit has been synonymous with transportation—admittedly, of the four-wheeled, rather than the airborne kind, but transportation nonetheless.

7. From Margarita Papandreou, president, Women's Union of Greece, "Women in Politics: Human Rights a Dominant Force," a speech delivered at the National Organization for Women in Denver, Colo., June 13–15, 1986. Reprinted in *Vital Speeches of the Day* 52 (1986): 744.

> Perhaps (during the early stages of the contemporary women's movement),we, didn't pay enough attention during our struggle for equal rights to that heavy sack, that sandbag, we carried on our backs . . . the responsibility for the house, the children, the oldsters. So, when the doors were finally opened to us . . . for education, for entry into so-called male jobs and professions, for political participation, etc., there we were, standing at the door, a man next to us, we—our bag—a staggering weight as we moved forward to take advantage of our new opportunities.

8. Ronald Reagan, President of the United States, "President's Response to the Tower Commission Report: Iranian Affair," a speech delivered to the American people in Washington, D.C., March 4, 1987. Reprinted in *Vital Speeches of the Day* 53 (1987): 323.

Let's start with the part that is most controversial. A few months ago I told the American people I did not trade arms for hostages. My heart and my best intentions still tell me that is true, but the facts and evidence tell me it is not.

As the Tower board reported, what began as a strategic opening to Iran deteriorated in its implementation into trading arms for hostages. This runs counter to my own beliefs, to Administration policy, and to the original strategy we had in mind. There are reasons why it happened but no excuses. It was a mistake.

Exercise 3 The goal of this exercise is to reach a consensus through collaborative debate.

Step 1: Students select a topic to serve as the proposition. Topics should be accessible to all members of the class. For example:

The University should eliminate grades.
The local community should fund a new library.

Step 2: Together, the students generate all the reasons for and against the proposition.

Step 3: These reasons are then distributed to members of the class for research purposes.

Step 4: In-class debate.

First speaker:	Affirmative—in support of the proposition. A student is selected to speak in favor of the proposition. It is his or her responsibility to argue the reasons. Class members may support and offer research materials.
Second speaker:	Negative—in opposition to the proposition. A different student is selected to speak in opposition. It is her or his responsibility to either (1) concede or (2) refute a reason offered by the previous speaker. This speaker may draw on the support and research of the entire class, including the first affirmative speaker.
Third speaker:	Affirmative. Yet another speaker is selected to speak in favor of the proposal. This speaker rephrases those points refuted by the opposition. This speaker must either concede or refute each one. Again, this speaker may draw on the support and research of the entire class, including the first opposition speaker.
Fourth speaker:	Opposition. A new speaker is selected to oppose. It is her or his turn to concede or refute the points established by the previous speaker. This person may also use the support of the entire class.

This process continues until all reasons are explored and considered. The goal of the process is for the class to reach consensus. The consensus will be one of three options: maintain the current system or state of affairs, accept the proposition outright, or create a modified plan. In the example of a university eliminating grades, these outcomes might be as follows: keep the current grading system (status quo), eliminate the grading system (affirm the proposition outright), or convert the grading system to pass/fail only (a potential modified plan).

Exercise 4 Originally, S.I. Hayakawa proposed an abstraction ladder with Bessie the Cow as the most concrete symbol on the ladder. In the following space, draw an abstraction ladder that has you as the most concrete symbol.

MOST ABSTRACT

10.

 9.

 8.

 7.

 6.

 5.

 4.

 3.

 2.

 1.

MOST CONCRETE

If you were introducing yourself to someone you had never met before, at what level would you begin?

Exercise 5 Each of the following words has a denotative and connotative meaning. Next to each word write the first definition that comes to mind, and then look up the word in the dictionary. Is there a large difference? Why? Do you think your peers' answers would be closer to the connotative definitions you generated or the denotative definitions you looked up? Test it on five friends. What did your test show?

	CONNOTATIVE	**DENOTATIVE**
school teacher		
Buick		
boss		
turkey		
sex		
trip		
work		
career		
education		
car		
emotional		

Exercise 6 The question of whether English should be the "official" language of the United States has been the subject of much debate. Read the following case study and consider the following questions:

- What functions of language are apparent in this argument?
- Based on what you know about how language affects our thoughts and perceptions, what would be the effects of making English our "official" language?
- Do you think that Bill Emerson used language effectively in his argument?
- Should the United States have an official language?

ENGLISH IS OUR COMMON THREAD

Mr. Speaker, many times before I have taken to the floor to speak about the importance of the English language. For decades, English has been the de facto language of the United States. In recent years, 19 States have designated English as their official language. Support for these efforts has been overwhelming. I strongly believe that English should be the official language of the United States Government. I have been a persistent sponsor of such legislation, and I will again today introduce the Language of Government Act.

At the same time, however, I want to recognize the important contributions of other languages through a sense-of-the-Congress resolution. In an increasingly global world, foreign languages are key to international communication. I strongly encourage those who already speak English to learn foreign languages.

As a nation of immigrants, America is comprised of people of all races, nationalities and languages. These differences make our Nation the wonderful place it is. While being different, all of these people can find a common means of communication in the English language. English is the common thread that connects every citizen in our great Nation.

Hon. Bill Emerson, House of Representatives, *Congressional Record* (January 4, 1995): E13.

ENGLISH LANGUAGE TAX CREDIT

Mr. Speaker, I rise today to introduce an important piece of legislation that I believe to be an integral part of the official English movement. As you may know, I am the author of H.R. 123, the Language of Government Act which seeks to make English the official language of the United States Government. This legislation is the perfect complement to the Language of Government Act. It recognizes the need for a highly skilled labor force and provides a tax credit to employers for the cost of providing English language instruction to their limited-English-proficient employees.

Many Americans lack the language skills and literacy necessary to take full advantage of roles as responsible citizens and productive workers. While many employers acknowledge the need to educate their workers and have demonstrated an interest in establishing on-site training programs for their employees, the high cost of doing so often prevents them from taking any concrete action. This legislation will provide them with an incentive to offer this crucial instruction to their employees and make the workplace a friendlier, and less daunting environment for non-English-proficient employees.

Hon. Bill Emerson, House of Representatives, *Congressional Record* (January 4, 1995): E24.

THE LANGUAGE OF GOVERNMENT

Mr. Speaker, today I am pleased to introduce once again the Language of Government Act. America is a nation of immigrants. As President Franklin Delano Roosevelt once said, "All of our people all over this country—except the pure-blooded Indians—are immigrants or descendants of immigrants, including those who came over here on the Mayflower."

Indeed, we are a diverse lot. We are a country of many peoples, each with an individual *cultural* heritage and tradition. It is not often that people of so many varying cultures and backgrounds can live together in harmony, for human nature often leads us to resist and fear those who are different from us. Yet despite our differences, we do have a common bond. We have a common tongue, the English language, that connects us to one another and creates our national identity. It is this unity in diversity that defines us as uniquely American.

The time is right for passage of this important, unifying legislation. H.R. 123 offers a balanced, sensible approach to the common language issue. This legislation states that the government has an affirmative obligation to promote the English language, elevating that goal to official capacity. At the same time, the bill seeks to set some common sense parameters on the number and type of government services that will be offered in a language other than English. We do not need nor should we want a full-scale multilingual government. But, if we do not address this issue in a forward-thinking, proactive manner, that is just what we would allow to develop.

I want to stress that the Language of Government Act is not "English only." It simply states that English is the language in which all official United States Government business will be conducted. We have an obligation to ensure that non-English-speaking citizens get the chance to learn English so they can prosper—and fully partake of all the economic, social, and political opportunities that exist in this great country of ours.

The late Senator Hayakawa, founder of this movement, was a profile writer, and I offer you one of my favorite quotes of his:

> America is an open society—more open than any other in the world. People of every race, of every color, of every culture are welcomed here to create a new life for themselves and their families. And what do these people who enter into the American mainstream have in common? English our shared, common language. . . .

As Americans, we should not remain strangers to each other, but must use our common language to develop a fundamental and open means of communication and to break down artificial language barriers. By preserving the bond of a unifying language in government, this nation of immigrants can become a stronger and more unified country.

Hon. Bill Emerson, House of Representatives, *Congressional Record* (January 4, 1995): E35.

NOTES

1. C. Perelman and L. Olbrechts-Tyteca, *The New Rhetoric: A Treatise on Argumentation*, J. Wilkinson and P. Weaver, trans. (Notre Dame, Ind.: University of Notre Dame Press, 1958).

2. Adapted from Theodore Newcomb, "An Approach to the Study of Communicative Acts," *Psychological Review* 60 (1953): 393–404.

3. R. Glen Hass, "Effects of Source Characteristics on Cognitive Responses and Persuasion," in *Cognitive Responses in Persuasion*, Richard E. Petty, Thomas M. Ostrom, and Timothy C. Brock, eds. (Hillsdale, N.J.: Lawrence Erlbaum Associates, 1981), 142–151. Hass's account is based on H. Kelman, "Compliance, Identification, and Internalization: Three Processes of Attitude Change," *Journal of Conflict Resolution* 2 (1958): 51–60.

4. Hass, 149.

5. Hass, 144.

6. J. Mills and E. Aronson, "Opinion Change as a Function of the Communicator's Attractiveness and Desire to Influence," *Journal of Personality and Social Psychology* 1 (1965): 173–177.

7. S. Chaiken, "Communicator Physical Attractiveness and Persuasion," *Journal of Personality and Social Psychology* 37 (1979): 1387–1397.

8. Hass, 143.

9. Hass, 153.

10. Richard E. Petty and John T. Cacioppo, *Attitudes and Persuasion: Classic and Contemporary Approaches* (Dubuque, Iowa: William C. Brown, 1981), 89–94.

11. Petty and Cacioppo, 64, report a study by S. Bochner and C. A. Insko, "Communicator Discrepancy, Source Credibility, and Opinion Change," *Journal of Personality and Social Psychology* 4 (1966): 614–621.

12. Hass, 159.

13. Irwin Mallin and Karrin Vasby Anderson, "Inviting Constructive Argument" *Argumentation & Advocacy* 36 (Winter 2000): 120–134.

14. Mallin and Anderson, 120; Gordon R. Mitchell, "Simulated Public Argument as a Pedagogical Play on Worlds," *Argumentation & Advocacy* 36 (Winter 2000): 134–151; David E. Williams and Brian R. McGee, "Negotiating a Change in the Argumentation Course: Teaching Cooperative Argument," *Argumentation & Advocacy* 36 (Winter 2000): 105–130.

15. There are several good resources that discuss the advantages of collaborative argument. These include J. M. Makau, *Reasoning and Communication: Thinking Critically about Arguments* (Belmont, Calif.: Wadsworth, 1990); David E. Williams and Brian R. McGee, 105–119; Carol K. Winkler and David M. Cheshier, "Revisioning Argumentation Education for the New Century: Millennial Challenges," *Argumentation & Advocacy* 36 (2000): 101–104.

16. Mallin and Anderson, 120–134.

17. Case study adapted from Michael Weisskopf, Joseph R. Szczesny, and Mile Eskenazi and Carole Buia, "Anatomy of a Recall: How a Small-Town Lawsuit in Texas Cascaded into the Biggest Consumer

Panic Since the Tylenol Scare, Plaguing Firestone and Ford with Allegations of Factory Flaws and Design," *Time* (September 11, 2000); "Firestone Tires," *Consumer Reports* 65 (November 2000): 10.

18. There are several good resources to help build listening skills. For instance, consider Paul J. Donoghue and Mary E. Siegel, *Are You Really Listening? Keys to Successful Communication* (Notre Dame, Ind.: Sorein Books, 2005); or Madelyn Burley-Allen, *Listening: The Forgotten Skill*, 2d ed. (New York, NY: John Wiley & Sons, 1995).

19. A discussion of listening types can be found at Larry Alan Nadig, "Tips on Effective Listening," http://www.drnadig.com/listening.htm (accessed May 27, 2008).

20. Stewart L. Tubbs, "Explicit versus Implicit Conclusions and Audience Commitment," *Speech Monographs* 35 (1968): 14–95.

21. Tubbs, 18.

22. This research is effectively summarized in Bert E. Bradley, *Fundamentals of Speech Communication*, 4th ed. (Dubuque, Iowa: William C. Brown, 1984), 346–348.

23. Ruth Anne Clark, *Persuasive Messages* (New York: Harper & Row, 1984), 28.

24. This research is summarized by Robert N. Bostrom in *Persuasion* (Englewood Cliffs, N.J.: Prentice-Hall, 1983), 178.

25. These studies are summarized in James C. McCroskey, "A Summary of Experimental Research on the Effects of Evidence in Persuasive Communication," *Quarterly Journal of Speech* 55 (1969): 169–170.

26. McCroskey, 172.

27. McCroskey, 174–175.

28. Aristotle, *Rhetoric*, 1356a.

29. Bradley, 66.

30. R. Brooks and T. Scheidel, "Speech as Process: A Case Study," *Speech Monographs* 35 (1968): 1–7.

31. See, for example, R. Glen Hass, "Effects of Source Characteristics on Cognitive Responses and Persuasion," in *Cognitive Responses in Persuasion*, Richard E. Petty, Thomas M. Ostrom, and Timothy C. Brock, eds. (Hillsdale, N.J.: Lawrence Erlbaum Associates, 1981), 141–172; Bostrom, 63–87; Gary Cronkhite and Jo Liska, "A Critique of Factor Analytic Approaches to the Study of Credibility," *Communication Monographs* 43 (1976): 91–107; Jesse G. Delia, "A Constructivist Analysis of the Concept of Credibility," *Quarterly Journal of Speech* 62 (1976): 361–375; and James C. McCroskey and Thomas J. Young, "Ethos and Credibility: The Construct and Its Measurement after Three Decades," *Central States Speech Journal* 32 (1981): 24–34.

32. Hass, 154.

33. Abraham Lincoln, "Gettysburg Address," as cited in Philip B. Kunhardt Jr., *A New Birth of Freedom* (Boston: Little, Brown, and Co., 1983), 240.

34. Harold Zyskind, "A Rhetorical Analysis of the Gettysburg Address," *Journal of General Education* 4 (1950): 202–212. For other analyses of the rhetorical effects of this speech, see Ronald F. Reid, "Newspaper Response to the Gettysburg Address," *Quarterly Journal of Speech* 53 (1967): 50–60; and Barbara Warnick, "A Ricoeurian Approach to Rhetorical Criticism," *Western Journal of Speech Communication* 51 (1987): 227–244.

35. Gilbert Highet, "The Gettysburg Address," in *Readings in Speech*, 2d ed., Haig A. Bosmajian, ed. (New York: Harper, 1971), 227.

36. George Orwell, "Politics and the English Language," in *Collected Essays* (London: Mercury Books, 1961), 357.

37. Howard Kahane, *Logic and Contemporary Rhetoric: The Use of Reason in Everyday Life*, 4th ed. (Belmont, Calif.: Wadsworth, 1984), 158.

38. Orwell, 357.

39. C. K. Ogden and I. A. Richards, *The Meaning of Meaning* (London: Kegan, Paul Trench, Trubner, 1923).

40. S. I. Hayakawa, *Language in Thought and Action* (New York: Harcourt, Brace, 1964), 180.

41. *Webster's New Collegiate Dictionary*, s.v. "fag."

42. Orwell, "Politics," 366–367.

43. Jack Kemp, "Why Abortion Is a Human Rights Issue," *Conservative Digest* (August 1986): 40.

44. Chaim Perelman and Lucie Olbrechts-Tyteca, *The New Rhetoric: A Treatise on Argumentation*, trans. John Wilkinson and Purcell Weaver (Notre Dame, Ind.: University of Notre Dame Press, 1969), 116.

45. Vilfredo Pareto, *The Mind and Society* (New York: Harcourt, Brace, 1935), vol. II, sec. 1135, p. 671, as cited in Perelman and Olbrechts-Tyteca, 116.

46. A wonderful little guide to making one's style more vivid is W. Strunk and E. B. White, *The Elements of Style*, 3d ed. (New York: Macmillan, 1979).

47. Haig A. Bosmajian, *The Language of Oppression* (Lanham, Md.: University Press of America, 1983), 118.

48. An excellent guide to how to avoid sexist and racist language is the *Publication Manual of the American Psychological Association*, 4th ed. (Washington, D.C.: American Psychological Association, 1994), 50–60.

49. Stokely Carmichael, Address to students at Morgan State College, January 16, 1967, cited in Bosmajian, 45.

CHAPTER EIGHT

ARGUMENT ANALYSIS AND CRITICISM

KEY CONCEPTS

Simple argument (p. 231)
Premise indicators (p. 232)
Conclusion indicators (p. 232)
Complex arguments (p. 236)
Argument chains (p. 237)
Compound arguments (p. 238)
Fallacy (p. 242)
Ad hominem (p. 245)
Ad populum (p. 246)
Presumption (p. 247)
Appeal to tradition (p. 247)

Straw argument (p. 248)
Equivocation (p. 248-249)
Amphiboly (p. 249)
Emotive language (p. 250)
Begging the question (p. 251)
Non sequitur (p. 252)
False analogy (p. 253)
Hasty generalization (p. 254)
Post hoc (p. 255)
Single-cause (p. 256)
Slippery slope (p. 256)

Just as we create and communicate arguments in support of various propositions, we are also a constant target of persuasive appeals by others. Campaign speeches, product advertising, editorials, business proposals, and even personal decisions require that we understand and evaluate arguments. In this process, it is important to be able to listen carefully, analyze, and evaluate the quality of arguments we receive. Analyzing and evaluating arguments involves critical-thinking skills such as understanding arguers' intended meanings, isolating their claims, deciding whether those claims are adequately supported by evidence, making unstated inferences explicit, knowing how those inferences work, pinpointing unstated assumptions, and detecting fallacies and erroneous reasoning.

The argument developed in Box 8.1 supports a policy proposition to remove the drug Accutane from the market. Representative Bart Stupak argued that the dangers associated with Accutane are far more damaging than the acne it is intended to treat. As you read his argument, ask yourself the following questions:

Does Stupak make a well reasoned, appropriately supported argument?

Is his argument strong?

What makes the argument compelling, or, what could have made it more compelling?

■ ■ ■ ■ ■

BOX 8.1
PUTTING PEOPLE FIRST[1]

I come tonight to put people first, to put our children first as I continue to speak out against the acne drug Accutane. As a legislator, I have called for more restrictions on the distribution and use of this drug, which is known to cause severe birth defects and a form of impulsive behavior and depression in young people taking this drug. This drug has devastated my family with the loss of our son BJ and more than 250 other families who have lost their young son or daughter across this nation while they were taking Accutane.

As we were flying back from Little Rock, Arkansas, CBS news ran a story tonight, and I quote an FDA safety reviewer, Dr. David Graham, when he spoke to the Senate Finance Committee. Dr. Graham said, "I would argue that the FDA as currently configured is incapable of protecting America against another Vioxx." He told the Senate Finance Committee that "there are at least five other drugs on the market today that should be looked at seriously to see whether they should remain on the market." He cited the acne drug Accutane.

Why Accutane? Because of the horrendous birth defects, but also because of a recent study by Dr. J. Douglas Bremner. He has demonstrated how Accutane mediates depression, causes impulsive behavior due to changes in the orbital frontal cortex in the front part of the brain. That mediates depression. Depression is found in this part of the brain. Over the course of our investigation of the Committee on Energy and Commerce research, it has indicated that the current formula of Accutane may be about 240 times greater than what is necessary to be effective.

Too much Accutane, a synthetic vitamin A, causes cerebra tumor or a pseudo tumor in some patients. This pseudo tumor is a warning that is found on the packaging, but what does it really mean? It means severe headaches. And while it acts like a tumor in the brain, it cannot be discovered. CAT scans will not show it. There is no evidence of a tumor. So what happens? As Dr. Bremner showed us here in a study of the orbital frontal cortex, there is a decrease in the metabolism of the brain. . . . It neutralizes or decreases the metabolism in this part of the brain. . . . The medical evidence is clear that Accutane causes changes in the brain, which leads some young people to take their own life through impulsive behavior.

(continued)

BOX 8.1   CONTINUED

Putting people first. Let us put children first. Let us join with the FDA drug safety reviewer and pull this drug from the market or, at a minimum, severely restrict the use and distribution of Accutane until we have all the answers about this powerful, dangerous drug. Is a decreased metabolism that we see here, is this reversible? Will the brain repair itself? How much Accutane is safe? What should the real dose be so we do not hurt the developing young brains of our children? Has the FDA done enough to protect our children? Has the FDA seriously looked at this study and similar studies in animal testing, which also demonstrate Accutane harms the brain? It is time to put our children first. It is time to pull this drug off the market until all of our questions are seriously answered. Put our children first. . . .

Chapter 7 focused on how arguers can develop their communication skills to effectively present arguments. This chapter concentrates on the role of the hearer as a critical and analytic recipient of arguments. Our goal is to develop tools for argument analysis and criticism that enable you to identify an argument's parts and how they are related to each other, building off of the models developed in Chapter 2. We will also explain common argument fallacies that undermine arguments and speaker credibility. Argument analysis enables us to identify an arguer's point of view, supply assumptions and inferences that may not be stated, and evaluate the adequacy of the argument as a whole. These are important critical-thinking skills that will be valuable as you assess the messages you hear and read.

BENEFITS OF ARGUMENT ANALYSIS

In Chapter 2, we introduced a model of argument including a co-orientational approach to understanding how arguments function in argument situations. In that model, an individual argument was said to have four components: a claim (expressed opinion), evidence (facts, beliefs, or premises supporting the claim), reasoning (the inference or link between the evidence and the claim), and level of dispute (the imaginary line dividing what is known and accepted from what is neither known nor accepted). Although arguments generally develop using these four components, they are often much more complicated than the simple model suggests. Arguments typically possess many kinds of statements and a complex structure.

When we diagram arguments, we attempt to illustrate how the statements that make up arguments support or reinforce one another. In this capacity, they function like blueprints or wiring diagrams and have many of the same uses and advantages.[2] Many methods for constructing diagrams of arguments have been proposed by philosophers and argumentation theorists.

Too often students (and critics and recipients of arguments) attempt to refute arguments or to criticize them without having undertaken the necessary preparation. Criticism requires that one first correctly understands an argument and carefully interprets it before attacking or responding to it. That can happen only when one can provide an account of the argument that is aligned with both the author's intended meaning and the interpretations of other recipients of the argument. The need for systematic understanding and interpretation will become more apparent if we consider two of the principal benefits of argument diagrams.

One benefit of argument analysis is that it helps us to better understand the arguments we encounter. Many arguments are not readily understandable when we first hear or read them. By diagramming and interpreting an argument, we come to a well-grounded comprehension of its language and structure. As an example, consider Daniel Webster's 1833 refutation of John C. Calhoun. Calhoun had earlier taken a strong states' rights position, arguing that the federal Constitution was a compact between states, not an instrument of "we the people," and that each sovereign state should retain its power to judge the constitutionality of an act of Congress. Webster strongly objected to Calhoun's interpretation, claiming that it attributed too much power to the states, and he questioned Calhoun's wording as follows:

> The first resolution declares that the people of the several states "*acceded*" to the Constitution. . . . The natural converse of *accession* is *secession*; and, therefore, when it is stated that the people of the States acceded to the Union, it may be more plausibly argued that they may secede from it. . . . *Accession*, as a word applied to political associations, implies coming into a league, treaty, or confederacy, by one hitherto a stranger to it, and *secession* implies departing from such league or confederacy. The people of the United States have used no such form of expression in establishing the present government. They do not say they *accede* to a league, but they declare that they *ordain* and *establish* a Constitution.[3]

A thorough consideration of this argument would lead us to ask the following questions: What is Webster's major claim in this portion of his address? Is it implied or explicitly stated? What basic premises does he state for his argument? How are they tied together? Answering such questions leads us to an understanding of the basic thrust of Webster's argument and an identification of the statements and inferences pivotal in tying his premises to his claim. (We will answer these questions and show how Webster's argument is diagrammed later in this chapter.)

The second benefit to argument diagrams is that they enable the recipient to judge and evaluate the argument. They enable one to identify the premises and evidence, ascertain the reasoning used by the arguer, and consider how these two forms of support are linked to the claim. Diagramming is thereby an intermediate step to testing an argument's evidence and reasoning, as our critique of various arguments in this chapter will illustrate. Diagrams also isolate secondary claims on which the primary claim depends, show how the premises are linked to support the claim, and reveal statements that are tangential or irrelevant to the claim. One can therefore avoid wasting time responding to incidental remarks or unimportant premises and go to the heart of the argument—its central inference—by noting the roles of vital subsidiary claims and essential premises.

AN APPROACH FOR ANALYSIS

The approach discussed in this section has for a long time been used by philosophers to portray the structure of practical arguments. In a rudimentary form, this model was introduced by Monroe C. Beardsley in his book *Practical Logic* in 1950. Beardsley used his model to identify the skeleton of an argument—the pattern in which its premises and claims were related to each other.[4] Variations of this model have recently appeared in books by Michael Scriven and Irving Copi, whose procedures we have adapted to a description of argument diagramming.[5]

Our variation of the general model divides arguments into four types or classifications. Arguments are classified according to the degree of complexity in their structure. By "complexity of structure," we mean how many statements there are in the argument and how they are linked together. This ranges from the simplest arguments (Type I), which comprise only one premise and one claim, to the most complicated (Type IV), which comprise many premises and many claims linked together in numerous ways. In addition, this section will explain five steps in analyzing arguments and constructing diagrams and illustrate them with examples.

Analysis of Type I Simple Arguments

The best way to become acclimated to argument analysis is to begin with simple arguments. *A simple (Type I) argument consists of one premise and a claim that follows from it.* The inference connecting the two may be stated or implied. Keep in mind that when we talk about the premise of an argument, we are talking about its foundation or the evidence used to support the claim. Reasoning, or the inference, is the way in which an arguer links the premise to the conclusion or claim. The first task is to recognize a text as an argument and not some other kind of communication event. The definitions and descriptions offered in Chapter 1 are helpful here. Unlike other kinds of communication, arguments advance a claim, offer support for it, and are made in a context of disagreement.

It is important to note that statements function as premises and as claims *relative to each other*. No statement in isolation is either one or the other:

> Because it's going to rain today, you should take your umbrella.
> Because you are taking your umbrella, it's probably not going to rain today.

In both statements, the presence or absence of rain is claimed to be causally connected to the presence of an umbrella (although the second argument is facetious and an example of *post hoc* reasoning). However, the fact that either clause can function as premise or as claim in relation to the other illustrates the point. *Premise* and *claim* are relative terms like *employee* and *employer*.[6] They function as they do only in context and in relation to each other.

The problem, therefore, is to be able to tell in any simple or complex argument which statements are premises and which are claims. There are two clues that can help you do this. One clue is that the premises (evidence) are generally *the most readily verifiable and least arguable statements in the argument*. In the first example just mentioned, the prediction that it's going to rain can probably be supported through reference to a weather report or conditions outside, and the arguer expects the arguee to agree that it will rain. In the second example, the arguee very likely has an umbrella in hand, a fact that can be observed by both parties. The most accepted statement, the one least likely to be questioned, then, serves as the premise of the argument.

The second kind of clue arises from the wording of the passage in which the argument occurs. Arguers often provide contextual cues called conclusion indicators and premise indicators to help recipients follow their arguments, and these can assist the analyst in structuring statements in the argument text. *Premise indicators are words like* because, since, for, *or phrases like* the fact that, by considering, *or* as shown by, *and they indicate that what follows is to be relied upon as a base for drawing a claim. Conclusion (claim) indicators include* therefore, so, consequently, it follows that, *and so forth, and they introduce statements by relating them to other, less-arguable statements.* Such transitional words or signposts should be noted, for they indicate how the arguer intended that recipients relate statements within the argument to one another. The reasoning linking the premises and the claim is often implicit and not expressly stated in the argument. If it is stated, it is stated in the form of an inference. In the process for analysis discussed here, an inference is simply a linking statement to be placed between the premise and the final claim. How this occurs in diagrams will become clear when complex and compound arguments and argument chains are considered later in this chapter.

For now, let us apply the diagramming procedure to the simplest possible form—the argument with one premise and one claim. As our example, we will again use a passage from Webster's reply to Calhoun:

> Where sovereign communities are parties, there is no essential difference between a compact, a confederation, and a league. They all equally rest on the plighted faith of the sovereign party.[7]

We will now explain the five steps in argument analysis according to this general model and apply them to this simple argument. The five steps are ascertaining the meaning, numbering the statements in the argument, identifying the argument's final claim, constructing a diagram, and criticizing the argument.

The first step is to figure out what the arguer means. This step is important because many arguments hinge on definitions of terms, and some arguments use technical or archaic language that is not readily understandable. The preceding argument, for example, is expressed somewhat archaically and relies on a defining characteristic of agreements between governments. Reference to a dictionary reveals that "to plight" means to pledge; "faith" means allegiance or duty; and a "sovereign community" is an independent government of some kind.[8] So, restated in contemporary language, the argument would say:

> Where independent governments are parties [to an agreement], there is no essential difference between a compact, a confederation, and a league. They all equally rest on the pledged duty and allegiance of each government.

Checking on and verifying the meaning in this way helps the analyst to understand the argument and to discover whether there was the kind of slippage in the use of terms or equivocal use of language discussed later in this chapter.

When longer arguments are involved, the analyst should begin by reading the entire argument straight through once or twice to grasp its overall meaning, then look up any specialized, technical, or archaic words. There are two things to keep in mind about interpreting the language of the argument during this step. First, one should interpret the argument in a way that is fair to the arguer. For example, Webster in his argument is not claiming that compacts, confederations, and leagues are exactly alike, only that they share the characteristic of pledge of duty and allegiance. If the analyst interpreted the argument's claim to be that the three types of agreement were exactly alike, he or she would overstate Webster's claim (and thus make the argument easier to criticize). When interpreting an argument, one should define terms as the arguer intended them to be defined, make the strength of the claim proportionate to the author's intention, and otherwise give the argument a fair and sympathetic reading. To do otherwise would be unfair to the arguer. Second, one should not prematurely evaluate or criticize the argument, but instead seek to understand it. If one moves to evaluation and criticism too quickly, there is a danger that the argument and the arguer's intent will be misconstrued and that the evaluation will be concerned with a claim other than the one the arguer intended.

The second step in analysis is to number the statements in the argument. Numbers should be assigned consecutively in the order in which statements occur in the text of the argument, like this:

> ① Where sovereign communities are parties, there is no essential difference between a compact, a confederation, and a league. ② They all equally rest on the plighted faith of the sovereign party.

The question of what counts as a statement to be numbered and what does not will invariably arise during this step. Different analysts may number statements in a given argument in different ways, and such variations are not a problem as long as the diagrams are clear and useful in displaying the structure of the argument.

Two guidelines are useful in numbering statements because they lead to diagrams that display the thoughtline of the argument clearly and increase the effectiveness of subsequent analysis. First, one should assign numbers only to complete thought units, not to partial thoughts. A "complete thought unit," whether it is a sentence, an independent clause, a noun phrase, or a participial phrase, will be expressible as a complete and fully formed idea. In the example we have been using, the phrase "where sovereign communities are parties" is not a complete thought unit because it depends on the rest of the sentence for its meaning. Any statement that is not understandable when it stands alone is a thought fragment and not a complete thought unit. Therefore, it should not be numbered separately. However, some phrases occurring in sentences are capable of being expressed as complete ideas with only minor changes and should be separately numbered. This is illustrated in the following argument:

> Despite the pessimism of the doomsayers, ① the economy will continue on the upswing this year. With ② low interest rates, ③ decreased energy prices, and ④ a booming stock market, ⑤ it's hard to visualize any cause for a slowdown.

The three noun phrases in the second sentence could easily be expressed as complete thoughts ("interest rates are low, energy prices are decreasing, the stock market is booming"). They should therefore be numbered separately.

The second guideline for numbering statements in arguments is also illustrated by the preceding argument. Rhetorical flourishes, editorial asides, repetitions, and other extraneous material should not be numbered. The phrase "despite the pessimism of the doomsayers" sets up the statement rhetorically but does not function as either premise or claim. It should not be included because it has no argumentative function and would detract from the clarity of the diagram. Any statement that is made merely to "set the stage," reinforce other statements, or digress from the main thoughtline of the argument should not be numbered because it is not a part of the central thoughtline of the argument taken as a whole.

The third step in analysis is to identify the argument's main claim. If there is more than one main claim, then there is more than one argument. The number of independent conclusions in a passage determines the number of arguments it contains.[9] This situation will be more fully discussed in the next section of this chapter. If conclusion indicators are present, circling them may assist in diagramming the argument. In this third step, it is advisable to consider the possibility that the argument's primary claim has not been explicitly stated. If the preliminary interpretation of the argument in step one indicated that the arguer left the principal claim unstated, it should be supplied now. The analyst should explicitly state the claim and supply it with a number in parentheses (to show the claim is implicit) prior to diagramming.

The fourth step in the analysis is to diagram the argument. Circled numbers representing the thought units and statements in the argument can be used. Those representing basic premises are placed at the top, and the diagram flows upward to the final, or main, claim. When diagrammed, Webster's argument looks like Figure 8.1. The second statement in the argument was the premise, and the first was the claim. Webster's conclusion that there is no essential difference between a compact, a confederation, and a league rested on the premise that the three share a common characteristic—the "plighted faith" (pledged allegiance) of a "sovereign party" (independent government). Thus, the second statement is placed at the bottom of the diagram, and the first statement is placed at the top.

The fifth and final step is to criticize the argument. Now that the argument's parts and their relation to one another have been identified, we are in a position to critique the argument's evidence and reasoning. In regard to the evidence, we can begin by observing that Webster cites no source for his observation that compacts, confederations, and leagues all rely on the pledged allegiance of the parties that agree to join them. Because Webster cited no source other than what he thought his audience already believed, he grounded the argument clearly below the level of dispute. There are times, however, when an analyst is less certain that evidence is truly evidence. In these cases, the analyst should employ the tests of evidence developed in Chapter 5. With this example, though, it would make sense to ask whether this "fact"—that all three alliances rest on voluntary agreement—is relevant to his argument about the Constitution. It would be worthwhile, too, to consider whether Webster's observations about various forms of government are consistent with the observations of other political figures of his day and with scholarship on government and politics of that time.

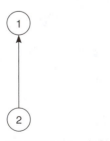

FIGURE 8.1   A Simple Diagram

Criticism also involves testing the arguer's reasoning. Here Webster emphasizes the similarity between compacts, confederations, and leagues; all rely on the voluntary actions of their members. Further, he argues that there is "no essential difference between" the three. The tests of quality, quantity, and opposition described in Chapter 6 could be applied to Webster's comparison. Clearly, the three objects compared are all forms of consensual agreement and thus are in the same class, so Webster's argument meets the test of quality. But Webster cited only one similarity between the three forms of agreement; he could have cited more.

Confederations, compacts, and leagues are formed voluntarily by parties of somewhat equal status who share a common purpose. Citing more similarities would certainly have strengthened Webster's argument and better met the test of quantity.

Diagramming and criticizing arguments using the general model for argument analysis therefore involves five steps. First, after identifying a statement as an argument with premises and claims, the analyst should carefully examine its terms and phrases to ascertain what the argument means. The resulting interpretation should be fair in recapturing its author's intended meaning and should refrain from evaluation and criticism. Second, the thought units in the argument should be assigned numbers in the order of their occurrence. Only sentences and phrases expressible as complete thoughts should be numbered, and tangential statements and digressions should not be assigned numbers. Third, the argument's main claim or primary conclusion should be identified. If implicit, it should be expressly stated and assigned a number in parentheses. Fourth, the argument's structure should be laid out in a diagram, beginning with the most accepted or easily verifiable premises at the top, and flow downward to the main claim. Fifth, the argument should be criticized and evaluated by using the tests of evidence and reasoning described in Chapters 5 and 6 of this book.

Analysis of Other Structural Patterns

The foregoing illustration of argument analysis has made use of the simplest form of argument, in which only one claim is stated and supported by a single premise. As might be expected, most arguments have a more complicated structure than this. Four categories or types of argument structures are illustrated in Figure 8.2. We have

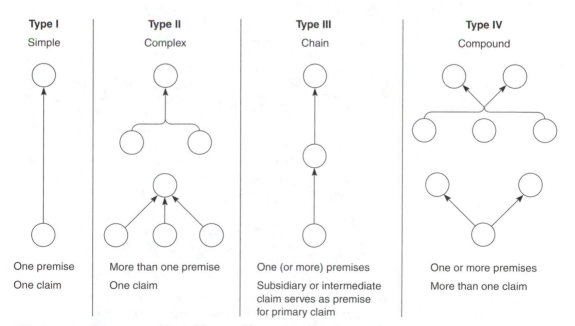

Type I	Type II	Type III	Type IV
Simple	Complex	Chain	Compound
One premise	More than one premise	One (or more) premises	One or more premises
One claim	One claim	Subsidiary or intermediate claim serves as premise for primary claim	More than one claim

FIGURE 8.2   Diagrams of Four Types of Argument Structures

already explained Type I (simple) arguments. The remainder of this section will explain and illustrate the other three types.

Type II Complex

Type II (complex) arguments have two or more premises supporting a single claim. The following argument is a good example of this pattern:

> ① Constitutionality aside, setting the minimum [drinking] age at 21 has been a practical disaster.
>
> Designed to attack drunken driving on the part of teenagers, ② it discriminates against a whole category of people, many of whom drink only moderately. ③ It penalizes female tenagers, whose DWI convictions are below the national average. ④ Furthermore, clandestine drinking has created mini-prohibition on college campuses.[10]

This argument makes a claim about the harmful practical effects of setting the drinking age at 21, and its premises describe three conditions resulting from the 21-year-old minimum. There are therefore three premises and one main claim, so the diagram would look like the one in Figure 8.3.

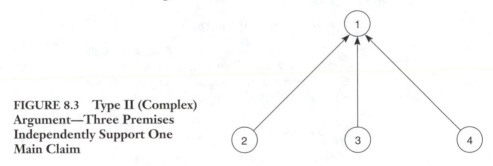

FIGURE 8.3   Type II (Complex) Argument—Three Premises Independently Support One Main Claim

There are two characteristics to note about this argument. First, the phrase "designed to attack drunken driving on the part of teenagers" provides background information and does not support the argument's conclusion, so it should not be numbered. Second, each premise supports the conclusion independently of the others. If one or perhaps even two of the premises were removed, the remaining premise(s) would still be sufficient to support the claim.

A second variation of Type II arguments is one in which premises work *in combination* to support the claim. In this pattern, the premises are interrelated and cooperate with one another. The following argument illustrates this pattern:

> ① Skier attendance figures on a national level have reached all-time highs during the past five years. Unfortunately, ② Washington state has not enjoyed the increase in market share over the past 15 to 20 years that other Western states have. ③ During the late 1960s, Washington enjoyed 18 percent of all skier visits in the Western states. ④ This has declined steadily to a current 6 percent of that market.[11]

Here the author's premises are interconnected. He claims that overall skier attendance is up, and simultaneously that the percentage of this market patronizing ski areas in Washington state has declined. The overall market has increased while

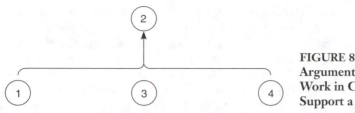

FIGURE 8.4 Type II (Complex) Argument—Three Premises Work in Combination to Support a Claim

Washington's share in it has decreased. If one disregards either the information about the national increase or the premises stating Washington's decline in the share, the conclusion is inadequately supported. To indicate the interdependence of the premises in the diagram, one can supply a brace or bracket to connect them, as in Figure 8.4.

This clearly shows that the claim that Washington has not enjoyed an increase in its share of the market is dependent on *both* a statement of the overall increase and an indication that the individual state share has declined.

Type III Chains

Type III arguments are also called argument chains. As we defined them in Chapter 2 *chains use proven claims as evidence for unproven claims.* Initial premises or evidence are used to support a claim that, once it is established and falls below the level of dispute, can itself be used to support a further claim. A simple example of an argument chain is the following:

> ① The weather's been warming up and ② there are buds coming out on my shrubbery. ③ These are signs I'll have to start mowing the lawn soon, so ④ I'd better get the lawn mower serviced.

When diagrammed, the argument's structure would look like that of Figure 8.5.

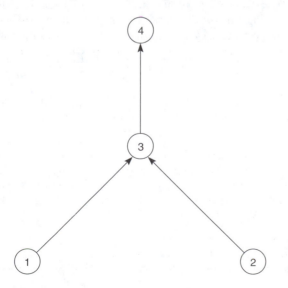

FIGURE 8.5 Type III (Chain) Argument—One or More Subsidary Claims Support the Primary Claim

This is a simple chain because the first two premises independently support a single intermediate claim that lawn mowing will soon be in order. Once supported, the claim that the lawn needs to be mowed is moved below the level of dispute and can in turn be used as a premise to support the main claim that the mower must be serviced. In Chapter 4, we call intermediate statements such as this subsidiary claims and note their importance in linking together extended arguments. When chains and subsidiary claims play a role in the structures of arguments, the resulting diagrams take the form of tree diagrams. Tree diagrams display the linkages between thought units in the form of branching and intersecting lines flowing from the bottom to the top of the diagram. In the diagrams illustrated here, subsidiary or intermediate claims appear in the middle of the diagram, between the basic premises and the main claim.

Type IV Compound

The most complicated argument structure is a *Type IV*, or compound, argument. *Compound arguments use one or more premises to support more than one conclusion.* Earlier in this chapter, we noted that the number of claims or conclusions in a text indicates the number of arguments present, and that if there are, for example, two claims, there are therefore two arguments. This is generally true, but Type IV arguments are exceptions to this rule. (Type IV arguments occur infrequently, but as a class they occur often enough to be considered as an exception.)

In a compound argument such as Type IV, one single premise leads to more than one claim or to a group of interdependent premises, which, taken together, lead to two or more further claims. Because the various premises cannot be isolated and assigned separately to individual claims, the argument must be considered as a whole. Here is an example of the simplest kind of Type IV argument:

> ① When asked on a recent survey what is most important to them on a job, teachers usually cite an opportunity to use their minds and abilities and a chance to work with young people. ② The vast majority of teachers are in their profession not for money but for all the reasons we hope they are. ③ Perhaps we should stop comparing teachers so quickly to high-priced professionals.[12]

The first statement, providing survey results about teacher attitudes, contains the evidence in this argument and states its premise—that teachers value aspects of their jobs other than salary. From this single premise, two conclusions are drawn—first, that teachers are not in their profession for money, and second, that they are not comparable to high-priced professionals. The argument when diagrammed, then, would look like Figure 8.6.

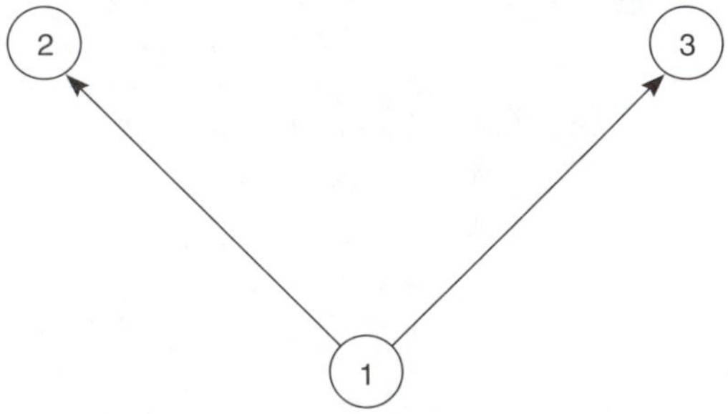

FIGURE 8.6   Type IV (Compound) Argument—A Single Premise Leads to More Than One Claim

The second variation of a Type IV argument groups a number of premises together and uses them in concert to support multiple conclusions. Here is a simple example of this type of compound argument from the same article on teaching:

> As it stands now, ① teachers under nine-to-ten-month contracts who earn $35,000 have salaries slightly below the median for males with four or more years of college who are working full time year round. ② That $35,000 is in the top quarter of salaries paid to college-educated women working full time year round. ③ Teachers no longer fare so badly in the marketplace. ④ Their salaries and nine-to-ten-month teaching year make an attractive professional option.[13]

The first premise taken alone does not support either conclusion. Only when both of the first two statements as premises are combined does one get a complete picture of the situation for the entire teaching profession. Furthermore, teachers' status in the marketplace and the attractiveness of teaching as an option are two separate, although related, conclusions. This compound argument would therefore be diagrammed as in Figure 8.7.

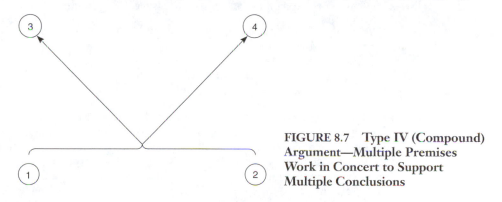

FIGURE 8.7   Type IV (Compound) Argument—Multiple Premises Work in Concert to Support Multiple Conclusions

Up to this point, this section of the chapter has described the general model for argument analysis, explained the steps to be followed in diagramming and criticizing simple arguments, and introduced three additional types of argument structures: the complex argument, the argument chain, and the compound argument. In order to bring the whole process together, let us consider the application of the five steps to an argument chain that includes complex arguments.

An Application

Because of its economy and flexibility, the procedure for argument analysis just outlined is useful in displaying and understanding the structure of long, complicated arguments. Let us return to Daniel Webster's lengthy argument cited at the beginning of this chapter to see whether argument analysis can assist us in understanding, interpreting, and criticizing it. Recall that the argument was stated as follows:

> The first resolution declares that the people of the several states "*acceded*" to the Constitution. . . . The natural converse of *accession* is *secession*; and, therefore, when it is stated that the people of the States acceded to the Union, it may be more plausibly argued that they may secede from it. . . . *Accession*, as a word applied to political associations, implies coming into a league, treaty, or confederacy, by one hitherto a stranger to it; and *secession*

implies departing from such league or confederacy. The people of the United States have used no such form of expression in establishing the present government. They do not say they *accede* to a league, but they declare that they *ordain* and *establish* a Constitution.

The steps for analyzing this argument are as follows:

1. *Ascertain the meaning.* To ensure an accurate interpretation of Webster's argument, we could check its context and the definitions of any terms that might be unclear. If we did this, we would discover that Webster is refuting John C. Calhoun's interpretation of the Constitution as summarized in three resolutions being considered by the Senate. Webster seems most concerned by the use of the term *accede* in Calhoun's first resolution. His concern grows out of the implications for using this particular term. On the whole, Webster opposes the use of the term *accede* for two reasons: First, "to accede" means to freely give consent to and implies, by means of its opposite, that "to secede," parties that have acceded to an agreement can withdraw from it at will; and second, no such term was used when the Constitution was established, so Calhoun's interpretation cannot be historically justified.

2. *Number statements in the argument.* All of Webster's statements appear to be straightforward and relevant to his claim. The conclusion indicator, "therefore," in the second sentence should be circled, and all thought units stated in sentences or independent clauses should be numbered separately in the order in which they appear in the paragraph:

> ① The first resolution declares that the people of the several states "*acceded*" to the Constitution. . . . ② The natural converse of *accession* is *secession*; and ⟨*therefore,*⟩ ③ when it is stated that the people of the States acceded to the Union, it may be more plausibly argued that they may secede from it. . . . ④ *Accession*, as a word applied to political associations, implies coming into a league, treaty, or confederacy, by one hitherto a stranger to it; and ⑤ *secession* implies departing from such a league or confederacy. ⑥ The people of the United States have used no such form of expression in establishing the present government. ⑦ They do not say they *accede* to a league, but ⑧ they declare that they *ordain* and *establish* a Constitution.

3. *Identify the argument's primary claim.* A consideration of each of the statements in this paragraph reveals that none of them articulates a claim or thesis that ties all the ideas together, so the claim must be implied. From the context, we know that Webster is attempting to refute Calhoun's strong states' rights position and his use of the term *accede*. Considering the thrust of Webster's statements in the paragraph, we are justified in supplying the following conclusion:

> The use of the term *accede* in Calhoun's first resolution should not be accepted.

The claim should be added and assigned the parenthetical number (9).

4. *Construct a diagram.* The first three statements in the argument can be grouped together because they are all related to the implications of the term *accede* and its opposite, *secede*. Furthermore, the first two statements are coupled together to support their conclusion, which then in turn serves as a premise for the final (implied) claim. Statements ④ and ⑤, which, respectively, define the terms "accession" and "secession," should be taken together to support statement ②, that one is the converse of the other. Statements ⑦ and ⑧ are again coupled together (the people do not say "accede" but

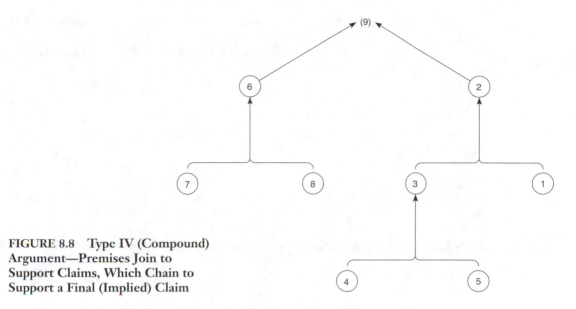

**FIGURE 8.8   Type IV (Compound)
Argument—Premises Join to
Support Claims, Which Chain to
Support a Final (Implied) Claim**

instead say "ordain" and "establish") to support the subclaim that no such expression was used. Therefore, the overall argument should be diagrammed as in Figure 8.8.

This diagram illustrates many of the important features of Webster's argument. By examining it, we know that the claim in the first complex argument (that, if Calhoun's interpretation is accepted, people will find it easier to argue for secession) rests on two interdependent premises. Furthermore, we know that Webster's claim is implied, not stated, and that it rests on four more or less independent premises. Therefore, if a critic or opponent of Webster's argument successfully undermined only one of the premises, the argument as a whole would still hold up.

5. *Criticize the argument.* Webster's argument rests on his definition of the terms *accede* and *secede* and on whether his interpretation of the intent of the authors of the Constitution is accurate. To test his evidence and premises, we might ask such questions as the following:

- Does Calhoun actually use the word *accede* in his first resolution?
- In the language of 1833, did the two terms *accede* and *secede* have the meanings Webster assigns to them?
- When the government was established, was any such term as *accede* used?
- Were *ordain* and *establish* the only words used in writing the Constitution?

Webster's reasoning in this argument is subtle but hinges on two unstated inferences: that use of a word implies its opposite, and that present interpretations of the Constitution should be governed by the intent of its authors. So, one might ask:

- Does the use of a word imply its opposite? What is the factual or cultural basis for this principle?
- How does Webster's argument about the intent of the authors differ from the fallacy of argument from tradition?
- Are the "people" referred to in statement ⑥ adequate authorities on this matter?

Diagramming the argument has enabled us to identify the aspects that should be evaluated. For example, if the claim in statement ③ that use of a term implies its opposite can be undermined, then the argument as a whole is questionable. Does use of a term *always* imply its opposite? If someone retreats from a position, could he or she as easily advance on it? If someone requires someone else to do something, could he or she as easily free that person from any obligation? Furthermore, by allowing us to identify the starting points of Webster's argument, the diagram reminds us that his account is an *interpretation* of the intent of the Constitution's authors and must be corroborated by considering all the language they used.

Tree diagrams are useful for discovering the pattern of claims and supporting statements in an argument. Tree diagrams help someone who wants to understand, criticize, or respond to an argument because they identify subarguments that relate to the conclusion and that link statements pivotal in supporting the claim.

UNDERSTANDING FALLACIES

As you analyze arguments you may discover that some of the relationships among the parts do not seem to work—they seem disjointed, confused, or simply incorrect. If this happens, you have probably found a fallacy in the argument. *A fallacy is an argument that is flawed by irrelevant or inadequate evidence, erroneous reasoning, or improper expression.* Fallacies can be persuasive because they are false arguments that may seem reasonable and acceptable but are based on erroneous assumptions or invalid reasoning. If recipients are not critically wary, they can be easily swayed by these arguments.

The ability to think and act critically depends in many ways on our ability to understand how arguments work as well as the ability to identify flaws that may appear. The first part of this chapter focused on understanding how arguments work. This section is intended to help understand how arguments fail. Identifying fallacies is an important skill for critics to develop because it helps them understand when an argument is flawed even if it is persuasive. Precisely because the purpose of argument is to persuade recipients to accept sound, well-supported claims, advocates should avoid practices that lead them to decisions based on erroneous inferences and assumptions.

Although fallacies represent a misuse of argument, someone who commits a fallacy is not necessarily evil or ethically corrupt. Arguers may commit fallacies unintentionally as well as intentionally. Unintentional fallacies occur when an arguer is unaware of proper argument construction or use and commits a fallacy without realizing it. In this sense, fallacies are not only deceptive to audiences, but to speakers and writers as well.

Some arguers, however, may intentionally commit a fallacy so as to persuade a listener rather than search out appropriate support for argument positions. Intentional fallacies represent a deliberate attempt to mislead an audience into taking some action based on false information. For example, an arguer might use a biased source, omit part of a quotation and thereby misrepresent what a source said, or attribute a statement to an opponent that was never made. Such intentional fallacies carry important ethical implications.

Consider the argument that develops in the following paragraphs. It illustrates how fallacies find their way into arguments and how we can justify contradictory premises.

Lawrence West's career has focused on developing nuclear weapons at the Lawrence Livermore National Laboratory. When he began, he expressed reservations about working on weapons of mass destruction and his role in their manufacture. Over time, however, he was able to dismiss his concerns and argued:

> Nowadays I would be quite willing to go and do full-time weapons work because I see the vast possibilities. . . . A tremendous amount of creativity is needed, and there are very few scientists willing to do it. Nuclear weapons can devastate the world. I recognize that. But we are making anti-weapons. My primary interest is not trying to find better ways to kill people, but better ways to kill arms. . . . I don't think I fall in that category of working on weapons of death. We're working on weapons of life, ones that will save people from the weapons of death.[14]

West's argument that building weapons of mass destruction save lives is interesting because it juxtaposes two seemingly irreconcilable premises. On the one hand, a recipient is faced with the premise that nuclear weapons can destroy the world and, on the other hand, with West's conclusion that such weapons made by the United States are not weapons of death but are instead weapons of salvation. The argument is almost Orwellian in the sense that "War is peace" and "Weapons of mass destruction save lives."

This is an example of a flawed argument because the arguer uses the way it is expressed to convince the audience to simultaneously hold two mutually exclusive beliefs. Although its surface meaning may seem apparent, closer examination of the argument reveals a flaw. The way it is expressed may seem reasonable, but its development is not.

For example, West says that bad weapons are weapons of death, which can result in world destruction. However, the weapons he helps build are weapons of life, weapon-killers, anti-weapons, which preserve world peace. The problem with the argument is that it assumes the positive attributes through assertion without any justification for or evidence supporting his claims. Instead, West uses strong and emotion-laden language to focus attention away from his lack of evidence and support. The resulting argument is fallacious.

Theorists who study argument agree almost unanimously that fallacies are deceptive and consequently dangerous.[15] Even Aristotle observed that honest speakers needed to prepare for spurious arguments and arguments that look genuine but are no more than shams.[16] All recipients of argument, therefore, need to develop a critical capacity to understand and assess the arguments directed at them.

The development of the capacity to recognize and diagnose the errors in fallacies depends on skills this section is intended to help you develop. These fallacies are described in Box 8.2. Although many theorists have identified countless types and variations of fallacies, our focus here is to help make you aware of how fallacies can infiltrate arguments and unsuspecting audiences and deceive them. Before we proceed, we have a final word of caution. Just because an argument is fallacious does not necessarily mean that the claim is incorrect. The claim may, in fact, be reasonable and valid, but not for the reasons and evidence expressed in the argument.

■ ■ ■ ■ ■

BOX 8.2
TYPES OF FALLACIES

AUDIENCE-BASED FALLACIES

- *Ad Hominem* — *Ad hominem* fallacies launch an irrelevant attack on the person or source originating an argument instead of responding to substantial issues raised in the argument.

- *Ad Populum* — *Ad populum* fallacies occur when the substance of an argument is avoided and the advocate appeals instead to popular opinion as a justification for the claim.

- Appeal to Tradition — Appeal to tradition fallacies occur when someone claims that we should continue to do things the way we have always done them simply because we have always done them that way.

- Straw Arguments — The straw argument fallacy attacks a weakened form of an opponent's argument or an argument the opponent did not dvance as a way to obscure the important issues.

LANGUAGE USE FALLACIES

- Equivocation — The fallacy of equivocation exploits the multiple meanings most words have by using secondary meanings to lead to a false conclusion.

- Amphiboly — The fallacy of amphiboly exploits ambiguity in grammatical structure to lead to a false or questionable conclusion.

- Emotive Language — The fallacy of emotive language manipulates the connotative meaning of words to establish a claim without proof.

GROUNDING FALLACIES

- Begging the Question — The fallacy of begging the question assumes as a premise or as evidence for an argument the very claim or point that is in question.

- *Non Sequitur* — The *non sequitur* fallacy contains a claim that is irrelevant to or unsupported by the evidence or premises purportedly supporting it.

REASONING FALLACIES

- False Analogy — A false analogy compares two things that are not alike in significant respects or have critical points of difference.

- Hasty Generalization — A hasty generalization draws a conclusion about a class based on too few or atypical examples.

- False Cause — False-cause fallacies occur when the arguer offers a cause for a consequence that is not directly related to the consequence.

- *Post Hoc* — *Post hoc* fallacies mistake temporal succession for causal sequence.

- Single Cause — Single-cause fallacies occur when an advocate attributes only one cause to a complex problem.

- Slippery Slope — The slippery-slope fallacy assumes, without evidence, that a given event is the first in a series of states that will lead inevitably to some outcome.

Types of Fallacies

The fallacies in this section are divided into four groups: (1) fallacies related to audience that focus the recipient's attention away from the relevant issues; (2) fallacies of language use that occur when words and grammar used by an arguer mislead or confuse the recipients; (3) fallacies of grounding that stem from a lack, poor quality, or incorrect use of evidence; and (4) fallacies of faulty reasoning that provide erroneous or insufficient connections between the evidence and the claim.

Audience-Based Fallacies

When arguers present arguments to direct a recipient's attention away from the central argument and to some other irrelevant argument, then the advocate has committed a fallacy to misdirect the audience's attention. Most often, fallacies of this type are called *ad* fallacies, *Ad* is Latin for "to," and fallacies of misdirection are often called *ad* fallacies because they appeal to the audience and not to the arguments. When an arguer shifts attention away from the argument and to the audience or something else, then the arguer has committed this fallacy.[17]

Such arguers may appeal to our stereotypes or prejudices about people, our tendency to go along with the crowd, our admiration for celebrities and famous people, or our respect for past practices. By appealing to such prejudices, which are often irrelevant to the claim, arguments circumvent the substantive issues that should be considered in reaching a decision. Various forms of this category of fallacies include personal attacks on the arguer, appealing to audience emotions, and taking advantage of the audience's ignorance and gullibility to get a claim accepted.[18] In this section, we will discuss four of the most common fallacies in this category—*argumentum ad hominem*, *argumentum ad populum*, appeal to tradition, and straw arguments.

Ad Hominem.   The issue an arguer raises and the meritoriousness of the arguer's claim are usually separate from the personal character, behavior, or characteristics of the arguer, yet the *ad hominem* fallacy diverts attention from the issue at hand and focuses instead on the personal character of the argument source. Translated literally as "to the person," *the ad hominem fallacy launches an irrelevant attack on the person or source originating an argument instead of responding to substantial issues raised in the argument.* For such an argument to qualify as a fallacy, the accusation must be irrelevant to the claim at issue and must be an effort to divert attention from it.

To illustrate this fallacy, consider the following example:

> **Parent:**   I am really concerned about your grades this past semester. You were always such a good student in high school and now you have slipped to straight Cs. I think you need to study more and forget about seeing so much of your friends.

> **Student:**   Why are you always on my back for not studying? *Your* grades in college were nothing to write home about!

In raising the issue of the student's grades, the parent makes three points—that the student had done well in the past, that his grades had slipped, and that he needed to cut back on his social life and study more. The student does not acknowledge or respond to any of these points, but instead accuses the parent of being a slovenly student so as to put the parent on the defensive.

One way to detect *ad hominem* responses such as these is to be alert to instances in which an indictment of an argument seems intended to divert the discussion away from the central issues it raises so as not to respond to them. There are, however, many occasions in which the arguer's character is and should be a central issue. Assessment of the integrity of political candidates in election years may be an important part of determining whether they are fit to hold office. Questioning the qualifications of a source is also legitimate when one is responding to argument from authority in which the evidence offered is the statement of a source other than the arguer. An argument is *ad hominem* and fallacious only when it is used to circumvent and avoid a legitimate issue by arbitrarily attacking the person who raised it.

Ad Populum.   Literally, *ad populum* means "to the people." *An ad populum fallacy occurs when the substance of an argument is avoided and the advocate appeals instead to popular opinion as a justification for the claim*. Consequently, the argument's claim is predicated on popular beliefs and opinions rather than on reason and evidence. Consider the following three examples:

> The president's approval rating has dropped to less than 35 percent. This is the first time during his term that his rating has dropped this low and proves, I think, that he is doing a very poor job.
> Most new parents buy Dr. Spock's *Baby and Child Care* book to learn about the care and feeding of newborn infants. So, it seems obvious that Dr. Spock has the best book available.
> Eighty-five percent of those polled believe fluoride in water causes cancer. Therefore, we should ban fluoride from our water supplies because of its consequences.

Each example presumes that if enough people believe something, it must be true. In fact, popular belief may even run counter to objective reality. Fluoridation does not cause cancer; at least there is no statistical validation for the popular conclusion. Appealing to popular beliefs, however, hides the reality of the argument and substitutes an extraneous issue.

As you can see in these three examples, just because many people agree about something does not necessarily mean it is true. The president's popular approval rating, taken alone, is not an absolutely reliable indicator of the quality of his work. Dr. Spock's book may contain no useful advice and still be a best seller. And fluoride may actually prevent cancer, yet popular opinion might say otherwise. The point is that public opinion cannot control the factual nature of the world; public opinion only reflects the opinions and attitudes of a large group of people. If the claim of the argument does not involve the attitudes and opinions of people, then arguments appealing to opinions commit *ad populum* fallacies.

We can think of many more examples to illustrate this point, and some have important social and economic consequences. Consider what happens when people stage a run on a bank or other financial institution. When this happens, depositors fear that the bank's financial situation is uncertain and a panic spreads throughout the depositors. When people begin withdrawing their money, others interpret this action as a sign of the bank's insolvency and begin to withdraw their money as well. The result is that the bank becomes insolvent because of popular opinion.

We are not suggesting here that arguments based on popular opinions are fallacious per se. Sometimes the argument seeks to focus on opinion. For instance:

> The latest Gallup Poll showed that *American Idol* is the most popular television show in history.
> Overwhelming popular support elected the president to office.
> Toyotta is the most popular automobile of all time.

In these cases, appeals to popular opinion are warranted because the crux of the argument is what the public thinks. The *ad populum* fallacy occurs only when the issues involved are not related to public opinion. Skillful argument critics should be able to discern the difference between arguments that depend on popular opinion and those that use popular opinion to avoid discussion of issues. Argument recipients who detect *ad populum* fallacies should attempt to redirect the arguments back to the issues at hand.

Appeal to Tradition.   *Presumption is the assumption in favor of existing beliefs and states of affairs when proposals for change are made.* Presumption exists as a convention of argument that reflects people's tendency to favor what is presently in practice until a good reason for changing it is offered.

Appeal to tradition attempts to convert that convention or practice into a right or a rationale for not making a change even when a good reason for doing so is offered. *The fallacy of appeal to tradition occurs when someone claims that we should continue to do things the way we have always done them simply because we have always done them that way.* Appeal to tradition takes advantage of people's reverence for past practice and attempts to avoid dealing with meritorious reasons for changing it.

Appeals to tradition are based on the often mistaken assumptions that what has worked in the past will work well in the future, that conditions have not changed, and that there is no better way of doing things. Consider the following true examples (from a college curriculum committee meeting):

> **Professor Smith:**   We should change the college grading scale to include plus and minus grading distinctions. A recent study by this committee indicates that there is a big difference between a B+ (94 out of 100 on most exam scales) and a B− (82 out of 100). Further defining the range of grades gives more precise information about a student's performance in the course.
>
> **Professor Jones:**   Why should we change? We've had simple letter grades without plus or minus distinctions in this college for over ten years and it's worked fine.

Professor Smith presented a good reason for changing the grading system—that the change will provide more precise information about student performance. Instead of responding to Smith's substantive argument, Jones merely appealed to tradition, saying that the way things have been done in the past should continue. When a cogent and meritorious argument for making a change occurs, then the fallacy of appeal to tradition ignores the rationale given for change and assumes that traditional practice is the best way of doing things.

Straw Arguments.   Straw arguments are often called strawperson or strawman arguments. They occur often in debates, discussions, and other situations where there is interactive argument. *The straw-argument fallacy attacks a weakened form of an opponent's argument or an argument the opponent did not advance.* In committing this fallacy, arguers use as evidence an argument not advanced by their opponents but nonetheless an argument that bolsters their own position. It is very well described by Edward Damer in his book on fallacies:

> There are several different ways in which one may misrepresent an opponent's argument or position. First, one may state it in a perverted form by utilizing only a part of it, by paraphrasing it in carefully chosen misleading words, or by subtly including one's own evaluation or commentary in it. Second, one may oversimplify it. An opponent's complex argument can be made to look absurd when it is stated in a simplified form that leaves out important qualifications or subtle distinctions. Third, one may extend the argument beyond its original bounds by drawing inferences from it that are clearly unwarranted or unintended.[19]

As we noted earlier, when we discuss the analysis and criticism of arguments, arguers should begin by grounding their arguments and criticisms on fair and reasonable representations of an opponent's argument. To do anything less is unethical. Consider the following examples of the straw-argument fallacy:

Mary: I think it's time for this university to start a Second Life campus. Just think, courses would be much more interesting and interactive. Plus, we wouldn't have to get up and go to a boring classroom and listen to a boring lecture. I think that Second Life is going to be the next generation of education. Professors can better integrate audio and visual aids; there are more opportunities for informal discussions and seminars. Our school is too stuck in the past.

Derrick: Yeah, but that idea will never work. I agree that the school is stuck in the past, but that means it would take forever to teach the professors how to use Second Life and we will end up wasting more time than we save. People will get frustrated and then they will stop using it.

Derrick took one aspect of Mary's proposal—that the school is stuck in the past—and discussed obvious problems with it. He did not, however, respond to the central issue she raised—whether Second Life is a good idea and the future of education. By ignoring the major thrust of her argument, he created a straw argument.

Language-Based Fallacies

Language plays an important role in the way arguments are perceived and interpreted. Most fallacies of language use are intentional and occur when arguers equivocate, use amphiboly, or use emotive language to get their claims accepted by deliberately trying to evade issues and avoid presenting solid evidence and reasoning in favor of what they advocate. How they succeed in these efforts will become clear as we examine the various strategies employed in arguers' fallacious use of language.

Equivocation.   Many words have more than one meaning, and occasionally arguers may exploit the ambiguity in language to make a fallacious claim. One way to do this through equivocation. *The fallacy of equivocation exploits the fact that a word has more than* *one meaning so as to lead to a false conclusion.* For example, someone might say, "You shouldn't take that course in reasoning that is supposed to improve your ability to argue; you argue too much with your friends now!" Here the meaning of the term *argue* has shifted from "reasoning and correctly supporting claims" to "engaging in interpersonal squabbles." The arguer has made a false causal connection between the two based on the ambiguity of the meaning of the term *argue*.

Equivocation is often used in deceptive advertising. For example, an advertisement that appeared in several national publications proclaimed that "Parents can receive a FREE college education" for their children. On its face, the bold letters across the top of the ad made a fairly spectacular promise that the average person might have a difficult time ignoring. For most people, the word *free* means without charge, cost, or obligation. But the word *free* means something very different to the producers of the ad. To them, *free* meant that parents needed to invest a substantial sum of money in their "tax-free open-end mutual funds and Unit trusts" and pay for a variety of administrative "charges and expenses." The point was that if enough money was invested, then the interest produced should be sufficient to send a child to college. But placing money into a long-term investment is not "free" because there is an opportunity cost to having the money committed, and there are administrative and other charges that are not free. Words mean different things to different people, and when word choice misdirects the audience's understanding of the argument, then an equivocation has taken place.

The question the recipient needs to ask is whether the argument contains any language that might be misconstrued by the arguer. If the answer is yes, then the recipient should ascertain what the words are intended to mean so that both recipient and arguer share a common understanding of the argument.

Amphiboly.   Equivocation exploits ambiguities in word meanings, but *amphiboly exploits ambiguity in grammatical structure to lead to a false or questionable conclusion.* Just as there are many types of grammatical structures, there are many forms of amphiboly. For example, an advertisement might claim:

> New, improved product X is unquestionably more effective.
> Our product is new and improved.

More effective than what? New and improved compared to what? Here we have comparative adjectives used but no object provided for comparison. Perhaps product X is being compared with the original product, or perhaps with other brands of the product. We don't know.

Here is another example. An arguer claims that "When we compare the danger of spreading AIDS with the incursion of privacy involved in widespread AIDS testing, we must conclude that it is a risk we have to take." Is the antecedent of "it" the spread of AIDS or the incursion of privacy? Until we know what the arguer is referring to, the meaning of the claim is unclear.

An excellent example of the exploitation of amphiboly appeared in an article on the writing of recommendation letters. The article was in response to a number of defamation suits that had been filed against people who wrote unfavorable letters of recommendation. Faced with the problem of writing an honest letter without subjecting themselves to lawsuits, many letter-writers are puzzled about what to do. Robert J.

Thornton, in his Lexicon of Inconspicuously Ambiguous Recommendations (LIAR, for short) recommends the circumspect use of amphiboly. Here are two examples:

> To describe a candidate who is woefully inept: "I most enthusiastically recommend this candidate with no qualifications whatsoever."

> To describe a candidate who is so unproductive that the position would be better left unfilled: "I can assure you that no person would be better for this job."[20]

Because of the ambiguity in the way the sentences are constructed, the reader of the first sentence assumes that the recommendation is unqualified (when it is actually the *candidate* who is unqualified). The reader of the second sentence may interpret it to mean that the candidate is the best alternative (when in fact hiring *no one* would be the best alternative). Such examples remind us to be on the lookout for intentional and manipulative ambiguity. If we are confused about what the arguer meant by the wording of a claim, there may be a good reason.

Emotive Language. The language used to express thoughts and ideas often is a potent force in influencing our opinions and actions. As one philosopher of argument observed, "An emotional appeal to us for some specific action may be so powerful as to inhibit our capacity to exercise critical judgment on the reasons offered in favor of the action urged."[21] *The fallacy of emotive language manipulates the connotative meaning of words to establish a claim without proof.* It attempts to persuade an audience by getting them to respond emotionally to images and associations evoked by the language used rather than by judging the quality of the arguer's evidence and reasoning.

Emotive language is often used by politicians, advertisers, and propagandists to gain acceptance for ideas that cannot be effectively supported through reasoning and evidence. The idea behind the fallacy of emotive language is to set up associations in the audience's mind with either pleasant or favorable values and attitudes (in order to win acceptance for an idea) or with unpleasant experiences or disfavored values (to get an idea rejected). Language is therefore used suggestively and can have an unconscious influence.

President Harry Truman can serve as an interesting example. In 1962, historian Herbert Feis contacted Truman with several questions about Truman's decision to use the atomic bomb on Hiroshima and Nagasaki during World War II. Truman had been the subject of much criticism on his decision, and he responded with an emotionally laden letter that he never sent:

> My dear Mr. Feis:
>   You write just like the usual egghead. The facts are before you but you'd like to garble them. The instruction of July 25th, 1945 was final. It was made by the Commander in Chief after Japan refused to surrender.
>   Churchill, Stimson, Patterson, Eisenhower and all the rest agreed that it had to be done. It was. It ended the . . . War. That was the objective. Now if you can think of any other "if, as, and when" egghead contemplations, bring them out. . . .
>   It is a great thing that you or any other contemplator "after the fact" didn't have to make the decision. Our boys would all be dead.[22]

Although Truman's response may be understandable, it does not address the criticisms posed by others, nor did it address Feis's request for information about the decision on whether to use the bomb to end the war. Instead, Truman used several emotionally charged words to place the researcher on the defensive. Terms such as "egghead," "contemplator 'after the fact,'" and "dead" all help charge the letter.

Advertisements for many "self-improvement" cosmetics and health products often use emotive language to appeal to the prospective buyer's desire for a sudden and dramatic improvement in personal appearance. An advertisement for tan accelerator claims that:

> Once in a generation there's a breakthrough so revolutionary it can change forever the way people tan.

Terms such as "breakthrough" and "revolutionary" are intended to convince consumers that the product's effects must be singular and a striking advance over other tanning methods. Or, consider this claim from a weight-loss ad:

> After years of research and testing, a scientist from Princeton University has finally developed a miracle weight loss formula which has clearly proven to be the strongest fat-burning compound in the entire world! [This product] is so radically powerful that it can actually make the slim and shapely figure of your dreams a reality.

Readers who are seeking a "radically powerful" "miracle" formula to make them "slim and shapely" may be persuaded by the emotive language of this advertisement. But the "Princeton scientist" is not identified, nor is the method used in the supposed study explained. Educated recipients of arguments should be skeptical of product claims that promise "revolutionary breakthroughs" and "miraculous results." Such language is often substituted for hard evidence and valid reasoning in order to make arguments and claims persuasive.

Grounding Fallacies

Fallacies that relate to evidence occur when arguments are poorly grounded. This happens when arguers use evidence that is of poor quality or, in some cases, nonexistent. Poorly grounded arguments tend to confuse reasoning or claims with evidence. When arguers commit it this type of fallacy, they are asking recipients to draw conclusions from premises that are either missing or inappropriate to the claim. As you may recall from our earlier discussion of evidence, there are many tests of evidence that help critics determine whether evidence is relevant, reliable, and valid. When arguers ground their arguments in evidence that fails these tests, then a fallacy of evidence occurs. Although many such fallacies are possible, the following are significant and prevalent forms of problems with evidence or lack of evidence.

Begging the Question.   *The fallacy of begging the question assumes as a premise or as evidence for an argument the very claim or point that is in question.* Often, when arguers beg the question they are accused of circular reasoning because they use the argument's premises as their claims and reason that one supports the other when, in fact, there is little or no difference. Arguers who beg the question fail to seek external support for their claims so that they assume the point they are expected to prove. Consequently, the evidence for such claims is not externally valid and, in fact, cannot be validated through external sources.

You may recall that when we discussed the level of dispute in Chapter 1, we pointed out that in an argument, one begins with evidence (statements that the audience accepts) and moves to prove a conclusion that is not yet accepted. Begging the question fallacies, however, are circular because they depend upon premises whose truth is assumed rather than established.

There are many ways to beg the question. Two of them are illustrated in the following examples.

> The soul is immortal because it lives forever.

In this example, the arguer has simply stated the claim in two different ways. "Living forever" may be a definition of "immortal," but stipulating a definition does not constitute proof of immortality's existence. Put simply, the evidence in the argument cannot possibly be verified.

> We must accept the traditions of men of old time who affirm themselves to be the offspring of the gods—that is what they say—and they must surely have known their own ancestors. How can we doubt the word of the children of the gods?[23]

The issue here is whether the ancestors' word can be trusted. To address the issue, the author commits an *ad verecundiam* (appeal to authority) fallacy to claim that we should trust their authority because their word on the matter is authoritative! This is a very clear example of the kind of circular reasoning often found in fallacies that beg the question.

When we suspect that a question-begging fallacy has been committed, we should determine whether premises independent of the claim have been offered to support it and, if they have, whether these premises are any more certain or acceptable than the claim itself. If the arguer has not offered established or accepted evidence to support the claim, then he or she has begged the question.

Non Sequitur.   This Latin phrase, literally translated, means "it does not follow." *The* non sequitur *fallacy contains a claim that is irrelevant to or unsupported by the evidence or premises purportedly supporting it.* In other words, the arguer grounds the argument in evidence that fails to support the claim advanced.

This fallacy, also known as "irrelevant reason," occurs very frequently. We are likely to be misled by it because the reasons or premises offered to support a conclusion somehow resemble the type of evidence that would be necessary to support it. People often present standards that *look* like evidence and connect them with claims in the same topic area, but actually the statements have no logical relation to each other. Consider the following two examples of *non sequitur* arguments:

> Plea bargaining affects many people. In 2004 in Pierce County, there were 3,115 burglaries, 85 robberies, 109 rapes, and 31 murders.

In this argument, the first sentence is intended to be the claim and the second the evidence for it. But they are unrelated. The evidence does not tell us how many perpetrators of the listed crimes were arrested or charged, nor does it contain any information as to whether the charges were plea bargained. The only claim the evidence proves is there was crime in King County in 1993. The argument is clearly a *non sequitur.* The next one is more subtle.

> The United States is the only industrialized country in the world where teenage pregnancy is increasing. The Guttmachur study found that the U.S. pregnancy rate is twice that of Canada, England, or France, and seven times that of the Netherlands.

The first sentence is intended to be the claim, and the second serves as evidence. Someone attending to this argument who is not aware of *non sequiturs* might easily be fooled. But notice that the evidence does not say that the pregnancy rate is *increasing*, only that it is higher than that in other countries. To prove there's an increase, we would need comparable rates for different time periods showing that rates have increased in the recent past.

Non sequiturs are often subtle and yet seem obvious when they are pointed out. To detect them, we need constantly to ask, "What kind of evidence would be needed to support this claim?" and "Does this evidence qualify?"

Reasoning-Based Fallacies

As we have noted elsewhere, there are many ways that arguments can go wrong and thus mislead or deceive an audience: Flawed arguments, known as fallacies, can grow out of inadequate evidence, emotive language, appeals to ignorance or prejudice, or inadequate reasoning. In this section, we will discuss fallacies of the last kind, those that result when an arguer uses an inference that fails to meet the tests of quality, quantity, or opposition discussed in the preceding section of this chapter. In particular, we will discuss standard types of fallacies in arguments from analogy, generalization, and cause.[24] These three types of fallacies occur very often in practical arguments.

False Analogy.   *A false analogy compares two things that are not alike in significant respects or have critical points of difference.* You may recall from the preceding section that one of the criteria for judging the adequacy of an analogy is whether it meets the test of quality, that is, whether it compares two things in the same class that share significant similarities relevant to the conclusion drawn by the arguer. Furthermore, it needs to meet the test of quantity, which requires that there be a significant number of similarities between the two things being compared. A false analogy does not meet these tests. Consider the following two examples:

> We should not teach socialism in the university any more than we should teach arson.

> The success of the forty-hour work week in making corporate America efficient and productive suggests that we should use it on farms as well.

In the first example, the arguer is comparing two things that share very few similarities. Socialism is a school of thought and political philosophy, a theory only potentially applicable to practice, whereas arson is an illegal activity. Indeed, the only way to see any similarity between the two would be to begin by assuming that socialism is patently illegal or aberrant, and there is no support for this assumption.

The second example does compare situations that are, in a sense, similar. Both corporate business and farming are lines of work that generate income and are productive for society. The question in this case is whether there are *enough* similarities to support the claim that a forty-hour work week would be equally efficient and productive on farms. Farming is quite seasonal, depends on temporary labor, and requires certain very labor-intensive actions at particular times. Someone seeking to refute this analogy might emphasize how vital the pattern and cycle of work in the two environments is to the viability of the comparison itself.

False analogies also result when someone attempts to use a figurative analogy to prove a point. Figurative analogies do not meet the test of opposition because they compare things in different classes. Their function in an argument is more illustrative and metaphorical than probative. Such comparisons enliven arguments and bring their points home. The state has been compared to an organism, the kingdom of God to a mustard seed, and life to a theatrical play. When figurative analogies are used as if they were literal comparisons, however, and are the only form of support offered for a claim, they may be fallacious.

Hasty Generalization.   The adequacy of a generalization, which reasons from some to all members of a class, depends on whether enough members of the class have been observed and whether those members possess the same characteristics as other members of that class. The argument based on too few examples fails the test of quantity for a generalization, and the argument based on an atypical example fails the test of quality. *A hasty generalization draws a conclusion about a class based on too few or atypical examples.*

Drawing general conclusions from too few examples is a common error of reasoning. For example, someone might say:

> I owned two MG cars—a midget and an MGB—and they gave me nothing but trouble. The choke and the batteries froze up on the "B," and the clutches went out on both cars. They were always in the shop. MGs are poorly constructed, and I think they should be avoided.

This generalization is unwarranted. The arguer's experience may have resulted from the way the two cars were driven and the care they received. Maybe the arguer rode the clutches and subjected the cars to excessively cold weather. We could only place confidence in the conclusion if we had performance and maintenance records for thousands of MGs and could compare them with other classes of cars comparable to the MG. Unwarranted generalizations of this type when applied to people are called "stereotypes." Someone who believes that all Southerners are slow or that all Californians are easygoing based on an acquaintance with just a few members of either class is committing this fallacy.

Likewise, hasty generalizations can be based on observed samples that are not typical of the class about which the arguer's observation is made. Consider the following example:

> The growth and success of cottage industries in the Appalachian Mountains suggest that other impoverished areas can build small industries to raise their people out of debt.

This generalization is hasty because businesses in areas other than Appalachia are not like businesses there. The Appalachian Mountains are rural and remote, travel in portions of that area is difficult, and settled areas are widely dispersed and located some distance from shopping malls and convenience stores. These characteristics make patronage of cottage industries more likely. In other geographical areas, however, people might prefer accessible, inexpensive, mass-produced goods, and cottage industries, which normally have a small profit margin, would fail.

Anyone to whom generalizations are addressed should ask the question, Are there other equally common examples that deny the conclusion? The key to discovering hasty generalizations is in discovering exceptions to the claim made. Stereotypes, for example, can always be undermined if one can cite instances of people who belong to the class in question but do not possess the characteristics attributed to the class.

False Cause.   People who make causal connections between one condition or event and another are prone to two types of error—*post hoc* and single-cause fallacies. The first misidentifies a cause, and the second fails the test of quantity by assuming that only one cause led to an effect when many causes, working together, might be necessary.

Post hoc comes from the Latin *post hoc ergo propter hoc*, which, literally translated, means "after this therefore because of this." *A* post hoc *fallacy mistakes temporal succession for causal sequence*. That is, one assumes that because two events are associated in time, one event must have caused the other. Consider three separate examples of *post hoc* reasoning:

> Serial killer Ted Bundy was found guilty of murder and executed in Florida. Before his sentence was carried out, he told an interviewer that he blamed pornography for causing his crime spree. Had it not been for pornography, he claimed, he would not have committed the crimes.

> John Hinckley shot President Reagan after seeing violent acts on TV. Therefore, violence on TV must have influenced his behavior.

> All people who have cancer drink milk. Therefore, drinking milk must cause cancer.

The arguer in each of these passages bases the claim on the assumption that some antecedent condition (pornography, TV violence, or milk) resulted in some consequent condition (murder, assassination attempt, or cancer). The connection between the antecedent and consequent, however, is temporal. In other words, the only apparent connection in each argument is that one condition followed the other, but in no argument does the advocate prove that there is a causal relationship that connects the antecedent with the consequent.

The sense in which antecedent and subsequent events in these examples are not causally connected can be clarified if one remembers the role of necessary and sufficient conditions. If a subsequent event can and often does occur without the so-called cause preceding it, then the two events are not necessarily causally related. They may be, but the information provided in the argument does not provide sufficient warrant for the claim. Do all people who see pornography act violently? Do people who do not watch violent television programming commit violent acts? Do people who never drink milk have cancer? If so, then the antecedent conditions cited are neither necessary nor sufficient for the effects claimed. Just because two events occur one after another in a sequence does not mean that they are causally related; they might be, but then again they might not.

Recipients of these arguments would need to seek out additional support to confirm or deny the reasoning. For instance, does TV violence cause violence, or are violent people predisposed toward violent programming? In other words, is TV violence simply a symptom and not a cause of violence in society? Do all people who drink milk get cancer? Why are there exceptions? What the argument critic needs to look for is the regularity with which the time sequence of events holds true for the argument. If there are exceptions or other unexplained conditions that might account for the conclusion, then a fallacy has probably been committed.

The second causation fallacy is single cause. *Single-cause fallacies occur when an advocate attributes a complex problem to only one cause.* There is almost never a single cause or explanation for any problem we face. Rather, most events in our complex society arise from myriad conditions and events. Yet advocates, hoping to simplify their arguments, attribute complex social problems to a single cause. This is misleading because it does not account for other, possibly important variables worth considering. Consider the following two examples:

Low interest rates are the reason for increased housing purchases.

Poor communication is the reason for the high American divorce rate.

In both cases only one cause is listed, but for an advocate to argue that there is only one cause for either housing purchases or the high divorce rate is naive at best. Increased housing purchases might be the result of a glut of houses on the market and higher individual incomes produced by a stronger economy. Financial problems and career choices may be alternative reasons for the high divorce rate. For any complex social, political, or economic problem we can think of, there is more than one cause, and an arguer should take care not to oversimplify.

Slippery Slope.   A frequent argument made against those who argue for change or propose a new policy is slippery slope. *The slippery-slope fallacy assumes, without evidence, that a given event is the first in a series of steps that will lead inevitably to some outcome.* This sort of erroneous reasoning assumes a "domino effect"—that once one event occurs, a whole series of subsequent events or developments will occur in an uncontrollable sequence. Slippery slope is thus a fallacy of evidence use because no support is given that the subsequent events will occur. It is also a form of causal reasoning, as Edward Damer has observed:

> [The name of this fallacy suggests that] when we take one step over the edge of a slope . . . we often find ourselves slipping down the slope, with no place to dig in and stop the sliding, once we start the downward movement. While this image may be insightful for understanding the character of the fallacy, it represents a misunderstanding of the nature of causal relations between events. Every causal claim requires a separate argument.[25]

In other words, to conclude that event A leads to event B, we must have substantial evidence that one cannot occur without the other and that event B will always be produced by event A. This is what constitutes a sufficient condition and thus a causal claim. In most instances of the slippery slope, however, the relationship and predicted outcome are much less certain. Consider the following example of a conversation between James and his father, Jason:

> **James:**   I was really struggling with Biology 101 and I needed to drop it. I'm sorry because I know college is expensive, but I just wasn't getting it and I was concerned about my grade point average. I went in and I spoke to the prof. She seemed to think that dropping it was a good idea because I am so far behind.
>
> **Jason:**   I don't care about the money as much as I care that you have dropped a class in your very first semester in college. It seems to me that once the going gets rough you're just going to quit. Is this going to be a pattern with you? Next time, will you drop the first class that is tough? I'm afraid that you might, and if you keep this up you may never finish your degree.

Jason is concerned about his son's welfare. He wants him to succeed in college and he wants him to finish his degree. However, Jason commits a slippery-slope fallacy. The implication here is that James will drop future classes if he is afraid of failure and that this one instance serves as a sign of a larger pattern of behavior. But Jason offers no proof for this claim. Instead, he discusses a particular event and reasons without evidence that it proves a larger pattern. The slippery slope is rarely accompanied by any evidence that the predicted series of events will in fact occur.

Argument theorists agree that fallacies have a significant potential to be deceptive and consequently dangerous because they may lead to poor decision making.[26] Recipients may make emotional decisions as opposed to reasoned ones. Arguers who intentionally use fallacies to trick an audience are behaving unethically. Arguers should strive to construct the strongest arguments possible based on their evidence and reason. At the same time, recipients need to understand which appeals are justified and reasonable and which are not. Aristotle once warned that honest speakers need to prepare for spurious arguments and arguments that look genuine but are simply shams.[27] Both arguer and recipient need to be able to tell the two apart.

It is important to recognize, however, that not all fallacies are the same. Just as arguments can be stronger or weaker, fallacies can be strong and weak as well. Identifying an argument as fallacious does not necessarily mean that the argument should be rejected. It might simply mean that the argument is weak. Many times, fallacious arguments can be made into strong arguments with further and better evidence or reasoning. For example, consider the following:

> The prohibition of smoking in public places in California has been a remarkable success. Physicians there have reported that respiratory illness among restaurant workers has decreased as a direct result of this ban. Since it has been so successful in California, we should support a smoking ban in New York.

A critical recipient might correctly point out that this arguer has potentially committed a fallacy of false analogy because there is not clear evidence that California and New York are substantially the same. And, for people who live in those two states, a better argument could probably be made that they are substantially dissimilar.

However, if the advocate were able to produce evidence and supporting arguments to demonstrate that California and New York are substantially similar in enough respects that are related to smoking and health, the argument would become stronger.

Finally, context can determine whether an argument that appears fallacious is truly fallacious. There are times in which speakers use arguments that might appear fallacious to motivate and inspire an audience. Consider, for example, a speaker at a political rally. When speaking to a group of recipients who are supportive of the political cause, a speaker might use emotive language to help the audience visualize the issues and ideas—to inspire, not to evade. Using rhetorical flourishes, emotive language, and other methods for delivering a powerful speech can be appropriate and persuasive, as long as the speaker focuses on the central issues of the argument and inspires people to act critically and through knowledge. When speakers act to reduce an audience's understanding of the central issues and dissuade them from critically evaluating the arguments, then fallacies are probably present.

Ultimately, fallacies depend on the relationship between an arguer and audience, whether they are intentionally or unintentionally deceptive, and the extent to which they weaken or divert attention away from an argument. Ethical arguers should strive to construct arguments that are not deceptive, that are as strong as possible, and that move the audience. Thinking critically about your own and others' arguments includes evaluating potential fallacies.

SUMMARY

Argument analysis can be used to understand, evaluate, and refute the arguments one hears and reads. By interpreting an argument's language and discovering how the statements within it are related to one another, one can identify equivocation, isolate the argument's primary claim, articulate implicit inferences, locate secondary claims, disregard irrelevant statements, identify fallacies, and perform other operations that lead to effective argument criticism and refutation. This chapter focused on a method for conducting argument analysis and an explanation of some of the most common forms of fallacies.

Arguments can be categorized into four types. Simple arguments (Type I) consist of one premise and a claim that follows from it. Complex arguments (Type II) have two or more premises supporting a single claim. These premises can support the claim independently or in concert. Argument chains (Type III) use one or more premises to support claims that, once proven, become premises for further claims. Compound arguments (Type IV) use one premise or two or more premises in concert to support more than one conclusion.

Having identified a statement as an argument, the analyst can use five steps to interpret and diagram it. These steps include determining what the argument means, assigning numbers to individual thought units in the argument, identifying the main or primary claim, displaying the argument's structure in a tree diagram, and evaluating the argument by using the tests of evidence and reasoning. During analysis, one should take into account the argument's context and the arguer's probable intent to render a fair interpretation of the argument.

Fallacies are arguments that are flawed by irrelevant or inadequate evidence, erroneous reasoning, or improper expression. We discussed the nature of fallacies and their types. Generally, fallacies can be identified by their type, and we identified four: audience based, language use, grounding, and reasoning. Each of these has several subtypes.

Audience-based fallacies divert the recipient's attention away from the main issues. These include *ad hominem*, *ad populum*, appeal to tradition, and straw argument. Language-based fallacies occur when arguers use language to mislead audiences. These include equivocation, amphiboly, and emotive language. Grounding fallacies are the result of arguments that use either no evidence or poor evidence. These include begging the question and *non sequitur*. Finally, fallacies of faulty reasoning occur when arguers make errors in their inferences. These include false analogy, hasty generalization, false cause, *post hoc*, single-cause, and slippery slope.

Although many theorists have identified countless types and variations of fallacies, our focus here is to make you aware of how fallacies can infiltrate arguments and deceive unsuspecting audiences. The treatment of specific fallacies in this chapter will make you sensitive to the factors that make fallacies dangerous and enable you to identify and accurately criticize the fallacies you encounter. One final word of caution: Just because an argument is fallacious does not necessarily mean that the claim is incorrect. The claim may, in fact, be reasonable and valid, but not for the reasons and evidence expressed in the argument.

GLOSSARY

Ad hominem (p. 245) launches an irrelevant attack on the person or source originating an argument instead of responding to substantial issues raised in the argument.

Ad populum (p. 246) occurs when the substance of an argument is avoided and the advocate appeals instead to popular opinion as a justification for the claim.

Amphiboly (p. 249) exploits ambiguity in grammatical structure to lead to a false or questionable conclusion.

Appeal to tradition (p. 247) occurs when someone claims that we should continue to do things the way we have always done them simply because we have always done them that way.

Argument chains (p. 237) use proven claims as evidence for unproven claims.

Begging the question (p. 251) assumes as a premise or as evidence for an argument the very claim or point that is in question.

Complex arguments (p. 236) have two or more premises supporting a single claim.

Compound arguments (p. 238) use one or more premises to support more than one conclusion.

Conclusion indicators (p. 232) include *therefore, so, consequently, it follows that*, and so forth and they introduce statements by relating them to other, less-arguable statements.

Emotive language (p. 250) manipulates the connotative meaning of words to establish a claim without proof.

Equivocation (p. 248-249) exploits the fact that a word has more than one meaning so as to lead to a false conclusion.

Fallacy (p. 242) is an argument that is flawed by irrelevant or inadequate evidence, erroneous reasoning, or improper expression.

False analogy (p. 253) compares two things that are not alike in significant respects or have critical points of difference.

Hasty generalization (p. 254) draws a conclusion about a class based on too few or atypical examples.

Non sequitur **(p. 252)** contains a claim that is irrelevant to or unsupported by the evidence or premises purportedly supporting it.

Post hoc **(p. 255)** mistakes temporal succession for causal sequence.

Premise indicators (p. 232) are words like *because, since, for*, or phrases like *the fact that, by considering*, or *as shown by*, and they indicate that what follows is to be relied upon as a base for drawing a claim.

Presumption (p. 247) is the assumption in favor of existing beliefs and states of affairs when proposals for change are made.

Simple argument (p. 231) consists of one premise and a claim that follows from it. *Premise* and *claim* are relative terms, like *employee* and *employer*.

Single-cause (p. 256) fallacies occur when an advocate attributes a complex problem to only one cause.

Slippery slope (p. 256) assumes, without evidence, that a given event is the first in a series of steps that will lead inevitably to some outcome.

Straw argument (p. 248) attacks a weakened form of an opponent's argument or an argument the opponent did not advance.

EXERCISES

Exercise 1 Diagramming

Diagram each of the following arguments using the process of argument analysis developed in this chapter. Based on what you know, how strong or reasonable is each of the arguments. Can you identify any fallacies? For example:

> Capital punishment for murderers is widely supported by the general population. A Harris Poll in 1975 reported 59 percent of the public in favor of capital punishment, and that proportion reportedly was increasing. Another poll in 1978 asked the question, "Are you in favor of the death penalty for persons convicted of murder?" The results showed 66 percent of the populace in favor of the death penalty.

Diagram

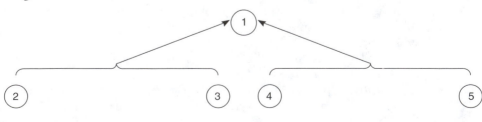

Statements

1. Capital punishment for murderers is widely supported by the general population.
2. A 1975 poll reported 59 percent of the public in favor of capital punishment.
3. The proportion of people favoring capital punishment was increasing by 1975.
4. A 1978 poll asked if people favored the death penalty for convicted murderers.
5. Sixty-six percent favored the death penalty.

Criticism

The polls are outdated. Perhaps pubic opinion has shifted since the 1970s. Besides, this is a form of *ad populum* argument that assumes that because the public supports something, it should be favored. Furthermore, the arguer does not report the source of the statistics or the method used to collect them. How large was the sample surveyed? Was the sample representative of the general population? Do other surveys and polls on this question (particularly those gathered since the mid-1970s) agree with the two polls cited here?

Arguments for Analysis and Criticism

1. [T]he data show that, if current trends continue, Social Security won't live to see another 60 years.

   The demographic trends that helped make Social Security so successful in its early years—plenty of workers paying in to support a few retirees—have started to work against it.

   In 1945, there were 42 workers for each Social Security beneficiary. Today, that figure is 3.3 workers. By 2030, it drops to two to one, according to the program's annual report.

   At current tax rates, Social Security starts to lose money by 2013—right around the time waves of baby boomers will start retiring.

   The deficits mount quickly. By 2070, annual Social Security shortfall will be more than $7 trillion.

   John Merline, "Should Social Security Retire? Public System Can't Stack Up to Market Returns." *Business Daily* (August 14, 1995): A1.

*2. Ladies make excellent teachers in public schools; many of them are every way the equals of their male competitors, and still they secure less wages than males. The reason is obvious. The number of ladies who offer themselves to teach is much larger than the number of males who are willing to teach. . . . The result is that the competition for positions of teachers to be filled by ladies is so great as to reduce the price; but as males cannot be employed at that price, and are necessary in certain places in the schools, those seeking their services have to pay a higher rate for them.

   Joseph Emerson Brown, "Against the Woman Suffrage Amendment," in *American Forum* (Seattle: University of Washington Press, 1960), 339.

3. Professor Smith: There is probably too much cheating going on in our department, and our faculty should do something about it.

   Professor Jones: I haven't noticed any evidence of cheating in my classes. What makes you say that it's widespread?

Smith: Well, I'm sure you remember that our colleague Adams found a lot of plagiarism on the course papers turned in to him last spring. Whole paragraphs were reproduced in more than one student paper. Then, of course, our graduate student proctors often have taken up crib sheets in the 100 course exam. And I've observed students during my own tests sharing information. These are signs of a pervasive problem throughout the department. Every time our faculty, teaching assistants, and proctors look for wrongdoing, they seem to find it.

Jones: I think you're exaggerating the extent of the problem; these are the behaviors of a small group of male students in their various courses who take pride in finding ways to "get around" the system.

Exercise 2 Read an editorial from the local newspaper and identify fallacies. Then, answer the following questions about each fallacy:

1. Why might this fallacy be persuasive to an audience?
2. What additional support or reasoning, if any, would you need to make the argument less fallacious?
3. Is it possible to make the argument less fallacious?
4. How would you change this argument to make it less fallacious?

Exercise 3 Read the following arguments and identify the fallacies.

1. In a debate about the benefits of a policy to reduce military spending, an arguer retorts, "You can't listen to him because he is an atheist."
2. The new Dave Matthews Band album is number one on the charts, so I think you should buy it.
3. We should not allow homosexual marriages because traditionally marriage is defined as being between a man and a woman.
4. The polls say that the president has a high popularity level, so I am going to vote for her.
5. Teachers and students are concerned with the quality of education. They should be trained more rigorously.
6. Dogs provide companionship to lonely individuals. All people living alone should have a cat.
7. California and Mississippi are both U.S. states that rely on farming, so the economies of these states must be the same.
8. I know about twenty-five students at the university who like The Shins. Therefore, The Shins must be popular among college students.
9. The cause of global climate change is human-caused carbon emissions.
10. Ellie is a college student who will graduate in four years, therefore all college students should graduate in four years.
11. I did well on that test because I was wearing my lucky shirt that day.
12. The reason there are so many teenage pregnancies is that kids don't get enough information at school about sex.

13. One student says, "I think that our professor is going to be a good teacher." The other replied, "Oh, I don't think so. Did you hear that he dodged the draft during the Vietnam war?"

14. A syllogism is a form of formal logic because it uses formal structures of logic.

15. It started raining right before I got into the car, so I think my accident resulted from the slippery and wet roads.

NOTES

1. Representative Bart Stupak, *Congressional Record* (November 18, 2004): H9992.

2. Irving M. Copi, *Informal Logic* (New York: Macmillan, 1986): 19.

3. Daniel Webster, "The Constitution Not a Compact between Sovereign States," in *American Forum: Speeches on Historic Issues, 1788–1900*, Ernest J. Wrage and Barnet Baskerville, eds. (Seattle: University of Washington Press, 1960), 136–137.

4. Monroe C. Beardsley, *Practical Logic* (New York: Prentice-Hall, 1950), 18–25.

5. See Michael Scriven, *Reasoning* (Point Reyes, Calif.: Edgepress, 1976). Copi's model is the simpler of the two and does not emphasize the interpretation and criticism of arguments as much as does Scriven's. To adjust our treatment of analysis to chapter length, we have eliminated steps Scriven recommends, such as formulating unstated assumptions and considering related arguments. The reader interested in a more complete and extensive treatment of analysis should consult the works of both these authors.

6. Copi, 7.

7. Wrage and Baskerville, 139.

8. *Webster's New Collegiate Dictionary*, s.v. "plight," "faith," and "sovereign."

9. Copi, 20.

10. Adapted from "More Big-Brotherism," *National Review* (December 31, 1986): 18.

11. Adapted from a letter to the editor, "New Destination Ski Resorts Could Boost Clean Industry," by Mel Borgersen, *Seattle Times* (December 21, 1986): A15. Used by permission of Mel Borgersen.

12. Adapted from Emily Feistritzer, "Balancing Act: Love and Money," *Seattle Times* (August 31, 1986): A16.

13. Adapted from Feistritzer, A16.

14. Fallacies of this type were identified as a group by C. C. Hamblin, *Fallacies* (London: Methuen, 1970):

135–176. He traced the origin of this group of arguments to Francis Bacon's *Advancement of Learning* in the early 1600s. Bacon identified four types of "idols," or prejudicial habits of thought, that affect reasoning. Hamblin (p. 146) noted that after Bacon the study of fallacies included the study of the influence of psychological factors on human reasoning.

15. Hamblin (p. 41) lists the Latin names for the first type of these as *Ad Hominem* and *Ad Passiones*. Hamblin noted that there are many varieties of "argument ad" and concluded that "We feel like adding: *Ad Nauseam*—but even that has been suggested before."

16. T. Edward Damer, *Attacking Faulty Reasoning*, 2d ed. (Belmont, Calif.: Wadsworth, 1987): 128–129.

17. Hamblin, pp. 40–41.

18. Hamblin, p. 41.

19. Damer, pp. 128–129.

20. Robert J. Thornton, "Lexicon of Inconspicuously Ambiguous Recommendations," *Chronicle of Higher Education* (February 25, 1987): 42. Copyright 1987: *Chronicle of Higher Education*.

21. Irving Copi, *Informal Logic* (New York: Macmillan, 1986), 114.

22. Monte M. Poen, ed., *Strictly Personal and Confidential: The Letters Harry Truman Never Mailed* (Boston: Little, Brown, and Co., 1982), 34.

23. From Plato *Timaeus*, cited in Irving Copi, *Informal Logic* (New York: Macmillan, 1986), 111.

24. The reasoning fallacies discussed here are included in many standard lists of fallacies. For discussions of fallacies, see C. L. Hamblin, *Fallacies* (London: Methuen, 1970), 135–176; Howard Kahane, *Logic and Contemporary Rhetoric*, 4th ed. (Belmont, Calif.: Wadsworth, 1984).

25. Damer, p. 94.

26. Copi, pp. 69–97.

27. Copi, p. 114.

DEVELOPING AND ARGUING EXTENDED CASES

CASE CONSTRUCTION AND ARGUING ABOUT FACTS

KEY CONCEPTS

Usually, when people argue they combine many individual arguments to develop extended exchanges that explore the issues in dispute. Arguments seldom occur in isolation. They are part of a larger context of discussion and debate. Each chapter in this book provides examples of how these extended arguments develop in conversations. Arguments are almost always part of complex exchanges in which people grapple with issues and ideas. When advocates interact with recipients and present arguments for changing beliefs, attitudes, and behaviors, they also face counterarguments and alternative claims, evidence, and reasoning supporting alternative views. Arguers use their skills to interpret, analyze, criticize, and refute counterarguments in complex exchanges.

Consider the topic developed in Box 9.1 focusing on whether parents should be allowed to select the sex of their children. The issues have been discussed for years, but because of technological advances they are becoming increasingly important and immediate. Most people who have read about and discussed this subject would probably agree with Katie: that the possibilities are frightening and potentially uncontrollable as the ability to manipulate genetics increases. The benefits of sex selection, as Jimmy alludes, are that these technologies offer the opportunity to diminish disease, create choice, and balance families.

■ ■ ■ ■ ■ ▉

BOX 9.1

SHOULD PARENTS BE ALLOWED TO SELECT THE SEX OF THEIR CHILDREN?[1]

Is it a boy or a girl? How many times have soon-to-be parents been asked that question? Historically, answers have been vague, but with technological advances it is now possible for parents not only to know the sex of their unborn child but to choose it. The development of new techniques such as sperm-sorting, prenatal testing, pregnancy termination, and the implementation of genetically tested embryos ensure the baby will be born the chosen sex. With genetic diagnosis, an embryo is created and analyzed in a test tube before being placed in the womb. Sperm-sorting organizes the sperm in a way that makes it more likely to fertilize the egg with the selected chromosome. Sex selection is technologically possible, but should it be done?

There are many possible advantages. Many families want to choose the sex of their child in an effort to balance families as well as to prevent gender-specific diseases from being passed on to offspring.[2] Some parents would prefer to raise a girl or a boy. And, as genetic technologies develop, it may soon be possible to do more than simply select a child's sex. Parents may be able to screen possible birth defects, improve IQ scores, and choose height and eye, hair, and skin color.

However, these advances have potentially negative consequences. In 1979, China announced its one child per family policy, developed in response to fears about rapid population growth and associated socioeconomic consequences.[3] Although policy successfully limited growth, more so in urban than in rural areas, it had the significant and serious consequence of creating a gender imbalance. In many cultures, boys are seen as more valuable than girls, and China is no exception. This bias led to a decrease in the numbers of girls born in China and a significant imbalance in the ratio of males to females in communities across the country.[4]

The statistics are disturbing. In 1981, shortly after the policy was adopted, there were 108 boys born for every 100 girls. By 1990 the ratio was 111:100. In 2005 the ratio had risen to 118:100. There are expected to be 30 million more men than women in China by 2020.[5] Many researchers have cautioned that China has created a "social time bomb."[6] China is not alone. Cultural biases assert themselves when technology allows

(continued)

BOX 9.1   CONTINUED

communities to limit the existence of one gender. Using ultrasound scanning for sexual selection is illegal in many places, but that does not stop its use.

Cultural factors represent just one set of issues in the discussion about sex selection. Social, scientific, and ethical issues are also involved. Socially, could gender selection produce a greater amount of gender inequality? Or would the opposite happen? Will scientific progress make birthing a business focusing on the production of genetically perfect babies? Or will we be able to eliminate significant diseases and birth defects from the gene pool? If given the opportunity, would you choose the sex of your child? Consider the following discussion between Jimmy and Katie and note how the arguments work together to develop an extended understanding of the issues.

Jimmy: The issue doesn't seem that complicated to me. Why shouldn't families be able to use whatever technology is available to choose and establish the kind of family they want to raise? I think choosing the sex of your child allows parents to be better parents because they are raising the sex they want and are more comfortable with. Given the choice, I would want to eliminate the possibility of having a child with a gender-specific disease. It's an issue of choice and freedom that we should be able to practice.

Katie: When you look at sex selection in terms of only America, it seems simple. But I think we have a social responsibility as human beings to protect rights. We need to protect the rights of children and women. Looking at the situation, I think the issues of gender inequality and aborted children would become larger and unmanageable, as it is in China. Women could easily become a minority around the world. Why is that right? Why should we allow it? If we are not careful, we will end up institutionalizing a gender bias that subjugates women.

Jimmy: I don't think giving women the ability to choose the sex of their child is producing gender inequality at all. It's giving women more control over their bodies and their families. I also think that many women will choose to have girls, thus balancing the effects of cultural values and preferences.

Katie: Maybe, but just the fact that there is a choice between genders, that one is possibly better than the other, illustrates inequality. Our society already has a hard time balancing gender inequalities as it is; I don't think we need another source to combat.

Jimmy: I don't think choosing a sex creates inequality at all. I think it's just an individual preference. Most people would choose a girl because they want to raise a girl, not because they think girls are better than boys. That's beside the point. In any case, don't you think it makes sense to develop technologies that help us reduce disease and birth defects?

Katie: Okay, but I think that sex selection might be balanced only if everyone is educated on population and gender percentages. But would that really affect their decision on what child to have? I can see some benefits if we find a way to regulate how technologies are used, but how do we regulate them? We have no control over other countries and what they choose to do. We don't have the right to push our cultural values and laws onto other cultures. And, how far do you push the technology? Do we start genetically engineering all of our children? This seems like a slippery slope that has the potential to end in disaster.

(continued)

BOX 9.1   CONTINUED

Jimmy: Again, I see the uses of these technological advances as ways to prevent dis-
              ease, mental illness, addiction problems, and other kinds of medical and
              social issues we face. If obesity ran in my family, I would want to take
              advantage of an opportunity to limit that gene from being passed to my
              children. Think of the decrease in obesity after generations that could
              occur in America?

Consider the following questions:

1. What types of claims, evidence, and reasons were used in this discussion?
2. Did the speakers adequately respond to the issues and arguments presented by the
   other?
3. Which speaker was more persuasive? Why?
4. How would you have organized this argument?
5. If you were going to present a ten-minute speech on this topic, which side would
   you choose? How would you outline the presentation?

The discussion between Katie and Jimmy is one type of extended discussion that
explores several different issues and offers a variety of argument types. In more formal
situations, though, advocates are often given an extended time to present their arguments. Arguers tend to give extended presentations in courts of law, legislative assemblies, and for most public presentations. They speak to other advocates and recipients
and then listen to responses.

In Chapter 7 we discussed how arguers can communicate more effectively when
presenting their arguments. This chapter focuses on how to construct extended arguments that prove or oppose a proposition. In particular, we will examine how to
analyze and use the relationships among claims, map issues, build extended argument
cases, and refute them. Finally, we will illustrate how to develop an argument using a
fact-based proposition.

ARGUING ABOUT FACTS, VALUES, AND POLICIES

Propositions establish an arena for argument. Figure 9.1 illustrates how a proposition
surrounds an area for argument that includes many potential issues for argument.
Propositional arenas contain many issues, and not all will be developed in an argument. The arguer's task is to analyze the proposition for the relevant issues and
develop an extended argument that either supports or denies the proposition. To
develop an overall position on a topic or proposition, you must know how to identify
the significant and controversial issues within the filed of argument. You further must
know how to find the relevant evidence to support your claims through research. You
need to be able to articulate your arguments and defend them against opposing points
of view. You also will need to know how to select from a large number of potential
arguments the ones that will be most effective with your audience.

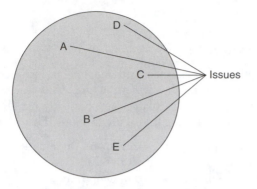

FIGURE 9.1   Propositional Arena

In completing these steps, you will construct an argumentative case. *A case is an extended argument supporting or opposing a proposition.* You may recall from Chapter 4 that a proposition is the "main claim" or "overarching claim" of an extended argument. Examples would be the following:

> Sex selection will create a global gender imbalance.
> John Doe is guilty of murder in the first degree.
> Euthanasia for terminally ill patients is desirable.
> The federal government should pass broadcast decency legislation.

Cases favoring such propositions might take the form of a speech in support of some legislation or a case for the defense or prosecution in a criminal trial; or they might develop as part of a conversation among business associates or friends. A network of claims and subclaims, each supported by further argument, characterizes extended argument cases. Box 9.1 provides a good illustration of many of the issues and claims that an arguer might use to support a proposition. Which of these arguments is developed and presented depends on the proposition and the context for the argument.

If the proposition were "Sex selection will create a global gender imbalance," then the propositional arena would include issues pertinent to this primary claim. These issues could include:

> Would China's experience be replicated on a global scale?
> Is there a global preference for one sex over another?
> Can these technologies assist with the elimination of diseases and birth defects?
> What are the moral and ethical implications for gender selection?
> Is choice the most important value?

Some of these issues are more important than others. As arguers construct their extended argument cases, they make decisions about which issues are most important for a particular context and to make the point they want to make. The important issues would then be developed into arguments.

We make extended arguments about fact-, value-, and policy-based propositions almost daily, and whereas value and policy cases are probably more common in public sphere argument, cases about propositions of fact are common in many private sphere arguments as well as certain fields of argument. Some fields, such as law, focus almost exclusively on fact-based propositions. For example, attorneys might argue whether:

> Chris Smith is guilty of theft.
> Anne Jones is guilty of reckless driving.
> Organization A violated export laws.

Each of these is a proposition for a case that will argue about historical facts. Lawyers, judges, and juries are then concerned with whether the case built by the prosecution is sufficient to prove the probable truth or falsity of the claim. Similarly, members of the medical field will diagnose or predict diseases using factual propositions. They might argue that:

> Smoking cigarettes has caused you to develop emphysema.
> Laser eye surgery will correct nearsightedness.
> Taking this prescription will alleviate your symptoms.

Other fields may also use fact propositions as a means of discussion and deliberation. Politicians often engage in fact-finding studies to determine whether certain policies work. Scientists will use fact propositions (such as hypotheses) to argue about the nature of the world and universe. Fact propositions, as with fact claims as discussed in Chapter 4, can be classified in three ways: historical, relational, and predictive. Argument cases can be developed using any of these types of fact propositions.

Most of us at one time or another have had the opportunity to develop extended cases based on fact propositions. Arguers use fact propositions to help establish what was, is, or will be. Consider, for example, the following propositions that might be part of an academic assignment:

> America's massive military buildup during the 1980s caused the collapse of the Soviet Union.
> Cutting financial aid means fewer students can attend college.
> Life on Earth began with living cells from Mars.
> Continued use of CFCs will result in the complete breakdown of the ozone layer.

RELATING FACTS, VALUES, AND POLICIES

As we discussed in Chapter 4, fact, value, and policy propositions are not separate and discrete entities. Rather, their characteristics blend with one another along a continuum of claims that ranges from facts to policies. They are related, and each implies the others. For instance, policy claims are based on underlying values and the existence of certain facts. If, for instance, sex-selection technology will cause global gender imbalance (predictive fact claim), then it makes sense to decide whether family, community, or national choice is more important than creating gender numerical inequity (value claim). If we find that sex selection might lead to an unwanted and unjustifiable gender inequity, then we may advocate banning the technologies and procedures that allow it (policy claim). The policy claim would not have been made or supported unless there were facts and values to back it up.

We make decisions about what course of action to take based on our assessment of potential benefits and costs. This means that policy decisions depend on our being able to make a factual assessment that some outcomes are likely and that those outcomes have value. A policy advocate, then, might engage in the following process to evaluate the benefits and disadvantages of a policy action, as illustrated in Box 9.2. Here the potential benefits are evaluated against the potential costs, and the comparison is directly related to our value system and our assessment of the facts. What is likely to happen? What is important? In this case, the factual assessment of the risks associated with genetic engineering and the value assessment of choice are the primary issues.

Just as policies are grounded in facts and values, facts and values imply policies. For example, if a patient were terminally ill, in tremendous pain, and with no hope of recovery (fact arguments), then we might decide that this person should have the right to decide if the continued struggle to live was more important than making the choice to die (value argument). If everyone could agree that certain forms of euthanasia were justified and desirable in certain circumstances, then lawmakers would enact legislation making those forms of euthanasia legal (policy argument). The reason that there is so much variation in abortion laws in different states is that there is no fact consensus about when life begins and no value consensus between pro-choice and pro-life factions in various parts of the country.

Although facts, values, and polices are tied to one another, the types of claims and evidence used in policy and fact arguments are different from those in value arguments. In selecting policies, people make decisions about what action to take based on their assessment of the risks involved and the potential benefits. In most cases, they are likely to choose policies that are more beneficial than the alternatives. If people perceive that protecting sex equity has a greater benefit than protecting choice, then sex selection technologies will continue to develop.

■ ■ ■ ■ ■

BOX 9.2
POLICY PROPOSITION: SEX SELECTION TECHNOLOGIES SHOULD BE BANNED

BENEFITS	COSTS
We avoid a "social time bomb."	Family and community choice will be thwarted.
Natural determination of sex ratios ensures survival of humankind.	Some families and communities will develop less safe, illegal technologies.
The sexes will be more equal.	Underlying bias is ignored when the only action is to ban technology.
Banning the technology prevents a "slippery slope" of genetic engineering.	We lose opportunities to eradicate some birth defects and genetic diseases.

Every policy decision makes assumptions about values and facts. Deciding whether or not to pursue a policy direction depends on a careful analysis of the potential benefits and costs. Cost-benefits analysis asks, "What are the potential outcomes?" and "How important or dangerous are they?" This assessment uses predictive factual claims to determine likelihood, and value claims to determine importance.

Policy arguments therefore concern action to be taken in the future, and they are based on empirical facts and on trends and projections. Value arguments, on the other hand, are usually based on the present and rely on social agreement concerning values. In Chapter 10 we define values as positive or negative attitudes toward certain end states of existence or broad modes of conduct. Examples of values are freedom, equality, self-respect, and family security. When we express our values, we express our own conceptions of the worth of objects or ideas. Values, then, regulate our orientations toward the objects and experiences in our lives.

ISSUE MAPPING

Writers on argument have pointed out that familiarity with multiple views on an issue improves one's own arguments as well as one's ability to anticipate and respond to others' views. As Josina Makau has observed, "The quality of deliberation on controversial issues depends, in large measure, on the arguers' ability to thoughtfully consider as many alternative perspectives as possible."[7] Many people who first approach a topic think they have their minds made up. As they conduct research on the topic and read the opinions of various authorities, they begin to see that the situation or the solution is not as readily apparent as they first thought. Often in the process of researching for a speech or debate, students will actually shift their opinions to the side opposite to the one they had favored in the beginning!

Researchers on critical thinking tell us this is a good thing. They have found that novice thinkers seek quick closure on a topic, neglect audience attitudes and possible objections, and fail to take into account obvious weaknesses in their own arguments. Experienced thinkers, on the other hand, withhold their opinions until they have gathered relevant information, begin by analyzing and interpreting the problem, study the attitudes of their potential audience and develop a broad range of lines and types of arguments to support a claim.[8]

To assist you in becoming an expert thinker of the latter type, we recommend that you construct an issues map when analyzing a proposition. *An issues map is a synthesis of the context, situation, participants, and issues associated with a proposition.* Issues maps are intended to help advocates explore as completely as possible the issues that define a propositional arena. A map allows advocates to consider more than one viewpoint in a context, and that is its value. It helps identify points of agreement, points of difference, and the context and situation for the argument. Box 9.3 is a template for an issues map.[9] As you will probably notice, the template draws on the theoretical framework for understanding arguments developed in Chapters 1, 2, and 3.

The first part of an issues map is the proposition that serves as the focus for discussion. An issues map should ensure that the proposition is clearly understood and that the parameters of the propositional arena are defined. The second part of the map provides a description of the propositional arena. In this section, an arguer identifies the situation, contexts, and parties involved in the arena. The intention is to describe the scope of the argument. In the third section of the map, an arguer describes the issues involved

■ ■ ■ ■ ■

BOX 9.3
ISSUES MAP

PROPOSITION

Proposition	Review the discussion of propositions in Chapter 4. What is the proposition for the current discussion?
Definition	Considering the discussion of propositional arenas in Chapter 4, what does this proposition mean? Define any terms that might be ambiguous. What is the propositional arena under discussion?

DESCRIPTION

Situation	Review the discussion of argument situations developed in Chapter 2. Provide a summary of the propositional arena. What happened? When?
Context	Consider the characteristics of spheres and fields in Chapter 1. What spheres are involved? Has this proposition been grounded mostly in personal, technical, or public arenas? What fields are involved? Are there any field-dependent standards that should apply?
Parties	The parties of an argument are the participants involved. Argument participants are developed in Chapters 2 and 7. Who is involved? Can you identify the primary parties who are affected by these issues? Can you identify secondary parties? Are any other groups or entities affected by this proposition?

ISSUES

Fact Issues	Based on the discussion in Chapter 4 and in this chapter regarding factual claims, identify the issues focusing on causal relationships, predictions of future events, and historical interpretation.
Value Issues	Based on the discussion in Chapter 4 regarding value claims as well as the material in Chapter 10, what are the issues that ask for evaluation or judgment? What are the comparisons of worth or importance within the propositional arena?
Policy Issues	Using the material from Chapters 4 and 11 about policy propositions, what actions or behaviors have been suggested to resolve the disagreement? What has been tried before? What worked, what didn't, and why?

ARGUMENT POTENTIAL

Goal	What would a successful outcome for this proposition be? What are the goals of the involved parties? Can the goals of the involved parties be met?
Parties	Can the identified parties achieve the goals? What other parties might need to be involved?
Resources	What resources are needed for the goal to be met? Are those resources available? What additional resources are needed?
Alternatives	Are there other ways of looking at the issues to find alternative approaches and solutions for the issues in the propositional arena?

in the proposition. Here the claims, evidence, and reasons developed by the advocate as described in Chapters 4, 5, and 6 are useful. This section of the map divides the research into three categories: issues related to the facts of the proposition, issues related to values, and issues related to policy implications. The goal is to find out what issues are important and what has been considered in the research. Finally, the map examines the argument potential. *Argument potential refers to the opportunity to influence the propositional arena through argument.* It involves questions such as: What would be an acceptable outcome for the argument? Are there opportunities for multiple parties to succeed? Are the people involved in the argument empowered to affect a positive change that can meet goals? What resources would be needed? What alternatives have been explored?

A well-written and developed issues map provides advocates with a way of understanding and interpreting a propositional arena. There are a couple of important points to keep in mind about using issues maps. First, maps do not take a position on a proposition. They are intended only to explore the issues within the propositional arena. Maps describe, they define, and they help focus arguments. In fact, if an issues map is prepared well, all the parties to an argument should be able to read it and agree with what it says. They may dispute some of the arguments developed in the issues, but they should agree that those are arguments made about the particular subject—not that they are correct, just that they are made. Second, issues maps serve as source material for extended case construction. An issues map may be used to develop a fact, value, or policy case and should also include the opposing arguments and issues. Therefore, when we use a map, we are using it to help shape both our advocacy and counteradvocacy.

PRINCIPLES OF CASE CONSTRUCTION

The process of decision making occurs in many venues and with many varied participants. Decisions are made in courtrooms, legislatures, boardrooms, and voting booths and among family and friends. They are made as part of a process of ongoing discussion about issues and topics and through the use of argument. Ideally, decisions are reached because the participants are informed about the issues being discussed and are able to advocate ideas and positions about those topics. Argumentation and decision making are the processes we use in our society to reach reasonable consensus about the issues we face. To some extent, the problems and issues that we consider significant change over time. In some years, we may be concerned about the economy, unemployment, inflation, and interest rates, whereas in other years we are worried about war and world peace. Different issues and concerns emerge each year as the contexts for argument change and evolve.

Issues such as abortion, capital punishment, environmental protection, and crime control are continuing sources of disagreement and debate in our society. If you wish to become seriously involved in the discussion of topics such as these, you will need to know how to research and construct an issues map to develop an understanding of the issues involved in each arena. Once you have completed an issues map, the next step is to draw on it to develop an extended argument case. Whether your case is oriented toward facts, values, or policies, there are certain recognized principles exemplified in legal briefs, legislative proposals, speeches, and academic debates that you should know. Before we discuss the specific methods of case construction, therefore, we need to pause to discuss the general principles of case construction.

Burden of Proof and Presumption

The person advocating change and challenging the existing framework for thinking and acting has the burden of proof and must overcome the presumption in favor of what currently exists or is accepted. Burden of proof is the obligation of the arguer advocating change to overcome presumption through argument. If the issues map has been developed well, in most cases it should be clear what changes are being advocated. Presumption "preoccupies the ground" of the controversy and will continue to do so until it is successfully challenged by some new belief, value, or action. Presumption, then, is the belief that current thinking, attitudes, values, and actions will continue in the absence of good arguments for their change. Essentially, presumption can be understood using the aphorism "if it ain't broke, don't fix it" (because you may end up making it worse than when you began). Therefore, the function of the burden of proof for the advocate is to prove that the risks inherent in change can be overcome by the benefits of change.

Copernicus, for example, once made the argument that the Earth revolved around the sun. Because his claim was not accepted by the church or majority of scholars at the time, he had the burden to prove his argument. The existing framework of beliefs (that the sun revolved around the Earth) had the presumption. Once the world came to accept (over a period of time) that his argument was correct, then a new reality—that the Earth revolves around the sun—was presumed to be correct, and any new subsequent interpretation of the facts would have the burden of proof.

It is important to note that people are predisposed to favor what they currently believe and what exists.[10] In other words, people are by nature conservative when it comes to making decisions based on argument; they will be persuaded to support a change only if they come to believe it is a good idea. The convention of presumption in argument thus does not imply that the present system of value *should* be favored; it only implies that an arguer should recognize the necessity of overcoming this conservative predisposition if he or she expects to make an argument effectively. In the field of law, for instance, the concepts of burden of proof and presumption form the foundation for much legal argument. An accused is presumed innocent unless proven guilty. In the absence of substantial argument that proves beyond a reasonable doubt that a defendant is guilty, to ensure a fair trial we will presume that the person is innocent.

There are times when it is unclear which side of an issue has the presumption and which side has the burden of proof, because facts, values, and polices may be inconsistent or not fully determined. On the topic of capital punishment, for example, different researchers dispute whether it deters crime. Some argue that people do not commit capital offenses because they fear the death penalty. Others contend that people who commit such crimes are not driven by concern for possible penalties but by their passions or disregard for the law. Studies conflict about whether capital punishment deters crime. Furthermore, public attitudes on capital punishment do not lie clearly on one side or the other of the issue. In the case of a topic such as this, the location of the presumption may be less important, and the convention of argument is that whoever asserts a position has the burden of proof for that argument.[11]

Extended Cases Should Be *Prima Facie*

Whenever an arguer develops an extended case, it is important that the central issues of the propositional arena be addressed. The issues map should provide a good guide toward the discovery of these issues. For example, if the main proposition of a fact-based dispute was that "Watching violence on television causes violence in children," certain issues are likely to come to mind (e.g., What is violence? Are children who watch violence predisposed toward being violent in the first place? Can we demonstrate that increases in violence on television are associated with increases in violence in children?). These issues must be addressed because audiences would expect to hear about them whenever media violence is discussed.

Assume that this topic was a value proposition: "Restricting violence in children's television is desirable." A somewhat different set of issues is suggested. Are these "restrictions" to be total or partial? What standards or criteria should be used to determine whether restrictions are desirable? What values would be fulfilled or furthered by restricting children's programming? How do current social values relate to a restriction on violence in television?

If the topic were a policy proposition, the kinds of issues argued would change again because the audience would expect different types of arguments to prove the proposition. Consider this proposition: "The federal government should ban all violence on television." Not only does this proposition assume prior discussion of relevant facts and values, it suggests an action to address the concerns developed in our assessment of facts and values. In this case, audience members would probably ask, what are the problems associated with violence on television? Are there less restrictive means available to manage the problems? Will this solution actually cure the problem? Do the benefits of this solution outweigh the costs (e.g., potential loss for First Amendment rights and freedoms)?

An arguer who initiates discussion of a topic by proposing a change must present what is called a *prima facie* case. *A* prima facie *case "on its face" presents good and sufficient arguments for adopting the viewpoint or action proposed by an advocate.* Cases are considered *prima facie* when their supporters satisfactorily address all of the major issues a reasonable audience would expect to see addressed. The issues that need to be addressed depend on the proposition and on what the audience knows about it. *Stock issues depend on the type of proposition and are the issues that recipients expect to see addressed in order for the arguer to meet the burden of proof.* For example, on the question of whether research funding should be granted for the investigation of AIDS, an advocate would probably not need to prove that there is a problem. If the arguer could prove that increased funding of a particular research application would dramatically reduce the incidence of AIDS, his or her case would be *prima facie*. Therefore, in the absence of opposition or significant questions regarding a proposal, it should be adopted.

Generally, each type of proposition implies its own stock issues. Fact, value, and policy propositions, then, each tend to have a set of issues relevant for that type of proposition. If, for example, a speaker advocated the policy of raising the gasoline tax to two dollars per gallon, an audience might want to know why—"What is the problem or ill you are trying to remedy?" That is a reasonable question and is one of the policy stock issues. If another arguer wanted to demonstrate that there are times when plagiarizing a research paper is justified, a professor might reasonably be expected to ask, "By using what criteria is that ever appropriate?" This is also a reasonable question for a value proposition, and it questions the standards used to assess the value. The stock issues for each type of proposition are detailed at the end of this chapter as well as in Chapters 10 and 11. Box 9.4 describes the stock issues related to each proposition.

■ ■ ■ ■ ■

BOX 9.4
STOCK ISSUES BY PROPOSITION

PROPOSITION TYPE	STOCK ISSUE	DEFINITION
Fact	Fact Definition	Fact definition consists of arguments that prove historical fact, causal relationships, and predictive facts. *Example:* Sex selection will result in gender imbalance.
	Threshold	The issue of threshold establishes the acceptable limits of definitions. *Example*: Gender imbalance exists once the ratio of men to women exceeds 110:100.
	Application	Application is the argument that the case examined is sufficient proof to verify the definition and its threshold. *Example*: Sex selection in China resulted in more than a 118:100 ratio and that would be expected for the rest of the world if we allow these technologies.
Value	Value	The stock issue of value is subdivided into two sets of issues: value object and value hierarchy. The value object is the central value, or term of the proposition, that will be debated. *Example*: Sex imbalance creates inequality.
		A value hierarchy is the ranking of values favored by each advocate or party in the debate. *Example*: Equality is more important than family or community choice.
	Criteria	Criteria are field- or sphere-dependent standards to be used to decide whether the value object fulfills certain values. *Example*: Any practice that causes inequality between sexes should not be supported, researched, or allowed.
	Application	The stock issue of application uses arguments, applied to the criteria, which demonstrate how the value object is supported or undermined. *Example*: Research demonstrates that there is a cultural bias toward male children, meaning that the birth ratio, if people have a choice, will exceed 118:100.

(continued)

BOX 9.4   CONTINUED

PROPOSITION TYPE	STOCK ISSUE	DEFINITION
Policy	Ill	An ill is a current wrong or harm the advocate is trying to resolve. *Example*: Sex selection will likely create a "social time bomb."
	Blame	Blame is the attribution of an ill to causes within the present policy system. *Example*: Because there are no current restrictions and people want a choice, they are beginning to use these new technologies.
	Cure	Cure demonstrates that some course of action can work to solve the ill. *Example*: Banning sex selection technology will prevent its use.
	Cost-Benefits	The cost refers to the problems or disadvantages associated with taking a policy action. Benefits are the positive consequences of policy action. *Example*: Although some will continue to use the technologies illegally, this plan will stop most of the problem.

Definitions Should Be Clear

One of the first issues over which advocates are likely to argue is that of definition of the proposition. Propositions are designed to establish a propositional arena that includes some issues while excluding others. Clarity, you may recall, is an essential requirement for a well-written proposition because if the language is not clear, then applicable issues are difficult to discern. This is why the issues map is so important in defining the scope of the propositional arena. Advocates need to be able to clearly define the important and potentially controversial terms both in the proposition and related to it. By defining the propositional terms, arguers establish their own views of the basic concepts on which the discussion will develop.

Some objects, practices, policies, and other phenomena may be readily understood, whereas others are more complex. If we were considering euthanasia, for example, arguers supporting the claim that the practice is desirable might provide a definition that includes only passive euthanasia—the withholding or removal of life-sustaining treatment from patients who are dying and have no hope of recovery.[12] Other advocates might disagree and challenge that the definition is insufficiently inclusive. Euthanasia is often said to include measures that bring about death ("mercy killing"). Before the discussion can move forward effectively, both advocates supporting euthanasia and opposing the practice must agree on the meaning of the central terms of the proposition for the outcomes to effectively address the central issues.

There are many methods that can be used to define terms. For example, one may provide actual examples of the value object with which the audience is familiar. (The removal of a feeding tube from the comatose Nancy Beth Cruzan is such an example.) The history of the status of the value object in society is another source for definitions. (One could cite a number of court cases and other situations in which euthanasia has occurred.) The term's etymology or derivation is another source. (Euthanasia comes from the Greek *eu* = happy; *thanatos* = death.) The opinions of authorities and experts who have studied the topic may function as a useful source for definitions. Finally, ordinary usage based on dictionary definitions can serve as a basis for definitions.

Arguers should avoid defining terms in ways that are incompatible with the propositions they are advocating. For example, those supporting passive euthanasia because it allows dying patients freedom of choice would not want to stipulate situations in which euthanasia *must* take place. This would deprive patients of freedom of choice by requiring actions mandated by the situation. The characteristics of the proposition that are identified should be compatible with the field of analysis and the issues that are applied within it.

Understanding Argument Situations

The placement of a proposition and argumentation case within the appropriate sphere and field is important because they provide the criteria for evaluating the arguments in the case. The issues map should provide some understanding of the contexts involved in making arguments from a particular propositional arena. Fields such as law, medicine, physics, and economics suggest standards of proof and evidence useful in making evaluations. The priorities, practices, and conventions in certain fields determine what issues are important and how judgments will be made about them. If two fields are applied in evaluating the same issues, the standards and rules drawn from each field may be in conflict. For example, at certain times in certain jurisdictions, the legal definition for death was "irreparable cessation of spontaneous cardiac and respiratory activity," whereas the medical definition was cessation of brain activity as indicated by a flat electroencephalograph. Furthermore, legal decisions are based on the letter of the law and precedent in similar court cases, whereas medical practice is based on medical ethics, which obligate a physician to do nothing to make the patient worse. Clearly, the fields of law and medicine have very different definitions, standards, and procedures for guiding decisions in euthanasia cases.

Arguers should keep their audience's attitudes and expectations in mind when they construct cases. If there is a clear presumption in favor of existing policy or in favor of a certain value orientation on a topic, advocates must take that presumption into account as they construct a case. Furthermore, they should be familiar with the major issues related to a topic and make sure they address them. If the case is based on a reasonable proposal and if the major claims relevant to a proposal are supported to the satisfaction of the audience, then the case will be *prima facie*. The general principles of case construction discussed in this chapter are based on reasonable audience expectations and the conventions of argument. Advocates who carefully take them into account will find that the cases they present will be persuasive and compelling to the audience for which they are intended.

PRINCIPLES OF REFUTATION

Anyone who opposes a *prima facie* case, once presented, has the burden of rejoinder. *The burden of rejoinder is the requirement that those who oppose a proposal respond reasonably to the issues presented by the original advocate.* For example, in a murder case, the state has the burden to prove beyond a reasonable doubt that the defendant committed the crime. The defense has a burden of rejoinder to refute the arguments presented by the state. And the defendant has the presumption of innocence until the burden of proof has been met by the state.

Types of Refutation

Meeting the burden of rejoinder means that the arguer must engage systematically in refutation of an opponent's case. *Refutation is the process of responding to someone's argument by revealing weaknesses in it or by presenting a counterargument.* Advocates have several options and strategies for refuting cases. First, refutation can be classified into case-level refutation (aimed at the entire case) or specific refutation (aimed at individual arguments). Second, refutation can be classified as destructive (intended to tear down the others' arguments), constructive (aimed at providing arguments to be weighed with the other case arguments), or bargaining (aimed at providing a middle ground or compromise between the case and any potential counterarguments).

Case-level refutation can be designed in three ways: direct refutation, counteradvocacy, or a combination of the two. Direct refutation systematically addresses an extended case by refuting the proposition as a whole, main claims within the extended argument, as well as sub-subclaims. When using direct refutation, an advocate refutes the claim and then synthesizes these individual responses into a rationale for rejecting the extended argument. Effective refutation shifts the burden of proof back to the original advocate.

Counteradvocacy involves offering alternative values or policies to be weighed in comparison with the original arguments. Counteradvocacy reflects real-life decision making in which various alternative proposals compete with one another. Refuting through counteradvocacy, however, means that the refuter, like the original advocate, assumes a burden of proof to support and defend the counterproposal. The most commonly used method of refutation is a combination of direct refutation and counteradvocacy in which the opponent attacks the arguments of the other person while offering an alternative proposal. For instance, with the sex selection argument, counteradvocacy might have focused on global regulation of the technology rather than an outright ban or completely free development and use.

Refutation Strategies

The five strategies discussed here and illustrated in Box 9.5 constitute a repertoire of approaches that can be used to indict extended case arguments and to defend your own position. In an extended debate, skilled arguers can use a variety of these strategies in combination to examine cases from multiple points of view and provide meaningful critiques and analysis. In Box 6.1 in Chapter 6, we discussed the Columbine shooting. Many advocates of gun control have used this case to support arguments for banning or severely limiting access to firearms. Proponents of gun control argue that over the past decade in the United States, more than 200,000 people have been killed by handguns, that criminals and unstable people have legal access to handguns, and that extending the waiting period for handgun purchases will help address these problems.

■ ■ ■ ■ ■

BOX 9.5
FIVE GENERAL REFUTATION STRATEGIES

STRATEGY	DEFINITION	EXAMPLE
Exploratory Refutation	Asking questions or raising objections designed to clarify an advocate's position and supporting evidence and reasoning.	How many of the 200,000 handgun deaths are attributable to the lack of a waiting period? How long must a waiting period be to be effective?
Develop Contradictions and Inconsistencies	Examining arguments for incompatibilities or discrepancies that weaken or diminish the position.	Your argument is based on the premise that stronger handgun control could have prevented the massacre at Columbine. Yet, rifles and shotguns could be used just as well and your plan doesn't prevent that.
Apply Tests of Evidence	Using the tests of evidence described in Chapter 5 to weaken or diminish the arguments.	The evidence you cite is not relevant because it only supports the argument that waiting periods will stop unstable people and criminals. Yet, at Columbine, the guns were purchased legally.
Apply Tests of Reasoning	Using the tests of reasoning developed in Chapter 6 to undermine and weaken the connections made in the argument between evidence and claim.	The argument you present is based on a *post hoc* fallacy. You assume that, because gun deaths decreased after waiting periods were established, longer waiting periods will result in fewer deaths. But you fail to take into account that other gun laws, including an assault rifle ban, contributed to less gun violence.
Constructive Refutation	Presenting counter-evidence and counter-arguments to be weighed against the arguments being refuted.	Waiting periods are not the answer. It is time simply to ban all handguns in the United States. Other countries have made handgun ownership illegal and credit those laws with making their citizens safer.

Exploratory Refutation

Exploratory refutation involves asking questions or raising objections designed to cause opponents to take a stand on issues an advocate hopes to refute. Exploratory refutation is intended to expose potential areas for argument. In response to the handgun argument, one might ask the following:

How many of the 200,000 handgun deaths were due to the lack of a waiting period?

How long of a waiting period do you want?

How will the mere existence of a waiting period ensure that criminals and unstable people cannot get guns?

Exploratory refutation is most effective when refuters take the time pursue and critique weak responses made by advocates in answer to their questions.

Expose Contradictions and Inconsistencies

A second effective refutation strategy is to note contradictions or inconsistencies in the arguments. Although it is factually accurate for gun control advocates to argue that people were shot and killed at Columbine, is it true that a waiting period might have prevented the tragedy? The argument could be refuted if one could show that a waiting period could not prevent such incidents because the handguns were purchased legally by people with no criminal record or history of mental instability. Further, a restriction on handguns would not have prevented Eric Harris and Dylan Klebold from purchasing rifles and shotguns. The advocates' original analysis of the problem could then be shown to be inconsistent with their call for a waiting period to screen out "undesirable" handgun purchasers. Similarly, if the case arguments focus on the dangers of handguns and the need to ban them to prevent Columbine-type massacres and then the proposal is a waiting period, that, too, is inconsistent because the evidence and reasoning support a ban whereas the claim is for waiting periods.

Apply Tests of Evidence

Arguers can apply the tests of evidence described in Chapter 5 to the extended case evidence. Evidence may be biased, outdated, irrelevant, inexpert, inconsistent, unreliable, inaccurate, or inaccessible. Criticizing opponents' evidence is usually not as damaging as some of the other refutation strategies and should not be overused. However, when biased or nonexpert evidence is used repeatedly, pointing out inadequacies in evidence can undermine the strength of the case claims. For instance, opponents of gun control often cite the National Rifle Association for support, but this lobbying group is biased on the topic.

Apply Tests of Reasoning

Advocates can also apply the tests of reasoning discussed in Chapter 6. An advocate may also examine arguments for the fallacies we discussed in Chapter 8. The refutation may charge that analogies were made between dissimilar phenomena; that generalizations were based on nonrepresentative samples; or that *post hoc* relationships were mistaken for causal relationships. The argument for a waiting period in obtaining handguns is based on a series of causal links: that the lack of a waiting period enables criminals and mentally unstable people to get guns, that these people substantially contribute to the number of handgun deaths, and that instituting a waiting period will therefore prevent deaths. These causal links could be successfully refuted if it could be shown that most handgun deaths are accidents or suicides or caused by people who know each other. The opponents of handgun control could show that merely instituting a waiting period will not substantially decrease gun deaths, because the presence or absence of a waiting period is neither a necessary nor a sufficient condition causing handgun deaths.

Develop Counterarguments

With counterarguments, advocates present counterevidence and counterclaims to be weighed against the arguments being refuted. Opponents of a waiting period might argue that increased restrictions on the legal sale of handguns will not decrease those handgun deaths that are caused by "undesirable" handgun purchasers. The *real* cause, they might argue, is the ease of illegally obtaining guns through sources supported by organized crime. They might then refute the waiting period by arguing with evidence that handgun deaths and injuries are largely the result of illegal firearms and that a waiting period will not control illegal possession of firearms.

The experience of preparing refutations of others' arguments and of anticipating others' refutations of our own arguments can contribute substantially to the development of critical-thinking abilities. Our arguments often seem quite strong and airtight until they are opposed by people who are skeptical of our viewpoint. By carefully considering objections that might be raised against our arguments, we can improve our reasoning and become more discriminating in our use of evidence.

DEVELOPING FACT-BASED CASES

Thus far, we have examined the interrelationships among facts, values, and policies, and we have discussed how to analyze a proposition through the use of an issues map. This section will explain how to put these concepts together with the principles of case construction and refutation to create an extended argument and an issues map. This approach can be used with any type of propositions, and in Chapters 10 and 11 we will apply it to cases supporting value and policy propositions. This section, however, focuses on developing extended arguments for fact-based propositions.

Arguing about Facts

People are inclined to believe that facts and statistics are true. However, as we observed in Chapter 4, there are many "facts" about which people disagree. Chapter 1, for instance, discussed the question of whether John F. Kennedy was killed by a single assassin. Because this assassination actually happened, there is only one "correct" answer to the question of who killed Kennedy. Yet, for years, various government agencies and other interested parties have debated about whether Lee Harvey Oswald acted alone or with someone else. It is a fact that China has a one child per family policy. It is also a fact that some families choose to ignore the law and that the ratio of boys to girls is increasing rapidly. But there is disagreement about why the ratio is increasing and whether illegal means are used to reduce the number of girls. Virtually all legal argument focuses on questions of fact. Does the U.S. Constitution allow gay marriage? Were steroids used illegally in setting baseball records? Should an accidental shooting be classified as assault in the first degree or the second degree?

Most extended arguments begin with questions about facts. For instance, we argue about the environment and our carbon footprints. There is disagreement about whether atmospheric pollution leads to global warming and climate change and, if so, to what extent this is a negative consequence of burning fossil fuels. In medicine, there are numerous debates about questions of fact. For example, to what extent do birth control pills and hormones lead to an increase in the rate of cancer among women? How harmful are elevated levels of cholesterol, and what are the most effective ways of lowering cholesterol levels? These are all potentially questions of fact—questions that might serve as the basis for extended arguments.

Stock Issues in Fact Propositions

When we argue about fact propositions, there are certain stock issues that must be addressed. These issues are the reasonable questions recipients have about the nature of any given fact proposition, and they should have been identified in the issues map. Although many issues can be used to develop fact-based cases, generally we can group

---

BOX 9.6

STOCK ISSUES IN FACT-BASED PROPOSITIONS

ISSUE	DEFINITION	EXAMPLE
Definition	The stock issue of fact definition consists of statements of historic fact, causal relationships, and predictive facts.	China's one child policy limits every family, which has resulted in more male than female births. Sex selection will result in gender imbalance.
Threshold	The issue of threshold establishes the acceptable limits of definitions.	Gender imbalance becomes very serious when the ratio of male to female births exceeds 110:100.
Application	Application is the illustration that the case examined is sufficient proof to verify the definition and its threshold.	China has now reached 118:100, meaning that it is experiencing gender imbalance. If technologies allow other countries to make the same choices, we can expect the same result.

---

them into three categories: issues of fact definition, threshold, and application. These can be seen in Box 9.6. To illustrate how these issues work, imagine the following conversation between a student, Hedda, and her advisor, Heather:

> **Hedda:** I took the art course to satisfy the university's art requirement. I don't understand why it doesn't count toward graduation.
>
> **Heather:** The university counts only certain art courses. The one you took is Art 351, and the art requirement is for any art course from the 100 or 200 level, not the 300 or 400 level.
>
> **Hedda:** So what you are telling me is that not all art courses satisfy the art requirement? Only some do? That makes no sense.
>
> **Heather:** Sorry, but the catalog is not always very clear about what counts and what doesn't count. But as you can see here, it does make a distinction about what kinds of courses count for the art requirement.

University catalogs, along with most contracts or agreements, are often rich sources of factual argument. Different parties may read the same documents and come to very different conclusions about what the documents mean. In this case, each of the primary stock issues of fact disputes is present.

Fact Definition

Definition is the first of the stock issues. It is important to distinguish between the two types of definitions presented thus far. Earlier in this chapter, we discussed definitions of proposition in general, as opposed to definitions of the fact. Before advocates can seek to interpret the meaning of a particular fact or set of circumstances, the nature of the facts must be clearly defined. The fact advocate must clearly define the facts of the case and explain their relevance to the proposition. *The stock issue of fact definition can consist of statements of historical fact, causal relationships, and predictive facts,* as was discussed in Chapter 4. The attorneys and judges in the field of law proceed by defining the relevant laws and then determining whether the issues in the case fit the laws of definition. Courts of law examine historical facts in which alleged crimes occurred. In the initial example, the student and advisor needed to clearly define which courses met the arts requirement and which courses did not. According to the university catalog, only courses numbered in the 100s or 200s met the requirement.

Definition is a part of any fact-based argument. If we argue about the existence of life on other planets, we need to define what we mean by *life*. Are we talking about intelligent life or microbes? If we argue that corporal punishment increases discipline and learning in schools, we need to decide if corporal punishment is physical punishment (such as a spanking), emotional punishment (such as humiliation), or some other form of punishment. Without a clear sense of definition, the arguers will not know how to develop the argument case. The stock issue of fact definition, then, provides a clear end point for the case. In other words, if the advocate can prove that some case meets the requirements of the definition, then the proposition is proven true or correct.

Threshold

The issue of threshold is closely related to the issue of definition. Because much of life and social action is not precise, there are many degrees of behavior and degrees of interpretation. *The issue of threshold establishes the acceptable limits of definitions.* A word or phrase can be defined in many ways. The definition of *life*, for example, has been subject to much debate for decades. Does life start at the moment of conception? Does it start at birth? Does life end when brain activity ends? Or does it end when the heart stops beating?

When we argue about the limits of a definition, we are arguing about its threshold. Although we know that a twenty-year-old, healthy, active college student is alive, we might debate the point at which life begins or ends. Beyond the threshold, we know life exists. The problem for advocates, however, is being able to argue at which point does life start or end. In the case of the student, the threshold was any art course numbered 100 to 200. The student could take multiple courses in that range, and upper-division courses in addition to the lower-division ones, but the threshold was any one course of lower-division work.

Threshold issues are common in our daily lives and in the workplace. If, for instance, you were planning to buy a new video game, you would encounter the issue of threshold on the side of the game's package. The package might say:

Minimum requirements include:
    3 gigahertz processor or higher
    Microsoft Windows Vista Home Premium

> Game Controller
> 100 gigabytes of available hard drive space
> 2 gigabytes of RAM

These requirements are threshold requirements. If the machine is a Macintosh or uses the Linux operating system, the game will not function properly. If any of these minimum threshold requirements is not met, the game will not run. Your machine may far exceed the threshold and be the latest, most up-to-date system, but unless it at least meets the minimum requirements set forth in the threshold, purchasing the game would not be wise.

Similarly, employers use threshold issues in developing want ads. Recently a newspaper ran an ad for the following position:

> Wanted: Public relations consultant. Must have a BA in Communication or closely associated area. Must have five years experience in public relations. Knowledge of computers is essential. Must know Microsoft Office products. Must be able to travel for work-related projects for periods up to two weeks. Should be good team player and self-starter. Salary competitive.

In this case, the organization is looking for a public relations consultant. For the organization, the threshold for an acceptable candidate centered on the degree earned, experience in the field, knowledge of computers, and travel. Candidates need to meet each of these requirements before they could be considered for the position.

Application

The third stock issue of application focuses on whether the example or phenomenon under consideration meets the requirements of definition and threshold. *Application is the illustration that the case examined is sufficient proof to verify the definition and its threshold.* In other words, application is the argument that some case or phenomenon meets the threshold for the definition. Suppose an applicant for the want ad mentioned earlier submitted a resume that highlighted the following abilities:

- Bachelor's degree in Communication, University of Washington
- Six year experience in public relations and marketing
- Microsoft Office trainer for current employer

This person has submitted an application—an argument that she or he meets the minimum threshold requirement for the position. The application is simply the argument that some instance—the applicant in this case—does or does not meet the requirements set forth in the threshold and definition arguments.

The student's academic record from the initial example provides another illustration of how an application might be argued. In considering her case, the advisor asks the question, "Did her record meet the requirements of the university?" To answer that question, the advisor could compare her transcript to the threshold to determine whether her performance met the definitional requirements. In other words, the advisor could examine her course, Art 351, to see whether it met the threshold requirements. It does not. Suppose, however, that her course had been Art 101. In that case, the course clearly would have met the threshold requirement because it was numbered in the 100 to 200 range, which in turn would have met the definitional requirement to complete one course of lower-division art. The same process could be used in buying software for a computer. If the computer meets all the threshold requirements to run the software, then the software in question should work.

The Issues Brief

The issues brief draws on the issues map and stock issues to provide a detailed and focused outline of arguments used to support and oppose a given proposition. *An issues brief is a synthesis of opposing views on the stock issues of a proposition.* The weakness of the issues brief is that it appears to assume that there are only two polarized sides, one supporting the proposition and one opposing it. Of course, on many controversial topics people's attitudes are more complex than that. For example, a person might oppose the death penalty in some cases and yet support it in others. We might favor some statements and positions of a politician and oppose others. Most often people do not take extreme positions on any given issue but instead admit exceptions or recognize the middle ground. The issues map is intended to illuminate these varied points of view. The brief, however, focuses arguments to show specific support and opposition to a proposition.

What follows is a brief about the difficulty level and rigor of the curriculum in American universities that articulates arguments on all the stock issues discussed in the previous section. Actually, the term *brief* is a misnomer, because a fully developed brief can be quite long. Notice the differences between the brief and the map. Whereas the map attempted to outline the issues available for argument within a propositional arena, the issues brief selects the best of those arguments to support or oppose the proposition for a given situation. Not all of the issues developed in the map are used; rather, the issues most appropriate for the situation are selected. When examining this brief, you should realize that each of the arguments is a claim that would need to be supported by further arguments and by evidence and reasons.

Are American universities tough enough? Jeffrey Walling does not think so. In his article "Colleges Should Change Course," he claims that standards for college graduates have declined so much that the value of a university education is now questionable. He says, for example:

> A . . . survey by the National Center for Education Statistics showed that half of 5,000 college graduates . . . could not read or interpret a simple bus schedule. Forty-four percent could not determine the contrast in a newspaper article featuring two opposing views. Seven out of eight could not figure the cost of carpeting a room (even with a calculator).
>
> Is it any wonder that, in a Roper survey conducted this year, 84 percent of college seniors couldn't say who was U.S. president at the start of the Korean War (President Harry S. Truman), and only 8 percent knew the source of "government of the people, by the people, and for the people" (Lincoln's Gettysburg Address)?[13]

Walling's conclusion is that U.S. schools have lost their rigor. They need to become much tougher. Included in Box 9.7 are the principal claims related to the proposition that U.S. universities are not sufficiently difficult.

The task of the advocate is to present each of the stock issues as clearly and articulately as possible. Each argument should include the relevant evidence and reasoning in support of the claims such that the audience is able to understand its meaning and relevance to the proposition. The opposition to the argument needs to do the same, with the exception that the opposition needs only to successfully refute a minimum of one stock issue. The reason is simply that if the opposition to a case can disprove any one of the stock issues, the case is rendered non–*prima facie*, which means it is no longer valid.

■ ■ ■ ■ ■

BOX 9.7

PROPOSITION: CURRICULUM AND INSTRUCTION IN U.S. UNIVERSITIES ARE INSUFFICIENT TO EDUCATE OUR STUDENTS

I. A "sufficient" curriculum should meet the following requirements. (definition)
   A. Curriculum and instruction should be rigorous and intensive to provide students with a needed discipline of learning.
   B. Curriculum and instruction need to provide a standardized knowledge base for our students.
   C. Students must be continually challenged—there should be no "easy" or "fluff" courses.

II. Minimally, a student should expect the following from a university education. (threshold)
   A. Mandatory, core courses should provide students with a general education and common base of knowledge.
   B. All students who hope to compete in the twenty-first century need to be equipped with knowledge of science and math.
   C. Students should be required to be physically present in class for their education.
   D. We should be looking for ways to increase classroom education time.

III. American universities are not adequately preparing our students. (application)
   A. Over the past 100 years, the number of mandatory or core courses has declined from 36% to 7%.
   B. Over the past 100 years, the number of colleges requiring science courses has declined from 86% to 34%.
   C. Over the past 100 years, the number of days students spend in a classroom has declined from 204 to 156.
   D. No university has looked for ways to increase days in class; rather, each has looked for ways to reduce the total time spent in class.

I. These definitions are wrong.
   A. Curriculum and instruction should be rigorous, but rigor does not necessarily mean a common curriculum or time in class.
   B. Standardization implies one way of thinking, and education should be about many ways of thinking.
   C. All courses should challenge students; however, students with different abilities find some courses easy and others difficult.

II. The standards set up to determine a sufficient education are wrong—they are very dated.
   A. Traditional core course model is Eurocentric and does not emphasize diversity of understanding.
   B. Technical skills for the twenty-first century include many other disciplines in which students take coursework, such as computer science, technical communication, and engineering.
   C. Classroom time should not be equated with learning, which includes many other things such as internships, study abroad, and service learning.
   D. We should look for ways to increase education, not time in a chair.

III. University students are better prepared now than ever before.
   A. Mandatory, core courses have been replaced with a superior, diverse curriculum.
   B. Students are selecting courses emphasizing critical thinking over rote knowledge.
   C. Number of days spent in a classroom does not determine educational success.
   D. Overall, student test scores and abilities are increasing.

SUMMARY

When advocates begin to connect individual arguments in support of a proposition, they are constructing extended argument cases. An extended case develops the issues associated with the proposition in a way that provides clear support for the proposition. Although propositions are classified as fact, value, or policy, advocates should be aware that each type of proposition is related to each other type—they are not exclusive of one another. Rather, policy propositions tend to assume certain facts and values. Similarly, facts exist within our interpretive frameworks of what is valuable or not. And values have implications for policy and tend to assume certain facts.

An issues map isolates and explores the issues within the propositional arena. The propositional arena is the area in which the issues for any given dispute exist. Arguers analyze these issues to determine the scope of the arena, its situation, the types of issues involved, and the potential for argument to affect meaningful change. From their analysis of the issues and their construction of arguments about the proposition, arguers begin the process of developing extended arguments.

Case construction focuses on the process we use to build a *prima facie* argument for the proposition. Central to the concept of case construction are four principles. The first principle is burden of proof and presumption. The burden of proof means that advocates have the responsibility to prove that a case and all of its associated risks are warranted beyond the current system. Presumption is the belief that current thinking, attitudes, values, or actions should continue to exist in the absence of compelling arguments to change them.

Second, advocates should construct cases that are *prima facie*. A *prima facie* case is one that meets the burden of proof and overcomes presumption. Generally, *prima facie* cases are composed of arguments that develop all of the stock issues for a proposition. Although the stock issues vary by proposition type, they are defined as the issues the recipients expect to see addressed in order for the arguer to have met the burden of proof. Third, cases should be clearly developed within a clearly defined propositional arena. And, finally, case development should be based on an understanding of the particular argument situation.

Once advocates have fulfilled the burden of proof and presented a satisfactory case for change, their opponents have the burden of rejoinder to respond reasonably to the issues raised in the case. In responding, the opponents engage in refutation. Refutation is the process of discrediting someone's argument by revealing weaknesses in it or by presenting a counterargument. Refutation can be divided into case-level (aimed at the opponent's case as a whole) or specific (aimed at individual arguments).

When refuting cases, opponents have three options. First, they can use direct refutation in which they tear down each of the arguments. Second, they can employ counteradvocacy, by offering an alternative point of view. Third, they can employ a combination of direct refutation and counteradvocacy by opposing arguments while offering their own alternatives.

Specific refutation, which is directed at individual arguments, can be implemented through five strategies that can be used singly or in combination. First, refuters can use exploratory refutation; they can raise questions and objections to draw out their opponents and make them take positions on issues on which their opponents might be vulnerable. Second they can note contradictions and inconsistencies in their opponents' case. Third, they can indict their opponents' evidence, showing it to be biased, outdated, irrelevant, inexpert, or unreliable. Fourth, refuters can attack reasoning by revealing fallacies and mistakes in their opponents' inferences. Fifth, refuters can produce arguments and evidence of their own that can be weighed against the arguments their opponents have made. Knowing these strategies of refutation and anticipated objections and criticism of one's own arguments can contribute substantially to critical-thinking ability and to the skills of advocacy.

With propositions of fact, there are three stock issues that recipients generally ask to have addressed. These are definition, threshold, and application. The stock issue of definition describes the major fact elements of the proposition. It focuses on what the end point of the case will be by offering a clear and concise definition of the terms in the proposition. The stock issue of threshold establishes the limits, or parameters, for the definitions. Threshold is intended to provide a clear way of distinguishing between what is included and excluded by the definitions. Finally, the stock issue of application is the argument that the phenomenon or example under consideration is included or excluded by the threshold arguments.

Finally, this chapter presented an issues brief as one way of understanding the process of advocacy. The issues brief is a way of examining two contrasting points of view and the arguments for and against a proposition. It provides a way for advocates to learn about and understand multiple views on a proposition, which is central to the process of developing critical thought.

GLOSSARY

Application (p. 286) is the illustration that the case examined is sufficient proof to verify the definition and its threshold.

Argument potential (p. 274) refers to the opportunity to influence the propositional arena through argument.

Burden of rejoinder (p. 279) is the requirement that those who oppose a proposal respond reasonably to the issues presented by the original advocate.

Case (p. 269) is an extended argument supporting or opposing a proposition.

Exploratory refutation (p. 281) involves asking questions or raising objections designed to cause opponents to take a stand on issues an advocate hopes to refute.

Fact definition (p. 285) are statements of historical fact, causal relationships, and predictive facts.

Issues brief (p. 287) is a synthesis of opposing views on the stock issues of a proposition.

Issues map (p. 272) is a synthesis of the context, situation, participants, and issues associated with a proposition.

Prima facie **case (p. 276)** presents good and sufficient arguments for adopting the viewpoint or action proposed by an advocate.

Refutation (p. 280) is the process of responding to someone's argument by revealing weaknesses in it or by presenting a counterargument.

Stock issues (p. 276) depend on the type of proposition and are the issues that recipients expect to see addressed in order for the arguer to meet the burden of proof.

Threshold (p. 285) establishes the acceptable limits of definitions.

EXERCISES

Exercise 1 Take any of the following propositions of fact and construct an issues brief. For the purpose of this exercise, the issues brief need contain only the claims that one might expect an arguer to make.

1. Computer skills increase grade point averages.

2. Strict vegetarian diets harm a person's health.

✳**3.** Third-party candidates cause diversity in the political process.

4. The welfare system makes people not want to work.

✳**5.** Leif Eriksson discovered America.

6. Restrictions on tobacco products in the United States have resulted in the export of tobacco products to lesser-developed nations.

7. Low-cost air-ticket prices have caused airline safety to decrease.

8. The Social Security system will be bankrupt in twenty years.

9. An asteroid caused the extinction of the dinosaurs.

10. Take-home tests improve student retention of subject matter.

Exercise 2 This chapter discussed different ways of refuting argument cases. First, we discussed strategies for refutation. These included the following:

- Case-level refutation, which is aimed at the entire case
- Specific refutation, which is aimed at individual arguments within the case

Second, we talked about styles of refutation, which included:

- Destructive refutation, which is aimed at tearing down the opponent's arguments
- Constructive refutation, which is aimed at offering alternatives through counterarguments
- Bargaining refutation, which attempts to provide a negotiated or compromise argument

Consider the following outlines for a fact-based case argument. Develop a refutation strategy for these cases:

CASE 1

***Proposition:* Banning handguns saves lives.**

CASE ARGUMENTS	REFUTATION

I. Definitions
  A. Handguns are personal weapons.
  B. A ban would prohibit private ownership.

II. Threshold
  A. We are talking about private guns, not guns owned by military or police.
  B. Handguns include any weapon that can be reasonably concealed on a person.

(continued)

III. Application
   A. Thousands die each year from the intentional
      discharge of private, concealed weapons.
   B. Thousands die from the unintentional use
      of handguns.
   C. Countries that have banned handguns have
      been successful at saving lives.

CASE 2

Proposition: **Sex education prevents teen pregnancy.**

CASE ARGUMENTS	REFUTATION

I. Definitions
   A. Sex education is instruction about human
      reproduction and birth control.
   B. Teen pregnancy is the unintentional
      pregnancy in people ages 13–19.

II. Threshold
   A. We are talking about instruction in middle
      and high schools.
   B. Instruction must include information about
      biology and birth control.
   C. Instruction is accompanied by access to
      birth control.

III. Application
   A. In countries where there is intensive sex
      education, teen pregnancy has decreased.
   B. Teen pregnancy has decreased where there is
      instruction in this country's schools.

Exercise 3 From the following collection of issues, develop an issues map. Based on
your map:

   1. What issues need further investigation?
   2. Develop a fact-based case.

ARCTIC NATIONAL WILDLIFE REFUGE DRILLING

The Arctic National Wildlife Refuge (ANWR) in northeast Alaska is meant to preserve
wildlife in its natural habitat, fulfill the international treaty of obligations of the United
States with respect to fish and wildlife, and allow local residents to continue subsistence
living (the ability to live off the land). A debate is under way about whether to authorize
drilling in 2,000 acres of ANWR. ANWR is federally owned land in the state of Alaska.
Oil drilling has been proposed there for several decades. To commit to this drilling it
would require an approval of the U.S. government, via the Congress and the president.

Arguments once made that the trans-Alaska pipeline would destroy the environment turned out to be false. North Slope caribou herds along the pipeline thrive despite these faulty predictions. Recent surveys of the central arctic caribou herd near the Prudhoe Bay oil field show the herd population at its highest level ever recorded in the past quarter century. The herd has grown more than sevenfold since development in the 1970s and the construction of the pipeline.

If their habitat is disturbed, the current count of roughly 130,000 porcupine caribou could be reduced by 40 percent, according to some sources.

Some scientists have demonstrated that thirty years of road building, noise, and oil exploration have adversely affected the behavior of animals, harmed vegetation, and caused severe erosion.

New technologies such as ice pads and new road construction techniques have minimized environmental impacts while reducing costs of exploration.

Drilling would pierce the surface of the refuge with oil wells and drill bits, forever altering the landscape. Many have pointed out that abandoned equipment and buildings are likely to mar the landscape for centuries. Currently, no one has developed a plan for restoring the landscape.

Drilling has been limited to only 2,000 acres in the North Slope of ANWR. It is a vast tract of peat bog and mud puddles. Oil could be extracted in winter, when it's night for fifty-eight straight days, and caribou would not come within 500 miles of the Arctic Ocean.

More than 180 bird species, 36 species of land mammals, and 36 species of fish in rivers and lakes live in ANWR. It is one of the few ecologically undisturbed locations in America.

The Alaskan people want it They are overwhelmingly supportive of responsible development of the Coastal Plain of the ANWR . . . Alaska's governor has urged Congress to take a balanced approach, and a recent poll shows 75 percent of Alaskans agree with balanced development plans.

Oil companies and well-financed lobbying groups are pushing for drilling in ANWR. Drilling only encourages this perversion of the legislative process.

A January 2004 poll showed that 51 percent of Americans oppose drilling, compared with 36 percent who support it.

With drilling the United States would have less dependency on foreign oil. Less money would be sent overseas to oil-producing nations. We would be less vulnerable to terrorism that threatens to disrupt foreign oil supplies.

The United States created ANWR in part to comply with environmental treaties it had signed. Destroying ANWR would violate these treaties and could cause other nations to begin destruction of their ecosystems.

Drilling in ANWR will not reduce U.S. dependence on foreign oil. Currently, the United States consumes about nineteen million barrels of oil a day and relies on foreign imports for more than half of its oil needs.

Fossil fuel drilling would create hundreds of thousands of jobs for the people who would work on the process. These paychecks would circulate to help our economy and save the economically struggling state of Alaska, which has to make cuts in many vital social services that particularly affect Native Americans in rural, isolated areas. In a broader view, drilling would help the U.S. economy by making oil cheaper for all Americans.

Adapted from www.savealaska.com, Save Alaska by Alaska Wilderness League, Natural Resource Defense Council, and Alaska Rainforest Campaign; www.anwr.org, Arctic National Wildlife Refuge Web site; and www.enn.com, Environmental News Network.

NOTES

1. Adapted from "Debate: Choosing Sex of Children," Debatepedia, http://wiki.idebate.org/index.php/Debate:Children%2C_Choosing_Sex_of (accessed May 27, 2008).

2. Summary: The YWL Discussion (June 2005) Boy or a Girl—Should You Choose? Sex Selection and Gender Equality. Association for Women's Rights in Development. http://www.awid.org/go.php?cid=373 (accessed on May 12, 2008). See also Margaret Talbot, "Jack or Jill," Atlantic.com, March 2002, http://www.theatlantic.com/doc/200203/talbot (accessed May 27, 2008).

3. Penny Kane and Ching Y Choi, "China's one child family policy," *British Medical Journal*, October 9, 1999, 319(7215): 992–994.

4. A good explanation can be found in Lesley Stahl, "China: Too Many Men," *60 Minutes*, April 16, 2006, http://www.cbsnews.com/stories/2006/04/13/60minutes/main1496589.shtml (accessed May 27, 2008).

5. Alice Poon, "China's Generation Without Women, Asia Sentinal, 25 March 2008, http://www.asiasentinel.com/index.php?option=com_content&task=view&id=1114&Itemid=34 (accessed May 27, 2008).

6. Poon, 2008.

7. Josina M. Makau, *Reasoning and Communication* (Belmont, Calif.: Wadsworth, 1990), 142.

8. Joanne G. Kurfiss, *Critical Thinking: Theory, Research, Practice, and Possibilities*, ASHE-ERIC Higher Education Report No. 2 (Washington, D.C.: Association for the Study of High Education, 1988), 25–34.

9. Adapted from William W. Wilmot and Joyce C. Hocker, *Interpersonal Conflict*, 6th ed. (New York: McGraw-Hill, 2001); and Paul Wehr, *Conflict Regulation* (Nashville, Tenn.: Westview Publishing, 1979).

10. Richard Whately, *Elements of Rhetoric*, Douglas Ehninger, ed. (Carbondale, Ill.: Southern Illinois University Press, 1963), 112–113.

11. For further discussion about burden of proof and presumption in advocacy, see Gary Cronkhite, "The Locus of the Presumption," *Central States Speech Journal* 17 (1966): 276; and Barbara Warnick, "Arguing Value Propositions," *Journal of the American Forensic Association* 18 (1981): 112–115. Permission to draw material from the latter article was granted by the American Forensic Association.

12. Richard Worshop, "Assisted Suicide," *CQ Researcher* 2 (1992): 148.

13. Adapted from Jeffrey Walling, "Colleges Should Change Course," *USA Weekend* (September 20–22, 1996): 4–6.

ARGUING ABOUT VALUES

Read the discussion in Box 10.1 and consider the underlying assumptions the speakers make. If you discuss with friends and colleagues what, if anything, should be done about Hollywood's influence over behavior or other cultures, you will probably find that they disagree with one another and that their differing opinions arise from their differing values. Issues related to freedom of expression, cultural diversity, the role of parents, and honesty may emerge, and some may come into conflict. Although most people generally agree that such values are important, disagreements, and thus argumentation, arise when they must choose between them. Is freedom of artistic expression more important than cultural integrity? Should parents or Hollywood be

■ ■ ■ ■ ■ ■

BOX 10.1

IS HOLLYWOOD DETRIMENTAL TO CULTURE?[1]

Hollywood has been described as having a heartbeat and a life of its own, affecting the world in seemingly endless ways.[2] In reality, Hollywood is simply a place where movies and television programs are made; yet the concept of Hollywood is much larger and more powerful. It is a collection of cultural media products that America produces for global distribution. Although many other countries export their media products, Hollywood is the most influential.[3] Even relatively successful European film industries struggle to maintain 30 percent of the total market share.[4]

Is Hollywood's global media dominance bad? Some argue that Hollywood plays a positive role around the world and provides inspiration and ideas that enrich our society and culture.[5] Hollywood helps us see and understand people and ideas we would not otherwise come to know. Critics, however, argue that Hollywood's media dominance has resulted in a cultural imperialism that undermines values and practices in other parts of the world.[6] Some have voiced concern that American media threatens to "dumb down" the rest of the world.[7] The issue is simply that with Hollywood's strength and resources, separate and distinct cultures will be lost.[8]

These perceived threats are significant because Hollywood, some analysts fear, may cause negative social and cultural behaviors by introducing falsehoods and misleading suggestions about people and cultures. Inaccurate media portrayals of significant social issues such as racism or terrorism have the potential to deepen cultural conflict and undermine efforts to build communities.[9]

Regardless of which side of the debate people support and believe, Hollywood's influence is tremendous. The following exchange between Angelina and Brad explores some of the issues related to Hollywood's dominance and the messages it sends. As you read it, consider the role of values—what is important, what is not? What are the most important issues or ideas in this exchange?

Angelina:	I can't imagine how anyone can believe the rights of Hollywood's artistic expression outweigh the negative social consequences. Hollywood has caused—or at least contributed to—significant increases in eating disorders, crime, misbehaving children, and violence.
Brad:	Hollywood has produced some remarkable material—some of which contributes to thoughtful discussion and reflection. *American Beauty* comes to mind because it illustrates literary value and provokes intense emotion and thought. Creating thought, evoking emotions, and shedding light on issues that are already present in society is something we shouldn't see as negative. I'm not saying that all of it is good, but it is only by allowing freedom to explore many different issues that we can produce truly inspirational or revealing art.
Angelina:	How do you explain the increase of eating disorders in America, which is directly correlated with the existence of eating disorders in Hollywood? The average woman is a size 10, and the average Hollywood woman is a size 4. The pressure to live up to a Hollywood "ideal" is intense. What about the increase in underage drinking and drug use, correlated to young starlets such as Lindsey Lohan? And even if they do not directly *cause* drug use and eating disorders, they *model* them. Hollywood highlights these

(continued)

BOX 10.1   CONTINUED

behaviors as acceptable signs of success and fun. And then we ship these "models" around the world, which, I suspect, undermines any respect other cultures may have for us. Most popular media seem to highlight the worst of who we are. Is this what we want our global image to be?

Brad: Eating disorders, underage drinking and drug use, even violence and crime have always been issues in America. Hollywood is simply a mirror; artists paint pictures of problems that already exist. The more problems our society has, the more we will see. And that is a good thing. We should be embarrassed by these portrayals; we should see these problems for what they are. That is the only way we, as a nation, will work for solutions.

Angelina: I see your point, but many children believe that what they see from Hollywood is real. Take, for example, the MTV show *Sweet Sixteen*. The children on the show are puppets of Hollywood, and other kids copy their outrageous behavior to achieve the same attention as their favorite celebrities.

Brad: Children copy the behaviors they see around them. We shouldn't be surprised by that. But, for the most part, it is not harmful, and parents should play a role here. Hollywood should not be a scapegoat for irresponsible viewers and parents.

Angelina: I agree. Children should not look up to Hollywood as models in any way. Hollywood represents roughly 10 percent of America, and therefore it is not representative of America as a whole. But its power is significant and it should be held responsible.

Many issues emerge in this conversation. Among them are values related to culture, responsibility, parenting, and individualism. Using this conversation as well as your own understanding of media influence, consider the following questions:

1. What values emerge in this discussion? Are some more important than others?
2. Are there any conclusions drawn here that are troubling? Why? What is challenging about them?
3. Do you think Hollywood's influence, on balance, is more positive than negative? How did you arrive at that conclusion? What is the basis for your judgment?

responsible for ensuring that children are exposed to positive messages? Such choices are not confined to our personal lives. Our leaders and legislators must often make similar choices between incompatible values when they decide on public policy or government spending. For example:

- Should we permit oil exploration in national forests to create jobs, augment energy resources, and promote the regional economy, or should we prohibit drilling and pipelines to preserve the environment?
- Should we raise taxes to provide for more social programs that benefit the poor, or should we cut taxes to give money back to the taxpayer?
- Should we trade with countries that have large potential markets that could help our industries and economy, even if those countries have poor records of protecting human rights?

Deliberating about such choices requires critical thinkers who see the value in premises and assumptions that differ from their own; who can critique their own deepest
prejudices, biases, and misconceptions; and who can develop well-grounded criteria
for choosing among competing values.[10]

The purpose of this chapter is to acquaint you with the basic dynamics of value
controversy. The first section will explain how choices are evaluated, how values are
prioritized by individuals, and how and why values change over time. The second section will explain the relationship between values and argumentation and the bases for
value arguments. The third section will orient you to the basic kinds of issues that
arise in value argumentation, and the last section will describe specific procedures for
constructing cases supporting and opposing value propositions. The formats suggested in this last section are particularly useful for essays, speeches, and debates in
which extended cases for or against value claims must be composed. But value disputes
also occur in conversations, discussions, and other argumentative situations. Because
such disputes revolve around issues similar to the ones we discuss, our strategies for
constructing cases should be useful in other communication situations as well.

VALUES AND VALUE SYSTEMS

Values are pervasive both in the life of society and the life of the individual. They help
guide our actions and provide a framework against which our decisions are evaluated
and understood. *Values can be defined as desirable, transituational goals, varying in importance, that serve as guiding principles in people's lives.*[11] In other words, we each have value
systems that we apply in different occasions and contexts to achieve certain personal
or social goals. Our individual values as well as our connection with cultural values
help us answer questions about whether Hollywood's influence is good or bad because
of how its actions affect our basic value assumptions.

Terminal and Instrumental Values

A value is a particular kind of belief. Rather than being descriptive or capable of being
true or false, a value is prescriptive; it helps us judge whether an action or state of
being is desirable or undesirable. Milton Rokeach, who researched American values
for three decades, divided values into two main categories: instrumental and terminal.
*Instrumental values concern modes of conduct or the means for fulfilling other values. Termi-
nal values concern desirable end states of existence.*[12] We get an education (instrumental
value) so that we can find a rewarding career (terminal value). We work hard (instrumental value) so that we can have a comfortable life (terminal value). Examples of
instrumental values are educational opportunity, leisure time, and economic prosperity. Instrumental values have a means–end relationship with certain terminal values
such as family security, an exciting life, a sense of accomplishment, and self-respect.
Rokeach estimated that, whereas an individual possesses a limited number of terminal
values—somewhere between one and two dozen—the total number of instrumental
values may be several times that number because we use many avenues or instruments
to reach our objectives or terminal value states.

Value Systems

Value systems can be described as having three significant characteristics: value content, value structure, and value consensus.[13]

Value Content

Value content refers to the motivational goals expressed in the value. Specifically, how do values guide and motivate our behaviors? Shalom H. Schwartz and Galit Sagie argued that there are ten distinct motivational value clusters that seem to remain consistent across cultures. Illustrated in Box 10.2 they are self-direction, stimulation, hedonism, achievement, power, security, conformity, tradition, benevolence, and universalism. Their argument is that we are motivated by power, the drive for achievement, or any of the other values they cluster together. Hollywood's actions and media production are driven by values from this list, including achievement, power, and tradition. Our actions reflect the values that are important to us, and the decisions we make reinforce their significance in our own mind-set.

■ ■ ■ ■ ■

BOX 10.2
VALUE CONTENT

DESCRIPTION	DEFINITION
Self-Direction	*Terminal values:* Independent thought and action (choosing, creating, exploring) *Instrumental values:* Creative, free, independent, curious, chooses own goals
Stimulation	*Terminal values:* A varied, challenging, and exciting life *Instrumental values:* Daring, novel, exciting
Hedonism	*Terminal values:* Pleasure and enjoying life *Instrumental values:* Sensual gratification, play
Achievement	*Terminal values:* Personal success through demonstrating competence according to social standards *Instrumental values:* Ambition, influence
Power	*Terminal values:* Social status and prestige, control or dominance over people and resources *Instrumental values:* Social power, authority, wealth
Security	*Terminal values:* Safety; harmony; and stability of society, relationships, and self *Instrumental values:* Family security, national security, social order, cleanliness, reciprocation of favors
Conformity	*Terminal values:* Restraint of actions, inclinations, and impulses likely to upset or harm others and violate social expectations or norms *Instrumental values:* Self-discipline, obedience, politeness, honoring parents and elders

(continued)

BOX 10.2   CONTINUED

DESCRIPTION	DEFINITION
Tradition	*Terminal values:* Respect for, commitment to, and acceptance of the customs and ideas that traditional culture or riligion provide *Instrumental values:* Accepting one's position in life, humility, devotion, respect for tradition, moderation
Benevolence	*Terminal values:* Preservation and enhancement of the welfare of people with whom one is in frequent personal contact *Instrumental values:* Helpfulness, honesty, forgiveness, loyalty, responsibility
Universalism	*Terminal values:* Understanding, appreciation, tolerance, and protection for the welfare of all people and for nature *Instrumental values:* Broad-mindedness, wisdom, social justice, equality, world peace, a world of beauty, unity with nature, environmental protection

Value Structure and Hierarchy

Value structure refers to the dynamic relations among the values in our individual value system. This means that some values are more important than others, and over time the relative importance of some values may change because the relative importance of values is dynamic. Rokeach made some important distinctions about the nature of types of values. He noted that each person has values organized into a value system. *A value system is an enduring organization of beliefs concerning preferred modes of conduct or end states of existence according to their relative importance.*[14] By this, Rokeach meant that each of us has values that are organized into hierarchies. A value hierarchy is an ordering of values so that some are ranked more highly than others. For example, people who want to prohibit logging in our national forests may value environmental preservation over jobs and growth. Or, Hollywood's right to artistic expression is more important than the consequences of modeling poor behavior.

From the 1960s through the 1980s, Rokeach conducted extensive studies of American value systems. Narrowing the list of terminal values to eighteen, he surveyed large samples of the American public to discover how these eighteen terminal values were ordered. These eighteen values are shown in Box 10.3. Three observations about this ranking of values are particularly noteworthy. First, American values appear to be stable across time. Although some value rankings may change, they do not change much. Concerning this stability, Rokeach and his coauthor noted that "such highly stable findings would seem to suggest that there is little, if any, value change occurring in American society, at least in the thirteen-year period under consideration. Many social scientists would probably interpret such findings as confirming the widely shared view that human values are deep-lying components of collective belief systems and are thus inherently resistant to change."[15]

Second, men and women as well as African Americans in the United States have similar rankings. In contrast to the stereotype that men value achievement and intellectual pursuits whereas women value love, affiliation, and the family, Rokeach found that these values were similarly ranked. In regard to race, the rank orderings of

■ ■ ■ ■ ■

BOX 10.3

ROCKEACH'S 18 TERMINAL VALUES HIERARCHY

1. Family Security
2. World at Peace
3. Freedom
4. Self-Respect
5. Happiness
6. Wisdom
7. Sense of Accomplishment
8. Comfortable Life
9. Salvation
10. True Friendship
11. National Security
12. Equality
13. Inner Harmony
14. Mature Love
15. Exciting Life
16. World of Beauty
17. Pleasure
18. Social Recognition

How would you hierarchically organize this list? Can you use this list to analyze whether Hollywood is a positive or negative global force?

African Americans and whites were similar, with the exception of the value of equality, which was ranked second by African Americans and twelfth by whites. Furthermore, when Rokeach matched African Americans with the whites in his survey according to education and socioeconomic status, the differences between the two races in value rankings either disappeared or became minimal, again with the exception of the different rankings of equality.[16]

Third, this ranking of terminal values was specific to American culture. Rokeach gathered information on value rankings from Australians, Canadians, and Israelis and found sizable differences among cultures. Israelis ranked national security second, whereas it was never ranked higher than tenth by Americans. Canadians ranked happiness, mature love, and true friendship much more highly than did Americans. Seymour Lipset, who has done extensive cross-cultural comparisons between Americans and Canadians, has noted that Americans are more religious, more patriotic, more populist and antielitist, and more socially egalitarian than Canadians and citizens of other developed countries. America is also more "antistatist" (distrustful of centralized government) than all other developed nations and thus is exceptional in the low level of support it provides for its poor in welfare, housing, and medical care. Lipset reports that among the developed nations, the United States has the highest proportion of its people living in poverty.[17] These studies of American values indicate that the orderings and priorities we place on various terminal values are culture-specific. People of different cultures and ethnicities will perceive and respond to value arguments in different ways. They will view as important those values that concern them most directly. The question of which values are ranked most highly by one's audience should always influence the design of one's value argumentation.

When our values come into conflict, we rely on our hierarchies to guide us toward appropriate actions. For example, what happens in a case in which parents want a student to major in business and the student wants to major in theater. The values of security (having college paid for) and conformity (honoring parents and obedience) are placed in opposition to the value of self-direction (choosing, creating, and exploring one's own goals). The choice will ultimately be based on the student's assessment of which values are most important and where they fit along a value hierarchy. With the Hollywood example, the freedom of artistic expression is considered more important than social recognition, equality, or a sense of harmony with other cultures.

Value Consensus

Value consensus is the degree of concurrence among members of a society concerning their values. If all the members of a society hold the ten value clusters in high agreement, then consensus is high. If there is little agreement, consensus is low. Consensus is important because it describes how well individual actions are tolerated or accepted in a given culture. Box 10.4 provides a case study of Ben & Jerry's Ice Cream, and it serves as a good example of how value consensus works. People and organizations

■ ■ ■ ■ ■

BOX 10.4
BEN & JERRY[18]

Ben & Jerry's Ice Cream has faithfully lived up to its three-part mission statement since it was founded. Its mission focuses on (1) making and distributing all-natural, high-quality ice cream; (2) making a profit for shareholders; and (3) facilitating innovations that improve the quality of life in the social community. Its ability to continue to live up to its mission was put into question in April, 2000, when Unilever, a large conglomerate that owns Dove Soap and Lipton Soup among many other businesses, purchased Ben & Jerry's for $326 million with plans to take the company global.

Initially, there seemed to be cause for concern that Ben & Jerry's would lose its identity. Some analysts warned that Ben & Jerry's, like many other companies before, would begin to conform to the less socially responsible, larger organization of Unilever. Warren Bennis, an expert on corporate culture and transformations, emphasized this point when he noted that most companies become "pretty much the color of the company" that acquires them. And in this case, the color of Unilever is not nearly as socially progressive.

Bomini Socila Investments is a New York mutual fund management firm that specializes in socially and environmentally responsible stocks. It lists Ben & Jerry's in its index as one of the top 400 companies in the world for its social agenda, but it doesn't include Unilever.

However, Unilever, which also owns other ice cream brands including Good Humor, Popsicle, and Breyers, promised to take the lead from the smaller company. It pledged to expand the Ben & Jerry's socially progressive mission and its active philanthropic philosophy. Early indications are that Unilever is working to transform its own mission to incorporate more of the Ben & Jerry's philosophy. It appears, Bennis noted, that the smaller company with its flower-child image and strong socially responsible agenda may well influence the larger company, which may help prove that the socially responsible choice is also the better choice for business. Twenty years ago, people would say they wanted to make money even at the expense of a socially progressive agenda. It appears now that organizations can do both at the same time.

often assume that although social responsibility and philanthropy are positive values that should be part of the corporate mission, these values are often fulfilled at the expense of the "bottom line." The value consensus is that profits come before social programs and that one often benefits at the expense of the other. Ben & Jerry's was founded on the premise that social activism was equally as important as profits and a quality product, and it succeeded in fulfilling both values.

THE PROCESS OF VALUE CHANGE

Most cultures experience some level of value consensus. They may believe in the importance of individual self-direction and independence. They may focus on the importance of traditions or the environment. For the United States, values of a world at peace, family stability and security, and freedom are all generally accepted and acknowledged core values. Nicholas Rescher observed that "there unquestionably exists (and will continue to exist) a prominent value consensus in America."[19] In our own society and in others, however, certain values are unstable and fluctuate in their importance and in the extent to which people adhere to them.[20] Because these fluctuations affect the hierarchies used in argumentation, advocates should be sensitive to them.

Values change in three ways. One type of value change occurs when a value that was held by a minority becomes more widely disseminated and becomes a majority value. Rescher has labeled this *value redistribution*, which is *a process in which a value becomes more and more widely diffused throughout a society until virtually all its members adhere to it*. In the period of the Vietnam war protests, for example, peace activists staged marches, rallies, draft card burnings, sit-ins, and other forms of protest against the war. The existence of peace logos, signs, and symbols along with speeches and rallies gradually raised the consciousness of the general population about peace as a value so that it came to be more widely held. Ultimately, American sentiment against the war was a major factor influencing political figures to bring an end to our involvement in Vietnam.

Rescher observes that in the normal course of events, values come to be emphasized or deemphasized; that is, they come to be more or less important to the people who hold them. *In value emphasis, values move upward in a value hierarchy. In value deemphasis, they move downward.* This increase or decrease in the extent of our adherence to values can be brought about by new information or by changes in our social or economic environment. For example, new information about the causes of cancer, heart attack, and stroke has noticeably changed Americans' awareness of good health in prolonging life. This increased emphasis on good health has changed our attitudes and behavior regarding exercise, smoking, and salt and cholesterol intake. Changes in the economic environment in the early 1990s led to a dramatic decrease in the number of professional jobs available to college graduates. As a result, college students came to value their education in terms of its "marketability" and sought degrees in business, engineering, and computer science in increasing numbers.

Rescher cites value restandardization as a third factor affecting the way in which values are applied within a society. *Value restandardization is a process in which standards used to measure whether a value is being met increase or decrease.* For example, the criteria to measure whether one has an adequate standard of living have changed over the years. In the late 1940s and early 1950s, costs and inflation were low; most families had only one car; and mortgages were well within the reach of middle-class incomes. Today, in many areas, even modest homes are expensive; cable television and telephones are considered basic utilities; lifestyles often require that most families have two cars; and many other costs have risen. Standards for an adequate income and lifestyle have changed dramatically over the past forty years.

In addition to cultural variations in value rankings, values vary in response to changing social conditions. As time passes, certain values may become more widely diffused in a society, may increase or decrease in importance, or may be restandardized. Value advocates should consider what factors—new information, technological development, or economic fluctuation—might affect the values they are discussing. Also, when incompatible values conflict, advocates should determine what standards audiences are likely to use to choose between them. As we shall see in the remaining sections of this chapter, audience adherence plays a major role in establishing basic premises in a value argument.

VALUES AND ARGUMENTATION

To support fact and policy claims, arguers can refer to truths and to facts that are verifiable and recognized by the audience. For example, if someone were to claim that "capital punishment deters crime," that person could use studies of the relationship between the existence of the death penalty and the incidence of first-degree murder and other capital crimes. But if the claim was that "capital punishment is justified," a different strategy would be required. Here, the advocate would have to draw upon value hierarchies and the relationship between values recognized in society to provide justification for capital punishment. This is why the research findings of Rokeach and others who have studied American values are so important to value argument. When people disagree about values, a choice must be made, and one criterion for deciding among competing values is their relative status in the larger society.[21]

Using Hierarchies

Chaim Perelman and coauthor Lucie Olbrechts-Tyteca, introduced in Chapter 6, have also studied Western society's values. They identified particular value hierarchies that seem to be widely accepted in Western cultures and therefore are used as a foundation for value arguments.[22] First is the hierarchy of *quantity*—whatever produces the greatest good for the largest number of people at the least cost is to be preferred. This hierarchy, which values more over less and judges alternatives based on effects and outcomes, comes from utilitarianism. ("We should subsidize health-care cooperatives to provide affordable health care for all citizens of the country.") Second is the hierarchy of *quality*, which values what is unique, irreparable, or original. Human life is often viewed from this perspective, as are great works of art. ("The Sistine Chapel is worth restoring, even at great cost, for the works of Michelangelo cannot be replaced.") Third is the hierarchy of *the existent*, which values the concrete over the possible. ("You should accept that job offer you have now rather than waiting for another one that might not materialize.") Fourth is the hierarchy of *essence*, which values what is at the core of a group or class rather than what is on the fringes. ("Free enterprise is central to what this country is all about, and we should do whatever we can to preserve free enterprise.") The fifth hierarchy, that of *the person*, values the dignity and autonomy of the person over all competing values.[23] ("Euthanasia allows a person death with dignity, and a dignified death is more important than life for a terminally ill person.") The hierarchies of quantity (more over less), quality (the unique over the common), the existent (the concrete over the merely possible), essence (the central over the peripheral), and the person (individual dignity and autonomy over all else) are commonly accepted throughout society and can be used as a basis for value claims.

Perelman and Olbrechts-Tyteca remind us that "when a speaker wants to establish values or hierarchies or to intensify the adherence they gain, he may consolidate them by connecting them to other values or hierarchies."[24] In the preceding examples, such things as affordable health care, the restoration of the Sistine Chapel, free enterprise, and euthanasia were said to be preferable because of their association with the values higher in these five pervasive hierarchies. Each of these five hierarchies is common and used frequently in arguments.

Principles for Constructing Value Arguments

The theorists whose work we have discussed, then, have suggested principles that can be quite useful in constructing arguments about values:

1. Generally, terminal values should be viewed as more significant and important than instrumental values.
2. When one is choosing between competing instrumental values (that is, choosing the most effective means to an end), the value that best meets the particular needs of the situation should be preferred.
3. In choosing one value over others, one should consider the hierarchies of quantity, quality, the existent, essence, and the person if they are applicable to a particular choice or course of action.
4. The results of Rokeach's value survey of terminal values indicate a rather stable value system that is accepted by the American public and that can be used to support value preferences.
5. Values are not entirely fixed, however. Because values tend to change slowly, the advocate should consider the possibilities of value redistribution, value emphasis, and value restandardization as described by Rescher.

When a choice must be made between competing values, or when an arguer seeks to defend a particular value hierarchy, these five principles can provide the means for justifying a shift or change in values or for opposing value orderings proposed by other arguers.

STOCK ISSUES FOR VALUE ARGUMENTS

When we argue to change values, we are attempting to persuade an audience to redistribute, emphasize/deemphasize, or restandardize some value within its value system. The process calls on an advocate to find persuasive means to enable the audience to reconceptualize its value hierarchies or value system. To argue for value change successfully, value advocates must address certain stock issues. As we noted in Chapter 9, stock issues are questions that must be asked and answered to construct a satisfactory case on a proposition. Propositions imply certain stock issues, and advocates seeking to persuade an audience should understand them. Stock issues are the standard issues that a general audience would expect an advocate to address in a particular argumentative case. The stock issues for a value case include values, criteria, and application.[25] These are illustrated in Box 10.5.

   The role of stock issues will be illustrated through examples from supporting and opposing arguments on the topic "euthanasia is desirable." Euthanasia, generically defined as a means for producing a gentle and easy death, is a controversial topic in America today. The law holds that patients have the right to refuse medical treatment and that patients with living wills can be allowed to die without specific measures (hydration, feeding tubes, resuscitation) to preserve their lives. However, when a patient becomes comatose and has not expressed preferences regarding treatment, the course of action to be taken is much less clear. Furthermore, laws applying to doctor-assisted death (induced death) are also inconsistent, particularly in regard to penalties for assisted suicide.[26] The public is aware of highly publicized cases in which an immediate family sued to have a relative removed from life-support mechanisms, or

---

BOX 10.5

STOCK ISSUES IN VALUE-BASED PROPOSITIONS

ISSUE	DEFINITION	EXAMPLE
Value ■ Value Object ■ Value Hierarchy	Defines the value and sets the goal or end point for the case arguments. Arguers must identify two value issues: value object and value hierarchy. Value object is the central value term of the proposition to be debated. Value hierarchy is the relative importance of the value.	Human dignity is an important value and is more important than even life. Existence without dignity or quality is meaningless.
Criteria	Field- or sphere-dependent standards to be used to decide whether the value object fulfills certain values. Criteria are the measures, norms, or rules used to judge whatever is being evaluated.	We should minimize physical pain and suffering, enhance dignity while avoiding degradation, and those affected should be free to make choices concerning what happens to them.
Application	The factual information and experience that can be used to support that the value object meets the criteria.	There are many people who are terminally ill, will not improve, and will suffer tremendous pain. These people should be allowed to avoid suffering and die with dignity.

severely deformed infants were allowed to die, or spouses and other loved ones ended the lives of suffering patients. Euthanasia dramatizes the conflicts between our religious beliefs, our humanitarian instincts, our legal codes, and our medical practices. As such, it is a highly appropriate topic for value controversy.

Value

The first of the stock issues in a value argument is value. The value stock issue defines the value and sets the goal or end point for the case arguments. Clearly identifying which value is most important in the discussion creates a common point of reference for all the participants. Therefore, if the case were about whether censorship should be permitted in school newspapers, advocates might argue that the value of freedom of speech is more important than other competing values. As long as the participants have a clear understanding of the relevant values involved, the discussion or debate can remain focused.

The stock issue of value requires the arguer to identify two issues: the value object and the value hierarchy. *The value object is an idea, practice, event, policy, or state of affairs that is to be judged by means of evaluation.* In addressing this issue, arguers should establish the value content of the object and define its primary features. In the example introduced at the beginning of the chapter, the value object, the thing being evaluated, was Hollywood's influence. With the proposition "euthanasia is desirable," the value object is euthanasia.

The second value issue an arguer needs to address is *value hierarchy, or the ranking of values favored by advocates or party in an argument.* In any extended value case, a certain value hierarchy is implied because, in defending any value orientation, advocates implicitly favor one value or certain values over others. The hierarchy applicable in any evaluation may become explicit only when that evaluation is challenged and contrasted to an alternative hierarchy. Therefore, explicit defense of a particular hierarchy may not be required when the value case is presented initially. However, if no value consensus is reached in the discussion, then the arguers may explicitly discuss value hierarchies and the relative importance of the values being discussed.

Naturally, supporters and opponents of euthanasia support different value hierarchies. Those supporting euthanasia would be likely to support freedom of choice and individual self-respect, whereas opponents might support the sanctity of human life and social responsibility. In defending their respective hierarchies, advocates of each position attempt to intensify their audience's adherence to and appreciation for the values at the top of their hierarchies. In other words, they attempt to persuade their listeners to rank values in the same way as they do. In defending a certain hierarchy, the value advocates can use the resources provided in the previous section: the distinction between terminal and instrumental values, the needs implied in the situation, Perelman's study of Western hierarchies, Rokeach's value survey, and Rescher's account of value change. In addition, advocates can seek out other studies of American values and value hierarchies.

Opponents of a value proposition can also reorder the audience's hierarchies by showing that the evidence and arguments the supporters used to support their own hierarchies were questionable. If euthanasia supporters argued that their own values were highly ranked by Americans, their opponents could respond that this is merely a form of argument *ad populum*. Keep in mind that just because the majority of the people believe that something is right does not mean that it *is* right. Many Americans in the South favored school segregation at one time, but it was not morally "right." Perhaps the values currently ranked highly by most Americans reflect excessive self-interest and ought not to be the ones most valued. Euthanasia opponents could argue that the social-welfare field they advocate is based on the idea that we should be more concerned with long-term consequences for the whole society than we are with the immediate interests of particular individuals.

Criteria

In addition to clarifying the value stock issue, advocates should carefully select the criteria by which they will evaluate the value object. *Criteria are field- or sphere-dependent standards to be used to decide whether the value object fulfills certain values. Criteria are the measures, norms, or rules used to judge whatever is being evaluated.* For example, if we say "this ice cream is good," we must have in mind certain criteria or standards (creaminess, good taste, natural ingredients) by which we will judge the good ice cream. Here the value would probably be pleasure or enjoyment; if the value object meets or measures up to the standards, it fulfills the value in question; if not, then it must be judged negatively.

The standards that advocates select should be taken from the field or sphere most appropriate to the occasion. Advocates supporting the desirability of euthanasia could select individual ethics as their field and argue that the greater good of the individual is its purpose. Within this framework, they could defend the values of physical well-being, self-respect, and freedom of choice. Therefore, the standards these values suggest are that physical pain and suffering should be minimized or avoided, that those affected should be able to maintain dignity and avoid degradation, and that those affected should be able to make free choices concerning what happens to them. If the advocates can establish these three standards, they then need only to prove that euthanasia enables those standards to be met in order to establish their case.

Their opponents could argue for an alternative sphere and a different set of criteria. For example, they could argue that social ethics should be the field for evaluation rather than just what is good for the individual. On a social level, alternative standards might come into play. In opposition to the three criteria just described, opponents might argue that the weak and the old should be protected, that life (the highest value) should be preserved, and that the medical profession should uphold its responsibility to preserve human life.

Both advocates and opponents of the desirability of euthanasia must validate their criteria through further argument, especially when those standards are questioned or challenged. Three strategies are available for establishing criteria. First, one can link them to more generally accepted and unquestioned standards and argue that because the more general standard is accepted, the audience should also accept the particular standard the advocate is supporting. For example, we put suffering animals out of their misery; why can we not allow a human being who is suffering to die? Or, we show compassion to strangers but refuse to allow our loved ones to end their own misery. Second, the standards can be justified by showing that no other standards take precedence over them. For example, in this country we believe that freedom of choice is more important than life itself. ("Live free or die" was a central motto of the colonial period, and Patrick Henry's "Give me liberty or give me death" is well-known.) Third, advocates can show the logical consequences of failing to apply the standards they advocate. Advances in medical technology have made it possible to "keep alive" individuals who are brain dead by artificially stimulating respiration and heartbeat. Once the machines have been activated, doctors are afraid to discontinue them because they fear malpractice suits and even criminal charges. The logical consequences of a complete refusal to sanction euthanasia would be the continued existence of thousands of patients who could be said to be "alive" only in a technical sense.

Application

The final stock issue deals with the application of the criteria the advocates have established. That is, does the value object meet the standards for fulfilling the values in question? Here is where factual information and experience can be used for evidence. Supporters of euthanasia should be able to show that passive euthanasia enables patients to avoid suffering and to die with dignity. The extent to which the criteria apply and the number of patients affected by the criteria are significant here. How many patients are terminally ill and on life-support mechanisms? What proportion of these patients are likely to be affected by the euthanasia practices the advocates favor? If the proportion is small or the use of passive euthanasia likely to be infrequent, the advocates' argument may lack significance.

On the other hand, opponents of euthanasia would have at least two options open to them on this stock issue. First, they might argue that the supporters' criteria do not apply. If many terminally ill patients are not sustained by life-support mechanisms, then passive euthanasia would not diminish their suffering. Furthermore, if most terminally ill patients are comatose and unable to express their wishes, then passive euthanasia would not provide death with dignity for those patients. Second, opponents might refer to the alternative criteria they have proposed and argue that applying those criteria better fulfills certain values. For example, if opponents of euthanasia established as a criterion that doctors should be able to uphold their responsibility to preserve life, then asking them to disconnect life-support mechanisms would work against that standard.

THE ISSUES BRIEF

Richard Paul and Gerald Nosich note that experienced critical thinkers know how to clarify the values and standards relevant to a situation, compare the values embedded in competing perspectives and interpretations, and question their own framework of thought.[27] Living as we do in a multicultural, diverse society requires us to understand and appreciate value orientations that differ from our own and to respect and incorporate the perspectives of individuals who come from religious and cultural backgrounds and personal experiences dramatically different from our own. Experience in value advocacy can enable many arguers to do this.

As a means of assisting you to incorporate divergent perspectives into your argument, we recommend that you construct an issues brief as we initially discussed in Chapter 9. Box 10.6 is a brief on the euthanasia topic that articulates arguments on all the stock issues discussed in the previous section. In this case, the value object, the subject of evaluation, is euthanasia. When examining this brief, you should realize that each

■ ■ ■ ■ ■

BOX 10.6

ISSUES BRIEF WITH DEFINITION, FIELD, CRITERIA, AND APPLICATION

PROPOSITION: EUTHANASIA IS DESIRABLE

I. *Value.*

A. *Definition. How should the value object be defined?*

Euthanasia will be defined as passive-withholding or removing life-support systems from moribund patients.

1. "Life-support systems" include equipment that provides basic life functions—respiration, heartbeat, etc.—through artificial means.
2. "Moribund" patients are people with no possibility of recovery who will die in the normal course of events.
3. This definition is supported by etymology and the opinion of experts.

This definition is overly restrictive and should include active euthanasia.

1. Active euthanasia has traditionally been included in the term.
2. Some "moribund" and comatose patients have, in fact, recovered consciousness.
3. *Merriam-Webster's Collegiate Dictionary* includes the act or practice of killing hopelessly sick or injured individuals in its definition of *euthanasia.*[28]

B. *Hierarchies. What ranking of values should apply to this value object?*

Euthanasia preserves and promotes personal freedom, comfort, and self-respect.

1. Freedom, comfort, and self-respect are three of the eight top-ranked values in Rokeach's value survey.
2. Freedom of choice and dignity are the essence of what it means to be human.

Euthanasia undermines our respect for life, which should be the highest value.

1. If life is not preserved and protected, all other values are moot.
2. Our Christian belief tells us that life is a gift, not ours to do with as we please.
3. A human life is unique and irreplaceable.
4. A society that does not value life becomes degraded and immoral.

II. *Criteria. What standards should be applied to determine whether the value object fulfills the desired values?*

To be beneficial, euthanasia should meet certain standards.

A. Euthanasia should allow free choice concerning the manner and timing of a person's death.
B. Euthanasia should prevent needless suffering and futile prolongation of life.
C. Euthanasia should prevent hardship for the families of terminally ill patients.

Other standards are more important.

A. Treatment of the terminally ill should protect and preserve life.
B. Treatment of the terminally ill should enhance the will to survive.
C. Treatment should not undermine the general respect for life in our society.

(continued)

BOX 10.6   CONTINUED
PROPOSITION: **EUTHANASIA IS DESIRABLE**

III. *Application. Do the proposed standards in fact apply to the value object?*

Euthanasia is beneficial and desirable.

A. It preserves freedom and dignity of the individual.

B. It ends patients' suffering.

C. It gives families a say in patients' treatment.

Euthanasia is harmful to society.

A. It puts pressure on terminally ill patients and undermines the will to survive.

B. In the absence of active euthanasia, patients will continue to suffer anyway.

C. Families can be distressed and torn apart by the responsibility to make these decisions.

D. Society's attitudes toward the preservation of life will be negatively affected.

---

of the arguments is a *claim* that would need to be supported by further arguments and evidence, such as the opinions of authorities or facts or statistics. What are included in Box 10.6 are the principal claim (the proposition), the major subclaims, and the sub-subclaims that constitute the two cases supporting and opposing the proposition.

SUMMARY

This chapter was intended to provide a systematic approach to value argument. Although some people have expressed the view that values are basically subjective and irrational, many contemporary theorists of argument have successfully provided the means for developing a rational approach to supporting value claims. They have recognized that many arguments in fields such as law and medicine are based on values and provide the grounds for making decisions and taking action. These theorists have explained how value arguments are structured, how they can be assessed, and how advocates can construct extended arguments supporting value claims.

Values are generally organized into value systems. A value system consists of value content, value structure, and value consensus. Value content refers to the clusters of values held as important by a culture. These include self-direction, stimulation, hedonism, achievement, power, security, conformity, tradition, benevolence, and universalism. Value structure describes the hierarchy, or relative importance, we place on values, and value consensus is the relative degree of acceptance values have within a given culture. Understanding value systems is important to value advocates who must gauge arguments to suit the values and attitudes of an audience. Furthermore, when individuals or groups of people disagree about values, it is often because their value systems are ordered differently.

In any society, value hierarchies are subject to fluctuation and change. Values may become more widely held because a persistent minority successfully argues for their importance. Because of new information or changes in the social or economic environment, values may become more or less emphasized. The standards that are applied to determine whether a value has been met may become more or less stringent. Because audience adherence is a vital factor in establishing the basic premises in a value argument, advocates should be aware of factors that may bring about changes in the importance and pervasiveness of values in society.

An arguer supporting a particular value proposition must advocate some orientation toward a value object. A value object is an idea, practice, event, policy, or state of affairs that has to be measured in an evaluation. To successfully support a value proposition, the value advocate must address three stock issues. First: How should the value object be defined? Second is criteria: What standards should be applied to determine whether the value object fulfills the desired values? Third is application: Does the value object in fact meet the standards that have been proposed by the advocate? The chapter concluded with an issues brief on the topic of euthanasia to illustrate how these five stock issues function in a value controversy.

GLOSSARY

Criteria (p. 308) are field- or sphere-dependent standards to be used to decide whether the value object fulfills certain values. Criteria are the measures, norms, or rules used to judge whatever is being evaluated.

Instrumental values (p. 298) concern modes of conduct or the means for fulfilling other values.

Terminal values (p. 298) concern desirable end states of existence.

Values (p. 298) are the desirable, transituational goals, varying in importance, that serve as guiding principles in people's lives.

Value consensus (p. 302) is the degree of concurrence among members of a society concerning their values.

Value content (p. 299) refers to the motivational goals expressed in the value.

Value deemphasis (p. 303) occurs when values move downward in a value hierarchy.

Value emphasis (p. 303) occurs when values move upward.

Value hierarchy (p. 307) is the ranking of values favored by advocates or party in an argument.

Value object (p. 307) is an idea, practice, event, policy, or state of affairs that is to be judged by means of evaluation.

Value redistribution (p. 303) is a process in which a value becomes more and more widely diffused throughout a society until virtually all its members adhere to it.

Value restandardization (p. 303) is a process in which standards used to measure whether a value is being met increase or decrease.

Value structure (p. 300) refers to the dynamic relations among the values in our individual value system.

Value system (p. 300) is an enduring organization of beliefs concerning preferred modes of conduct or end states of existence according to their relative importance.

EXERCISES

Exercise 1 Box 10.3 provided a hierarchy of values for 1981. Rank these values as you believe they are hierarchically ordered today. Consider the following questions:

1. Are the values ordered the same now as they were then?
2. What explains any difference?
3. What process of value change do you think occurred, if any?

*Exercise 2 What follows is an excerpt from a Supreme Court decision on flag burning (*Texas v. Johnson* 491 U.S. 397 [1989]). In this case, a man named Johnson participated during the 1984 Republican National Convention in Dallas, Texas, in a political demonstration to protest the policies of the Reagan administration and some Dallas-based corporations. After a march through the city streets, Johnson burned an American flag while protesters chanted. He was convicted of desecration of a venerated object in violation of a Texas statute, and the state court of appeals upheld the conviction. However, the Texas court of criminal appeals reversed the ruling, holding that the state could not punish Johnson for burning the flag in this situation because his action was expressive conduct protected by the First Amendment provisions protecting freedom of expression. The decision was appealed to the U.S. Supreme Court, which ruled in favor of Johnson. Following is an excerpt from the majority opinion, which was authored by Justice William Brennan. In regard to his value-based argument, answer the following questions:

1. What values does Justice Brennan affirm in this opinion?
2. What values does Brennan view as opposed to his position?
3. What criteria for evaluation does Brennan apply in the decision?
4. What is your own value position in regard to Brennan's specific argument?

MAJORITY OPINION IN *TEXAS V. JOHNSON*

The State asserts an interest in preserving the flag as a symbol of nationhood and national unity. . . .

Johnson was prosecuted because he knew that his politically charged expression would cause "serious offense." If he had burned the flag as a means of disposing of it because it was dirty or torn, he would not have been convicted of flag desecration under this Texas law: Federal law designates burning as the preferred means of disposing of a flag. . . . The Texas law is thus not aimed at protecting the physical integrity of the flag in all circumstances, but is designed instead to protect it only against impairments that cause serious offense to others. . . . Whether Johnson's treatment of the flag violated Texas law thus depended on the likely communicative impact of his expressive conduct.

Texas argues that its interest [is] in preserving the flag as a symbol of nationhood and national unity. . . . Quoting extensively from the writings of this Court chronicling the flag's historic and symbolic role in our society, the State emphasizes the " 'special place' " reserved for the flag in our Nation. . . . The State's argument is not that it has an interest simply in maintaining the flag as a symbol of *something*, no matter what it symbolizes; indeed, if that were the State's position, it would be difficult to see how that interest is endangered by highly symbolic conduct such as Johnson's. Rather, the State's claim is that it has an interest in preserving the flag as a symbol of *nationhood* and *national unity*. . . . According to Texas, if one physically treats the flag in a way that would tend to cast doubt on either the idea that nationhood and national unity are the flag's referents or that national unity actually exists, the message conveyed thereby is a harmful one and therefore may be prohibited.

If there is a bedrock principle underlying the First Amendment, it is that the government may not prohibit the expression of an idea simply because society finds the idea itself offensive or disagreeable. . . .

Texas' focus on the precise nature of Johnson's expression, moreover, misses the point of our prior decisions: their enduring lesson, that the government may not prohibit expression simply because it disagrees with its message, is not dependent on the particular mode in which one chooses to express an idea. If we were to hold that a State may forbid flag burning wherever it is likely to endanger the flag's symbolic role, but allow it wherever burning a flag promotes that role—as where, for example, a person ceremoniously burns a dirty flag—we would be saying that when it comes to impairing the flag's physical integrity, the flag itself may be used as a symbol—as a substitute for the written or spoken word. . . . We would be permitting a State to "prescribe what shall be orthodox" by saying that one may burn the flag to convey one's attitude toward it and its referents only if one does not endanger the flag's representation of nationhood and national unity.

We are tempted to say, in fact, that the flag's deservedly cherished place in our community will be strengthened, not weakened, by our holding today. Our decision is a reaffirmation of the principles of freedom and inclusiveness that the flag best reflects, and of the conviction that our toleration of criticism such as Johnson's is a sign and source of our strength. Indeed, one of the proudest images of our flag, the one immortalized in our own national anthem, is of the bombardment it survived at Fort McHenry. It is the Nation's resilience, not its rigidity, that Texas sees reflected in the flag—and it is that resilience that we reassert today.

The way to preserve the flag's special role is not to punish those who feel differently about these matters. It is to persuade them that they are wrong. . . . We can imagine no more appropriate response to burning a flag than waving one's own, no better way to counter a flag burner's message than by saluting the flag that burns, no surer means of preserving the dignity even of the flag that burned than by—as one witness here did—according its remains a respectful burial. We do not consecrate the flag by punishing its desecration, for in doing so we dilute the freedom that this cherished emblem represents.

Exercise 3 Read the following three situations and analyze the values that clash:

SITUATION 1

Your parents are paying for your university education. Paying the tuition and housing bills can be a hardship for them, but their hope is that you succeed with your education and complete a degree in business. Although you appreciate their sacrifice and are loyal to them, your passion is to become an actor and attempt to find a career in entertainment. Therefore, you wish to major in theater. Unfortunately, when you shared this wish with your parents, they not only opposed your choice, saying it was "unrealistic" and "very unlikely," but they also told you that if you chose to major in anything but business, they would end their financial support for your education.

SITUATION 2

Your university is a large research institution that conducts studies in cancer and AIDS prevention and treatment. You were attracted to the school in the first place because it has the best premedical program in the state, and your goal is to become a doctor. Although you support finding cures for these diseases, you are also very opposed to the live animal research conducted in university laboratories. You become even more concerned when you discover that part of the required coursework in your biology and premed major will be assisting with some of these research projects and conducting vivisections on the animals. Yet you know that a biology major is the first step toward a medical degree that will help you find cures for people later on.

SITUATION 3

You are a member of a group in a business communication class. Your final project, worth half of your grade, is to conduct an analysis of a local business, write a research paper focusing on marketing strategies and suggestions for improving the business, and present your project to the class at the end of the term. Four of the five members of your group worked hard to produce a quality paper and design a thoughtful presentation. One member, however, rarely showed up at meetings, came unprepared when he did come, and failed to do his fair share. Everyone in the group is angry with him, but no one is willing to confront him or tell the professor about his lack of effort. This is particularly disturbing to the other group members because the final grade for the paper and presentation will be the same for everyone—even the person who didn't work. The presentation is in two days.

Based on each of the situations and your understanding of values, answer the following:

1. Using Rokeach's hierarchy of values, what is the "correct" course of action in each situation?

2. What do you think is the correct course of action for each situation? What values support your conclusions?

3. How would you organize the terminal value hierarchy in a way that is consistent with your own decision making?

Exercise 4 Develop an issues brief using the proposition "Hollywood is detrimental to society."

NOTES

1. Adapted from Katie Pickett, Communication & Theatre Department, Pacific Lutheran University, May 21, 2008.

2. J. Marrero, "Does Hollywood have a negative impact on the world?" *Helium.* http://www.helium.com/items/448145-hollywood-changed-world-times (accessed May 10, 2008).

3. Jessica C. E. Gienow-Hecht (February 2006), "A European Considers the Influence of American Culture," *E-Journal USA,* http://usinfo.state.gov/journals/itgic/0206/ijge/gienowhecht.htm (accessed May 28, 2008).

4. A. Enderby (2006). Hollywood's Impact. International Debate Education Association, http://www.idebate.org/debatabase/topic_details.php?topicID=57, (accessed May 10, 2008).

5. J. Overstreet (2003). "Hollywood: Thumbs Up or Down?" Seattle Pacific University Response. http://www.spu.edu/depts/uc/response/summer2k3/faithfilm.html (accessed on May 10, 2008).

6. Gienow-Hecht, 2006.

7. Gienow-Hecht, 2006.

8. Gienow-Hecht, 2006.

9. C. Roberto (2007). "Hollywood's decay." *Merinews: Power to People.* http://www.idebate.org/debatabase/topic_details.php?topicID=57 (accessed May 10, 2008).

10. Richard W. Paul and Gerald M. Nosich, "A Model for the National Assessment of Higher Order Thinking," in A. J. A. Binker, ed., *Critical Thinking; What Every Person Needs to Survive in a Rapidly Changing World* (Santa Rosa, Calif.: Foundation for Critical Thinking, 1992), 85; and The Foundation for Critical Thinking, www.criticalthinking.org (accessed February 1, 2001).

11. Shalom H. Schwartz and Galit Sagie, "Value Consensus and Importance: A Cross-National Study," *Journal of Cross-Cultural Psychology,* 31 (July, 2000): 465–468; see also Bradley R. Agle and Craig B. Caldwell "Understanding Research on Values in Business: A Level of Analysis Framework," *Business & Society,* 38 (September 1999): 326–388; Soyeon Shim and Pitti Shim, "A Personal Value-Based Model of College Students' Attitudes and Expected Choice Behavior Regarding Retailing Careers," *Family & Consumer Sciences Research Journal* 28 (September, 1999), 28–52.

12. Milton Rokeach, *The Nature Human Values* (New York: The Free Press, 1973), 7–8.

13. Schwartz and Sagie, 465–470.

14. Rokeach, 7–8. Another theorist who divided values along these lines is Donald Walhout, who distinguished between social values (political stability, equality, freedom, etc.) and individual values (social participation, friendship, proper self-love). See his *The Good and the Realm of Values* (Notre Dame, Ind.: University of Notre Dame Press, 1978), 45–46.

15. Milton Rokeach and Sandra J. Ball-Rokeach, "Stability and Change in American Value Priorities," *American Psychologist* 44 (1989): 777.

16. Rokeach, 57–59 and 66–72.

17. Seymour Lipset, *Continental Divide: The Values and Institutions of the United States and Canada* (New York: Routledge, 1990), 37–39.

18. Adapted from Lauren Coleman-Lochner, "Ben & Jerry's Plans to Stay Cool," *The Record* (April 19, 2000): 1; Carl M. Cannon, *Policy: Charity for Profit*, (June 17, 2000); Gary Dessler, "How to Earn Your Employees' Commitment," *The Academy of Management Executives* 13 (May 1999): 58–67.

19. Nicholas Rescher, *Introduction to Value Theory* (Englewood Cliffs, N.J.: Prentice-Hall, 1969), 115. See also Rokeach and Ball-Rokeach, 777.

20. The account of value change in this section is drawn from Rescher, 111–118.

21. For other studies of American values, see Gail M. Inlow, *Values in Transition: A Handbook* (New York: John Wiley, 1972); and Ben J. Wattenberg, *The Good News Is the Bad News Is Wrong* (New York: Simon & Schuster, 1984). Many studies of contemporary American values are available.

22. Chaim Perelman and Lucie Olbrechts-Tyteca, *The New Rhetoric: A Treatise on Argumentation*, trans. John Wilkinson and Purcell Weaver (Notre Dame, Ind.: University of Notre Dame Press, 1969), 83–99. In addition to the hierarchies stated here, these authors noted the hierarchy of order—that the cause, or that which comes first, should be valued over that which comes later.

23. For further explanation of these hierarchies, see Gregg B. Walker and Malcolm O. Sillars, "Where Is Argument? Perelman's Theory of Values," in *Perspectives on Argumentation*, Robert Trapp and Janice Schuetz, eds. (Prospect Heights, Ill.: Waveland, 1990), 143–145.

24. Perelman and Olbrechts-Tyteca, 83.

25. The stock issues suggested here are taken from Paul W. Taylor, *Normative Discourse* (Englewood Cliffs, N.J.: Prentice-Hall, 1961): 14–103. An earlier version of this explanation appeared in Barbara Warnick, "Arguing Value Propositions," *Journal of the American Forensic Association* 18 (1981): 109–119. Many points in the euthanasia example appeared in Stanislaus J. Dundon, "Karen Quinlan and the Freedom of the Dying," *Journal of Value Inquiry* 4 (1978): 280–91. This journal has many useful articles on value-oriented issues such as abortion, euthanasia, and human rights.

26. Richard Worshop, "Assisted Suicide," *CQ Researcher* 2 (1992): 148.

27. Paul and Nosich, 101.

28. *Merriam-Webster's Collegiate Dictionary*, s.v., "euthanasia," Merriam-Webster OnLine, 2001. www.m-w.com (accessed February 9, 2001).

CHAPTER ELEVEN

ARGUING ABOUT POLICIES

KEY CONCEPTS

Systems perspective (p. 321)
Ill (p. 324)
Qualitative significance (p. 324)
Quantitative significance (p. 324)
Blame (p. 325)
Structural blame (p. 326)
Structures (p. 326)
Attitudinal blame (p. 326)
Cure (p. 327)
Plan of action (p. 327)

Effects (p. 327)
Cost (p. 327-328)
Benefits (p. 328)
Needs-analysis case (p. 328-329)
Direct refutation (p. 329)
Comparative advantages (p. 333)
Goals argument (p. 335)
Defense of the present policy system (p. 338)
Minor repairs (p. 338)
Counterproposal (p. 339)

The decision to act or not to act involves a process of policy argumentation. For example, consider the following three claims:

All US citizens should be subjected to mandatory AIDS screening
The United States should permit the sale of organs.
I should study tonight.

These statements are policy propositions that focus arguments around specific choices and actions. Each asks recipients to behave or cooperate in certain ways and, presumably, if the arguments supporting the claims are sufficient, then recipients will support or pursue particular courses of action.

This chapter examines how policy arguments work and how arguers construct and refute extended policy cases. When you have finished reading this chapter, you should be able to recognize, write, and respond to policy arguments and extended policy cases.

THE FUTURE NATURE OF POLICIES

Policy arguments differ from fact and value arguments discussed in Chapters 8 and 9. If we argue that US citizens should be tested for AIDS or that we should allow organ sales, we promote a future action. Policy arguments are future-bound. Because historical policies and actions cannot be changed through argument, when we make policy proposals we focus on what should be done from this time forward. The future-action nature of policy arguments is fundamentally different from value arguments because fact and value arguments can examine and evaluate whether current and past conditions were true, justified, or reasonable. In value-oriented discussions, we can say:

> Testing all US citizens for AIDS is justified.
> Allowing the sale of organs is beneficial.
> Studying is a good idea.

In fact-orientated discussions we could argue:

> Testing for AIDS is widespread in the United States.
> The number of organ transplants will double in the next ten years.
> When I have studied in the past, I have received good grades.

Fact and value propositions can study what currently is, what should have been in the past, or even what facts and values we would hold as true or reasonable in the future because the focus of such argumentation is definition or evaluation—not action. We can evaluate the past and present to learn, but we cannot act differently in the past. Policy propositions are bound to future actions.

Because the future is uncertain, policy arguments ask hearers to predict what will work or what will not work. Box 11.1 provides a good illustration. Each year, thousands of people die waiting for organ transplants. Although transplants have become increasingly successful, many people remain reluctant to become organ donors. Increased supplies have the potential to save up to 100,000 lives in the United States alone. The question of how to increase organ availability has prompted some to begin arguing that the sale of organs should be permitted.

The proposition "The United States should allow the sale of organs" is a policy proposition. It is based on the factual assessment that current, donated supplies are insufficient and that thousands of people die while waiting on transplant lists. Although allowing the sale of organs might seem to be a reasonable approach for saving lives, we really have only a probable idea of what the result will be if we change the

BOX 11.1
SHOULD ORGANS BE SOLD ON THE OPEN MARKET?[1]

Would you sell a kidney to pay for graduate school? What if selling a lung or skin could help make house payments during economic downturns? Would you be willing to sell an organ of a deceased loved one if it could financially help your family? Most countries have laws prohibiting the sale of organs. The United States outlawed selling organs with the passage of the National Organ Transplant Act in 1984.[2] There are very few places in the world where organs can be sold legally, even though demand has increased steadily for decades.

With surgical advances, improved antirejection drugs, and new diagnostic and tissue-matching techniques, transplant procedures have become much more common and have much better survival rates. More than 2,300 patients receive hearts each year, with about 85 percent surviving for at least a year.[3] And more than hearts are transplanted. Surgeons have successfully replaced kidneys, lungs, livers, corneas, pancreases, and even faces.[4] In 2006, almost 29,000 transplant operations were performed in the United States, up from just over 28,000 one year earlier.[5] Success stories continue to multiply, as do the number of operations performed and the survival rates.[6]

Despite the increase in successful surgeries, a significant need remains.[7] Each day, about 74 people receive a transplant, but more than 97,000 remain on waiting lists. Seventeen people die daily waiting for organs to become available.[8]

Many organizations have made extensive efforts to promote organ donations. Even so, many potential donors remain reluctant. Their reasons vary from religious to personal to a misunderstanding of how organ donations work. The Mayo Clinic, for instance, has provided a list of myths that seem to make potential donors reluctant.[9] These include:

- If I become a donor, doctors won't work as hard to save my life in an emergency.
- Maybe I am not really dead when they harvest my organs.
- Organ donation is against my religion.
- I am too young to make this decision.
- I am too old; no one would want my organs.
- My family wants an open-casket funeral and that can't happen if I donate my organs.
- I am in poor health, which makes me an unsuitable candidate.
- Rich people always seem to move to the front of the line when organs become available; I don't want to support the rich.
- My family will have to pay for the hospital bill and surgery if I donate.

Although education and donation campaigns have worked hard to overcome myths such as these, organ donations lag far behind the need. For every 100,000 transplant operations needed each year, fewer than 30,000 are performed due to lack of supply.[10] Because of shortages, there has been growing pressure among many to allow people to sell their organs; the hope is that monetary incentives might overcome reluctance and myths.

Even though most of the world prohibits the sale of organs, a significant underground market has developed in many countries, including South Africa, Brazil, and Israel. Some governments and "entrepreneurs" sell organs under the table, including organs harvested from executed prisoners. Brian Handwerk reported in *National Geographic* that organ recipients can pay as much as $100,000 for illicit organs.[11] The poor and the imprisoned are often targeted as potential donors, and this problem is projected to increase.

(continued)

BOX 11.1   CONTINUED

With inadequate supplies and a growing underground market, the question of whether to allow legal organ sales has reemerged. Many fear that legally putting a price on organs ultimately gives the rich an advantage to health care, creating unequal distribution of health benefits. The market for organs could ultimately put pressure on the poor to endanger their lives and health for economic gain.[12] The following discussion explores some of these issues. As you read the arguments, think about what proposal makes the most sense. What should be done? How do we help move 100,000 people off the waiting list?

Thomas: I wish I had the opportunity to sell my kidney and pay for school. It seems to be a win-win. I can save a life, I don't need the extra kidney, and I can eliminate my college debt.

Hanne: I would love to be able to save a life as well as pay off my college debt. But we need to consider the implications for the poor. They can be easily exploited for the sale of their organs by the rich, thus abusing their dignity and creating a market that benefits only the rich. And what about families who might be pressured to stop medical treatment of loved ones so that organs can be harvested?

Thomas: Dignity isn't really the issue when you consider the huge underground, illegal market. All our current policies have done is make illegal activity profitable and unsafe. If we could sell our organs, it could be done safely and fairly. The most vulnerable people in society could have a real choice that could help them out.

Hanne: The issue is much larger than getting paid to save a life. But there needs to be a way to increase the number of donors in the United States. I know my grandpa had to wait three years to get a kidney, and during those three years, the dialysis treatments were expensive and painful. My family would have done anything to prevent that kind of suffering.

Thomas: I think one thing to consider is that we already allow the sale of blood and sperm. Commercial markets have increased the number of those donors. So far, we seem to have managed these markets well. It seems to me we could do the same thing with organs.

Hanne: I understand what you are saying, and the idea is making its way into the media. Have you seen *Baby Mama*? The movie illustrates a women getting paid for the use of her womb. Even so, I think there are more safety issues to be considered with organ selling because transplants are much riskier surgery than donating blood, giving sperm, or even carrying a baby. The safety factors and risks of the surgery make the market for organs more dangerous.

Thomas: We need to remember how many lives would be saved with more donors. I know I personally wouldn't really think of donating an organ unless I was given money. How else are we going to increase organ donations?

This discussion focuses on a policy proposition, and the two arguers try and find ways to address the significant issues of organ donation. As you read it, consider the following questions:

1. Is there a clear course of action that could be taken to resolve the problem?
2. What issues seem to be the most important in addressing the proposition?

(continued)

BOX 11.1   CONTINUED

3. Are there other issues or questions you would raise before you could make a decision about whether or not to allow the legal sale of organs?
4. If you were going to design a ten-minute policy presentation on this proposition, how would you organize it?
5. If you were Hanne, what would be your next argument?

law.[13] Some experts support organ sales as a means to increase the supply and argue it is the only available near-term solution. Others quickly point out that these organs may not go to the neediest and that there may be undue pressure placed on families and poor people to sell. Ultimately, whatever decision is made about the sale of organs will depend on a careful assessment of the potential benefits and the potential costs.

Policy propositions are simply a prediction of what we believe will occur. Accepting a policy proposition commits a hearer to a future call to action—what should be done. The decision to act, in turn, depends on the listener's assessment of how successful or reasonable the argument *probably* is. In this case, is the prediction that allowing organs to be sold will increase the supply reasonable and probable? Or, could it have the opposite effect if donors opt to stop donating?

POLICY SYSTEMS

This section examines how policy arguments function as part of a system. We take the position that extended policy arguments function systematically, which means that as we seek to change one part of the system through our arguments, we change the overall nature of the system. Such changes carry with them both benefits and costs that arguers should understand and consider.

It is not always clear how policy arguments affect our lives. Obviously, we make decisions about how our lives will be conducted, but we may not always be aware of the short- and long-term consequences and benefits of the actions we take. *A systems perspective recognizes that the world is a complex and interconnected set of relationships between and among component parts that compose a whole, and that one change in any part of the system changes the other elements of the system.* This means, then, that a system is a set of parts that are interrelated and form a whole unit.[14]

Changes in policies and practices can have widespread effects throughout a system. This is because most systems have many parts, each of which has a particular role and function. Since all the parts of a system are interconnected and affect one another, some consideration must be given to the extent to which a change in one part of the system will affect the others. Furthermore, most systems operate within a larger environment, and that environment can affect or be affected by changes in the system.

For example, consider the growth in online and distance-education courses. These programs have many interrelated parts, such as faculty, course designs, teaching resources, available technology, and students. Providing more money for instruction might provide better resources and more qualified faculty, but it might also increase the price such that many students cannot afford the courses. Simplifying course design or lowering admission standards might increase student access, but it also might decrease the amount students learn. Relying on technology might offer a flexible learning environment while excluding students who are not technologically literate. The larger environment might be affected if state legislatures cut back on funding for colleges and universities because they view distance learning as a better means of providing continuing education.

What affects one part of the system can be felt throughout the system. Any policy decision carries benefits and costs for the entire system. People act in contexts, and the actions we take affect our contexts. When we take actions in a system, we experience both benefits and costs. The benefits are all the advantages associated with the decision, and the costs are all the associated disadvantages. Online learning, for instance, has the advantage of providing access to education for millions of students who could not otherwise earn a degree. It helps break down barriers for nontraditional students in terms of both cost and ability to attend classes. There are also costs associated with online learning. Those same students do not receive the benefits of working with other students or professors. Their education may not be as rich as it might have been if they were on campus. The quality of the relationships among faculty and students may not be as good, and resources devoted toward distance learning may take away from other educational programs for on-campus students.

When we evaluate whether we should engage in a particular action, we evaluate the likelihood of the benefits as well as the likelihood of the costs throughout the system. Presumably, most people act when the net benefits are perceived to be greater than the net costs or disadvantages associated with an action.

STOCK ISSUES IN POLICY ARGUMENTS

When a policy is proposed, it must address certain issues—the reasonable questions recipients have about the validity of any action. These issues were introduced in Chapter 9 as stock issues—questions that must be asked and answered to construct a satisfactory case. Although many issues may serve as stock issues for policy analysis, we can generally group them into four categories: ill, blame, cure, and cost-benefits.[15] The discussion between Hanne and Thomas in Box 11.1 explored each of these issues as they related to the sale of organs. These issues and the supporting arguments are illustrated in Box 11.2.

However, even with much less formal and significant policy conversations, the same groups of issues are explored. Imagine the following exchange between two roommates:

Juli: I think we should go to Alaska and work in a fish cannery. That might sound like a strange idea, but I've always heard that there is a lot of money to be made, and they are always looking for people to work there.

Nancy: Wait a minute! That's an awfully long way from home. Why don't we just find something around here for the summer instead of making such a long trip? I know of two or three fast-food places that are hiring.

Juli: I'm out of money, and I need to find a good-paying job for the summer. Otherwise I'm just not going to be able to stay in college. Besides, we've decided that we want to work together this summer, right?

Nancy: Right. But still, can't we just stay around here? It would be more fun and we know people.

■ ■ ■ ■ ■

BOX 11.2

STOCK ISSUES IN POLICY-BASED PROPOSITIONS

ISSUE	DEFINITION	EXAMPLE
Ill	An ill is a current wrong or harm that needs to be resolved.	There are too few organs to meet the needs of almost 100,000 people on waiting lists. Thousands die each year because of an inadequate supply of organs.
Blame	Blame is the attribution of an ill to causes within the present policy system.	The National Organ Transplant Act of 1984 prohibits the sale of organs. Many potential donors have strong attitudes against donating organs, ranging from religion and family issues to misunderstanding how donations work.
Cure ■ Plan of Action ■ Plan Effect	Cure represents the ability of a policy action to overcome the ill and blame. It consists of a plan of action and plan effects.	The National Organ Transplant Act should be modified to allow for the regulated sale of organs. By providing a safe, legal means for selling organs, this plan should have the effect of increasing the supply.
Cost-Benefits	The cost refers to the problems or disadvantages associated with taking a policy action. Benefits are the positive consequences of policy action.	A potential cost to this plan is that people may be willing to sacrifice their health to make money from the sale of their organs. Additionally, families may be under increased stress to sell organs of recently deceased loved ones. The potential benefits include saving lives by ensuring a greater supply, and the illicit, unsafe harvesting and sale of organs by organized crime will diminish.

Juli: We could, but I have a friend who said in her first summer up there she made more than $7,000, and that is much more than we could ever hope to make around here. Besides, it would be fun to get away for a summer.

Nancy: Maybe, but I've heard jobs up there are difficult to get.

Juli: Not unless you know someone, and I do. She said we could get hired without any problem.

This conversation presents an extended policy argument about the proposition "We should work in an Alaskan fish cannery this summer." The friends can either accept or reject it, and through the exchange the stock policy issues are explored.

Consider the order of the questions and answers. Juli began with a proposition for going to Alaska to work. It was phrased as a declarative sentence, and Nancy did not need to respond. So why did she answer the sentence with a question? Her reason is the same as any listener's reason might be. People often do not accept propositional statements without asking for specific supporting arguments from the speaker. Nancy pointed out that they could find jobs nearby, so what made Juli think they needed to travel to Alaska? She also said that a few places were hiring. A correct answer to each question was important: If Juli had not thought her plan through sufficiently, or if her answers were unsatisfactory, Nancy would have rejected her idea because it would not have been *prima facie* (acceptable at first glance).

This conversation is typical of many policy arguments, even very complex arguments about legislation, such as legalizing the sale of organs. Advocates need to be aware of the stock issues and prove them reasonably before recipients can be expected to take action. This section develops each of these stock issues in detail, enabling you to identify them and build arguments supporting each type.

Ill

When Nancy asked Juli what was wrong with their current plan for summer work, she was asking Juli to supply an argument proving the stock issue of ill. *An ill is a current wrong or harm the advocate is trying to resolve.* Likewise, if we ask, "What is the problem with policies related to organ donation?" we are also asking for the ill or the harm associated with the current system. Before we legalize organ sales, legislators as well as public audiences will need to be convinced that a problem exists. People act in the presence of a need—the reason to act. The argument of ill is generally a factual presentation of that need.

Before people are persuaded to act, they look for a significant ill or need. Most people do not act without some significant cause. For example, we might drive by litter scattered along a road. Although most of us agree that litter is a problem (an ill), we would probably not stop to pick it up and dispose of it properly; however, if the litter found its way into our front yard, we would be more inclined to do something. It is a question of significance. If the ill is seen as significant for us, we are more likely to act.

Qualitative Significance

The difficult question to answer is whether an arguer is presenting an ill that is significant enough to warrant the type of action proposed. Significance can be either qualitative or quantitative. *Qualitative significance is related to the intensity of the effect; we assess something as significant to the extent that it strengthens or diminishes life.* Evaluating qualitative significance usually requires comparative consideration of values.

An example of a value conflict of this type is shown in controversies about species preservation. To protect fish runs and spawning grounds, some legislators have proposed removal of dams that block fish migration and affect water quality. Those who have opposed dam removal believe that the dams are important for irrigation and production of relatively green hydroelectric power. Which is more important: protection of the environment and endangered species or preservation of farms and power sources? The significance of these competing interests is qualitative and value-based; it cannot be reduced to quantitative terms.

Quantitative Significance

Quantitative significance is related to the scope of the effects claimed; it asks how many people will be affected and how frequently. Quantitative significance is often more easily evaluated than qualitative significance because it simply involves statistical comparison.

As long as the evidence available is reliable and accessible, quantitative significance can usually be more easily weighed than qualitative significance. For example, if Juli argued that going to Alaska for two months would yield $10,000, the quantitative comparison of $10,000 to $3,000 at any other summer job is easier than evaluating the effect of such income on their lifestyles.

Arguing Significance

Most often, when we argue that something is significant, we blend both qualitative and quantitative measures. We do so because issues related to significance involve our understanding of the scope of an ill (how many are affected) and the value of the ill (how important this issue is to us). Is it significant that selling organs helps only one person? How many people constitute a significant ill? How many additional lives will be saved if we make organ sales legal? The answers to these questions are difficult because much depends on the context of the proposed policy. An ill is generally considered significant enough to warrant action if life or the quality of life is threatened. Of course, significance is a relative term, and it depends on how we value life or quality-of-life issues.

For example, preserving a right to free speech or free association has value only to the extent that it helps or hurts people.[16] Or, when we express outrage against animal testing for cosmetics, we argue that it unnecessarily destroys the quality of animal life. But what happens in a case in which animal experimentation is necessary for human survival? In 1992, for example, a baboon liver was transplanted into a human to save that person's life. Is a human life worth more than a baboon's life? These qualitative issues can be difficult questions to answer, but generally they involve the use of a value hierarchy. One of the ways of measuring the significance of an ill is by its impact on living beings.

Blame

We assume that most people in the world are relatively honest and caring and would not intentionally allow an ill to exist. We do not want people to die while waiting for a transplant. But why, then, do we allow people to die when most of us could donate a kidney or sign a donor registration card? Although we may attempt to avoid ills and strive to overcome them, we continue to allow significant ills to exist. We allow thousands to go without needed transplant surgery. We allow people to starve in other parts of the world even while many nations have enough food to feed them. The United States has a tax system that is viewed by many as privileging the wealthy at the expense of the middle class and indigent. Why do we allow such ills to continue?

The stock issue of blame helps explain why people are unable to resolve or diminish ills. Put simply, *blame is the attribution of an ill to causes within the present policy system.* Blame points to the person, people, or agencies responsible for the ill. For the ill to be corrected, the blame must be removed. If the blame for Juli and Nancy's lack of money is lack of jobs, then they must find good summer jobs to provide them with income and to alleviate the ill. If Food and Drug Administration rules are written in such a way that encourage animal testing, then they must be rewritten to overcome the ills associated with animal testing. If the legal prohibition for selling organs is the cause of an organ shortage, then we should make sales legal.

Structural Blame

There are two types of blame that act as barriers to resolving ill: structural and attitudinal. *A structural blame is the result of a defect that is an integral part of the nature of the current policy system.*[17] Understanding a structural blame requires understanding a structure. *Structures are the fixed elements or features of a policy system.* Examples of structural elements of policy systems are laws, contracts, treaties, rules, and orders. Taken as a whole, structures reflect the formally accepted rules governing our society and political system. Such structures are "fixed" because they can be removed only by means of formal action taken to replace them with other structures.

In 1896, for instance, the issue of racial discrimination was brought before the Supreme Court, and it ruled in *Plessy v. Ferguson* that separate-but-equal facilities did not discriminate. Consequently, separate white and African American lavatories, schools, and restaurants were seen as fair and just, so long as the facilities were provided equally. In 1954, however, over the issue of equal educational opportunity, the case of *Brown v. Board of Education* was brought before the Supreme Court. This case charged that because of the separate-but-equal rule established in *Plessy*, an ill of educational discrimination existed and African American students were unfairly deprived of educational opportunities. The Supreme Court found for Brown on the grounds that separate was inherently unequal.[18] The Court noted, "We conclude that in the field of public education the doctrine of separate but equal has no place. Separate educational facilities are inherently unequal."[19] The blame for our inability to provide equal educational opportunity was attributed to a fixed structure—the Supreme Court decision in *Plessy v. Ferguson.* To correct the problem of discrimination, the decision had to be overturned—the structure had to be removed.

Attitudinal Blame

A second type of blame is attitudinal. *Attitudinal blame arises from people's beliefs and values, rather than from a law or some other structure of the present system.* Typically, we assume that good people would not allow unnecessary evils to exist. However, if an ill is allowed to exist because of prevailing beliefs or value hierarchies, then an attitudinal blame has been identified. In Box 11.1, the list of myths compiled by the Mayo Clinic provided a good list of attitudes preventing people from donating organs. A concern is that organ donation might be prohibited by religion. Another concern was the fear that doctors would not expend much effort to save the life of a donor. These, among the other myths, are all attitudes that inhibit actions.

Attitudinal problems may contribute to the continuance of defective structures or failure to adequately support good structures within the system. For example, people smoke even though they know it will damage their health and eventually kill them. The blame does not rest in some law or structure forcing them to smoke; rather, it rests in their attitudes toward smoking. Similarly, although the United States adopted civil rights legislation in 1964, attitudes continue to perpetuate *de facto* segregation in some regions.

Cure

Being able to isolate and attribute blame for a given ill is not particularly useful unless the advocate has some way of resolving the problem. This is the role of cure. Cure is the third stock issue for policy cases and is the one asked for by Nancy when she said she heard that jobs in Alaska were difficult to get. *Cure demonstrates that some course of action can work to solve the ill.* In other words, if Juli and Nancy go to Alaska, will they find jobs? If we legalize organ sales, will lives be saved? How much of the ill does it cure? How can we change attitudes about donating organs? If it is legal to sell organs, will attitudes still result in too few organs available for transplant? If we mandate desegregation in the schools, do we alleviate discrimination? How much of the ill can the policy action cure?

Plan of Action

Cures consist of two parts: a plan of action and its effect on the ill. *A plan of action is the specific program advocated in support of the proposition.* Examples include Juli's plan to work in Alaska and the government's plan to allow students of many races to attend the same schools to overcome segregation. When advocates specify direct and definite courses of action, they are specifying plans of action.

Plans of action can be very detailed or very simple. Almost any legislation passed by Congress, from the budget to foreign assistance programs, involves extremely detailed plans of action that specify almost every action associated with the legislation. These plans can often take many volumes and thousands of pages to describe. On the other hand, Juli's plan for Nancy and her to work in Alaska is very simple and informal. Unlike congressional legislation, her plan is not a law or a contract; it is simply an agreement between two friends to take a particular action to alleviate an ill.

Effects

Having a plan, however, does not mean it will work. When the U.S. government passed legislation to provide incentives for the production of biofuels based on corn, the hope was that it would alleviate rising fuel prices. The effect was that fuel prices stayed high and the cost of food, particularly corn-based food, rose rapidly. Juli says working in Alaska will give her enough money to stay in school, but she needs to advance arguments to prove her claim that her plan will work.

This is the role of effects. *Effects is the argument that the plan of action can solve or cure the ill.* In other words, what effect does the plan have on the ill? Too often, people assume that if a plan is designed to address an ill, it will automatically work. For example, busing was designed to alleviate the ill of school segregation, but it didn't entirely work. Aside from creating its own myriad problems, the plan in many cases did little to reduce segregated neighborhoods, differences in socioeconomic status, or any of the other variables that contribute to and perpetuate segregation.

Effects, then, is the argument presented about the relative effectiveness of a plan. If the plan worked a little, is that preferable to nothing? The problem that remained beyond the structure of segregation was the attitude of segregation. Although integration of public schools following *Brown* promoted racial accord in some areas of the United States, in other areas it did not. If the plan of action cannot overcome prejudiced attitudes, then the ability of the plan to affect the ill is diminished because the social system will seek to undermine it.

Cost-Benefits

Recognizing that policies are adopted within a larger system is an important step in understanding cost. *The cost refers to the problems or disadvantages associated with taking a policy action.* The assumption is a simple one: For any action we take, we give up or pass by other actions or cause systemic changes that may not be beneficial. Therefore, the issue of cost asks, "What are the negative consequences of this action?"

If Nancy and Juli decide to go to Alaska, their costs might be giving up social activities and friends at home, or they may get homesick. School districts that were forced by *Brown* to bus students had to spend money on transporting students instead of on instruction. Students also had to leave their neighborhoods and spend time being bused to schools farther from their homes. If we legalize organ sales, will that put undue pressure on people to sell organs? All of these are consequences or costs of a policy action.

Benefits are the positive consequences of policy action. There are many examples of how enacting a policy will result in positive outcomes.[20] For example, busing can provide greater cultural diversity in the classroom. Students can have an educational opportunity that is superior on average because of a greater mix of teachers, students, and facilities. The worth of the benefits depends on the value structure. How much value do we place on the benefits, and how much value do we place on the cost? If integrating the U.S. educational system is a highly placed value, then the benefits of busing in some areas might outweigh the associated costs.

Cost and benefits are interrelated. When we make decisions, we examine both sides of the system and consider the cost and benefits of competing system alternatives. On the one hand, we look at the cost and benefits associated with the present system. On the other hand, we look at the cost and benefits associated with the proposed system. Whichever system has the greatest net benefits will, presumably, be the system we support. Cost and benefits act as a fulcrum on which policy decisions are weighed. Arguers use this fulcrum to decide which system is most beneficial.

THE ISSUES BRIEF

As observed earlier, policy advocacy may occur in many settings—conversations, discussions, debates, editorials, and so on. The advocate may have extended time for speaking and presenting a case, or may have only intermittent speaking times and may have to develop a policy argument in several sections at different times. The situation may have an effect on how the policy argument is developed, structured, and presented. Regardless of situational constraints, policy advocates persuade their audiences that the benefits of their proposal outweigh its cost by showing the consequences of action and inaction through the development of extended arguments. This section will introduce and explain how a needs-based policy argument can be developed and refuted. Other approaches to arguing policies will be discussed in the following section; however, the needs-based approach is the most commonly used means of advocating policy decisions. This section will introduce you to needs-based policy arguments and illustrate how such arguments can be refuted.

Needs-Analysis Approach

On occasion, an advocate will find a problem that is caused by a defect in the current system that can be resolved. When such is the case, a needs case is appropriate. *A needs-analysis case claims that the ill existing in the current system cannot be corrected within the pres-*

ent system, but can be cured by the advocate's policy proposal.[21] Needs arguments are very common in persuasive speeches as well as more extended debates because the format and requirements for the argument are simple and straightforward. All that is required of an advocate is proof that a significant ill exists, that it is caused by some feature of the present system, and that it can be resolved through the proposed plan of action.

An extended needs argument is developed in two distinct clusters of arguments. The first establishes a significant ill and blame. The ill and blame are developed together to reveal that the present system suffers a significant problem that cannot be resolved for structural or attitudinal reasons. The second cluster presents a plan of action and proves that the proposed plan can cure the ill presented.

Often, needs-based cases will develop a third cluster of arguments that focus on the benefits of the plan. Although the plan achieves benefits by reducing the ill and overcoming the blame, it may also have additional benefits. For instance, busing students will have the effect of curing (at least in part) racially segregated schools. This functions as a benefit. However, there are additional benefits that are not related to the ill or the blame but occur as a natural consequence of changing the system. For instance, beyond integration, students will have the benefits of learning about other cultures and customs and preparing to live and work in a diverse society. These "spin-off" benefits add to the desirability of the plan of action, although they are not necessarily related to the ill as identified.

Refuting Needs Cases

In response, an arguer who opposes the proposal may use the strategy of direct refutation. Although other refutational strategies will be discussed later, direct refutation is a common and effective means for an opponent to respond to proposals. *Direct refutation is an approach used by policy opponents that is designed to argue and disprove at least one of the stock issues in the proposal.* In using a direct refutation approach to a proposal, opponents attack it on one or more of the stock issues of ill, blame, cure, and cost-benefits. In order to be *prima facie* (acceptable on its face), a policy proposal must meet all the issues implied in the stock issues of ill, blame, cure, and cost-benefits. If its opponents can show that the proposal falls short in any of the areas, it can be rejected. Direct refutation does not require the opponent to support any current or proposed policy system, only to argue against the one presented. Essentially, with direct refutation, the advocate takes the position, "I am not going to defend any policy system, but I will challenge everything my opponent has said and show the case to be insufficiently proven."

Fundamentally, arguers using this strategy take advantage of the issue of presumption. Because audiences are naturally predisposed to favor the current, known policy system, arguers using direct refutation simply must show that the policy proponents have failed to fulfill their burden of proof on one or more stock issues to show that the proposed plan should not be adopted.

Arguers using the strategy of direct refutation generally parallel the case they oppose in organization and argumentation. If the case presents significant ills, the advocate claims that these ills are caused by certain attitudes or structures, that a certain plan will correct the ills, and that it will produce certain benefits; then the person using direct refutation would attempt to show that the ills do not exist or are insignificant, that the causes for them have been misidentified, that the proposed plan is flawed and unworkable, that it will not correct the ill, and that the claimed benefits will not be produced. Box 11.3 is an outline of how a needs case can be developed and opposed.

The emphasis with the needs-based organizational pattern is how well the plan of action can cure the ill. The stock issue of cost-benefits is not readily apparent in this format. Although the opposing side argues for specific costs, the benefits in the case are inherent in the plan's ability to cure the ill. This means that if the case is true, then the benefits will be realized when the plan works and the significance of the ill is diminished and a blame is removed.

Direct refutation presents a clear counterargument for each of the significant arguments developed in the case being opposed. Although the illustration in Box 11.3 shows refutation against every case argument, a solid refutation may be conducted with less detail and breadth. Minimally, the advocate needs to disprove any one of the stock issues because, in doing so, one of the elements of a *prima facie* case is disproved. Notice too that beyond simply answering the case argument, an opponent would also describe the costs associated with a system change.

There are many significant issues that require policy action that might use a needs-based approach. For example, consider the problem of tobacco. Since the surgeon general first warned us about the dangers inherent in smoking, the tobacco industry has been attacked, and increasing regulations have been placed on smoking—

■ ■ ■ ■ ■

BOX 11.3

NEEDS CASE AS DEVELOPED AND OPPOSED

I. There is a need for a new system.
  A. There are significant ills.
  B. The present system is to blame.

II. There is a plan that can solve the problem.
  A. This plan of action will resolve the ill.
    1. What agent should act?
    2. What mandate should be given to the agent?
  B. This plan will have the effect of curing the ill.

III. In addition to solving the ill, the following benefits will accrue. (optional)
  A. Benefit 1
  B. Benefit 2

I. There is no need for a new system.
  A. The ills are insignificant or do not exist.
  B. The present system is capable of handling any ills should they arise.

II. The plan should not be adopted.
  A. The plan is unneeded or won't work.
    1. This agent is incapable or unqualified to act.
    2. This mandate won't work to cure the ill.
  B. Even if this plan worked, it cannot cure the ill.

III. This plan will receive no benefits.
  A. Benefit 1 won't come true.
    1. The benefit is exaggerated.
    2. The plan of action does not get this benefit.
  B. Benefit 2 won't come true.

IV. The case will accrue many costs.
  A. Cost 1
  B. Cost 2

how old people have to be, where they can smoke, and increased insurance premiums for those who do smoke. Is it fair?

Most of the evidence suggests that smoking is very dangerous. Smoking increases the risk of getting various types of cancer, including throat and lung cancers. Because it increases the heart rate by 10 to 25 beats per minute, or up to about 36,000 beats a day, smokers risk heart disease and heart attack as well as stroke. Smoking constricts the blood vessels in the arms and legs and leads to a greater risk of amputation. On average, therefore, every cigarette costs smokers between 5 and 20 minutes of life, and tobacco is the underlying cause of more than 420,000 deaths each year.

Smoking is deadly. It kills the equivalent of three Boeing 747 planeloads of people each day, which is 17 times more people each year than are victims of homicide for all of the United States, and 50 times more than die from illegal drugs. In addition, smoking contributes to up to 40,000 nonsmoker deaths from heart disease and lung cancer. More than one-third of the people who die in cigarette-related house fires are nonsmokers whose cigarette did not cause the fire. All told smoking costs the United States about $50 billion each year in medical costs.[22]

For years the federal government has struggled over what to do about tobacco. In 1996 the federal government moved to regulate it as a drug and placed it under the jurisdiction of the Food and Drug Administration (FDA). Yet smoking continues to increase among 15- to 30-year-olds and has its highest growth rate among young women. Tobacco is a $45 billion industry, and it is fighting to at least maintain its grip on the market share of the United States as well as that of other nations.

The case argument in Box 11.4 is fairly simple. A problem exists (smoking) that has a clear and direct solution (a ban). The important feature of this argument is that the plan of action must cure the ill and the blame. If the ills cannot be cured, then the plan is irrelevant. While this might seem obvious, often advocates offer plans that will only partly solve a problem or only partly overcome the blame. In such cases, the need is only partially satisfied, and the significance of the case is reduced.

It is important to note in this issues brief that we have outlined only claims. Each of these claims is part of an argument, and the advocates on both sides of the proposition would need to produce supporting arguments, reasons, and evidence to prove that their claims are true. Also, there are many other possible arguments in support of the claims. Advocates may choose as many or as few as they perceive are necessary to support the proposition and persuade the recipients.

The viability of a needs case rests on the advocate's ability to correctly identify an ill within the present system, to locate the features within the present system that cause the ill, and to remove the deficiencies in the present system through a plan of action that will work. In other words, the needs analysis rests on the premise that the present system has important defects that contribute to a significant ill. The needs approach offers a clear analysis of each stock issue and presents beneficial alternatives for the present policy system. The focus of a needs case is that the current system is unsatisfactory and the best solution is to adopt the advocate's course of action.

Because the needs case seeks to replace the current structure, an arguer should use it when the ill is particularly significant and can clearly be cured through an alternative to the current system. Needs cases must overcome a greater presumption than other types of cases because they are a new system that seeks to replace the old system.

■ ■ ■ ■ ■

BOX 11.4

PROPOSITON: THE UNITED STATES SHOULD BAN THE SALE OF ALL TOBACCO PRODUCTS

I. Thousands of people are dying every day. (ill)
   A. Cancer and heart disease are on the rise.
   B. Nonsmokers are being severely harmed.

II. Current efforts are not adequate to solve the problem. (blame)
   A. People want to smoke and circumvent the laws. (attitudinal)
   B. Individual state efforts are fragmented and inadequate to reduce the consumption of tobacco. (structural)
   C. Current federal and state laws are inadequate to stop tobacco consumption. (structural)

III. A ban on the sale and consumption of tobacco products will eliminate the problem.
   A. The federal government should render all tobacco products illegal. (plan of action)
   B. A ban will prevent the consumption of tobacco products and eliminate the harms. (effects)

IV. The benefits to this action are tremendous. (benefits)
   A. Because of reduced medical expenditures related to smoking, the health care system will be saved.
   B. We have the potential to save thousands of lives each year.
      1. Nonsmokers will be saved.
      2. Smokers will be saved.

I. The estimates of death and dying are exaggerated.
   A. Cancer and heart disease come from many sources, and tobacco is only one of them.
   B. The evidence supporting the harms to nonsmokers is suspect.
   C. Consumption is beginning to decrease.

II. Current efforts are reasonable.
   A. The laws as they exist effectively protect children.
   B. Adults should be able to make their own choices.

III. The proposed cure will not work.
   A. We have tried prohibition before without success.
   B. Historically, prohibition has resulted in an increase in consumption.
   C. People will still find a way to smoke because the plan of action does not overcome the attitudinal barriers.
   D. Tobacco growers will find other markets in Asia, and the harms will just be transferred elsewhere.

IV. The costs associated with the plan outweigh any potential benefits.
   A. The tobacco industry will fold, and many workers will be unemployed.
   B. All people lose their freedoms when we lose our ability to choose options relating to personal health.

Therefore, the evidence and reasoning supporting the cure (that the effect of the plan will be to cure the ill) is particularly important. This means that the role of the opponent is to cast as much doubt on the proposal as possible. Unless the benefits of the plan (through curing the ill as well as additional benefits) are sufficient to overcome the risk inherent in changing systems, the case will probably not be adopted by the audience.

ALTERNATIVE FORMATS FOR ARGUING POLICIES

In the previous section, you were introduced to a particular case format, the needs case. Needs arguments are based on the premise that the current system is a failure because it has been either unwilling or unable to redress a significant ill. On occasion, however, the present system is attempting to address a problem or is addressing a problem in a way that, in the advocate's view, is inappropriate. Such situations may require the use of alternative argument formats. This section will introduce and explain two alternate approaches to presenting and supporting policy propositions: comparative advantages and goal. Although other approaches are possible, these two are commonly used and widely adaptable for many different situations. How they are used in policy argument will depend on the nature of the topic being discussed and the situation in which the argument is made.

Comparative-Advantages Case

Often, there are problems that have no clear-cut or easy solutions. Sometimes, the present system is already attempting to cure the ill, and there is no obvious deficiency in the way the system is dealing with a problem. In such cases, an advocate may want to argue for a new system that is superior to the present system. The case argument that is developed compares the advantages and disadvantages of two competing system alternatives and, hence, is called a comparative-advantages case.

The comparative-advantages argument develops the position that in comparison with the current system, the proposed system has more benefits. Instead of isolating a problem and offering a cure (as with the needs case) the focus of a comparative-advantages argument is to argue that the advocate's proposal is comparatively stronger or more beneficial than the current system.

In a comparative-advantages argument, the ways stock issues are developed differ from a needs argument. Furthermore, the systems approach in particular underlies the logic of the case. For instance, in a needs argument, the ill was a harm that the current system could not cure. But if the present system has already identified the problem and is trying to cure it, then such an analysis would be redundant because both sides would agree that such an ill exists. For example, there is probably agreement that discrimination exists and that school segregation is bad. The present system is already attempting to solve the problem through mandatory busing and other programs designed to integrate education. An advocate wanting to reduce racial discrimination would probably not have to prove that discrimination is bad because the current system already embraces that view. With a comparative-advantages case, however, the advocate would argue that there are more effective ways to reach a goal and address problems than those in the present system. With school busing, then, the advocate might claim that there are better ways to achieve equal educational opportunity than busing. In a comparative-advantages case, the ill is interpreted as inadequacies in existing plans and policies. The blame in such an argument rests on the way the current system seeks to cure the ill; the cure is the alternative.

Costs and benefits become an important argument in a comparative-advantages case. Whereas the needs case proved benefits by alleviating the ill, in a comparative-advantages case, the advocate makes the argument that there are many benefits associated with the proposed system and costs associated with the current system. Comparative-advantages cases seek to be accepted because they are, on balance, better than the current system. This approach does not attempt to identify a single ill or set of ills or their causes; rather it emphasizes the policy proposed and its effects in comparison to the present system.[23] This means that even if the proposal is not perfect and cannot entirely remove the blame or cure the ill, it is *comparatively* better than the present policy system.

An advocate using a comparative-advantages approach would cluster arguments in the following areas:

   I. Plan of action
      A. Agent: Who should act?
      B. Mandate: What action should be taken?
  II. Benefit 1
      A. The scope and effectiveness of the present system is limited. (ill)
      B. The present system cannot remedy the ill. (blame)
      C. The proposed plan of action will solve the problem. (effect)
 III. Benefit 2

A comparative-advantages case fulfills its burden of proof by successfully arguing that the proposed plan is an improvement over the present system and can be favorably compared with other competing systems. To understand how this works, consider a conversation between two college roommates, Kyle and Andrew.

> **Kyle:**   I think it is time to move off campus. I hate living in the dorms and I hate eating cafeteria food. In general, I hate, living on campus. So many freshmen, so much noise.
>
> **Andrew:**   Yes, but living on campus has many benefits. If we move into an apartment, who will cook our meals? Who will clean the bathrooms? Who will we socialize with? It seems to me that what we are doing now is the best alternative.
>
> **Kyle:**   You're wrong. Look at it this way—if we move off campus, we will save a lot of money. In fact, I figure that our housing cost will drop by about a third. Besides, the freedom to come and go without worrying about dorm rules and regulations far outweighs any reason to stay in the dorms. Besides, I like the idea of just having time to get away from campus and relax.
>
> **Andrew:**   Well, I hadn't thought of it like that. I especially hadn't thought about the cost savings, and I suspect that between you and me, we can cook better than the cafeteria. Let's move!

In this conversation, Kyle develops a comparative-advantages argument. Both Kyle and Andrew want a comfortable place to live, they want to save money, and they want freedom. But Kyle points out that living off campus will achieve these ends better than living in the dorm. Even though the present policy system, living in dorm rooms, was not bad per se, changing policy systems, living off campus, produced more net benefits than net cost.

Consider the problems associated with using cell phones while driving. Many studies have demonstrated that any distraction while driving contributes to a risk of traffic accidents. Cell phones, in particular, represent a significant distraction. What should be done to alleviate this problem? In response, some countries and some states have moved to prohibit mobile phone use while driving. Others are considering similar action. Some car manufacturers integrated hands-free and voice-activated communication systems in their vehicles so that drivers will have less to distract them.

In this case, there is a problem that has been recognized internationally and by auto manufacturers. The current system is working to reduce the risks associated with distracted driving, and some laws have been passed regulating cell phone use. Because the status quo has already initiated a series of policies to alleviate the problem, does this mean that an advocate has no grounds on which to argue about banning cell phones? Clearly a needs case wouldn't be appropriate here because the current system is not to blame—it is attempting to do something. There are laws and manufacturing programs designed to solve the problem. The broader question, however, is, "Is there a better solution?" If there is a better alternative than the present systems, a comparative-advantages approach is warranted and might take the following form:

I. The United States should ban the use of cell phones while driving. (plan)
   A. Congress should enact the ban. (agent)
   B. The plan should make the use of cell phones while the vehicle is in motion illegal. (mandate)
II. This plan of action will help save lives. (benefits)
   A. Many accidents are caused by distractions including cell phones. (ill)
   B. Present policies fail to decrease distractions. (blame)
      1. There are very few laws restricting cell phone use. (structural blame)
      2. Existing laws fail to regulate hands-free phones. (structural blame)
      3. People will ignore the law and continue to use their phones. (attitudinal blame)
   C. A complete ban will reduce accidents. (cure)
      1. The plan will deter at least some drivers from using their phones.
      2. A complete ban will make enforcement easier.
      3. Some accidents will be prevented.

In this example, only the claims have been outlined. If this extended case were presented in a policy discussion, the advocate would include evidence and reasons supporting each of the claims.

This case contrasts what is being done currently with what could be done—the comparison of alternative systems. The ill analysis in the benefits focuses on a deficiency in the current system. It would be inappropriate to argue that cell phone use while driving is bad, because both sides of the discussion would agree and the argument would simply be a restatement of common ground. Instead, the ill focuses on the deficiency of the present system. The blame, then, becomes the reason why the present system is unable to remedy its own ill, and the cure is the proof that the alternative will overcome the systemic defects identified in the ill and blame.

Goals Case

Extended policy arguments using a goals approach have a focus that is very different from either the needs or comparison approaches discussed earlier. *The goals argument presents a significant goal and the case revolves around a comparison of systems attempting to achieve the goal.*[24] This means that an advocate using a goals approach must identify and defend a specific goal that is or should be a focus in the current system. This goal is something that is or should be highly valued in the context of the policy system (see Chapter 10 for more detail on how values function). For example, a goal of the legal system is justice. A goal of the Supreme Court is to uphold the Constitution. A goal of families is to provide a comfortable life for one another. There are many different goals that operate from a social, political, or economic level.

The goals approach functions on the premise that a particular goal is not being met because of a structure or attitude (blame) in the present system. Therefore, the proposal in a goals case seeks to eliminate factors that prevent the system from achieving the goal.

The goals case should prove that the present system cannot achieve the goal because of structural or attitudinal blames. The argument progresses by presenting a plan of action that overcomes the blame and better achieves the goal than the present system. This approach makes the assumption that eliminating inconsistencies between important goals and policies is a sufficient warrant for change.[25]

Generally, a goals argument develops in the following organizational pattern:

I. An important goal exists.
II. Flaws in the present system are to blame for its inability to achieve the goal.
III. There is a plan of action that will better achieve the goal.
IV. The proposed plan of action will better meet the goal.

With this format, the ill takes the form of an unmet goal. The case does not argue that the present system is bad per se, but that it is missing an opportunity by failing to achieve an important objective. The blame argues that some feature or flaw in the present system prevents it from achieving the goal. The cure is a plan that removes the barrier to the goal, and the benefits are the ability of the plan to better meet the goal. The case argument may also offer additional benefits from altering the present system.

Identifying the appropriate goal, however, can be difficult. The goal must either be accepted by the parties of the dispute or the advocate must argue that it should be an important goal. In our complex system of values and policies, it is not uncommon for different values to overlap and conflict. There are many instances in which individual rights conflict with social rights. Consequently, what has value and is an important goal for one person might be unimportant or a bad goal for another. It is important, therefore, to recognize that what is a reasonable goal for a given audience is largely dependent on the fields and for the argument. (Refer to Chapter 1 for a description of fields and how they influence arguments.)

Different groups of people often have goals that conflict. For several years, the goal of environmental protection has clashed with the goal of economic development, and this has been a particularly heated issue with regard to the spotted owl controversy. The spotted owl is indigenous to the old-growth forests of the Pacific Northwest. It is an endangered species that does not appear to nest in newer forests. For it to survive, according to many environmentalists, we need to protect the ancient forests. On the other hand, people in the logging industry argue that placing the old-growth forests off limits to harvesting could result in up to 700,000 jobs lost and will have the effect of destroying many small Washington, Oregon, Idaho, and Montana towns. Which value is more important? The protection of the spotted owl, or the protection of jobs? This can be a difficult issue to resolve, and President George H. W.

Bush, faced with deciding how to proceed, in 1991 called upon a group of investigators called the "God Squad" to determine whether logging should be allowed even at the expense of the owl. Logging won. In this case, the goal of protecting U.S. economic interests outweighed the goal of protecting species.

If we wanted to construct a goals argument, there are two ways we could proceed. First, we could argue that the goal of economy over species is an important goal, but that the present system is unable to meet that goal because of some blame. In fact, this was the argument made by many loggers who claimed that the owl's status as a threatened species prevented the United States from achieving important economic goals. An alternative way of arguing this issue would be to prove that another goal is superior and should be supported. Such a case might be organized as follows:

  I. Protecting species should be our most important goal.
    A. Species diversity guarantees our own survival.
    B. We don't have the moral right to justify the extinction of a species.
 II. The present system is allowing the spotted owl to become extinct. (blame)
III. We should guarantee the right of owls and other protected species to live. Congress (agent) should eliminate the "God Squad" and place biodiversity as our highest priority. (mandate)
 IV. Such a program has many advantages. (benefits)
    A. The spotted owl will survive.
    B. We set a much more reasonable precedent.
    C. We help our economy become more diverse with less reliance on logging as the sole industry of many towns.

With the goals case, the present system's inability to meet the goal serves as the ill. The blame is the barrier that prevents the system from meeting the goal. The cure is the plan of action and its effects in guaranteeing better species diversity, and the benefits are the positive consequences associated with acting and better meeting the goal.

ALTERNATIVE FORMATS FOR REFUTING POLICIES

As there are many approaches for supporting policy proposals, there are also many approaches for opposing them. As we noted in Chapter 9 listeners who choose to respond to the issues presented by the original advocate assume a burden of rejoinder. In other words, they must address the central stock issues as originally presented and provide a sufficiently strong reason for rejecting the case as originally presented. The central question guiding the response is, Why do we reject policy systems? You have already been introduced to one strategy—direct refutation—based on the premise that the proposal is incoherent or inadequate in itself. It may have flaws, or it may fail to address all the stock issues adequately.

Beyond direct refutation, an opponent may employ three other macrolevel strategies to counter an extended policy case. These strategies are defense of present policy, minor repairs, and counterproposals. The remainder of this section will describe each of these options and illustrate how each can be used to oppose policy cases.

Defense of the Present Policy System

When advocates elect to defend the present policy system, they commit themselves to the argument that the present policy has greater systemic benefits than the proposal. *Defense of the present policy system rests on a comparison of the proposal and the present system, and argues that the present system is superior.* Opponents of a proposal who use this strategy take the position that "compared with the proposed alternative, the present system is more beneficial." Arguers using this approach focus primarily on the issues of ill and blame, and they argue that present structures and attitudes are sufficient to cure the ill identified in the proposal.

Defense of present policies can be effective for any case approach. As with the strategy of direct refutation, it parallels the organization of the extended case and seeks to disprove at least one of the stock issues. The difference between this approach and direct refutation is that the utility and benefits of the current system become arguments against the proposal. In a sense, what is good about the present system is a reason not to replace it.

Respondents defending the current policy system will show that the present system is adequate, and that any deficiencies have been erroneously identified or exaggerated by those advocating change. After all, any change involves risk and may result in disadvantages that outweigh the supposed benefits of correcting an ill or problem. As with those who use direct refutation, advocates of present policies take advantage of the presumption in their favor. It is advisable to assume that most audiences would prefer to stay with known policies than to assume the risk of adopting an untested policy, unless the present policy is proven to be inadequate or problematic.

Defending current policies requires the arguer's commitment to support structures as they exist and currently function. When an arguer chooses to defend current policies, a commitment is made to adopt a consistent and systemic view of the argument. With direct refutation, any responsive argument could be made; with support of present policies, the answers should not contradict present policies. This approach should be used when the systemic benefits of the present system are greater than the benefits of the proposed system.

Defense of the Present Policy System with Minor Repairs

Occasionally, people opposing policy proposals may recognize that the current policy, if left unaltered, cannot correct the ill or solve the problem. They believe, however, that if minor flaws such as inadequate funding, lack of information, or improper administration were corrected, the present policy could be made adequate. The premise of this strategy is that "the present system is basically fine, but it could be streamlined and improved with minor additions or changes that don't involve wholesale systemic changes." *The defense of present policies with minor repairs strategy offers small changes to existing policies to improve their effectiveness and efficiency in meeting the needs.*

Minor repairs are by definition minor. As such, they should not involve significant structural or attitudinal changes to the policies or their administration. To do so involves a fundamental change in the nature of the policy system and means that the arguer is no longer defending the present system, but is proposing a new and different system. Advocates using this strategy should defend the integrity of the present system. Offering minor repairs means that the essential characteristics of the present policy must remain intact.

For example, consider the case for preserving ozone. Perhaps the present system's failure lies in the cost of implementing programs and not in the programs themselves. An advocate using minor repairs might argue to reprioritize funding so that the current structures are allowed to work. The system is not changed, just its implementation.

The strategy of defending present policies with minor repairs focuses on the blame issue. If the respondent can prove that minor system changes can accomplish the same objective as the proposed case, there is no reason to act. The present system cannot be held accountable for shortcomings if it has the capacity to adapt to new challenges and ills. The minor-repairs approach argues for a flexible system.

Defense of present policies with minor repairs is advisable when you believe that the blame has been exaggerated and that the change proposed by the opponents is greater than what is needed to correct the ill. Making minor modifications in an existing policy, it can be argued, is surely less risky than implementing an entirely new policy system.

Counterproposals

The strategy of counterproposal argues that the alternative presented should supersede the proposed policy. Consequently, an arguer presenting a counterproposal develops an extended case independent of the original case argued. For example, with the case of banning cell phone use while driving to reduce accidents, an advocate might argue that allowing hands-free systems will achieve the same benefits. The counterproposal does not disagree with the needs or blame analysis presented in the original extended case. Instead, the argument centers only on the relative ability of the two systems to achieve the benefits. If the counterproposal is better able to cure the ill and overcome the blame than the original proposal, then it should be adopted instead.

When should a counterproposal be used? A counterproposal does not enjoy the same presumption of strategies using present policies because it offers a new plan of action. As with any new plan of action, there is risk involved with change. When you put forward a counterproposal, you assume the burden of proof to demonstrate that the proposed counterpolicy system can cure the ill and blame better than the originally proposed system. Therefore, a counterproposal probably should be used only when there is consensus that something must be done about a problem, but disagreement about the nature or scope of the policy that will be necessary to correct it.

The three macrolevel argument strategies for refutation presented in this section are not mutually exclusive. Nor do any of these case-level arguments preclude using direct refutation. Depending on the respondent's analysis of the proposal, it may be appropriate to use two or more of the strategies in combination. Each offers different options for the arguer, and each addresses different issues. The objective of the respondent is to provide an argument against adoption of the proposed policy system. As long as using multiple strategies does not lead the arguer to contradict his or her own arguments, a combination of approaches is useful.

SUMMARY

This chapter examined how to construct and refute extended policy arguments. It began by discussing the nature of extended policy arguments and important policy concepts.

Extended policy arguments are composed of subsidiary claims supporting a policy proposition and the reasoning and evidence that support them. Policy arguments, unlike other types of argument, ask audiences to make decisions about future actions based on their expectations of what is probable or likely to occur. When we decide between different policy alternatives, we base our decisions on our assessment of net benefits and net cost associated with various competing policy systems.

Understanding systems is important because policy arguments seek to change the complex nature of our social, economic, and political systems. A systems approach to policy argumentation begins with the assumption that policies are interconnected and that changes in one part of a system have effects in other parts of the system. When we examine the relative merits of any particular policy system, we need to assess not only the policy, but also the extended system of changes it represents and the system it is designed to replace. No action occurs in a vacuum, and advocates as well as listeners need to be aware of the consequences of action or inaction.

Before listeners are likely to accept extended policy arguments, they expect certain issues to be addressed. Stock issues are issues that must be addressed adequately before a listener will accept a proposition. With policy propositions, we can discuss four categories of stock issues: ill, blame, cure, and cost-benefits. The ill is a current wrong or harm associated with the present system that the advocate is trying to resolve. The blame is the attribution of the ill to some deficiency in the present system, and blame may be both structural and attitudinal. The cure demonstrates that some course of action can work to solve the ill, and it consists of a plan of action and its effects. The cost is the problems or disadvantages associated with taking an action, and the benefits are the positive consequences of action.

When an advocate constructs an extended policy argument, all these issues must be addressed. However, depending on situational variables of audience and proposition, the advocate may choose to focus on different aspects of the proposition. This chapter discussed three different strategies for arguing in favor of policy propositions: needs, comparative advantages, and goals. A needs case maintains that the current system is unsatisfactory and that the best solution is to adopt a new system to replace the defective one. The comparative-advantages approach argues that the proposed system can achieve greater advantages than the current system. The goals approach claims that the elimination of blame precluding the attainment of important goals is a warrant for change.

This chapter also discussed four possible strategies that can be used to oppose extended policy arguments: direct refutation, defense of present policies, defense of present policies with minor repairs, and counterproposals. The strategy to be chosen depends on the nature of the topic, the characteristics of the case to be opposed, and the beliefs and attitudes of the audience. The first strategy, direct refutation, does not involve defending any particular positions, but instead tests each of the significant arguments presented in the opponent's case. Defense of present policies, however, defends existing structures and proves that such structures are of greater utility and benefits than the plan of action proposed in the case. When existing policies have minor flaws that prevent them from functioning correctly, a respondent may offer a defense of present policies with minor repairs. The minor repairs are intended as modifications designed to overcome minor problems in existing policies. Finally, advocates may use counterproposals. Counterproposals are an effective strategy if the opponent's case fails to understand the nature of the problem or if the respondent has a better proposal for curing the problem. These strategies are not mutually exclusive, and an arguer may draw from multiple strategies to refute a policy case.

Taken as a whole, policy arguments are an important element in our daily lives. We decide whether or not to take action based on individual assessment of the cost and benefits derived from different extended policy arguments. This chapter was intended to help describe and systematize a process familiar to all of us and fundamental to the process of our decision making.

GLOSSARY

Attitudinal blame (p. 326) arises from people's beliefs and values, rather than from a law or some other structure of the present system.

Benefits (p. 328) are the positive consequences of policy action.

Blame (p. 325) is the attribution of an ill to causes within the present policy system.

Comparative advantages (p. 333) is a strategy that develops the position that in comparison with the current system, the proposed system has more benefits.

Cost (p. 327-328) is the problems or disadvantages associated with taking a policy action.

Counterproposal (p. 339) argues that the alternative presented should supersede the proposed policy.

Cure (p. 327) demonstrates that some course of action can work to solve the ill.

Defense of the present policy system (p. 338) rests on a comparison of the proposal and the present system, and argues that the present system is superior.

Direct refutation (p. 329) is an approach used by policy opponents that is designed to argue and disprove at least one of the stock issues in the proposal.

Effects (p. 327) is the argument that the plan of action can solve or cure the ill.

Goals argument (p. 335) presents a significant goal and the case revolves around a comparison of systems attempting to achieve that goal.

Ill (p. 324) is a current wrong or harm the advocate is trying to resolve.

Minor repairs (p. 338) offer small changes to existing policies to improve their effectiveness and efficiency in meeting the needs.

Needs-analysis case (p. 328-329) claims that the ill existing in the current system cannot be corrected within the present system, but can be cured by the advocate's policy proposal.

Plan of action (p. 327) is the specific program advocated in support of the proposition.

Qualitative significance (p. 324) is related to the intensity of the effect; we assess something as significant to the extent that it strengthens or diminishes life.

Quantitative significance (p. 324) is related to the scope of the effects claimed; it asks how many people will be affected and how frequently.

Structural blame (p. 326) is the result of a defect that is an integral part of the nature of the current policy system.

Structures (p. 326) are fixed elements or features of a policy system.

Systems perspective (p. 321) recognizes that the world is a complex and interconnected set of relationships between and among component parts that compose a whole, and that one change in any part of the system changes the other elements of the system.

EXERCISES

Exercise 1 For each of the following propositions, outline a needs case, a comparative-advantages case, and a goals case using the formats discussed in this chapter:

   1. Proposition: I should buy a new car.

   2. Proposition: I should live with my parents until I have established myself in a career.

   3. Proposition: The federal government should provide more student financial aid.

 *4. Proposition: I should attend a different school.

Exercise 2 Select two of the cases you constructed in Exercise 1. For each of them, construct an opposing case. Use a different opposing strategy for each of the propositions: direct refutation, defense of present policies, defense of present policies with minor repairs, and counterproposal. After you have completed your outlines, explain how each differs from the others. What are the advantages of each, and in what type of situation would each be most appropriate?

*Exercise 3 Following is a set of scrambled claims supporting the proposition, "The federal government should legalize the sale, possession, and use of marijuana." Some claims could be used to outline an extended argument using needs analysis, others could be selected to construct a comparative-advantages case, and still others could be used to make up a goals case. Organize the scrambled statements to make up a needs-analysis case, a comparative-advantages case, and a goals case. Note that some of the statements will be used in all three cases, others twice, and some only once.

   1. A benefit of regulating marijuana will be to decrease the youth smoking problem.

   2. A great deal of money is wasted enforcing present laws; hundreds of millions of dollars are spent, and only 10 percent of marijuana is confiscated.

   3. Funds will no longer be spent needlessly enforcing an unenforceable law.

4. The plan will be financed by reallocating money presently spent for marijuana control.

5. There is a significant need to change marijuana laws in this country.

6. Legalization of marijuana will be beneficial.

7. A major goal of our society is to eliminate illegal drug use.

8. One-fourth of all marijuana users are under the age of 17.

9. By regulating marijuana, present laws divert law enforcement officials from pursuing and prosecuting hard drug traffickers, and thereby undermine our efforts to control hard drugs.

10. Marijuana sale and consumption will be regulated by the Food and Drug Administration.

11. Harmful substances such as paraquat will be eliminated, protecting consumers.

12. By focusing enforcement efforts on harder drugs, the proposed plan would enable us to better meet our goals of eliminating use of hard drugs.

13. The possession, sale, and use of marijuana will be legalized.

14. Experts estimate that marijuana regulation will prevent a significant percentage of the 10 million underage smokers from trying marijuana.

15. These problems are caused by present marijuana laws that are vaguely worded and in-consistently enforced.

16. Monitoring and regulating of marijuana sales are the only ways to decrease youth con-sumption.

17. Some of the illegally sold marijuana contains paraquat, which causes physiological damage.

18. Young people will no longer be affected by marijuana and other harmful side effects.

19. The following plan of action should be adopted.

20. Decreasing usage has significant beneficial effects.

Exercise 4 Following are two sets of scrambled claims for cases opposing legalization of marijuana. The first is a direct refutation opposing the needs-analysis case included in Exercise 3. The second set of statements develops a counterproposal. Unscramble the claims in each case, and construct an outline from them.

DIRECT REFUTATION

1. The plan to legalize marijuana won't work.

2. Two-thirds of high school seniors oppose marijuana use.

3. Reallocating present enforcement funds will not provide sufficient revenue to support the plan.

4. There is no need to change marijuana laws.

5. Young people who wish to experiment with marijuana will still be able to obtain it after it has been legalized.

6. Use among young people is decreasing.

7. Because marijuana is not physically or psychologically harmful or addictive, regulating its use will provide no benefits.

8. Funds spent on marijuana enforcement are insignificant; only 4 percent of drug arrests are for marijuana violations.

9. No benefits will result from the plan.

10. Paraquat is no longer used to destroy marijuana plants.

11. Personal and funding to regulate and control marijuana distribution are unavailable.

COUNTERPROPOSAL

1. The counterproposal is a better proposal than legalization of marijuana.

2. It is true that there is a significant need to change marijuana laws.

3. Revenue collected from these fines will be given to law enforcement agencies for control of hard drugs.

4. Under decriminalization, we no longer need to use resources and time prosecuting people for a minor, victimless offense.

5. People found to possess marijuana in small amounts for personal use will be subject to minimal fines.

6. Decriminalization allows redirection of funds to areas in which enforcement is most needed.

7. Decriminalizing marijuana, continues to indicate society's disapproval of substance abuse.

8. Instead of legalizing marijuana, we should decriminalize its use through following proposal.

NOTES

1. Adapted from Katie Picket, "Selling Organs," Communication and Theatre, Pacific Lutheran University, May 29, 2008.

2. Debate: Human Organs, Sale of Debatepedia. http://idebate.org/index.php/Debate:Human_Organs%2C_Sale_of.html (accessed May 12, 2008).

3. Peggy Saari, "Medicine and Disease: When Did the First Heart Transplant Take Place?" History Fact Finder, Julie L. Carnagie, ed. UXL-GALE, 2001, *eNotes.com*. 2006 http://www.enotes.com/history-fact-finder/medicine-disease/when-did-first-heart-transplant-take-place (accessed May 29, 2008) and American Heart Association, "Organ Donation," http://www.americanheart.org/presenter.jhtml?identifier=4697 (accessed May 29, 2008).

4. Jo Revill, "The Right patients for a face transplant is out there today," guardian.co.uc, October 29, 2006, http://www.guardian.co.uk/science/2006/oct/29/medicineandhealth.theobserver (accessed May 29, 2008).

5. U.S. Department of Health and Human Services, HRSA News Room, April 16, 2007, http://newsroom.hrsa.gov/releases/2007/OrganDonationRates2006.htm (accessed May 29, 2008).

6. The Case for Selling Human Organs. Reasononline. http://www.reason.com/news/printers/34799.html (accessed May 12, 2008).

7. The Case for Selling Human Organs. Reasononline. http://www.reason.com/news/printers/34799.html (accessed May 12, 2008).

8. Mayo Clinic, "Transplant Programs at May Clinic," http://www.mayoclinic.org/transplant/organ-donation.html (accessed May 29, 2008).

9. Mayo Clinic, "Organ donation: Don't let these 10 myths confuse you," http://www.mayoclinic.com/health/organ-donation/FL00077 (accessed May 30, 2008).

10. Kidneys For Sale. Santa Clara University. http://www.scu.edu/ethics/publications/iie/vln2/kidneys.html (accessed May 12, 2008).

11. Brian Handwerk, "Organ Shortage Fuels Illicit Trade in Human Parts," National Geographic, May 29, 2008, http://news.nationalgeographic.com/news/2004/01/0116_040116_EXPLorgantraffic.html (accessed May 29, 2008).

12. Human Organ Selling/Buying. CollegeNET: It Pays to Think. http://www.collegenet.come/elect/app/app?service=external/Forum&sp=4286 (accessed May 12, 2008).

13. Jerome R. Corsi, "The Continuing Evolution of Policy System Debate: An Assessment and Look Ahead," *Journal of the American Forensic Association* 22 (1986): 158.

14. Ludwig Bertalanffy, "General System Theory—A Critical Review," *General Systems* 12 (1962): 1–20.

15. George W. Ziegelmueller and Charles A. Dause, *Argumentation: Inquiry and Advocacy* (Englewood Cliffs, N.J.: Prentice-Hall, 1975), 32–37.

16. William L. Benoit, Steve R. Wilson, and Vincent F. Follert, "Decision Rules for the Policy Metaphor," *Journal of the American Forensic Association* 22 (1986): 141.

17. Austin J. Freeley, *Argumentation and Debate: Critical Thinking for Reasoned Decision Making*. 8th ed. (Belmont, Calif.: Wadsworth, 1993), 196–199.

18. Richard Kluger, *Simple Justice: The History of Brown v. Board of Education and Black America's Struggle for Equality* (New York: Vintage Books, 1975), 781–782.

19. *Brown, et al. v. Board of Education of Topeka, Shawnee Co., Kansas*, 347 U.S. 483 (1954).

20. Many authorities have examined the nature of policy benefits and advantages. For more information, see Russel R. Windes and Arthur Hastings, *Argumentation and Advocacy* (New York: Random House, 1965), 229.

21. Freeley, 215.

22. Michael Castleman, "A Life in Smoke: How Cigarettes Work on Your Body as They Destroy It," *Mother Jones* (May/June 1996): 57–58.

23. W. Scott Nobles, "Analyzing the Proposition," in Douglas Ehninger and Wayne Brockricde, *Decision by Debate*, 2d ed. (New York: Harper and Row, 1978), 169.

24. John D. Lewinski, Bruce R. Metzler, and Peter L. Settle, "The Goal Case Affirmative: An Alternative Approach to Academic Debate," *Journal of the American Forensic Association* 9 (Spring 1973): 458.

25. Lewinski, Metzler, and Settle, 458.

ANSWERS TO SELECTED EXERCISES

CHAPTER 1

Exercise 1

1. This an argument. The first sentence, that "there is a plethora of credible scenarios for achieving human-level intelligence in a machine," is the claim. The rest of the paragraph provides examples of this to prove that the claim is true.

5. This is an argument. Eakin makes the claim that our ability to think has become impaired. It is backed with evidence from a linguistics professor who supports that formal English is on the decline and then reasons from this that it will begin to undermine our cognitive abilities.

10. This is not an argument. Although there is clear evidence, there is no claim or attempt to influence.

Exercise 3

■ *What kinds of grounds do medical doctors use . . . ?*
   The medical profession in general and doctors specifically ground their arguments in many different ways. These include patient case studies, patient charts, and laboratory experiments. Generally, the medical profession uses evidence that is verifiable and observable and tends to generalize from specific cases or experiments to understand how different diseases or injuries affect people.

■ *What constitutes acceptable evidence for medical arguments?*
   Medical evidence needs to be verifiable. In other words, if one doctor conducts a study and finds evidence of a cure for AIDS, other professionals will attempt to verify those results through replications. Much medical research makes use of "double-blind" studies, in which a large number of people receive a medicine or a placebo and then their subsequent condition is studied. Also, long-term studies of particular populations reveal whether a given treatment has been effective.

■ *In what spheres do medical doctors operate?*
   Doctors operate in all three of the spheres discussed in the text. When medical professionals brainstorm ideas about treatment or discuss in relatively informal settings how their cases have gone, they are arguing in the personal sphere. When they discuss experimental evidence or debate the merits of various treatments, they are making arguments in the technical sphere. And when they

talk with a patient's family members about the costs and benefits of a particular treatment, they adapt their arguments to a public sphere so they can be better understood.

- *What are audience expectations of this field?*
  Patients want doctors to be correct. Because much of the medical profession is mysterious and frightening to patients, doctors need to be reassuring and speak from experience and knowledge. Patients, then, want their doctors to know what the appropriate answer is.

- *What are some conventions or rules followed by doctors?*
  There are many. Typically, doctors advise their patients to get second opinions. They look for strong empirical support for conclusions. They consult with the family members and patient about the proper methods of treatment. And they live by the Hippocratic Oath, which governs the medical profession's ethics.

CHAPTER 2

Exercise 2

Note: There is often more than one correct way to diagram an argument using either model. Since there may be individual variations in the way various analysts number and connect statements and supply principles as warrants in the Toulmin model, there are often two or three correct ways to diagram an argument. There are, however, in-correct diagrams. The claim should not be mistaken for data, for example. The following diagrams are therefore suggestive. Further refinements should be made through class discussion and consultation with your instructor.

1. ① It is the chemical firms that release the most troubling types of molecules into the environment. ② In Baton Rouge, according to company data, an Exxon chemical plant was leaking 560,000 pounds of benzene yearly, while just south of there, ③ according to a survey by the Sierra Club, eighteen plants in and around St. Gabriel and Geismar dumped about 400 billion pounds of toxic chemicals into the air during the first nine months of 1986.

Co-Orientational Model

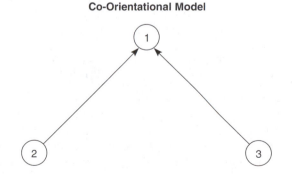

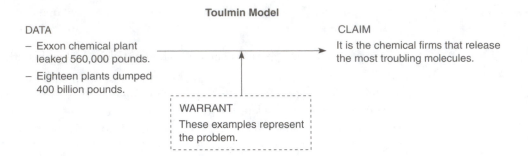

Toulmin Model

DATA

– Exxon chemical plant leaked 560,000 pounds.

– Eighteen plants dumped 400 billion pounds.

CLAIM

It is the chemical firms that release the most troubling molecules.

WARRANT

These examples represent the problem.

Criticism

The argument seems too ready to indict chemical plants as the main source of the problem. The evidence focuses on only two examples, and one of those is water and the other air pollution. What other sources of pollution (such as nonpoint pollution) might there be? Have the impacts of the various possible sources been compared?

CHAPTER 3

Exercise 1

1. This is an inductive pattern. The authors' point is that there are gaps between the rich and the poor in every society; they differ only in degree. To prove this, they provide statistical information about how these gaps have changed in the United States over time.

4. This is a narrative pattern. The author's point is that the person's determination and faith in oneself is the key to accomplishment, and she uses the story about learning how to read to illustrate that point.

CHAPTER 4

Exercise 1

1. Noncontroversial. This is a factually true statement.

5. Double-barreled. Whether a practice is "desirable" and whether it is "necessary" are two different issues. Here they have been combined in one claim.

14. May or may not challenge the present system. Whether or not this claim is well formulated will depend on the jurisdiction in which it is made. If there are legal limitations on abortion availability—parental consent or limitation on trimester, for example—the claim would challenge the present system. But if abortion is generally available, then it would not challenge the system.

Exercise 2

1. Past fact

CHAPTER 5

Exercise 1

1. *Expertise:* Is Kause an expert? What are his credentials? Neither, his title nor his position is cited.

   Statistical method: No information is given about the size or representativeness of the sample or the method used.

5. *Relevance* and *Accuracy of citation:* Is Kennedy's quotation relevant to the military draft? In what context was it made? The crucial part of this argument—that the country is in a military force crisis—is not supported by any evidence.

   Non sequitur: Kennedy's claim (in his inaugural address) was made in relation to volunteer service. Since he was not calling for mandatory service (which is just the opposite of his point), the claim here is unsupported by the quote cited because the quote is irrelevant to it.

10. *Expertise:* Who is Dr. Harvey Brenner? His credentials are not given.

    Recency: This study was conducted in 1975. It is questionable whether it applies to current conditions.

    Relevance: The argument assumes a causal connection between unemployment and death, but the evidence does not state a causal relation, only a correlation.

CHAPTER 6

1. *Analogy*

   Evidence: A painter paints his painting so that light shines on all parts of the work.

   Claim: The listener should . . . be shown the conclusion contained in the principle.

   Inference: (implied) [The speaker's task is like the painter's.]

   Questions: Is writing a composition or giving a speech like painting a picture in this sense? How is aesthetics like composition?

5. *Analogy*

   Evidence: North America did not remain empty of cities; the continent is not a poorer place now than 20,000 years ago.

   Claim: We have more practical reasons for not burning Amazon forests than to stave off natural catastrophe.

   Inference: (implied) [The forests of the Amazon are like the natural state of the North American continent 20,000 years ago.]

   Questions: Were the original North American forests as essential to environmental preservation as Amazon forests? Have conditions changed in 20,000 years such that destruction of Amazon forests would have more impact now?

11. *Dissociation*

    Evidence: We could act through bitterness and hatred; we could allow our protest to degenerate into violence.

Claim: We must struggle on the high plane of dignity and discipline; we must meet physical force with soul force.

Inference: (implied) [Effective response to oppression need not be violent; it can be dignified yet forceful.]

Questions: Should not oppression, which is a form of violence itself, be responded to by violence? Are not bitterness, hatred, and violence justified in such circumstances?

20. *Generalization*

    Evidence: Asian Americans denied entrance; impossible job market in academia; people seek treatment as disadvantaged minorities; Chicago firm fined; white teacher fired.

    Claim: Affirmative action for qualified minorities has turned into affirmative discrimination. . . .

    Inference: (implied) [The instances cited are representative of a general pattern of reverse discrimination.]

    Questions: What about the issue of underrepresentation in certain schools and occupations; how is this to be corrected? Are the instances cited atypical?

CHAPTER 7

Exercise 2

1. Lamkin cites the author Rosabeth Moss Kanter to give credibility to her own claim that women must work to gain organizational power. By focusing on the specific sources and methods of gaining power, Lamkin keeps her audience interested in her topic. She emphasizes a feminist perspective by citing a female authority when addressing an all-female audience.

   Because of her lively content, similarity in attitudes with the audience, and focus on a topic the audience is probably interested in, Lamkin will probably be able to hold audience attention and win acceptance for her ideas.

5. First and foremost, Ms. Crooks stresses her long and intensive experience with the topic. She stresses the American value of consensus-building through open exchange—a value her audience shares.

   One problem with this treatment is that the author's purpose is vague. Her audience may wonder what her point is and lose interest in what she has to say.

CHAPTER 8

Exercise 1

2. ① Ladies make excellent teachers in public schools; many of them are every way the equals of their male competitors, and still they secure less wages than males. ② The reason is obvious. ③ The number of ladies who offer themselves to teach is much larger than the number of males who are willing to teach. . . . ④ The result is that the competition for positions of teachers to be filled by ladies is so

great that it reduces the price; but ⑤ since males cannot be employed at that price, and ⑥ are necessary in certain places in the schools, ⑦ those seeking their services have to pay a much higher rate for them.

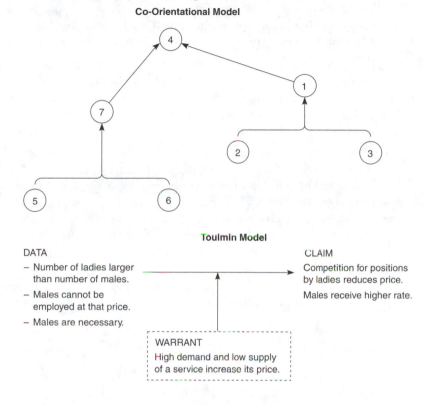

Co-Orientational Model

Toulmin Model

DATA
– Number of ladies larger than number of males.
– Males cannot be employed at that price.
– Males are necessary.

WARRANT
High demand and low supply of a service increase its price.

CLAIM
Competition for positions by ladies reduces price.
Males receive higher rate.

Criticism

The argument rests on a "supply–demand" relationship: that a larger supply of a commodity (in this case, female teachers) decreases its value. First, for the argument to hold up, the assumptions made by its author must all be true: Male teachers must be "necessary" in certain places, and there must be a much larger supply of females competing for positions than there are males. Second, other causes (rather than supply–demand) are not considered. For example, females might simply be willing to accept lower pay than males, or the pay differential might be the result of systematic discrimination.

CHAPTER 9

Exercise 1

3. Third-party candidates cause diversity in the political process.

    I. Definitions
       A. Third parties are parties that field presidential candidates for the presidential election.
       B. Third parties are not Democrats or Republicans.

C. Diversity means multiple points of view.

D. Diversity means focus on many issues.

II. Threshold

  A. At a minimum, the third parties must be beyond the existing two parties.

  B. At a minimum, the issues must be outside the mainstream issues of the two parties.

III. Application

  A. The Green Party is outside the Republican and Democratic sphere.

  B. The Green Party contributes many unique issues related to environmentalism.

5. Leif Eriksson discovered America.

I. Definitions

  A. Definitions of *discovery*

    1. He must have landed on North American soil.

    2. He must have been the first nonnative to land.

    3. He must have recorded the incident.

  B. Definitions of *America*

    1. This refers to the North American continent.

    2. This refers to the mainland only.

II. Threshold

  A. The minimal requirement is to have landed somewhere in North America.

  B. The minimal requirement is to have provided some lasting record of the discovery.

III. Application

  A. Leif Eriksson landed in what is now Maine in North America.

  B. Leif Eriksson recorded the discovery in his ship's logs.

CHAPTER 10

Exercise 2

Values affirmed by Brennan: freedom of expression, inclusiveness of all ideas

Values opposed to Brennan's position: loyalty to the country first and foremost, patriotism

Criteria for evaluation:

- To respect legal principles for treatment of the flag
- To avoid offense to others
- To protect any behavior construed as "communication"
- To preserve the principles on which the nation was founded
- To preserve free expression
- To allow various views to be heard
- To preserve the dignity of the flag

CHAPTER 11

Exercise 1

4. *First proposition:* I should attend a different school.

NEEDS CASE

I. My personal situation is such that I should transfer to another college.
   A. Northeast Exclusive College no longer meets my needs.
      1. It does not offer a program in my chosen major.
      2. The high tuition is causing me to go into debt.
   B. The prospects of getting the education I want here are dim.
      1. No curriculum changes in my interest area are planned.
      2. The high tuition will force me to drop out of school.

II. Transferring to another college seems the best plan.
   A. My parents and I will discuss my options during spring break.
   B. Next fall I will probably transfer to State University.
   C. This action will allow me to stay in school in my chosen major.

III. A transfer to another college will be beneficial.
   A. It will save thousands of dollars in tuition.
   B. It will broaden my educational experience.
   C. It will allow me to enroll in a major department that is highly ranked nationally.

COMPARATIVE-ADVANTAGES CASE

I. Transferring to another college next year is my plan.
   A. I will consult my parents about the decision.
   B. I will transfer to State University next year.

II. The transfer will be economically beneficial.
   A. I will save $4,000 in tuition next year alone.
   B. Neither my parents nor I will have to go into debt to finance my last two years of college.
   C. $4,000 is a significant proportion of my family's annual income.
   D. Only a transfer will avoid indebtedness since I do not qualify for financial aid or scholarships.

III. The transfer will be educationally beneficial.
   A. State University offers the major program I've selected.
   B. This major is exciting to me and offers excellent career opportunities.
   C. Northeast Exclusive College does not offer this major and has no plans to do so.

GOALS CASE

I. My goal is to obtain a bachelor's degree in dental hygiene in a quality program at reasonable cost.

II. Northeast Exclusive College does not offer this program, and its tuition is very high.

III. Transfer to State University seems advisable.
   A. I will discuss this with my parents during spring break.
   B. I will transfer into the hygiene program at State University next fall.

IV. In two years, I will receive a degree in a field with good career opportunities.

Exercise 3

NEEDS-ANALYSIS CASE

   I. (5)
     A. (2)
     B. (8)
     C. (15)
     D. (17)

  II. (19)
     A. (4)
     B. (10)
     C. (13)

 III. (6)
     A. (1)
     B. (3)
     C. (11)

COMPARATIVE-ADVANTAGES CASE

   I. (19)
     A. (4)
     B. (10)
     C. (13)

  II. (6)
     A. (3)
     B. (11)

 III. (1)
     A. (14)
     B. (16)
     C. (18)
     D. (20)

GOALS CASE

   I. (7)

  II. (19)
     A. (4)
     B. (10)
     C. (13)

 III. (9)

 IV. (12)

INDEX